OXFORD STUDIES IN EUROPEAN LAW

Series Editors

PAUL CRAIG
Professor of English Law at St John's College, Oxford

GRÁINNE DE BÚRCA
Professor of Law at New York University School of Law

Saving the European Union from Its Illiberal Member States

OXFORD STUDIES IN EUROPEAN LAW

The aim of this series is to publish important and original research on EU law. The focus is on scholarly monographs, with a particular emphasis on those which are interdisciplinary in nature. Edited collections of essays will also be included where they are appropriate. The series is wide in scope and aims to cover studies of particular areas of substantive and of institutional law, historical works, theoretical studies, and analyses of current debates, as well as questions of perennial interest such as the relationship between national and EU law and the novel forms of governance emerging in and beyond Europe. The fact that many of the works are interdisciplinary will make the series of interest to all those concerned with the governance and operation of the EU.

OTHER TITLES IN THIS SERIES

Compliance with European Consumer Law
The Case of E-Commerce
Felix Pflücke

Legislative Authority and Interpretation in the European Union
Martijn van den Brink

Secession and European Union Law
The Deferential Attitude
Núria González Campañá

Fiscal State Aid Law and Harmful Tax Competition in the European Union
Dimitrios Kyriazis

The Abuse of Constitutional Identity in the European Union
Julian Scholtes

Judging European Democracy
The Role and Legitimacy of National Constitutional Courts in the EU
Nik de Boer

EU Values Before the Court of Justice
Foundations, Potential, Risks
Luke Dimitrios Spieker

Postnational Constitutionalism
Europe and the Time of Law
Paul Linden-Retek

The Legislative Priority Rule and the EU Internal Market for Goods
A Constitutional Approach
Eadaoin Ní Chaoimh

The Jurisprudence of Constitutional Conflict in the European Union
Ana Bobić

Reflexive Governance in EU Equality Law
Emma Lantschner

Enhanced Cooperation and European Tax Law
Caroline Heber

Legal Pluralism in European Contract Law
Vanessa Mak

Europe's Passive Virtues
Deference to National Authorities in EU Free Movement Law
Jan Zglinski

Accountability in EU Security and Defence
The Law and Practice of Peacebuilding
Carolyn Moser

Accountability in the Economic and Monetary Union
Foundations, Policy, and Governance
Menelaos Markakis

Saving the European Union from Its Illiberal Member States

ANDRÁS JAKAB
European Court of Human Rights/University of Salzburg

&

LANDO KIRCHMAIR
University of the Bundeswehr Munich

OXFORD
UNIVERSITY PRESS

OXFORD
UNIVERSITY PRESS

Great Clarendon Street, Oxford, OX2 6DP,
United Kingdom

Oxford University Press is a department of the University of Oxford.
It furthers the University's objective of excellence in research, scholarship,
and education by publishing worldwide. Oxford is a registered trade mark of
Oxford University Press in the UK and in certain other countries

Published in the United States of America by Oxford University Press
198 Madison Avenue, New York, NY 10016, United States of America

British Library Cataloguing in Publication Data

Data available

Library of Congress Control Number: 2024952152

ISBN 978–0–19–895460–6

DOI: 10.1093/oso/9780198954606.001.0001

The manufacturer's authorised representative in the EU for product safety is
Oxford University Press España S.A. of El Parque Empresarial San Fernando
de Henares, Avenida de Castilla, 2 – 28830 Madrid (www.oup.es/en or
product.safety@oup.com). OUP España S.A. also acts as importer into Spain
of products made by the manufacturer.

Series Editors' Preface

The problems posed by democratic backsliding and authoritarian populism have been discussed in academic literature, by political scientists and legal scholars. Such developments have posed serious problems for, inter alia, the rule of law and judicial independence, with negative implications for the EU.

The present volume makes an important contribution to this topic. It analyses the malaise that has beset certain EU Member States, which deteriorated from fragile liberal democracies to illiberal regimes. The authors examine the range of factors that contributed to this situation from an institutionalist perspective, identifying the factors, both formal and informal, that led to the resultant illiberalism. The book also considers the ways in which existing vulnerabilities and weaknesses of democracy and the rule of law at the EU law level have been exacerbated by illiberal Member States, and vice versa.

Having identified the problem, and the causes thereof, the authors then consider three possible ways in which the situation could be alleviated. The first is through development of an epistemological tool to identify illiberal elements, suggesting that the EU Justice Scoreboard could be developed to serve this purpose. The second suggestion is to strengthen the protection of fundamental rights, through completion of a European Fundamental Rights Union, whereby the EU Charter of Rights would also be available for purely domestic cases. The third suggestion is to strengthen and develop the *Spitzenkandidaten*-system, to enhance the democratic accountability of the Commission, and reduce the gap between it and the European Parliament.

The rule of law crisis and its implications for the functioning of the legal and political institutions of the EU is of concern and significance to all those interested in EU law. This book is a welcome addition to this discourse.

Paul Craig and Gráinne de Búrca

Preface

This book was born out of various frustrations. First of all, we were frustrated by the *lack of effective EU measures* concerning the erosion of the rule of law and democracy in some of its MSs. Even though recently the EU has indeed adopted some (mainly financial) measures concerning some of these issues, they not only fall significantly short of what could have been done, but have also been adopted too late to effectively tackle the problem. We are confronted with a story of missed opportunities, half-hearted, smokescreen, and postponed EU actions. There was always some other crisis (financial crisis, humanitarian challenges of supporting refugees, Brexit, the pandemic, Russian war of aggression against Ukraine, etc) that seemed to consume all the energy. Especially in order to maintain unity, the issue of erosion kept being swept under the rug. And with every delay and every omitted action, the erosion grew more severe.

Second, we were frustrated by the discourse that overly focused on new enforcement methods against illiberal EU MSs. We are convinced that this is not (and has never been) the main reason why the EU has been ineffective in dealing with these states. It has been a *lack of political will* that has resulted in existing enforcement methods not being triggered. Consequently, we wanted to discern how the institutional context could be shaped (possibly without formal treaty changes) to make EU action more likely.

Third, we were frustrated by the usual framing of these developments, both in the political and in the academic discourse. According to the usual framing, two EU MSs have *accidentally* been taken over by illiberal forces, so we just need to wait it out until this problem goes away. We think that this problem is not going to go away, as most former socialist countries have deep-seated cultural vulnerabilities to such developments. It was *not an accident*; there were severe risk factors present that were widely ignored. As a matter of fact, it is more likely that further EU MSs will fall victim to erosion. While we focus our analysis on former socialist countries, there are cultural risk factors in the legal and political culture of further EU MSs as well (such as tolerating/accepting corruption, strong affective polarization, prioritizing substantive justice of outcomes delivered by a strongman over procedural fairness—just to name a few potential vulnerabilities).

Fourth, we were frustrated by the search for illiberal legal rules in these regimes. While there are indeed a few formal legal rules which can be 'caught', the vast majority of the problems lie in the area of *informality*. Politically biased or selective application of the laws, combined with political rhetoric that trickles down to everyday life, is way more important. A liberal constitutional mask still predominately exists (even in Hungary where a new Fundamental Law has been adopted), but under this mask illiberal practices flourish. Without this liberal mask, the situation would be even worse. The normativity of the (formally largely still liberal) constitutional rules of these illiberal regimes is slowly getting weaker and weaker. With a traditional legal doctrinal mindset, we cannot conceptualize the nature of these regimes: they are not programmed in their formal legal rules.

Fifth, we were frustrated by the terminology 'rule of law crisis', as if the erosion of democracy in illiberal EU MSs was less bad or less important. We are in fact convinced that the rule of law and democracy are mutually dependent, as neither of them can flourish without the other. It is therefore a *twin crisis* of both democracy *and* the rule of law that should better be referred to as the *illiberal regime crisis* of the EU.

Sixth, we were frustrated by the idea that the erosion affects the EU only at the MS level. We wanted to show that the erosion of democracy and the rule of law at MS level unavoidably also poisons EU institutions. Furthermore, we wanted to highlight that, paradoxically, the EU strongly contributed to the formation of these regimes (through financial subsidies and by draining liberal cohorts of voters to Western Europe). In fact, what we are seeing is an unfortunate dynamics of *mutual poisoning*.

Despite all this frustration, we do want to be constructive. While the first part of the book is roughly an analysis of what has been happening, the second part aims to offer three underrated *antidotes*. Whether the illiberal erosion in the EU will actually be reversed, and whether it is even reversible at all, is unclear at this point. We would like to believe that it is reversible and that it will in fact be reversed, but unfortunately we cannot be certain. A number of sobering events and a series of unfulfilled hopes over the last couple of years have reminded us to remain cautious about being overly optimistic about *reversal*. We are, however, absolutely certain that the implementation of our proposals would make the chances of a reversal at least considerably higher. And we are equally certain that it would be essential, as a minimum strategy, for the *containment* of further illiberal erosion within the EU, and, thus, for saving the EU from its illiberal MSs.

András Jakab and Lando Kirchmair
Salzburg and Munich, 24 July 2024

Acknowledgements

As always, completing a book takes a lot of work and a lot of time. During such a long process, debts accumulate. Many colleagues have enriched our thinking and work with countless discussions during and outside academic events, and we have received helpful detailed comments on parts or even the entire manuscript. We would like to mention some of them and signal our gratitude to the participants of our online presentation on 'Measuring the rule of law—How to do it?' at the re:constitution seminar on 'Rule of Law Methodologies' on 22 April 2022; our online lecture on 'Methodological Problems of Measuring the Rule of Law' at the Pontificia Universidad Católica de Chile on 21 April 2022; our presentation on 'Democracy in the Member States: Hungary as an Example' at the Common Market Law Review Workshop on 'European Democracy' at the LMU University of Munich on 8 April 2022; our online presentation on 'Lage und Aussichten der Rechtsstaatlichkeit in Ungarn' at the event 'Ungarn vor den Parlamentswahlen' of the German Society of South-East European Studies (Südosteuropa Gesellschaft) on 31 March 2022; our presentation on 'Institutioneller Alkoholismus und der Abbau der Rechtsstaatlichkeit in früheren sozialistischen Staaten' at the conference 'Rechtsstaat und Demokratie unter Druck' of the University of Vienna on 25 March 2022; our Global Governance Lecture on 'Wer Rechtsstaat sagt, muss auch Grundrechte meinen: Die Grundrechtecharta als Instrument effektiver Durchsetzung des Rechtsstaatsprinzips' at the University of Graz on 23 June 2022; our lecture on 'Why the Rule of Law and Democracy Have Been Declining in Hungary and What Can Be Done About This?' at the Norwegian Institute of Foreign Affairs on 30 August 2022; our presentation on 'Können Rechtsstaatsdifferenzen und staatlich organisierte Korruption aus dem gemeinsamen europäischen Rechtsraum eliminiert werden?' during the conference on 'Lernt Europa aus seinen Krisen?' at the Distance-Learning University Hagen on 19 November 2022; our presentation on 'How to Develop the EU Justice Scoreboard into a Rule of Law Index' at the workshop on 'The Rule of Law in the Face of Contemporary Global Transformations: Challenges and Opportunities' at the Technical University Munich on 21 November 2022; our presentation on 'Constitutional Resilience in the EU' a SCEUS 'jour fixe' on 15 January 2023, our presentation at an online event on the *Spitzenkandidaten*-system at the

Global Constitutionalism Colloquium of the Wissenschaftszentrum Berlin on 18 January 2023; our presentation on 'The Role of Law: Formality vs Informality' during the workshop 'Informality, electoral and organizational clientelism in the East and the West of Europe' at the Andrássy University Budapest on 31 March 2023; our online presentation on 'EU Constitutional Resilience' at the Judicial Studies Institute of Masaryk-University Brno on 16 January 2023, as well as in particular to Sebastian Ambros, Larissa Bley, Sarah Deisl, László Detre, Borbála Garai, Stefan Griller, Viktoria Jachmann, Marcus Klamert, Christoph Krenn, Lisa Lechner, Florian Lehne, Aistė Mickonytė, John Morijn, Rainer Palmstorfer, Benedikt Pirker, Isabel Staudinger, Attila Vincze, Paul Weismann, Edvin Zukic, and the two anonymous reviewers.

We are very proud that our book has been accepted for publication in the prestigious Oxford Studies in European Law series. We would like to thank Paul Craig and Gráinne de Búrca for all their efforts in bringing us to this point. Thanks are also due to the staff at OUP, especially to Rachel Kavanaugh for her professional work. We are also grateful to Viktoria Jachmann for preparing the index.

Two of the chapters were (in somewhat different forms) previously published with Cambridge University Press under the terms of the Creative Commons Attribution licence (<https://creativecommons.org/licenses/by/4.0/>). These are Chapter 5 ('How to Develop the EU Justice Scoreboard into a Rule of Law Index: Using an Existing Tool in the EU Rule of Law Crisis in a More Efficient Way' (2021) 22 *German Law Journal* 936–55) and Chapter 6 ('Two Ways of Completing the European Fundamental Rights Union: Amendment to vs. Reinterpretation of Article 51 of the EU Charter of Fundamental Rights' (2022) 24 *Cambridge Yearbook of European Legal Studies* 239–61).

Even if it is often just an excuse for not having spent enough time with our families, we would like to express our deepest gratitude to our loved ones. After all, they are the ones who give us hope and encourage us to keep thinking about how we can contribute to making things better, without giving in to frustration. Therefore, we would like to dedicate this book to Lisa and Emily, and Christina and Theoneri.

Outline Contents

Detailed Contents

Figures

Tables

Table of Cases

(1) COURT OF JUSTICE OF THE EUROPEAN UNION

(a) European Court of Justice: Cases

(b) European Court of Justice: Opinions

(c) **General Court: Cases**

2. AUSTRIA

3. GERMANY

4. HUNGARY

5. POLAND

Abbreviations

AB	Alkotmánybíróság (Hungarian Constitutional Court)
AG	Advocate General
BEEPS	Business Environment and Enterprise Performance Survey
BTI	Bertelsmann Transformation Index
BVerfG	Bundesverfassungsgericht (German Federal Constitutional Court)
BVerfGE	Entscheidungen des Bundesverfassungsgerichts (Decisions of the German Federal Constitutional Court)
CEPEJ	Commission européenne pour l'efficacité de la justice (European Commission for the Efficiency of Justice)
Cf	conferatur
CFR	Charter of Fundamental Rights of the European Union
Ch	chapter
CJEU	Court of Justice of the European Union
COE	Council of Europe
COVID-19	Coronavirus Disease 2019
CPIA	Country Policy and Institutional Assessment
CPR	Common Provisions Regulation
CR	Conditionality Regulation
EC	European Commission
ECB	European Central Bank
ECJ	European Court of Justice
ECR	European Case Reports
ECHR	European Convention on Human Rights
ECtHR	European Court of Human Rights
eg	exempli gratia
ENCJ	European Network of Councils for the Judiciary
EP	European Parliament
EPP	European People's Party
EU	European Union
EUJS	European Union Justice Scoreboard
FIW	Freedom in the World
ie	id est
MEP	Member of the European Parliament
MPIL	Max Planck Institute for Comparative Public Law & International Law
MS(s)	Member State(s)
NGO(s)	Non-Governmental Organization(s)

OECD	Organization for Economic Co-operation and Development
OHCHR	Office of the High Commissioner for Human Rights
OSCE	Organization for Security and Cooperation in Europe
PM	Prime Minister
PSPP	Public Sector Purchase Programme
RLI	Rule of Law Index
RRF	Recovery and Resilience Facility (EU)
RRFR	Recovery and Resilience Facility Regulation
RRP	Recovery and Resilience Plan (EU)
TCE	Treaty establishing a Constitution for Europe
TEU	Treaty on European Union
TFEU	Treaty on the Functioning of the European Union
TK	Trybunał Konstytucyjny (Polish Constitutional Court)
UN	United Nations
US(A)	United States (of America)
VfGH	Verfassungsgerichtshof (Austrian Constitutional Court)
VfSlg	Sammlung der Erkenntnisse und wichtigsten Beschlüsse des Verfassungsgerichtshofes (Collected Decisions of the Austrian Constitutional Court)
WGI	Worldwide Governance Indicators
WJP	World Justice Project

Introduction

Mutual Poisoning and Three Underrated Antidotes

Nowadays criticism of the (often missing, belated, and mostly called for) European Union (EU) measures to improve the rule of law and democracy in Europe is commonplace in EU law scholarship. Too often, the European Commission (EC) in particular has failed to meet expectations for a strong commitment to the EU's core values (enshrined in Article 2 of the Treaty on the European Union, TEU) in light of the actions of Hungary and Poland, two illiberal Member States (MSs) in the EU.

While the nature of the erosion of the rule of law and democracy was unclear for a long time, which meant that grounds for hope existed that the solution to the problem was simply a lack of understanding of the current situation, or at least of its gravity or long-term impacts, this explanation is no longer accurate. This sounds surprising, considering the number of years that have passed since the slow demise of the rule of law and democracy began. Perhaps, the reason why one or more EU organs have failed to act is because they still do not fully grasp the long-term dangers emanating from illiberal MSs. As an explanation for an entire organization like the EU, however, this is no longer convincing.

There are, we contend, three major misconceptions concerning the EU 'rule of law crisis' that we want to address in this book. The first misconception is expressed in the denomination, as the name 'rule of law crisis' is actually misleading (cf especially Chapters 1 to 4), the second is to conceive of it as a 'crisis only in the MSs affected' (cf Chapters 3 and 4), and the third is to believe that 'the EU does not have the necessary legal tools' (cf chapters 5, 6, and 7). We address these issues in seven chapters. We begin by explaining our theoretical framework, namely institutionalism, which highlights--besides formal rules--important elements of the rule of law and democracy often overlooked by lawyers: de facto practices and narratives (Chapter 1). Using this framework, we are well placed to provide detailed insights into the decline of the rule of law and democracy in Hungary. We will see that the reasons for this erosion are not specific to Hungary, as has already been demonstrated by Poland

Saving the European Union from Its Illiberal Member States. András Jakab and Lando Kirchmair,
Oxford University Press.
DOI: 10.1093/oso/9780198954606.003.0001

and very recently by Slovakia (Chapter 2). But it is not just some MSs that are in trouble. The EU itself suffers from rule of law and democracy deficits, which have a negative impact on the EU's ability to confront its illiberal MSs (Chapter 3). This leads to the diagnosis that the rule of law and democracy are interdependent, not only within a single country but across the multi-level system of the EU and all its MSs (Chapter 4). In Chapters 5, 6, and 7 we then offer antidotes to what we diagnose as the mutual poisoning of the EU and its illiberal MSs.

First, in Chapter 1, we lay out our theoretical framework. We hold that institutionalism provides important insights for understanding legal systems. Institutionalism highlights that formal legal rules work in interplay with informal elements of de facto practices and narratives. To be more precise, institutions are made up of the interplay of three components: formal rules, actual practices, and narratives. From this we draw lessons to be learned for institution-building. In the first chapter, we aim to lay the groundwork for answering the question as to how to get former socialist EU MSs back on track.

In Chapter 2, we revisit the emergence of illiberal regimes in post-socialist EU MSs and make the argument that it is far too simplistic to talk about the EU's 'rule of law crisis'. We are convinced that it is more fitting to call it an 'illiberal regime crisis'. Institution-building concerning the rule of law and democracy has been a moderately successful feat in post-socialist EU MSs like Hungary and Poland. To put it more pessimistically, it has partially failed since the end of socialism, in particular when it comes to actual practices and narratives, that is, when it comes to informal institutional elements.

The erosion of democracy and the rule of law is usually caused by an unfortunate combination of various factors that can include political, sociological, cultural, and economic trends and circumstances. Certain countries have a weaker immune system against erosion than others, with post-socialist MSs particularly likely to appear amongst the problematic cases. Lawyers have a tendency to not pay enough attention to the informal elements (practices and narratives) in this failure, even though they have been much more important than formal legal norms. Inherited cultural patterns from socialism (and even from the times before) are much more informative about what has happened and why. The nature of such regimes cannot be understood based on their formal legal rules, as the typical modus operandi is exactly the biased application of laws. We can observe a growing gap between written laws and legal reality: the normativity of formal legal norms is slowly deteriorating in these regimes (especially in politically sensitive legal areas) and informal extra-legal practices are becoming increasingly stronger, often (at least partially) contrary to existing laws. The forms are still there, but slowly they are being hollowed out. Captured institutions (such as constitutional courts and the prosecutorial services) are independent on paper, but in reality they follow the wishes of the central government. All this is possible because of the inherited legal and political culture of these countries that serves as a breeding ground for such developments.

In the last decade, at least two EU MSs have degraded from (fragile) liberal democracies (which they indeed became after socialism) to illiberal regimes (Hungary and Poland). These are not full-blown dictatorships, at least not yet, even though the situation is getting worse year by year in Hungary, with no end in sight. Poland, on the one hand, has become a cause for hope after the last elections in 2023. However, we should not get our hopes up about the rule of law and democracy in the EU, because, on the other hand, another country, Slovakia, seems to have been infected. The illiberal EU MSs are currently in-between in the grey zone. Not only key elements of the rule of law, like judicial independence, but also mechanisms of democratic accountability have been eroded, albeit to a different degree: 'elections are free, but not fair', and both private and public media are centralized and used as propaganda machines. The extent to which these phenomena occurred differ in various MSs. Most of our examples of illiberal MS practices are from Hungary, as this country has eroded the furthest and it has the longest history of erosion. We consider, however, our analysis also applicable to other MSs, especially to post-socialist MSs: the phenomena are characteristic for the entire region, even if they are less dramatic and less obvious elsewhere. Also the pre-democratic cultural explanatory factors are similar in our opinion. This is why we prefer the terminology 'illiberal', as this shows the deliberate negation of the post-war liberal constitutionalist consensus of democracy and the rule of law. The terminology 'hybrid regime' already presupposes a severe deterioration (which in the case of Poland has never been achieved).[1]

In Chapter 3 we make the case that it is wrong to conceive of all this 'purely as a crisis of the MSs affected'. The illiberal regime crisis is actually a symptom of the EU's own constitutional malaise. We argue that what we have seen is an unfortunate dynamic of mutual poisoning: existing vulnerabilities and

[1] Leonardo Morlino, 'Hybrid Regimes' in András Sajó, Renáta Uitz, and Stephen Holmes (eds), *Routledge Handbook of Illiberalism* (Routledge 2022) 142. Cf also Gábor Halmai, 'Illiberalism in East-Central Europe' in András Sajó, Renáta Uitz, and Stephen Holmes (eds), *Routledge Handbook of Illiberalism* (Routledge 2022) 813; Dániel Hegedűs, 'An Externally Constrained Hybrid Regime: Hungary in the European Union' (2018) 25 Democratization 1173.

weaknesses of democracy and the rule of law at EU law level are being made even worse by illiberal MSs, and also the other way around.

On the one hand, doubts about the democratic credentials of the EU are made more plausible by illiberal MSs influencing EU decision-making procedures. Members of the European Parliament (MEPs) are elected in increasingly unfair national procedures (as European Parliament (EP) elections are organized by MS authorities and largely according to MS legal rules), MS governments with doubtful democratic credentials can delegate EU officials, and border-crossing judicial cooperation becomes more and more difficult if MSs appoint fake judges. The EU on the other hand misses opportunities (fails to launch infringement procedures, delays the application of the conditionality regimes) and actually finances (still, up to this day) the erosion of its basic values--to a large extent due to problems of democratic accountability at EU level.

In short, in recent years we have witnessed the dark side of the strong entanglement and interconnectedness that the European integration process has created. It is not only the case that the transition to constitutional liberal democracy can be strongly supported by institutions like the EU. The opposite is also possible. Illiberal tendencies can take advantage of this interconnectedness and help spread illiberalism throughout the EU. This dark side of the interconnectedness of European integration poses challenges to democracy and the rule of law. It has so far been understudied and underemphasized; we suspect this is the case because it is rarely acknowledged that the EU itself is affected.

To elaborate this insight, we recount the history of the constitutional dimension of the EU in Chapter 3 as intertwined stories: the development of the rule of law and democracy. After briefly recounting the evolution of the doctrines of direct applicability and primacy at the European Court of Justice (ECJ), the most important institutional driving force of European constitutionalism, we address the history of enforcement and supremacy conflicts. As the rule of law continued to develop, the need for democratic legitimacy grew stronger, that is, this has actually contributed to democratization. By democratization we refer to the establishment and the process of enhancing the effectivity of political accountability of political decision-makers, both in the executive (EC) and the legislative (EP, and the Council of the EU). This intertwined development is key to understanding how the relationship between the institutions of the EU and the legislation procedures have changed over the decades.

When the EU is perceived in this manner, it is clear that we are not entirely dealing with a success story. After we have spelled out these important strands of development, it becomes obvious that the challenge of a stable rule of law and democracy does not only concern the MSs but also the EU itself. Among other things, a wave of crises of the EU—namely the financial crisis, the refugee situation, the COVID health crisis, and the Russian aggression resulting in the largest security and humanitarian crisis since the Second World War—have left their marks on the functioning of the EU too. There has even been an erosion of the rule of law and democracy at EU level impacting all EU organs. In other words, it is not only that the EU needs to be saved from its illiberal MSs: the EU also needs to be saved from itself. To give just another example: the democratic deficit of the EU was a major point of discussion in the 1980s and 1990s up until the Treaty of Lisbon secured some important improvements to this end, for instance by strengthening the role of the EP. Yet the 2019 elections to the EP, which were presented very much as though the *Spitzenkandidaten*-system was to be implemented for the first time, and the process by which the current President of the EC was finally selected, were a major disappointment for democracy at EU level. This comes at a massive cost. Trust, a major political resource when handling crises, is sorely lacking, and legitimacy, a key source of political authority, is wanting. More importantly, the central political figure in the EU is not really accountable to the EP. The EC President was promoted in 2019, almost out of the blue, and crowned by the—or rather some of the—governments of the MSs in the Council (at a high cost), and the EP did not have much say. The point is not that the *Spitzenkandidaten*-system, a quite specific way of designing political accountability, is the miracle solution to all democracy problems in Europe. Rather, the profound lack of directly attributable democratic political accountability for a key European institution, the EC, is an important shortcoming which could have been addressed by complying with the *Spitzenkandidaten*-system after the elections for the EP. The elections to the EP in 2024 have indeed shown the potential for the reintroduction of the *Spitzenkandidaten*-system. After all, the *Spitzenkandidat* of the party that received the most votes (again Ursula von der Leyen, but this time as the top candidate of the European People's Party, EPP) was able to collect the majority of votes in the EP and was once again elected as President of the European Commission on 18 July 2024. This is a victory for the *Spitzenkandidaten*-system, which raises hopes that it will help to make the EC more accountable.

The legal tools to tackle the illiberal regime crisis are there, but the Commission has so far been applying them half-heartedly, selectively, late, or not at all. The present book aims to shine a spotlight on those areas that have been somewhat neglected so far and thereby shed new light on why this has been happening.

In Chapter 4, we suggest that what has been happening in the EU's illiberal regimes is more of a twin crisis, namely, a slow erosion of both democracy and the rule of law. By focusing exclusively on the rule of law, the debate is missing the point of how democracy and the rule of law mutually support each other. It has been commonly known for some time that the rule of law, and especially certain political fundamental rights, are preconditions for a democratic process. However, one should not forget the reverse causality either: namely, that the rule of law is itself a product of democratic rotation; if governing parties have no fear of being outvoted and finding themselves in opposition, they will inevitably be less and less inclined to respect the separation of powers, particularly judicial independence, and fundamental rights. Moreover, if we understand the rule of law as the negation of unlimited government power, then democratic accountability contributes to it, itself being a limitation on government power.

In Chapter 4, we reap the benefits of our analysis to this point. The insights of the first three chapters are brought together by highlighting specifically how and why inherited cultural (informal institutional) factors in several post-socialist countries in combination with certain unforeseen side-effects of an EU membership have contributed to erosion. This was brought about through various mechanisms: it has been suspected for a while now, albeit not without criticism, that an abundance of natural resources, such as oil and the revenues gained therefrom contribute to the strengthening of autocratic regimes: the *ceteris paribus* low economic performance of the autocracy, it has been claimed, is masked by oil revenues. The EU funds apportioned to new EU MSs play a similar role. Because it is easy to immigrate to Western Europe, citizens believing in Western values and being free to move are leaving their home countries in a proverbial 'brain drain', thereby facilitating the dismantling of institutions of the rule of law and democracy. It is therefore important to note that it is not only the EU that needs to be saved from its illiberal MSs (and from itself). It is also the MSs that need to be saved from the EU. Hence, the rule of law and democracy at EU and MS levels are complexly and deeply intertwined in many ways. This is the consequence of decades of European integration.

In addition, illiberal MSs do not isolate. The erosion of the rule of law and democracy in specific MSs is poisonous for other MSs, and the EU itself. Just consider these examples: by investing into various foreign media assets or by ruining judicial cooperation through fake judges, illiberal MSs look out for allies and seek to expand their influence in other MSs. It is not only that illiberal regimes are poisoning other MSs, but they are also infecting the EU too. If the elections in an MS are not free and fair, the political actors voted into power will be acting like Trojan horse officials on the EU level too—in the Parliament and the Commission alike. The EU must ensure the rule of law and democracy for itself before it is too late. The more MSs turn into illiberal regimes, the more difficult it will be to stop the further spread of this poison.

This development is unfortunate because we have witnessed now for years that in a situation in which the rule of law and democracy are declining, nothing improves by itself and in fact everything is much more likely to get worse. One thing is for certain, burying your head in the sand, averting your gaze, crossing your fingers, or waiting until the storm might pass are not a great idea. If nothing is done to prevent attacks on the rule of law and democracy, the situation will simply get worse and worse.[2] Going beyond a diagnosis of how the rule of law and democracy are mutually dependent across the multi-level system of the EU and its MSs, and building upon the institutionalist framework in Chapter 1, we wish to offer guidelines in Chapter 4 for future institution-building in illiberal MSs. A key insight is that lack of foreign pressure to observe democratic and rule of law standards can be dangerous. This was exactly what happened when the new MSs joined the EU, for post-accession conditionality is much weaker than pre-accession conditionality. Once a country joined the EU, hardly any measures were taken which exerted pressure and demanded or enforced democratic or rule of law standards. The authoritarian cultural traits of a society are like alcoholism: although it is theoretically possible to kick one's addiction alone, normally one needs external help or pressure, given the empirically evident great danger of relapsing (ie institutional alcoholism). While the equality of MSs before the law might have hampered interventions given that MS politicians were especially eager to protect remaining national spheres of sovereignty, to successfully cure alcoholism it is important that everyone involved accepts the tragic truth that a family member is an alcoholic.

The EU, however, will only be able to restore the rule of law and democracy in all its MSs when it faces its own deficits. This is important to understand when considering how the EU could fix, first, its own constitutional problems (Chapter 3) in order to, second, master the illiberal regime MS challenge (Chapter 2). An important insight in relation to addressing this challenge is that the rule of law and democracy are mutually dependent and can therefore only be protected and fixed together.

[2] See also Gráinne de Búrca, 'Poland and Hungary's EU Membership: On not Confronting Authoritarian Governments' (2022) 20 International Journal of Constitutional Law 13, 34 speaking of 'risks of non-confrontation'.

Fortunately, and third (Chapters 5, 6, and 7), it is outright false to say that the 'EU does not have the necessary enforcement tools' to fix all this. As a matter of fact, it does. It always has. The problem has rather been that the application of these enforcement mechanisms depends at one point or another on political discretion. Just to provide a few examples: first, in the Article 7 procedure the Council (of foreign ministers) and the European Council decide at key points of the procedure. Second, releasing EU funds, which was considered to be a key leverage in the illiberal regime crisis, also depends on political discretion. The decision of the EC on 13 December 2023 to release funds (€10.2 billion) to Hungary[3] has even prompted the EP to initiate proceedings at the ECJ, presumably because the release of funds was more closely linked to Orbán not vetoing another aid package to Ukraine than to significant rule of law reforms in Hungary. In a strictly legal sense, the EC has likely acted within its discretion when releasing the money. Third, also in the case of infringement procedures, the EC has political discretion whether to launch them or not—and what we have seen in the last two decades is a stark decline in the number of new infringement procedures. MSs have not become more law-abiding, but the willingness of the EC to launch infringement procedures has declined. The situation increasingly resembles horse trading: if an MS is in violation of EU law in, for example, four matters, then the EC is often willing to look the other way in two cases, if at least the remaining two will be solved quickly. Political expediency rules over law enforcement.

This can be changed. We propose antidotes which (largely) already exist and which would only have to be adapted and applied to resolve the illiberal regime challenge. First, we need to better evaluate the situation without whitewashing it. We need an epistemological tool to this end which we identify in an *adapted* EU Justice Scoreboard (Chapter 5). Second, we need to strengthen the protection of fundamental rights in all MSs. A solid guarantee of fundamental rights is important to uphold or restore the rule of law, which in turn also positively influences a democratic culture. We therefore make the case for *completing* the European Fundamental Rights Union, which can be achieved in two ways: treaty amendment or a reinterpretation of Article 51 (1) of the EU Charter of Fundamental Rights (CFR) (Chapter 6). Third, the *Spitzenkandidaten*-system needs to be further strengthened and stabilized for the long term—not only to ensure the democratic accountability of the

[3] Commission Decision, on the reassessment, on the Commission's initiative, of the fulfilment of the conditions under Article 4 of Regulation (EU, Euratom) 2020/2092 following Council Implementing Decision (EU) 2022/2506 of 15 December 2022 regarding Hungary 13 December 2023, C(2023) 8999 final.

Commission, but also because this has the potential to approximate the so far undecided and hesitant stance of the Commission to the clearly anti-illiberal-regime stance of the EP. In the long run, the *Spitzenkandidaten*-system can create an effective institutional incentive for the coherent application of the already existing enforcement tools by the EC against the EU's illiberal regimes (Chapter 7). These antidotes, however, are not meant to be an encyclopedic analysis of all possible tools, but rather serve as examples of certain hitherto underrated ones which could be used quite easily and would have a long-lasting effect on improving institutional structures.

We are not suggesting that these three antidotes are the only ones that might prove effective, but (1) they have been underrated (ie underemphasized in the discourse, as they are less obvious than the usually suggested tools), and (2) they are realistic in the sense that no treaty amendment is necessary for them (which is less realistic in our opinion as illiberal MSs would clearly oppose them). There may be other tools that could help. For example, withholding large sums of financial aid, as is done today, can be a somewhat effective incentive to correct certain illiberal policies––even if these are not applied to their potential (and in order to apply them fully, again, the *Spitzenkandidaten*-system and the establishment of indices can be helpful).[4] However, the three antidotes that we present in this book are less discussed and provide for important structural improvements that can have long-lasting effects.

The most important—but so far largely overlooked—reason why the performance of the EU in restoring and protecting core European values internally has fallen short is that the EU itself suffers from severe shortcomings precisely regarding the rule of law and democracy. What the antidotes we propose have in common is that they directly address these shortcomings. In other words, they are a more comprehensive treatment because they address not only the symptoms but also the deep-rooted institutional mechanisms of the illiberal regime crisis. On a more positive note, the legal tools are there, even though the EC has so far been unwilling to apply them. The present book aims to unfold why this has been the situation and, importantly, what can be done about it to save the EU from its illiberal MSs.

[4] For problems in the application of various conditionality regimes, see László Detre, András Jakab, and Tamás Lukácsi, 'Comparing Three Financial Conditionality Regimes and Their Application to Hungary: The Conditionality Regulation, the Recovery and Resilience Facility Regulation, and the Common Provisions Regulation' (2023) 23 Max Planck Institute for Comparative Public Law & International Law (MPIL) Research Paper No 2023-23.

1

Legal Institutionalism as a Conceptual Frame for Understanding and Confronting the Current EU Illiberal Regime Crisis

1. Introduction

Institutionalism provides important insights for understanding legal systems. Institutionalism, old and new alike,[1] highlights the importance of (institutional) context.[2] Taking context seriously is something which has been lost to some extent by legal doctrine. Hans Kelsen's *Pure Theory of Law* is a prime example of focusing on formal rules while consciously excluding 'legal reality' from scientifically studying the law. The so-called institutionalist legal theories (Savigny, Santi Romano, Hauriou, Schmitt, Weinberger, MacCormick) show a very diverse picture, however, partly criticizing each other as well. These studies are using a terminology different from that of the present book to describe the nature of law.[3] A typical tenet in many of these theories is that besides the concepts of positive law, there are also metaphysical 'institutions' (eg marriage) that are realized through positive law (this tenet has no necessary connection to our considerations in the present book).[4] As the present book's focus

[1] Emphasizing the continuities between 'old institutionalism' and 'new institutionalism', see eg Philip Selznick, 'Institutionalism "Old" and "New"' (1996) 41 Administrative Science Quarterly 270, 273 and 276, by pointing at one of the key works of New Institutionalism: Walter W Powell and Paul J DiMaggio (eds), *The New Institutionalism in Organizational Analysis* (University of Chicago Press 1991), by highlighting what is also of the essence for us here (at 274), 'Attention to myths and symbols is hardly new', and (at 274) by stating that '"new" is the reconception of formal structure as "thickly" institutionalized ... On this understanding, the official design is created within a received and constructed framework of culture and constraint.' Cf, however, also James G March and Johan P Olsen, *Rediscovering Institutions: The Organizational Basis of Politics* (Free Press 2010) 2: 'The new and old are not identical, however. It would probably be more accurate to describe recent thinking as blending elements of an old institutionalism into the neo-institutionalist styles of recent theories of politics.'

[2] See eg Gretchen Helmke and Steven Levitsky (eds), *Informal Institutions and Democracy: Lessons from Latin America* (Johns Hopkins University Press 2006) preface, describing the astonishing differences between formal institutions and the informal realities in Latin America during the mid-1990s.

[3] For more details see Massimo La Torre, *Law as Institution* (Springer 2010) 98–121.

[4] For more detail and criticism see Bernd Rüthers, *Institutionelles Rechtsdenken im Wandel der Verfassungsepochen: Ein Beitrag zur politisch-kritischen Funktion der Rechtswissenschaft* (Gehlen 1970) 33–7.

Saving the European Union from Its Illiberal Member States. András Jakab and Lando Kirchmair, Oxford University Press. © András Jakab and Lando Kirchmair 2025.
DOI: 10.1093/oso/9780198954606.003.0002

is not the history of legal theories, but the current situation, we are not going to critically analyse these legal theories. The concept of institution that is used in the present book does not stem from any of these institutionalist legal theories (and it is also not a doctrinal concept), but rather from political science.

There are various definitions for the concept of 'institution'. For the purposes of the present inquiry, the most suitable definition describes institutions as consisting of three components or, more precisely, an interplay of these components: (a) formal rules, (b) actual practices, and (c) narratives.[5] The latter two (ie practices and narratives) are referred to jointly as 'informal' components (and we refer to a large part of de facto habitual behaviour and beliefs vaguely as legal culture[6]), when juxtaposed with 'formal' rules. Such informal elements may operate (unwritten) institutions which may prove to be even more powerful than formal institutions. In Helmke and Levitsky's words: 'They reinforce, subvert, and sometimes even supersede formal rules, procedures, and organizations.'[7] A typical example would be institutionalized corruption. While the different components may mutually reinforce one another, producing resilient institutions, in case of discrepancy they may actually weaken each other, leading to weak institutions.

One of the main functions of any institution is to increase predictability, to reinforce law-abiding behaviour, and thus promote long-term thinking. This, however, is in stark contrast to the current Hungarian regime, which stands out due to its ad hoc, short-term driven, pragmatic power politics which almost completely neglects actual public policy considerations.[8] On several occasions, the government has violated the formal rules of the very legal order that it runs. Hence, an actual practice which is focused on completely 'controlling the political moment' resists any substantive narrative (in this case, theoretical foundation).[9] If we want to understand how to address the illiberal regime in Hungary, we submit that the perspective of (legal) institutionalism

[5] Vivien Lowndes and Mark Roberts, *Why Institutions Matter: The New Institutionalism in Political Science* (Palgrave Macmillan 2013) 46, 77: 'power is exercised through regulation, practice and storytelling'. Thus by institution we do not mean the mere sum of different legal rules about a social issue, but emphatically more than that.

[6] For an interesting analysis of the relationship between culture and institutions from an economic perspective, see eg Alberto Alesina and Paola Giuliano, 'Culture and Institutions' (2015) 53 Journal of Economic Literature 898, 899–901 showing awareness for the 'arduous task' of defining culture.

[7] Gretchen Helmke and Steven Levitsky, 'Introduction' in Gretchen Helmke and Steven Levitsky (eds), *Informal Institutions and Democracy: Lessons from Latin America* (Johns Hopkins University Press 2006) 1, 2.

[8] See Chapter 2.

[9] Theoretical foundations are, by their nature, futile in this regime. For such attempts, however, see eg Z András Varga, *Eszményből bálvány? A joguralom dogmatikája* (Századvég 2015); Ádám Rixer (ed), *Állam és közösség: Válogatott közjogi tanulmányok Magyarország Alaptörvénye tiszteletére* (Patrocinium 2012).

in general and institution-building in particular is instructive. Legal institutionalism provides, furthermore, important insights for improving the rule of law and democracy at EU level.

2. Key Insights of Legal Institutionalism: We Ought to Be Aware of Informal Institutional Elements like Practices and Narratives

Both the entire legal system and its individual elements (eg judicial review or private property) may be conceptualized as institutions. These institutions do not exist in isolation, but instead reinforce, complement, or even weaken each other ('institutional environment').[10] An institution will be considered 'strong' when it is capable of efficiently influencing human behaviour in a permanent and predictable manner. While this, on its own, is not a sufficient condition for the state's (economic) success, strong institutions bolstering the rule of law and democracy (both referred to here as constitutional institutions) will significantly contribute to economic success.

The present book does not deal in detail with definitions of the rule of law or theories of democracy. Rule of law here means its formal elements—in particular, predictability, effectiveness, and clarity—as well as substantive elements such as separation of powers and the protection of fundamental rights both formally and in reality. By democracy we simply refer to the possibility of making elected officials responsible for not promoting the citizens' interests—by not re-electing them, that is, by making them compete on the basis of who could promote the citizens' interests best. Governments could be forced by their electorate to change measures that are harmful to their interests (trial and error). In other words, for the purpose of this book, democracy is understood as the concurrent presence of the following qualities of any regime: (a) periodically organized fair and free elections, (b) general and equal suffrage, (c) an actual and legally realistic chance of voting the incumbent government out of office, and (d) voters having a real opportunity and the legal means to inform themselves about the performance of the government. It is evident from these definitions that the two notions include factual and legal elements. Of course,

[10] Elinor Ostrom, 'An Agenda for the Study of Institutions' (1986) 48 Public Choice 3, 7–8; Gretchen Helmke and Steven Levitsky, 'Informal Institutions and Comparative Politics: A Research Agenda' (2004) 2 Perspectives on Politics 725.

this is not the only way to define democracy and the rule of law; however, it is a useful definition for our purpose here.[11]

These virtues of democracy eventually also made these communities economically stronger, which was necessary for successfully fighting international conflicts. Empirical studies have confirmed that (except for extremely poor countries) democracy makes economic growth more likely (all other factors being equal). The idea of equal freedom itself also has economic implications, as it helps competition. Non-discrimination means that the most capable should do the job, and that only his or her individual achievements count. Protection of private property is necessary for capitalist economic growth. Protection of privacy and freedom of thought contribute to a fearless and creative working environment. Political freedoms ensure democracy, so their economic impact is relatively indirect.[12]

From an institutionalist perspective, the constitution is not merely a sum of constitutional rules, but also the actual practice of constitutional bodies and narratives surrounding the constitution. The latter can be, for instance, that the 'purpose of the constitution is to restrict the power of the state' or that 'the purpose of the constitution is to guarantee human rights', etc.

It is typical for lawyers around the world to focus primarily on the first, formal element of institutions: the rules. While we consider this too strong a focus on formal rules it is, precisely in the context of post-socialist EU MSs, misleading. It is, one could say, a post-socialist trait to consider it a virtue to proudly ignore the other elements.[13] The failures of institution-building in post-socialist countries experienced in the past three decades shed light on the downsides of this approach.[14] This may also be discerned in typical post-socialist legal training where legal education is confined to reciting existing legislation or reproducing legal-doctrinal constructs.[15] The same goes for the

[11] On dilemmas about the definition of the rule of law and democracy, see András Jakab, *European Constitutional Language* (CUP 2016) and Jørgen Møller and Svend-Erik Skaaning, *Requisites of Democracy: Conceptualization, Measurement, and Explanation* (Routledge 2011).

[12] For a deep analysis of these questions with further references, see Robert D Cooter, *The Strategic Constitution* (Princeton University Press 2000); Sigrid A Koob, Stinne S Jørgensen, and Hans-Otto Sano, *Human Rights and Economic Growth: An Econometric Analysis of the Rights to Education and Health* (Report of the Danish Institute for Human Rights 2017).

[13] Cf the reasons explained in detail in Chapter 2.

[14] For these phenomena in Hungarian parliamentary law see eg Péter Smuk, 'Az Országgyűlés' in András Jakab and György Gajduschek (eds), *A magyar jogrendszer állapota* (MTA TK 2016) 617: 'In several cases, we cannot blame the respective rules of the Standing Rules, but the [lack of] democratic and constitutional culture of the actors responsible for running the legal institutions' [translation AJ]; for post-Soviet failures, see Dennis J Galligan and Marina Kurkchiyan (eds), *Law and Informal Practices: The Post-Communist Experience* (OUP 2003).

[15] András Jakab, 'A magyar jogi oktatás megújításához szükséges lépések: Reformjavaslat összehasonlító áttekintésre alapozva' (2010) 4 Magyar Jog 204.

realm of legislation, where narratives—like 'what is the true purpose and the public policy aim of legislation?'—are largely neglected. In addition, *ex ante* and *ex post* impact studies on actual practices are not carried out. Thereby the task of legislation is reduced to the adoption of a formal act.[16] In György Gajduschek's words:

> the specification of public policy goals [in our terminology: legislative narratives—AJ/LK] is almost completely missing, questioning the rationality of the whole process. The way these tools are employed—which are almost exclusively of legalistic nature, or are considered as such—is ill-conceived. The shortcomings of implementation are particularly striking. With no planning or allocation of necessary resources, implementation is doomed to fail already from the outset. Public policies change so rapidly and to such a great degree, often taking a complete U-turn, that they have no time to 'run their course'. At times the system for implementing the policy has not even been set up and is already subject to change, but in general, there is hardly ever enough time for the impact and results of policies to take effect.[17]

Institutions are systems of different man-made, non-physical factors that 'generate regularities of behaviour'.[18] From among these, some (indeed perhaps even the majority) are unwritten and presupposed, stemming from narratives about actual practices. For example, when playing cards, one shall not punch one's opponent, pour boiling soup on the opponent's cards, etc. A formal description of possible card moves is not enough to thoroughly know the game, as there is much more involved. We must adhere to certain civilizational customs, which make the game even possible. This involves not only adherence to the formal rules, but also informal elements such as a common cultural understanding of the game. Poorly designed formal rules may of course result in weak institutions, but—and this seems to be more relevant here—officials' cultural shortcomings may contribute just as much. A republic without

[16] György Gajduschek, 'Előkészítetlenség és utólagos hatásvizsgálat hiánya' in András Jakab and György Gajduschek (eds), *A magyar jogrendszer állapota* (MTA TK 2016) 796.

[17] György Gajduschek, 'A közpolitikai célok megjelenése a jogban' in András Jakab and György Gajduschek (eds), *A magyar jogrendszer állapota* (MTA TK, 2016) 43

[18] Avner Greif, *Institutions and the Path to the Modern Economy: Lessons from Medieval Trade* (CUP 2006) 21. For a somewhat different terminology (institutions as a combination of formal and informal rules), though with a similar content, see Douglass C North, *Institutions, Institutional Change and Economic Performance* (CUP 1990) 3. It would be possible to introduce a fourth component of institutions between formal rules and actual practices: informal (unwritten) rules. This would definitely be more precise, but for the actual points that we would like to make in the present book, it did not seem necessary and, at the same time, it would have considerably complicated the explanations. Therefore, for the sake of simplicity, this conceptual component has not been introduced here.

republicans or a bureaucracy without (Weberian) bureaucrats is simply not going to measure up.

Authoritarian rules can make use of a mismatch between formal rules and informal elements in perfidious ways. Ozan Varol, for instance, summarizes Erdoğan's rule with a motto also attributed to various Latin American rulers: '"For my friends, everything, for my enemies, the law."'[19] What he coins 'stealth authoritarianism' makes use of the law, for instance, by conducting criminal prosecutions for non-political crimes which are selective, but may be formally in conformity with the law. He offers the example of someone who has been sentenced to sixteen years in prison for violating building codes. While he assumes that the convictions 'may have been legally accurate', he adds that 'in Turkey, illegal construction is the norm, not the exception'. Hence, the formally correct application of legal rules is misused in order to cut back on political opponents. Erdoğan's own 'thousand-room presidential palace', Varol adds, 'was constructed in violation of numerous zoning laws and court decisions'.[20]

Without analysing the informal practices, that is, in this case that illegal construction is formally against the law but de facto an accepted practice, it would not be possible to understand that the legal conviction was apparently politically motivated instead of an act of equal application of the law for all citizens. To study informal practices and narratives is, thus, of the essence if we want to understand what is actually going on in illiberal EU MSs. This is the very first step before we can think of how to (re-)construct institutions in order to (re-) align formal and informal elements of the law.

3. Lessons to Be Learned for Institution-Building

Institution-building is a more complex process than envisaged by the majority of lawyers. This is true everywhere but is of particular importance in post-socialist countries. Lawyers typically concentrate on formal elements, that is, written rules and perhaps the relevant implementing acts. This focus, however essential, is not sufficient to ensure the successful operation of legal institutions. The failure of numerous well-crafted constitutions may be explained by the naivety of the legal profession.[21] At the same time it is also true that

[19] Ozan O Varol, 'Stealth Authoritarianism in Turkey' in Mark A Graber, Sanford Levinson, and Mark Tushnet (eds), *Constitutional Democracy in Crisis?* (OUP 2018) 339, 344.

[20] Varol (n 19) 345. Despite that example, after the tragic earthquake in February 2023 with tens of thousands of victims, violating construction laws might not appear as a minor crime anymore.

[21] In certain situations, institution-building is an impossible mission. See eg the Transitional Constitution of the Republic of South Sudan (2011) which was a well-crafted text that also tried to

unsophisticated constitutions may be successful, if the right social practices and narratives replace and correct faulty formal rules'. Until most recently, the Constitutions of the United States[22] and the United Kingdom[23] were good examples for systems where patchy formal rules are supplemented by informal institutional elements. As Helmke and Levitsky put it:

> Informal [institutional elements] also shape formal institutional outcomes in a less visible, but equally important, way: by creating or strengthening incentives to comply with formal rules. In other words, they may do the enabling and constraining that we usually attribute to the formal rules.... [F]ormal [rules] often work because they are embedded in implicit and informally shared expectations, or 'grammatical rules', about the particular behavior governed by the explicit formal or 'game' rules. For example, the effectiveness and stability of the United States' presidential democracy is not only a product of the rules laid out in the Constitution, but is also rooted in a set of 'paraconstitutional' rules that prevent formal checks and balances from deteriorating into severe interbranch conflict ... The absence of such norms of restraint and accommodation may help explain why similarly designed presidentialist systems have often proven more crisisprone in Latin America.[24]

consider the local social reality, but which due to the civil war environment sadly failed. Despite the Constitution containing smart formal rules, South Sudan is a typical example of what we call a failed state. For more detail see Thilo Marauhn and Hatem Elliesie (eds), *Legal Transformation in Northern Africa and South Sudan* (Eleven 2015). For an interesting perspective, see also Adam Day, *States of Disorder, Ecosystems of Governance: Complexity Theory Applied to UN Statebuilding in the DRC and South Sudan* (OUP 2022) 6–8 providing thought-provoking insights based on complexity theory such as that (1) 'longer term socially focused engagement during periods of relative peace [rather than 'moments of violent conflict'] looking to gradually shift relationships when the system is not under immense pressure, may yield better results'; (2) 'a focus on the relationships that constitute systems, on the quality of exchange that sustains them, and how they might be gradually reconfigured'; (3) 'Complexity suggests it is important to be willing to work with the grain, understanding that underlying rules take time to shift, while accepting that some levels of "bad" governance may be necessary in the short term'; (4) instead of regretting a '"lack of political will"' on the level which ought to be transformed it is important to ask 'How much are individual actors able to change systems of governance?'; (5) 'a willingness to embrace the mystery of socio-political systems, even those that appear dysfunctional to outsiders, rather than trying to reduce them to single, simple narratives or fit them into external ... models' is finally important according to Day in the work of the UN when aiming at transforming states of disorder.

[22] The US Constitution is a very imperfect legal document, containing plenty of contradictions and loopholes; see for more detail William N Eskridge Jr and Sanford Levinson (eds), *Constitutional Stupidities, Constitutional Tragedies* (New York University Press 1998).

[23] In the UK some of the informal components of constitutional institutions are called 'constitutional conventions', see Jakab (n 11) 78, 147, and 200–1 with further references.

[24] Helmke and Levitsky (n 7) 3. The difference between the terminology of the present chapter and that of Helmke and Levitsky is that we differentiate between formal and informal elements (or components) of the same institutions, whereas they rather talk about 'formal institutions' and 'informal institutions' interacting with each other. While we think that this terminological difference is actually not central, we do believe that conceptualizing the phenomena as informal and formal elements of the same

Since these institutions have multiple components, they more often than not depart from the ideals envisioned by the makers of the formal rules. In other words, due to this complexity, legislation often takes recourse to the method of trial and error. Therefore, these institutions cannot actually be precisely traced back to the will of a single policy-designer, but instead combine several, in part contradictory, visions.[25] While this is bad news for the incumbent constitutional founding fathers at the time policy is conceived, they may later deny responsibility, and rightly so, in the event that the constitution fails.

3.1 The Difficulty of Institution-Building

Institution-building is particularly difficult in societies marked by strong value divisions, for narratives are already fraught by contradictions and will resist new formal rules more than in societies boasting a more homogeneous value order.[26] Discussing how divided societies produce weak constitutional institutions and what the resulting consequences are, Daren Acemoglu writes the following:

> [W]hen [constitutional] institutions are strong, citizens have the power to punish politicians by voting them out of power; when institutions are weak, politicians pursue clientelistic policies that punish citizens who fail to support them.... [M]any disastrous kleptocracies last for long periods; Mobutu ruled for thirty-two years, Trujillo for thirty-one, and the Somozas for forty-two years. This longevity is made even more surprising by the fact that many kleptocratic regimes lack both a core constituency of supporters and a firm command of the military....[27]

According to him, there are certain strategies for rulers to compensate for this lack:

institution generally better captures the interwovenness of the different elements—at least in areas that are the focus of the present book.

[25] Robert E Goodin, 'Institutions and Their Design' in Robert E Goodin (ed), *The Theory of Institutional Design* (CUP 1996) 28.

[26] Elinor Ostrom, *Understanding Institutional Diversity* (Princeton University Press 2005) 27.

[27] Daron Acemoglu, 'Constitutions, Politics and Economics: A Review Essay on Persson and Tabellini's The Economic Effects of Constitutions' (2005) 43 Journal of Economic Literature 1025, 1046.

> [O]wing to the absence of strong [constitutional] institutions, rulers can deploy strategies, in particular 'divide-and-rule' to defuse opposition to their regime. The logic of the divide-and-rule strategy is to enable a ruler to bribe politically pivotal groups off the equilibrium path, ensuring that he can remain in power against challenges. By providing selective incentives and punishments, the divide-and-rule strategy exploits the fragility of social cooperation in weakly-institutionalized polities: when faced with the threat of being ousted, the kleptocratic ruler intensifies the collective action problem and destroys the coalition against him by bribing the pivotal [social] groups....[28]

While he speaks of division along ethnic lines, his observations may be generalized, vividly portraying ideological opposition between social groups defined by twentieth-century history, like the case of the Hungarian left- and right-wing elites:

> Ethnic divisions are the key feature in [this] model. Each ethnic group is afraid of replacing their own leader when in power, because this increases the probability of a switch of power from their own ethnic group to a rival group. This makes the standard method of controlling political elites ... ineffective, and enables leaders to not only exploit other ethnic groups but also their own ethnic group.[29]

3.2 A Successful Example: Germany after the Second World War

Perhaps the most widely known example is the transformation that took place in Germany following the Second World War. Among the elements bolstering this success story are—without claiming to provide an exhaustive list—the following:

(a) Well-designed formal rules are important. German legal scholarship, traditionally of a high standard, contributed greatly to the creation of

[28] Acemoglu (n 27) 1046.

[29] Acemoglu (n 27) 1046. Even in societies which have strong institutions, strong ideological divides can have destructive effects, see eg the United States, Geoffrey C Layman, Thomas M Carsey, and Juliana M Horowitz, 'Party Polarization in American Politics: Characteristics, Causes, and Consequences' (2006) 9 Annual Review of Political Science 83.

well-designed formal legal rules;[30] although this was not a decisive factor as it seems to be possible to design excellent constitutional systems built on the rule of law despite a relatively weak legal scholarship background.[31] The intellectual matrix of German legal doctrine and the knowledge of crafting a formidable constitution certainly helped to build the *Rechtsstaat*.

(b) An honest narrative is a stable ground for the rule of law and democracy. Instead of indulging in self-pity, Germans confronted—albeit with a considerable delay, from the 1960s onwards—their mistakes and sins (*Vergangenheitsbewältig ung*).[32] Of course, populists and demagogues are always quick to offer simplistic narratives, serving up excuses instead of the painful truth. After the Second World War, however—somewhat belatedly, facilitated also by the ageing of the previous generation, but nevertheless-–, both the West German elite and society at large chose honesty. This moral stance towards the past helped forge a *credible* narrative for the legal order and, in particular, the *Grundgesetz*. The new regime built on human dignity, democracy and the rule of law.[33] The honesty and credibility of the social and political order further increased—as a self-reinforcing process—the social trust essential for success. Although facing the past in this way is not an indispensable condition for successful constitutional institution-building,[34] it certainly helps to achieve it.

(c) External pressure, and to a considerable degree, military occupation of the country made a backlash to authoritarianism impossible—although, admittedly, on its own this would not have been enough. Erstwhile Nazi views were not eradicated. In fact, some former Nazis kept their high offices and helped each other as a network. A notorious example would be the West German Ministry of Foreign Affairs until as late as the 1970s. Certain university faculties of law and the deeds and attitudes of specific jurists of famous legal scholars have been passed over in total silence or remained uncovered

[30] Cf on this eg Charles J Friedrich, 'Rebuilding the German Constitution, I' (1949) 43 American Political Science Review 461, 478 stating that 'According to all accounts, the experts [drafting the Basic Law on Herrenchiemsee from August 10 to 23 in 1948] worked in an objective spirit free from party antagonism. Indeed, the matters on which they split resulted not from party divisions, but from genuine disagreement dividing the members regardless of party.'

[31] Scandinavian states would be an example for such a constellation.

[32] For an overview, see Peter Reichel, *Vergangenheitsbewältigung in Deutschland: Die Auseinandersetzung mit der NS-Diktatur in Politik und Justiz* (CH Beck 2001).

[33] For a discussion of the role of moral legitimacy in making legal systems more efficient, as shown by the example of the Hungarian legal system, see Boda Zsolt, 'Bizalom, legitimitás és jogkövetés' in András Jakab and György Gajduschek (eds), *A magyar jogrendszer állapota* (MTA TK 2016) 837.

[34] Just take the example of Austria, which took much more time until the mid-1980s to confront its role in the Second World War. See Heidemarie Uhl, 'Das "erste Opfer": Der österreichische Opfermythos und seine Transformationen in der Zweiten Republik' (2001) 30 Austrian Journal of Political Science 19.

for a long time.[35] Nevertheless, new political values became unquestionable in public debates, that is, there was no public counter-narrative rejecting the rule of law and democracy. Germans were afraid of themselves, their dark side, and consciously undertook international obligations while also trying to pacify other Western European nations with their eagerness to comply. European integration—including the conception of the European Court of Human Rights (ECtHR)—may partly be explained by this very conscious German approach. Taking their cue from Ulysses, who tied himself to the mast for fear he should yield to the temptation of the Sirens, Germans set to work on building supranational European institutions with great fervour.

(d) Economic success (ie output) greatly contributed to legitimizing these values as well as their internalization by society. Precisely this point shows the interconnectedness of the different elements, as economic success was of course not unrelated to the democratic and rule of law institutions enshrined in formal rules. The above cited Daron Acemoglu has already written extensively about this in his best-selling book, *Why Nations Fail*.[36]

(e) There was a consensus among the German elite to adhere to democracy and the rule of law. Indeed, without the self-restricting consensus of the elite, liberal democracies will likely be dysfunctional.[37] This consensus was underpinned by the physical extinction of former opposing elites including the partial exclusion of Nazis from public life, American pressure, fear of the Soviet Union, and the taste of economic success. Based on these elements, a legal culture developed which fostered the formal rules instead of compromising them.

[35] See eg Stephan H Lindner, '"Sich eingereiht"? Wolfgang Hefermehl und der Nationalsozialismus' (2016) 17 Jahrbuch der Juristischen Zeitgeschichte 326. It also took until 2021 (!) for the most important German legal publisher, Munich-based CH Beck, to rename several important legal commentaries and collections of statutes in order to ban the names of prominent Nazi jurists like Palandt, Schönfelder, Maunz, and Düring.

[36] Daron Acemoglu and James A Robinson, *Why Nations Fail: The Origins of Power, Prosperity and Poverty* (Crown Business 2012). For a methodologically more sophisticated analysis, with similar results see Roberto Rigobon and Dani Rodrik, 'Rule of Law, Democracy, Openness, and Income: Estimating Interrelationships' (2005) 13 Economics of Transition and Institutional Change 533, 533: '[D]emocracy and the rule of law are both good for economic performance, but the latter has a much stronger impact on incomes. Openness (trade/GDP) has a negative impact on income levels and democracy, but a positive effect on rule of law. Higher income produces greater openness and better institutions, but these effects are not very strong. Rule of law and democracy tend to be mutually reinforcing.' On the effect of liberal democracies in helping economic growth see eg Moshe Yanovskiy and Tim Ginker, 'A Proposal for a More Objective Measure of De Facto Constitutional Constraints' (2017) 28 Constitutional Political Economy 311.

[37] John Higley and Michael Burton, *Elite Foundations of Liberal Democracy* (Rowman & Littlefield 2006).

3.3 A Relatively Successful Example from the More Recent Past in the EU: Romania

In general, for successful institution-building, several conditions must be given. These are *inter alia* an elite consensus, favourable international conditions, smartly designed formal institutions, economical pressure, and a fitting narrative as well as de facto practices which do not compromise formal rules.

When looking at examples of successful constitutional institution-building from the recent past, it is clear that some form of external pressure played a part in this success.[38] In some cases, such as Austria and Japan, this took the form of direct military pressure; in others, it was the fear of possible foreign occupation that changed the mindset of local elites and pushed them towards a consensus. Estonia is a case at hand, which had its well-founded fear of the Russians to thank for its success story starting in the 1990s.[39]

As stated in the introduction, one should consider corrupt and authoritarian practices and narratives as being similar to alcoholism: in theory it is possible for the patient to cure themselves, but normally, complete recovery requires not only the will to get better but also external support.[40] Moreover, once the patient seems to have recovered, they still need supervision so as not to regress. This is exactly what is happening in several former socialist countries which, after having joined the EU, are no longer subject to the strict and continuous supervision ('pre-accession conditionality') that they experienced before accession. As a consequence they no longer feel like they need to adhere to the civilizational norms of Western liberal democracies.[41]

[38] Michael J Gorges, 'New Institutionalist Explanations for Institutional Change: A Note of Caution' (2001) 21 Politics 137.

[39] This, however, also had the negative consequence of excluding the local Russian population from Estonian democracy. See, with reference to the ethnic background of the local communist elite before 1990, Dorothee Bohle and Béla Greskovits, *Capitalist Diversity on Europe's Periphery* (Cornell University Press 2012) 99. The relatively good performance of Baltic states (as compared to other post-Soviet states) can partly be explained by the consensus of the local elite, see Martin Mendelski, 'The EU's Rule of Law Promotion in Post-Soviet Europe: What Explains the Divergence Between Baltic States and EaP Countries?' (2016) 7 Eastern Journal of European Studies 111.

[40] On the necessity of international pressure in order to successfully clamp down on institutionalized corruption see eg Alina Mungiu-Pippidi, 'Corruption: Diagnosis and Treatment' (2006) 17 Journal of Democracy 86. For the metaphor of alcoholism in a narrower context ('fiscal alcoholism') see George Kopits, 'Saving Hungary's Finances: Budapest's Four Step-Plan for Fiscal Alcoholics' (4 December 2008) *Wall Street Journal Europe* <https://www.wsj.com/articles/SB122833696970376717> accessed 24 October 2024.

[41] On the deficiencies at EU level to keep them in line, see Chapter 3. On deficiencies of EU enforcement mechanisms, see also András Jakab and Dimitry Kochenov (eds), *The Enforcement of EU Law and Values: Ensuring Member States' Compliance* (OUP 2017); Laurent Pech and Kim Lane Scheppele, 'Illiberalism Within: Rule of Law Backsliding in the EU' (2017) 19 Cambridge Yearbook of European Legal Studies 3.

Romania is a positive counter-example in this respect: here, the institutions or certain aspects of the rule of law became stronger following EU accession. Although this strengthening is minimal, taking into consideration the general decline in the region, it is still relatively significant. However, this improvement is not down to the sudden enlightenment of the Romanian elite or their lesser affinity for corruption, but much rather to the fact that the accession treaty of Romania includes a clause concerning the period following accession.[42] Namely, it introduces a so-called 'cooperation and verification mechanism', which basically means that Romania will be evaluated annually based on a set of predefined criteria. Should Romania fail to take the necessary measures against corruption, the EC will adopt 'appropriate measures'.

While the specific substance of such measures, eg cancelling payments, has not been determined, and indeed such measures have never been applied, it is actually not the possibility of formal sanctions that has rendered this mechanism so effective. Rather the informal tying of entry into the Schengen zone by certain Western states to the results reflected in the annual reports and the high prestige of the EU—and consequently of these annual reports—in the eyes of the Romanian public are key.[43] Annual reports are a point of reference in Romanian public discourse, and their content and recommendations carry significant weight. For example, when the Romanian elite sought to relax corruption rules in February 2017, mass demonstrations erupted. Perhaps even more important for abandoning the amendment—although it was less spectacular and received less coverage in the media—was a formal condemnation of the planned amendment by the EC, which expressly referred to the cooperation and verification mechanism.[44]

[42] Radu Carp, 'The Struggle for the Rule of Law in Romania as an EU Member State: The Role of the Cooperation and Verification Mechanism' (2014) 10 Utrecht Law Review 1.

[43] This mechanism also applies to Bulgaria according to its EU accession treaty, but because of the unfortunate developments in Bulgarian domestic politics it seems less effective. There is no guarantee that the Romanian improvement will persist; the attempts to curb anti-corruption measures continue—the improvement has been the result of a lucky constellation of Romanian domestic politics (power balance, personal relationships, mass protests) and external pressure from the EU. For more detail, see Ingi Iusmen, 'EU Leverage and Democratic Backsliding in Central and Eastern Europe: The Case of Romania' (2015) 53 Journal of Common Market Studies 593; Ulrich Sedelmeier, 'Anchoring Democracy from Above? The European Union and Democratic Backsliding in Hungary and Romania after Accession' (2014) 52 Journal of Common Market Studies 105; Corina Lacatus and Ulrich Sedelmeier, 'Does Monitoring without Enforcement Make a Difference? The European Union and Anti-corruption Policies in Bulgaria and Romania after Accession' (2020) 27 Journal of European Public Policy 1236.

[44] Jean-Claude Juncker and Frans Timmermans, *Joint Statement on the Fight against Corruption in Romania* (1 February 2017) <www.europa.eu/rapid/press-release_STATEMENT-17-195_en.htm> accessed 24 October 2024.

4. Reshaping Informal Elements of Institutions in Illiberal EU MSs Is Key

A successful learning process takes considerable time, the consistent control of requirements, and also a positive affirmation like experiences of economic and moral success. In the case of Hungary and most other former socialist countries, however, these conditions were not given. To put it another way: the scaffolding was dismantled too early and the half-ready institutions of the rule of law partially collapsed in several post-socialist countries. This is clearly shown by the different rule of law indices (Bertelsmann, World Justice Project, Freedom House), which all indicate a slow erosion in former socialist countries since their accession to the EU.[45] While this is most apparent in the case of Hungary, Croatia, and Poland, it is discernible in other states as well.[46]

A Western style legal order can only function successfully in the long run if those operating the system also internalize these Western values. Adequate informal elements may be established, but only painstakingly slowly. The mere adoption of new formal laws will, in itself, most certainly not suffice. When the internalization of such values does not take place and the citizens do not feel invested in the new system, meaning they have nothing to gain by it, then as soon as the external pressure lapses, the (pre-rule of law and pre-democratic) pagan reflexes resurface and the mask falls: first, on the level of narratives (rhetoric) and practice, with the destruction of formal institutions soon to follow.[47]

In light of the above it is worth considering how the (constitutional) changes of the past few years in Hungary may be addressed from the point of view of institution-building. What role do formal rules, actual practices, and narratives play? Considering the discussion in Chapter 2, we can summarize this question as follows: the constitution-making of 2010/11 was a (successful) attempt to gain dominance over the legal culture in Hungary, even though the formal text of the new Fundamental Law largely still conforms to standards of democracy and the rule of law. Actual practices, however, to which the new Constitution contributed, deteriorated the legal culture in Hungary and hastened the decrease in the rule of law and democracy. The pre-democratic historical origins

[45] Cf Chapter 2. On the methodology of these indices, see Chapter 5.

[46] For similar considerations see James Dawson and Seán Hanley, 'What's Wrong with East-Central Europe? The Fading Mirage of the "Liberal Consensus"' (2016) 27 Journal of Democracy 20. On the erosion of Slovenian constitutionalism (explaining it with inherited cultural deficiencies and hoping for external, mainly EU, help), see Matej Avbelj, 'The Sociology of (Slovenian) Constitutional Democracy' (2017) 1 Hague Journal of the Rule of Law 35. For a general overview see Martin Brusis, *Illiberale Drift und Proliferation: BTI-Regionalbericht Ostmittel- und Südosteuropa* (Bertelsmann 2018).

[47] Timothy Snyder, *On Tyranny: Twenty Lessons from the Twentieth Century* (Penguin 2017) 32: 'The symbols of today enable the reality of tomorrow.'

of the current legal narrative come once again to the forefront—ironically despite the fact that a reason as to why Hungary would have needed a new constitution was to get rid of socialist legal culture.

5. Conclusion

A key insight from the above is that we lawyers should pay more attention to the informal elements of the rule of law and democracy. Informal elements (ie de facto practices and narratives) are inextricably linked to formal legal rules, and all three together are crucial to ensuring the rule of law and democracy. Institutionalist approaches comprise both formal and informal elements: they are essential for understanding erosion phenomena which lie at the heart of the present book. They are also key in finding the way back to liberal democracy after erosion by ensuring that de facto practices and narratives support formal rules. Taking elements beyond mere formal rules more consciously into account, such as actual practices and narratives, would lead to different results in the realm of legislation as well as in the application of the law. Legal training could contribute to that and would ideally result in the gradual reinforcement of the substantive cultural elements necessary for the rule of law and democracy.

2
The Emergence of Illiberal Regimes in Post-Socialist EU Member States

1. Introduction

'Since 1989, post-socialist transformation has changed the world.'[1] After the fall of socialism and with the dissolution of the Soviet Union the idea emerged that the 'end of history'[2] was close. The pull of the EU (ie the hope of membership) contributed to a steady development of the rule of law and democracy in post-socialist European states and in 2004 many of them (including Hungary and Poland) acceded to the EU. The continent seemed to be reunited after the fall of the Berlin Wall and the collapse of the Soviet Union.

In the last decade, however, this transformation has turned from a success story into the opposite. The erosion of democracy and the rule of law in Hungary and Poland is one of the largest worldwide. The reasons for this development are complex and there is no single explanation available. We contend that the role of socialist cultural legacy has been underestimated so far. Legal culture, which comprises in our understanding here both de facto practices and narratives (ie attitudes, beliefs, political rhetoric), shapes institutions as much as formal legal rules. Little noticed in Western Europe, but all the more important, is the fact that post-socialist legal culture is still present in post-socialist MSs in the EU. This is problematic as this culture suffers from special diseases. This inherited socialist legal culture partly comprises the attitudes, beliefs, and practices both of the general population (which is remarkably and measurably different from Western Europe concerning the demand for human rights and the refusal of corruption) and of the legal profession (eg specific features in legal thinking).

[1] Raj Kollmorgen, 'Post-Socialist Transformations in the Twentieth and Twenty-First Centuries' in Wolfgang Merkel, Raj Kollmorgen, and Hans-Jürgen Wagner (eds), *The Handbook of Political, Social, and Economic Transformation* (OUP 2019) 348, 364.

[2] Francis Fukuyama, 'The End of History?' (1989) 16 The National Interest 3, notably still with a question mark, and then three years later Francis Fukuyama, *The End of History and the Last Man* (Free Press 1992).

Saving the European Union from Its Illiberal Member States. András Jakab and Lando Kirchmair, Oxford University Press.
DOI: 10.1093/oso/9780198954606.003.0003

One of the latter is that which, for lack of a better term, we will refer to as rule-fixation.[3] This means that the vast majority of legal scholars and practising lawyers perceive law as a mere jumble of rules, or perhaps a system of rules. In other words, they completely ignore all other aspects of a functioning legal system. By this we do not necessarily mean the interpretative judicial practice (case law), although on occasions this is also disregarded. We are rather referring to the actual practices of the rules' addressees, as well as the narratives underpinning these rules. This broadly comprises everything from the *raison d'être* and goal of the institution to its symbolism, the public discourse surrounding it, and social attitudes towards the institution.[4] Rule-fixation as criticized in this chapter therefore does not refer to absolute compliance with the law (in fact, what happens is very often quite the opposite), but much rather a conscious blindness towards the actual practices and narratives affecting the operation of the legal order. By abandoning the rule-fixation perspective and giving consideration to the consequences of this approach, the situation can be seen more clearly (an accomplishment in its own right), and in the medium term this may also strongly promote a willingness to comply with the law.

Of course, the current problems present in post-socialist legal systems are not only caused by rule-fixation of legal professionals. They are in fact partly a result of general attitudes present in the entire population. Partly they are a result of the concrete individual or collective decisions taken by politicians. Partly (and paradoxically) the EU accession of these countries contributed to the erosion of the rule of law and democracy, as enormous amounts of uncontrolled money arrived (ie EU subsidies made the corruption situation even worse) and the free movement of persons resulted in those social cohorts leaving the country which were culturally more favourable to the mentioned constitutionalist values.

We will elaborate on this below by taking Hungary as an example. The study of the Hungarian case concentrates first on a recapitulation of the erosion of the rule of law and democracy in order to search for the reasons explaining this erosion. We argue that this can be instructive for understanding the reasons behind the weakening of constitutional institutions in several countries all

[3] For more details, see András Jakab and Miklós Hollán, 'Socialism's Legacy in Contemporary Law and Legal Scholarship: The Case of Hungary' (2004) 11 Journal of East European Law (Columbia University) 95; András Jakab, 'Informal Institutional Elements as Both Preconditions and Consequences of Effective Formal Legal Rules: The Failure of Constitutional Institution-Building in Hungary' (2020) 68 American Journal of Comparative Law 760.

[4] Narratives in the sense used here also include unwritten rules of legal interpretation, see eg John Bell, 'The Importance of Institutions' in Maurice Adams and Dirk Heirbaut (eds), *The Method and Culture of Comparative Law: Essays in Honour of Mark Van Hoecke* (Hart 2015) 207.

around the world during the last couple of years and particularly for post-socialist EU MSs.[5] Finally, in order to corroborate our thesis about the negative effects of pre-democratic cultural legacies in the context of erosion of the rule of law and democracy, we offer a comparative outlook on other former socialist countries in the EU. We diagnose in this chapter a generally low immune system against erosion and forecast that beyond the most well-known examples (Hungary and Poland) without effective external pressure further post-socialist countries are very likely to follow in the future.

2. Recapitulating the Erosion in Hungary

In 2011 László Sólyom, the first President of the Hungarian Constitutional Court 1990–98 and also a former President of the Republic 2005–10, wrote that he believes in the survival of institutions of constitutionalism. He voiced this belief despite both the objectionable provisions of the new Fundamental Law and government practices. He put his hopes especially in the constitutional culture and, not surprisingly given his role as first president, in the future Constitutional Court case law.[6] Unfortunately, however, his optimistic vision did not become reality. We submit that exactly the opposite happened: while there were some unfavourable changes in the legal system, the vast majority of the erosion can actually be explained by unfavourable cultural factors. While a small group of Hungarian (mostly constitutional) lawyers had the internalized culture to run the legal system according to Western liberal standards of democracy and the rule of law, the average Hungarian lawyer did not. When

[5] From the bourgeoning literature on these recent challenges, see eg Mark A Graber, Sanford Levinson, and Mark Tushnet (eds), *Constitutional Democracy in Crisis?* (OUP 2018); Tom Ginsburg and Aziz Z Huq, *How to Save a Constitutional Democracy* (University of Chicago Press 2018); Tom Ginsburg, Aziz Z Huq, and Mila Versteeg, 'The Coming Demise of Liberal Constitutionalism' (2018) 85 University of Chicago Law Review 239; Edward Luce, *The Retreat of Western Liberalism* (Atlantic Monthly Press 2017); Yascha Mounk, *The People vs Democracy: Why Our Freedom Is in Danger and How to Save It* (Harvard University Press 2018); Wojciech Sadurski, 'How Democracy Dies (in Poland): A Case Study of Anti-Constitutional Populist Backsliding' (2018) Sydney Law School Legal Studies Research Paper No. 1 <https://papers.ssrn.com/sol3/papers.cfm?abstract_id=3103491>; Gero Erdmann and Marianne Kneuer (eds), *Regression of Democracy?* (VS 2011); Ozan O Varol, 'Stealth Authoritarianism' (2015) 100 Iowa Law Review 1673; David Landau, 'Abusive Constitutionalism' (2013) 47 University of California Davis Law Review 189; Roberto Stefan Foa and Yascha Mounk, 'The Danger of Deconsolidation: The Democratic Disconnect' (2016) 27 Journal of Democracy 5; Paul Howe, 'Eroding Norms and Democratic Deconsolidation' (2017) 28 Journal of Democracy 15; Steven Levitsky and Daniel Ziblatt, *How Democracies Die* (Random House 2018); Yascha Mounk and Roberto Stefan Foa, 'The End of the Democratic Century: Autocracy's Global Ascendance' (2018) 97 Foreign Affairs 29.

[6] László Sólyom, 'Előszó: Az alkotmányos kultúra szerepe' in András Jakab (ed), *Az Alaptörvény keletkezése és gyakorlati következményei* (HVG Orac 2011) 11–14.

negative influences came from politicians (who had equally pre-democratic cultural traits), most lawyers did not resist. Rather the opposite: many of them felt comfortable with the new situation as it very much reminded them of how they were socialized before 1990. The same was true for the average voter, especially (but not only) in rural areas.

2.1 In What Sense Is Hungary an Illiberal Regime?

According to most democracy indices, Hungary is no longer a fully-fledged, that is, well-functioning, consolidated, and embedded, democracy—but not yet a dictatorship either.[7] It is something in-between, in the grey zone: an 'electoral autocracy' (V-Dem), a 'partly free' country (Freedom House), or a 'defective democracy' (Bertelsmann Transformation Index, BTI). So-called rule of law indices capture various details in a single indicator.[8] Such indices clearly reflect the ongoing erosion of the rule of law in Hungary in recent years.

For instance, the Political Transformation Index of the BTI includes the rule of law as a sub-index. It measures four elements of the rule of law, and a total of seventeen rule of law criteria with forty-nine different partly overlapping questions, from the point of view of traditional legal doctrine. This includes *inter alia* (1) the separation of powers, (2) judicial independence, (3) prosecution of abuse of power, and (4) fundamental rights. Figure 2.1 clearly shows a gradual and steady erosion of the rule of law and democracy in Hungary.

Despite the different methodology of various rule of law indices, they all show a significant and steady erosion in Hungary. Another example is the World Justice Project Rule of Law Index (WJP RLI). Its explicit aim is to measure elements of the rule of law in operation, as experienced by individuals. In other words it measures the de facto practices, or the perception of de facto practices, not primarily the body of laws. On a conceptual and methodological level, this is probably globally the most refined rule of law index. Relying primarily on UN documents it defines the rule of law with the following four principles: (1) the government, its officials and representatives, as well as private

[7] Simplistic binary descriptions about Hungary (democracy vs dictatorship) are unsuitable for analytical purposes. For sophisticated evaluations you need graded systems, such as rule of law indices or democracy indices, see Chapter 5.

[8] For methodological details of the mentioned (and further) rule of law indices see Chapter 4. The different rule of law indices are using different data sources, namely hard data (eg judicial budget), expert opinions (of constitutional lawyers), and/or public opinion polls (eg corruption perception). The use of these indices does not make traditional (doctrinal) legal analysis obsolete, but for situations with a large number of changes and for problems of growing discrepancy between facts and norms they are particularly useful (in the expert opinions, traditional doctrinal opinions are included anyway).

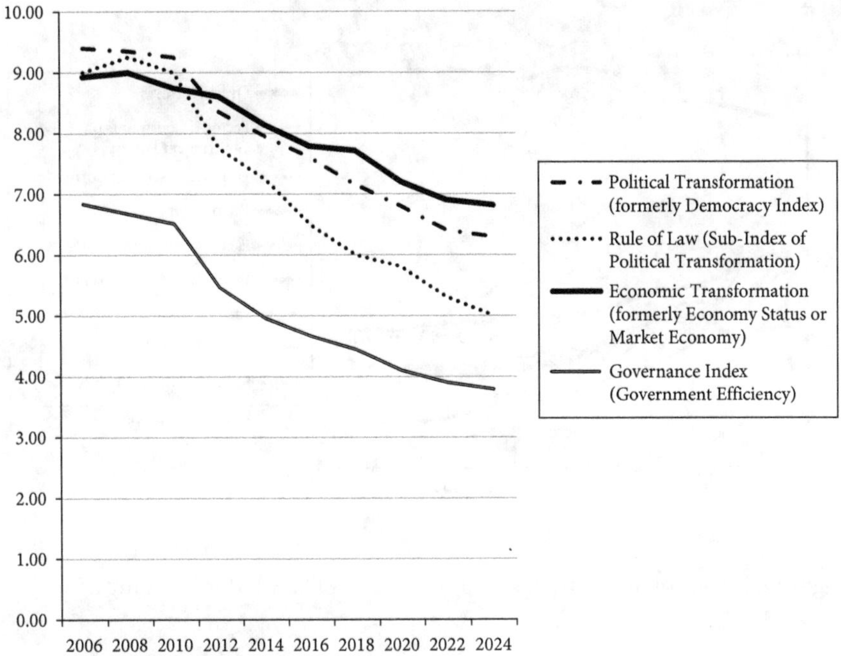

Figure 2.1 The Bertelsmann Transformation Index depicted on a diagram, data on Hungary from the period 2006–24

persons and companies are held accountable under the law; (2) laws are clear, publicized, stable, and just, serving to protect fundamental rights, including the security and property of persons; (3) processes by which the laws are enacted, administered, and enforced are accessible, fair, and efficient; (4) justice is delivered in timely fashion by competent, ethical, and independent persons, who are impartial, accessible, have adequate resources, and reflect the make-up of the communities they serve. Based on these principles, the index measures nine factors (comprising forty-seven subfactors): (1) constraints on government powers, (2) absence of corruption, (3) open government, (4) fundamental rights, (5) order and security, (6) regulatory enforcement, (7) civil justice, (8) criminal justice, and (9) informal (traditional) justice (the latter is hard to measure and is therefore not included in the aggregate result).

The higher the points achieved, the better; the maximum is one, the minimum is zero (Figure 2.2). The Hungarian results reflect gradual erosion in the constraints on government power (separation of powers), absence of corruption, open government, fundamental rights, regulatory enforcement, and criminal justice. The results for order and security have, however, shown a

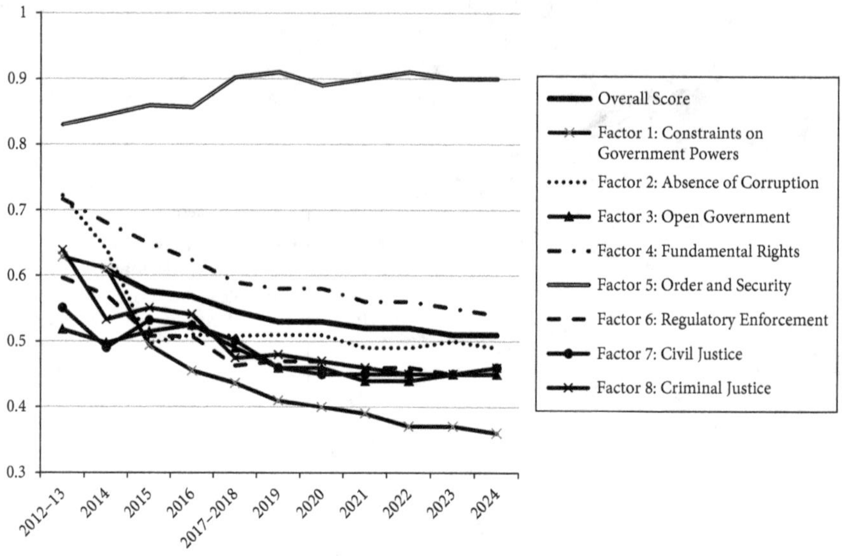

Figure 2.2 Data of the World Justice Project Rule of Law Index for Hungary 2012/13–24

slight improvement. The aggregate result of these changes shows a clear downward trend (there is no data for the period preceding 2012/13 since the project is relatively new).

In this book we avoid the terms 'autocracy' and 'authoritarian regime', because in certain conceptualizations they are used as synonyms for 'dictatorship', while in others they are defined more broadly (ie considering dictatorship as its worst case), and in some cases they are even explicitly distinguished from dictatorship (ie in a graded category system, a regime that is one degree less oppressive than dictatorship). Unfortunately, the multiplicity of definitions of 'autocracy' and 'authoritarian regime' also allows some authors to alternate different meanings even within a single writing.[9] Using the name 'illiberal regime' makes it easier to avoid such conceptual misunderstandings, which will hopefully contribute to the transparency of the arguments offered in this book.

By illiberal regime we wish to refer to a political entity which explicitly refuses (at least partially) the narrative of liberal values,[10] *and* at the same time

[9] For this reason we are not using the term 'authoritarian enclave' either, and instead we are using the more generic term 'deep state'. On authoritarian enclaves in the Chilean context, see Andrew Arato, 'Democratic Legitimacy and Forms of Constitutional Change' (2017) 24 Constellations 447.

[10] For an overview of various illiberal regimes like 'dictatorship, despotism, tyranny, autocracy, totalitarianism, and authoritarianism', see Nenad Dimitrijevic, 'Illiberal Regime Types' in András Sajó, Renáta Uitz, and Stephen Holmes (eds), *Routledge Handbook of Illiberalism* (Routledge 2022) 121, 121,

shows strong signs of erosion in democracy and the rule of law in the de facto practices of officials.[11] Whether also formal legal rules increasingly contradict liberal values we consider secondary (and as we will see, this is in fact not a good *differentia specifica* for some of these regimes). An illiberal regime can already have deteriorated to a hybrid regime (Hungary), or it might only be on its way to becoming a hybrid regime (until very recently Poland was on its way there; at the moment when we are finishing this manuscript, Slovakia seems to have taken its place).[12]

In our opinion 'illiberal regime' describes best the nature of the Hungarian regime.[13] In order to justify this choice, we will lay bare the 'ideological agnosticism' of the current regime by concentrating on the dishonest narrative which accompanied constitution-making in 2010/11 (2.2), before analysing (changes to) the formal text (2.3), and the de facto practice (2.4).

By erosion we simply mean the (slow) deterioration of either democracy or the rule of law. Erosion is not necessarily major; it can be minor and it can also affect only certain aspects of democracy or the rule of law. Moreover, erosion is not necessarily illegal: even within the framework of legality, new laws or de facto measures can cause a deterioration of certain aspects of democracy or the rule of law.

comprising under illiberal regime an entity which is 'not based on the primacy of individual liberty' and in institutional terms does 'not recognize the supremacy of rights, limited government, or the rule of law'. Emphasizing the 'gradual suppression of democratic rights and subordination of a pre-existent autonomous civil society to the state', as elements of illiberal regimes, see Benjamín García-Holgado and Aníbal Pérez-Liñán, 'The Weaknesses of Illiberal Regimes' in András Sajó, Renáta Uitz, and Stephen Holmes (eds), *Routledge Handbook of Illiberalism* (Routledge 2022) 925, 925.

[11] Martin Krygier, 'Illiberalism and the Rule of Law' in András Sajó, Renáta Uitz, and Stephen Holmes (eds), *Routledge Handbook of Illiberalism* (Routledge 2022) 533, 533 contrasting 'illiberalism with the rule of law', differentiating 'eliminationist illiberalism', which seeks 'to do away with differentials of power altogether' while '"unbinding"' forms of illiberalism 'seek to concentrate power in the state and remove the independence of all sorts of intermediary forces, institutions, and groupings'.

[12] For hybrid regimes, see eg Leonardo Morlino, 'Hybrid Regimes' in András Sajó, Renáta Uitz, and Stephen Holmes (eds), *Routledge Handbook of Illiberalism* (Routledge 2022) 142. Cf also Gábor Halmai, 'Illiberalism in East-Central Europe' in András Sajó, Renáta Uitz, and Stephen Holmes (eds), *Routledge Handbook of Illiberalism* (Routledge 2022) 813.

[13] For further references on the terminological debate focusing on the hybrid regime in Hungary, see András Bozóki and Dániel Hegedűs, 'An Externally Constrained Hybrid Regime: Hungary in the European Union' (2018) 25 Democratization 1173. They characterize the Hungarian hybrid regime with 'the presence of one-sided and unfair political competition as well as the formal existence of a liberal constitution but with serious deficiencies in its actual functioning'.

2.2 A Dishonest Narrative of an Ideologically Agnostic Regime

From a purely technical point of view, it is not necessary to adopt a new constitution in order to entrench policies or to enforce personnel changes in the state organization. The technique of amendment can, at the end of the day, achieve the same result. But constitution-making is not only about legal technique; it is, maybe even more importantly, about controlling the narrative behind formal rules. While the tool of amendment is just as viable, if not an easier means of implementing political will, and it could have surely made the formal adoption of an entirely new document obsolete, introducing the new Fundamental Law was important for constructing a new narrative—irrespective of whether this narrative was true or not. In addition to cementing the government's power via the new Fundamental Law, introducing the Fundamental Law 'successfully' facilitated staffing policies. A case at hand is making court-packing less obvious and therefore politically less costly by introducing a symbolic political rupture.

From the outset, the governing parties abandoned the plan to persuade opposition voters and to create a text that could be 'likeable' for them, functioning as a symbol for the entire political community. They deliberately chose not to heal polarization (rather the opposite: they deliberately made it more severe in order to politically weaken democratic accountability structures). They opted for total victory, of which the Fundamental Law has now become a symbol. Yet without open violence—something that is not characteristic of the present Hungarian regime—total victory cannot be achieved, and the embers will continue to smoulder under the ashes. Even if an opposition party disappears it will be replaced by a new one, perhaps one that is even without the historical (post-socialist) baggage. Comprehensive empirical analyses show that only those constitutions that are more or less based on a compromise between the entire political elite survive long-term, that is, at least two decades.[14] The Fundamental Law definitely lacks this support, and were we to accept the findings of the analyses cited, it is most likely that the text would not survive a change of government (once the necessary two-thirds constitution-amending majority was reached).

While in 2010, there was no detailed roadmap or systematic planning on how to build up the Hungarian illiberal regime, the power-hunger of the

[14] Zachary Elkins, Tom Ginsburg, and James Melton, *The Endurance of National Constitutions* (CUP 2009). Or more generally, for the success of a liberal democracy, a certain degree of consensus of the elite is needed; see the case studies in John Higley and Michael Burton, *Elite Foundations of Liberal Democracy* (Rowman & Littlefield 2006).

regime and sheer possibility allowed to slowly but steadily accumulate steps towards illiberalism. The end result, however, has been reached by a series of improvised decisions instead of following a systematic plan.[15] The only consistent pattern of behaviour of the regime has always been to accumulate more power—at best unrestricted. The rest are narratives constructed only after the fact[16] (ie ad hoc, for the specific task)—this is what cognitive scientists call 'rationalization', the process 'when a person has performed an action and then concocts the beliefs and desires that would have made it rational'.[17] Ideology is only an interchangeable 'political product'[18] for the regime.[19] In fact the regime is deeply agnostic in terms of ideology.[20] Whatever serves the purpose of defending and extending power and decreasing restrictions upon power is ideologically welcome.

At the time the Fundamental Law was drafted, several different official reasons were given as to why Hungary needed a new constitution.[21] In the end, two main arguments prevailed, both of which have been red herrings. The first argument (a) claimed that the 'communist Constitution of 1949' had to be replaced, while the other argument stated that (b) the new Constitution would mark the closure of the two decades of 'confusion' following the end of socialism in 1989/90.

Ad (a). The argument relating to the replacement of the 'communist Constitution of 1949' does not hold water either formally or substantively: as to its content, the 1949 Constitution was replaced in 1989/90 and apart from a few insignificant phrases which could have been weeded out with a simple constitutional amendment, there were no socialist remnants left in the text by

[15] On this style of politics, see Tilo Schabert, *Boston Politics: The Creativity of Power* (Walter de Gruyter 1989).

[16] See eg Jerome Bruner, 'The Narrative Construction of Reality' (1991) 18 Critical Inquiry 1.

[17] Fiery Cushman, 'Rationalization Is Rational' (2020) 43 Behavioral and Brain Sciences e28; see also Vadim Cherepanov, Timothy Feddersen, and Alvaro Sandroni, 'Rationalization' (2013) 8 Theoretical Economics 775 pointing to Ernest Jones, who 'described human beings as rationalizers whose behavior is governed by "the necessity of providing an explanation"' in 1908.

[18] Explicitly so by an influential pro-government ideologue, public intellectual, and journalist Gábor Gergely Fodor, '"A rendszer igazságait védem"—Interjú G. Fodor Gáborral' <https://magyarnarancs.hu/belpol/a-rendszer-igazsagait-vedem-93802>.

[19] It is not simply 'thin' ideologically (as populist politics in general, see Ben Stanley, 'The Thin Ideology of Populism' (2008) 13 Journal of Political Ideologies 95, but its loud ideological elements are a self-contradictory bunch of *interchangeable* elements, none of which is actually meant substantively by the apex of the regime.

[20] On the 'ideological flexibility' of the regime see Dóra Győrffy and József Péter Martin, 'Legitimacy and Authoritarian Decline: The Internal Dynamics of Hybrid Regimes' (2022) 70 Problems of Post-Communism 593, 601.

[21] Narratives are 'not just of how we do things around here, but also why we do things the way we do'. See Vivien Lowndes and Mark Roberts, *Why Institutions Matter: The New Institutionalism in Political Science* (Palgrave Macmillan 2013) 64.

2010/11. The main formal argument was that the Constitution's title still contained a reference to the year 1949 (it was entitled 'Law No XX of 1949'). In this respect it is worth recalling that the governing party had already proposed remedying this problem in the year 2000 by way of a simple amendment, which was not accepted at the time. The rewriting of the title, hence, did not make the adoption of a new constitution necessary.

A further formal argument referred to the 'patched up' character of the old text, while another claimed that instead of the existing long and technical text, containing highly detailed rules, there was a need for a 'short and likeable' constitution. The same objections may, however, be raised against the current Fundamental Law: compared to the status of the text in April 2011, the ensuing seven amendments changed the original text on several points resulting in its growth by 30 per cent. To put it another way, the text is now just as patched up as its predecessor. At present, the Fundamental Law is already one and a half times longer than the 2010 text of the old Constitution, and therefore the requisite brevity was also not met.

Ad (b). The symbolic closure of the previous two decades (from 1989/90 until 2010) was, however, an argument that the governing parties may have taken at least partially seriously.[22] These two decades, in particular the second, were in fact less of a success for the country: the neighbouring countries in the Central European region caught up with the once leading Hungary, some even outperforming it in terms of economic indicators. Even though politicians should have in fact been taking a close look at themselves in the mirror, blaming the Constitution (or pointing the finger at each other) seemed to be a more comfortable solution for them. Hungarian society got stuck and sank deeper and deeper into this national version of a cold war where victory over the opposition justified all the means: corruption, running the country into debt, low-quality government, or even a lack of governing. This troubled and unsuccessful period was to be closed by the new Constitution.

The characteristic ideological element carrying the Constitution is, rather, ideological agnosticism. Contradicting stories underpin that the narrative only served to enthuse the regime's own followers and to deliberately provoke the opposition. Thereby polarization is increased, and, as a conscious result, the rational public discourse that would be necessary for effective democratic accountability is damaged.[23]

[22] For its symbolism see László Sólyom, *Das Gewand des Grundgesetzes: Zwei Verfassungsikonen—Ungarn und Deutschland* (Berliner Wissenschaftsverlag 2017).

[23] See also Lando Kirchmair, 'Demokratische Legitimität, die EU-Rechtsstaatlichkeitskrise und Vorüberlegungen zu einer transnationalen Gewaltengliederung' (2019) 6 Zeitschrift für praktische Philosophie 171, 190–91 for the notion of 'cuckoo politicians' who deceive and manipulate the

There are several examples of blatant contradiction. Despite the officially Christian rhetoric, the pro-government press regularly scolds and mocks the Pope.[24] While the government conducts the anti-Soros propaganda campaign with anti-Semitic overtones,[25] it allies itself with the populist Israeli right wing.[26] Even with official anti-immigration, the system of settlement bonds (financially benefiting cronies near to the government and allowing criminal and/or secret service elements from Russia and Arabic countries to acquire Schengen status) is maintained.[27] The sovereigntist rhetoric is not disturbed by long-term indebtedness towards Russia or China with unfavourable conditions.[28] Despite the smear campaign against international capitalism, the government concludes so-called strategic agreements with the largest multinational companies,[29] whereby it provides them with privileges, while the legal nature of the agreements is not clear.[30]

Whether planned from scratch or rather an adaption little by little, since the creation of the new Constitution, a new general and official narrative of the legal order has emerged, namely, the idea of the 'illiberal state'.[31] The Prime Minister launched this concept at his notorious Tusványos speech in 2014 and although its precise substance—apart from it being national and based

population in order to pursue their own, individually motivated interests or the interests of a small group within the population.

[24] See Zsolt Bayer, 'A pápa esze' (2 August 2016) *Mandiner* <https://mandiner.hu/velemeny/2016/08/bayer-zsolt-a-papa-esze>; Balázs Bozzay, 'Bencsik András: Ferenc pápa keresztényellenes, meg akarta alázni Magyarországot' (8 June 2021) *telex* <https://telex.hu/belfold/2021/06/08/bencsik-andras-ferenc-papa-meg-akarta-alazni-magyarorszagot-es-keresztenyellenesen-viselkedik>.

[25] Lily Bayer, 'Hungary to Take Down Controversial Soros Posters' (12 July 2017) *Politico* <https://www.politico.eu/article/hungary-to-take-down-controversial-soros-posters/>.

[26] This included secret service help by Netanjahu against Hungarian journalists and opposition politicians, see Szabolcs Panyi and András Pethő, 'Hungarian Journalists and Critics of Orbán were Targeted with Pegasus, a Powerful Israeli Cyberweapon' (19 July 2019) *Direkt 36* <https://www.direkt36.hu/en/leleplezodott-egy-durva-izraeli-kemfegyver-az-orban-kormany-kritikusait-es-magyar-ujsagirokat-is-celba-vettek-vele/fffff>.

[27] For concrete examples see 'Hungarian Journalists and Critics of Orbán Were Targeted with Pegasus, a Powerful Israeli Cyberweapon' <https://adatbazis.k-monitor.hu/adatbazis/cimkek/letelepedesi-kotveny-biznisz>.

[28] See Bálint Ablonczy, 'Ezermilliárdos kínai adósság: a magyar szuverenitást veszélyezteti a Fudan és a Belgrád-vasút' (21 April 2021) <https://www.valaszonline.hu/2021/04/21/fudan-egyetem-kina-magyarorszag-adossag-geopolitika-elemzes/, https://www.napi.hu/magyar-gazdasag/paks-ii-hitel-orosz-hitel-tartozas-suli-janos.674586.html>.

[29] As of today, there are officially ninety-three strategic partnership agreements; see the government website <https://kormany.hu/kulgazdasagi-es-kulugyminiszterium/strategiai-partnersegi-megallapodasok>.

[30] See eg the analysis by Transparency International <https://transparency.hu/wp-content/uploads/2016/03/A-v%C3%A1llalatok-%C3%A9s-a-korm%C3%A1ny-k%C3%B6z%C3%B6tti-strat%C3%A9giai-meg%C3%A1llapod%C3%A1sok-Magyarorsz%C3%A1gon-Tanulm%C3%A1ny-a-lobbiz%C3%A1sr%C3%B3l.pdf>.

[31] For the concept, see Fareed Zakaria, 'The Rise of Illiberal Democracy' (1997) 76 Foreign Affairs 22.

on labour—is unknown, it is presented as an alternative to (liberal) Western democracies built on the protection of fundamental rights. Meanwhile, the Fundamental Law formally continues to guarantee fundamental rights conducive to a democracy.[32]

However, not even the proclaimed illiberalism seems to be 'pure'. Instead it is mixed with the language of liberal fundamental rights, and, more recently, even the protection of sovereignty (conceptualized as 'constitutional identity') is derived from human dignity.[33] The regime mingles Marxist egalitarian statements with conservativism. It talks about the Ten Commandments in public, but behind the scenes it tramples on all of them—especially the Seventh and Eighth.[34] It poses as the international defenders of Western Christianity while openly bashing the West, regularly sabotaging its international institutions from within in line with Russian and Chinese interests, and cosying up with the Christian-persecuting Chinese and the Islamist Turkish regimes.[35] And of course, the all-pervasive, systemic corruption,[36] which according to one of their ideologues is their main policy,[37] best demonstrates the extreme pragmatism of the regime. Rhetoric and actual government action have little to do with each other: that is, they typically say something different from what they actually do.

Those critics of the regime who still treat the regime's provocative rhetoric and ideological fragments at face value after thirteen years have still not understood its profound cynicism. It is the specific purpose of outrageous statements to divert attention from the real government performance by provoking angry reactions. That is why the use of labels such as 'fascist', 'Christian fundamentalist', or 'nationalist' does not simply miss the point, but is fundamentally

[32] András L Pap, *Democratic Decline in Hungary* (Routledge 2017) 47–65 with further references.

[33] The result is doctrinally quite confusing, but the aspiration is clear, see Hungarian Constitutional Court, Decision 32/2021 (XII.20.). For a smart analysis, see eg Nóra Chronowski and Attila Vincze, 'Full Steam Back: The Hungarian Constitutional Court Avoids Further Conflict with the ECJ' (15 December 2021) *Verfassungsblog* <https://verfassungsblog.de/full-steam-back/>.

[34] See eg Reuters Staff, 'Hungarian ex-Olympic Champion and Mayor Resigns over Sex Tape' (6 November 2019) *Reuters* <https://www.reuters.com/article/us-hungary-fidesz-mayor-idUSKBN1XG1L8>; Nick Thorpe, 'Jozsef Szajer: Hungary MEP Quits after Allegedly Fleeing Gay Orgy' (1 December 2020) *BBC News* <https://www.bbc.com/news/world-europe-55145989>.

[35] See eg Ariel Cohen, 'Viktor Orban's Goulash Energy Policy Makes Hungary Putin's Trojan Horse in Europe' (17 May 2022) *Forbes* <https://www.forbes.com/sites/arielcohen/2022/05/17/viktor-orbans-goulash-energy-policy-makes-hungary-putins-trojan-horse-in-europe/>; Wilhelmine Preussen, 'Orbán Backs China's Ukraine Peace Plan' (27 February 2023) *Politico* <https://www.politico.eu/article/viktor-orban-hungary-ukraine-china-peace-plan-russia-invasion/>.

[36] See the detailed documentation and case studies in Maria Csanádi and others, *Dynamics of an Authoritarian System: Hungary 2010–2021* (CEU Press 2022).

[37] Interview with András Lánczi, 'A viccpártok színvonalán áll az ellenzék' (21 December 2015) *Magyar Idők* <www.magyaridok.hu/belfold/lanczi-andras-viccpartok-szinvonalan-all-az-ellenzek-243952/> (translation AJ).

harmful. With such categories polarization is increased as they radicalize the opposition as well as the supporters of the regime. Thereby, albeit unwittingly, the socio-psychological infrastructure of the regime is strengthened. Thus, paradoxically, those who shout 'fascism' at the doubtless illiberal current Hungarian regime actually bolster the polarization strategy of the regime.[38]

The ideological elements used by the regime are in fact eclectic, inconsistent, contingent, and essentially irrelevant. They are not held together by consistent ideological foundations, but only by the Prime Minister: by his consciously nurtured personal charisma, by his inexhaustible energy, by his network of domestic and international contacts, by his three-decade-old political brand, by his immeasurable wealth controlled through his cronies and family members, and by the fact-resistant adoration of a significant mass of voters. With the rhetorical excuse of protecting national sovereignty and national interest, the government made a new Constitution that is less in line with the traditional principles of democracy and the rule of law than the old Constitution.

2.3 Keeping (Mostly) the Liberal Mask: The Formal Text of the New Fundamental Law

Compared to the large amount of institutional changes, the changes made to formal rules from the 1989/90 Constitution to the 2011 Fundamental Law were relatively minor. The 2011 Fundamental Law basically follows the regulatory system and text of the previous Constitution even with some codificatory improvements. On the one hand, this was favourable, as liberal democratic traditions (especially case law) had a higher chance of survival. On the other hand, however, this was also unfavourable, because superficial observers, that is, those who only considered the legal norms but not the actual practices and narratives, might have had a false impression that the changes were only minor.[39] For instance, the leading politicians did not—for whatever reason—introduce

[38] Such regimes are especially embarrassed if we refuse their tribal-polarized logic. See the Istanbul mayoral election as an example: F Michael Wuthrich and Melvyn Ingleby, 'Pushback Against Populism: Running on "Radical Love" in Turkey' (2020) 2 Journal of Democracy 24.

[39] For more detail see Pál Sonnevend, András Jakab, and Lóránt Csink, 'The Constitution as an Instrument of Everyday Party Politics: The Basic Law of Hungary' in Armin von Bogdandy and Pál Sonnevend (eds), *Constitutional Crisis in the European Constitutional Area* (Springer 2015) 33; Attila Vincze and Márton Varju, 'Hungary: The New Fundamental Law' (2012) 18 European Public Law 437; Kim Lane Scheppele, 'Autocratic Legalism' (2018) 85 University of Chicago Law Review 545; Kim Lane Scheppele, 'The Rule of Law and the Frankenstate: Why Governance Checklists Do Not Work' (2013) 26 Governance 559; Miklós Bánkúti, Gábor Halmai, and Kim Lane Scheppele, 'Hungary's Illiberal Turn: Disabling the Constitution' (2012) 23 Journal of Democracy 138; Matthijs Bogaards, 'De-democratization in Hungary: Diffusely Defective Democracy' (2018) 25 Democratization 1; Istvan

a semi-presidential or a bicameral system. Hungary, thus, continues to be a unicameral parliamentary system.

Beyond rules of mere symbolic relevance, the text was, however, scattered with ad hoc exceptions, the drafters tinkering with the rules on both state organization and fundamental rights to align them with their real or perceived daily party interests. This particularly pertains to the provisions governing the ordinary courts, the Constitutional Court, or churches. Sometimes the desired outcome was not achieved on the first attempt, so even exceptions had to be amended and then re-amended (there have been thirteen amendments to the Fundamental Law since its adoption). These repetitions were actually due to the fact that the majority of constitutional law experts informing the constitution-making project simply fled the decision-making process in close procession. This was down to the fact that on the one hand their opinions were not really taken into consideration, and on the other hand they faced a situation where their ethos of restricting state power conflicted with the line they were asked to take.

In this context, all intellectual checks placed on the decision-makers gradually melted away. The pressure exerted by EU institutions and foreign actors such as the USA and international financial markets constituted the only form of effective restraint. Besides this, exercise of the power was unrestricted due to the constitution-making majority which existed up to 2015. While this supermajority has been lost for three years, since April 2018 the governing parties have retained their two-thirds constitution-making majority.[40] This trend was already visible at the time of the 2010/11 process, becoming particularly conspicuous with the Fifth Amendment to the Fundamental Law, forced upon the government by Brussels, Venice, Strasbourg, and Luxembourg, seeking to remedy the gravest constitutional flaws affecting European norms. In fact, this was even acknowledged in the official reasoning attached to the amendment: 'Therefore, in order to prevent certain constitutional issues to be used as a pretext for attacks against Hungary, the Government, without abandoning its original intentions ... proposes a different solution.'

Pogany, 'The Crisis of Democracy in East Central Europe: The 'New Constitutionalism' in Hungary' (2013) 24 European Public Law 341, 352.

[40] The 2018 elections were heavily criticized by the Organization for Security and Cooperation in Europe (OSCE), see Statement, OSCE/ODIHR, Limited Election Observation Mission (8 April 2018) <www.osce.org/odihr/elections/hungary/377410?download=true>: 'The 8 April parliamentary elections were characterised by a pervasive overlap between state and ruling party resources, undermining contestants' ability to compete on an equal basis. Voters had a wide range of political options but intimidating and xenophobic rhetoric, media bias and opaque campaign financing constricted the space for genuine political debate, hindering voters' ability to make a fully-informed choice.'

2.4 The Devil Is in the De Facto Practices of Officials That Hollowed out Formal Institutions

An essential feature of the Hungarian regime is that the regime is not using open and brutal methods of oppression, and also legal rules in most cases remain within the limits of Western constitutionalism—with a few exceptions, which only explain a minor fraction of the erosion.[41] There is no legal rule which would explicitly exclude the opposition from winning the elections. However, there is a series of nasty and mostly illegal tricks like biased application of campaign finance laws, a state-run propaganda machine, using the secret services to spy on opposition politicians, gerrymandering, etc. These make the playfield uneven and unfair and, thus, getting the current government voted out very unlikely.[42]

The nature of the regime, hence, cannot be understood based on its legal rules. Although there are indeed some problems with certain laws and with certain provisions of the Fundamental Law,[43] the suffocating nature of the regime is not a direct and necessary consequence of its written laws. The problems rather stem from the application of the law and from de facto practices by various officials. For example, law enforcement agencies either do not or extremely slowly and incompetently apply existing criminal laws to obvious corruption cases if they happen in the environment of politically shielded personalities.[44] The blatantly arbitrary disciplining practices of the Speaker of the Parliament applied to Members of Parliament,[45] or certain tax authority raids on political and economic opponents, can be cited as examples. Chasing away the Central European University was also carried out predominantly with such means. It was primarily not the text of the law that forced the university

[41] Erica Frantz and Andrea Kendall-Taylor, 'The Evolution of Autocracy: Why Authoritarianism Is Becoming More Formidable' (2017) 5 Survival 57.

[42] Or to put it differently, the elections are 'free but not fair', see (without using the expression explicitly but describing in detail the phenomenon along these lines) eg OSCE Office for Democratic Institutions and Human Rights, *Limited Election Observation Mission Final Report on the Parliamentary Elections in Hungary 8 April 2018* (27 June 2018).

[43] For an overview of these problems see András Jakab and Eszter Bodnár, 'The Rule of Law, Democracy, and Human Rights in Hungary: Tendencies from 1989 until 2019' in Tímea Drinóczi and Agnieszka Bień-Kacała (eds), *Rule of Law, Common Values, and Illiberal Constitutionalism: Poland and Hungary within the European Union* (Routledge 2020) 105; András Jakab and Eszter Bodnár, 'Agonie eines jungen Verfassungsstaates: Die ungarische Verfassung 1989 bis 2019' in Ellen Bos and Astrid Lorenz (eds), *Das politische System Ungarns* (Springer 2020) 55.

[44] See eg Erdélyi Katalin, 'Elszabotált nyomozások: 20 fontos ügy, ami megakadt az ügyészségen' (16 September 2021) *Atlatszo* <https://atlatszo.hu/kozpenz/2021/09/16/elszabotalt-nyomozasok-20-fontos-ugy-ami-megakadt-az-ugyeszsegen/>.

[45] Zoltán Szente, 'The Twilight of Parliament—Parliamentary Law and Practice in Hungary in Populist Times' (2021) 1 International Journal of Parliamentary Studies 127.

to leave the country, but the way it was applied and the political context.[46] The Hungarian illiberal regime is—in addition to the concentration of financial resources—mostly a combination of creative, occasionally illegal (selective) law enforcement, as well as informal, extra-legal (ie not legally prescribed), sometimes illegal, practices. Compared to these, the problems that can be discovered in written laws are relatively minor. The character of the regime as a whole is therefore not primarily determined by formal (legal) norms, but by informal practices.[47] The following list is not exhaustive, providing merely a few examples:

(a) It is clear that in certain cases the Constitutional Court is simply afraid or unwilling to render a decision that would necessarily follow from the Fundamental Law. A vivid example would be the use of in the strict sense lawful, but hitherto never used delaying tactics, for example the setting up of special analysis groups of law clerks to prepare a lengthy preliminary report on the case, while practically suspending the procedure, in respect of the manifestly unconstitutional *lex CEU*, which served to expel the Central European University (a liberal private university) from Hungary.[48] Although from a formal legal point of view this cannot be objected to, on the level of actual practices, however, it definitely amounts to institutional destruction. It undermines the belief in the independence of the Constitutional Court (and rightly so), gradually discrediting the narrative of the separation of powers.[49] That the Hungarian government was constitutionally empowered to disapply EU law if it considers that EU law would violate Hungarian constitutional identity has been the result of another problematic Decision 32/2021.[50]

[46] For a detailed example of how this works at the Constitutional Court through failure to act see Nóra Chronowski and Attila Vincze, 'The Hungarian Constitutional Court and the Central European University Case: Justice Delayed is Justice Denied: Decision of the Hungarian Constitutional Court of 6 July 2021 and the Judgment of the ECJ of 6 October 2020, Case C-66/18' (2021) European Constitutional Law Review 1.

[47] On the role of formal legal rules see Scheppele (n 39). On 'stealth authoritarianism', see Varol (n 5) and Ozan O Varol, 'Stealth Authoritarianism in Turkey' in Mark A Graber, Sanford Levinson, and Mark Tushnet (eds), *Constitutional Democracy in Crisis?* (OUP 2018) 339.

[48] On the unconstitutionality of *lex CEU* see László Sólyom, Miklós Lévay, Zoltán Szente, and András Jakab, 'Amicus Curiae a Lex Ceu ügyében' (12 June 2017) *Amicus Curiae in the case of Lex CEU* <www.public.mkab.hu/dev/dontesek.nsf/0/af27b40ba3b0b821c1258109003f9b19/$FILE/II_1036_5_2017_%C3%A1ll%C3%A1sfoglal%C3%A1s.002.pdf/II_1036_5_2017_%C3%A1ll%C3%A1sfoglal%C3%A1s.pdf>. For an empirical analysis of government influence on the Hungarian Constitutional Court, see Zoltán Szente, 'The Political Orientation of the Members of the Hungarian Constitutional Court between 2010 and 2014' (2016) 1 Constitutional Studies 123.

[49] On another move by the Constitutional Court, this time clearly also a breach of its own procedural rules, see Gábor Halmai, 'The Hungarian Constitutional Court betrays Academic Freedom and Freedom of Association' (8 June 2018) *Verfassungsblog* <www.verfassungsblog.de/the-hungarian-constitutional-court-betrays-academic-freedom-and-freedom-of-association/>.

[50] See Hungarian Constitutional Court, Decision 32/2021 (XII.20.). Cf for an analysis, Attila Vincze, 'Unsere Gedanken sind Sprengstoff—Zum Vorrang des Europarechts in der Rechtsprechung des ungarischen Verfassungsgerichts' (2022) 49 Europäische Grundrechte-Zeitschrift 13.

(b) There is a host of credible accounts, some of them also reported by the media, regarding the selection of court leaders (who continue to play an important role in allocating cases within the respective court), evidencing that on the level of actual practices a personal relationship with the head of the National Office for the Judiciary was considered as being more important than the official criteria of merit. This practice, in the majority of cases, does not breach the relevant procedural rules (in some exceptional cases it does), since these were largely drafted by the National Office for the Judiciary; it much rather infringes general (and in the specific statutes uncodified) principles of the rule of law that prohibit the abuse of powers. This leads to an organizational culture that constitutes unfavourable institutional context for judicial independence.[51]

(c) While the Fundamental Law formally upholds the idea of self-government, this is actually hollowed out in service of the complete and general centralization of the state, partly through formal statutory implementing rules and the re-regulation of competences, and partly through the practice of financing (discretional or non-transparent distribution of funds).[52]

(d) While formal rules on corruption have been maintained, the prosecuting services continue to operate without transparency or guarantees. Meanwhile, a string of unrefuted press reports have been published indicating that the Chief Prosecutor's Office fails to take action or delays and/or spectacularly blunders the indictment when a person close to the government is suspected of committing a crime. Indeed, corruption in a broader sense may even appear on the level of legislation, as in the regulation of gambling and tobacco retail.[53]

(e) Although formal legal provisions stipulate that it is one of the goals of the National Media and Infocommunications Authority and of the Media Council to promote media pluralism, on the level of actual practices they are visibly steering the entire media landscape into the government fold, partly through

[51] Mátyás Bencze and Attila Badó, 'A magyar bírósági rendszer hatékonyságát és az ítélkezés színvonalát befolyásoló strukturális és személyi feltételek' in András Jakab and György Gajduschek (eds), *A magyar jogrendszer állapota* (MTA TK 2016) 441.

[52] See the most recent report 'Monitoring of the European Charter of Local Self-Government in Hungary', CG-FORUM(2021)01-03final from 12 February 2021 by the Congress of Local and Regional Authorities (Rapporteurs Marc Cools and Jean-Pierre Liouville) <https://rm.coe.int/monitoring-of-the-european-charter-of-local-self-government-in-hungary/1680a129f6>. Cf Ilona P Kovács, 'Modellváltás a magyar önkormányzati rendszerben' in András Jakab and György Gajduschek (eds), *A magyar jogrendszer állapota* (MTA TK 2016) 583.

[53] With detailed documentation see Miklós Ligeti, 'Korrupció' in András Jakab and György Gajduschek (eds), *A magyar jogrendszer állapota* (MTA TK 2016) 727. Moreover, as to the narrative, the obvious systemic corruption is openly defended by some intellectuals near to the government in friendly media outlets as building a new national capitalist class, see the infamous interview with András Lánczi in *Magyar Idők* (21 December 2015) <www.magyaridok.hu/belfold/lanczi-andras-vic cpartok-szinvonalan-all-az-ellenzek-243952/>.

an incomplete application of legal rules, but partly also through overt breaches, as established by the court.[54]

(f) Formally, the protection of private property continues to form part of the Hungarian legal order, yet this has significantly deteriorated or at least become patchy on several points. Besides that, (since 2010) the relevant competences of the Constitutional Court remain incomplete to this day. The Court is barred from reviewing tax or budgetary laws from the perspective of the right of private property and one may repeatedly read about instances where a company is stripped of its market share with state effort. Usually, a legislative amendment is introduced first (which, on its own cannot be formally objected to), then passing them on to private persons at the level of actual practices, like the case of laws on gambling. Finally strict formal rules as a next step are introduced to protect the new incumbent. In fact, it is the very concept of private property that becomes relative when trying to get a clear picture of the true financial situation of senior politicians. And not just because of the different contract options, but also because of the political dependency of certain types of private property ownership it is a mere formality as to who happens to be registered as the owner.[55] We have witnessed since 2010 several occasions when oligarchs (Simicska, Spéder) have lost a large part of their wealth after they fell out with the regime. Sustained pressure by police raids, tax authority controls, informal blacklisting for public procurements, etc ruined their businesses.[56] In another example, all media assets owned by government-friendly businessmen have been 'donated' to a centrally organized private foundation at the same time, forming since then the largest media conglomerate in Hungary.[57] In general, government-near businessmen are very much aware of the fact that despite formal ownership, their assets are de facto under the disposal of the political leadership—if they are 'asked' to sell their assets under market price or even to donate them, then they will normally do so. Further, thanks to the tragicomic way politicians' asset declarations are handled, we also do not have a clear picture of politicians' wealth, even where assets are in their name. While there is

[54] Gábor Polyák and Krisztina Nagy, 'A médiatörvények kontextusa, rendelkezései és gyakorlata' (2014) 20 Jura 127 <www.mediakutato.hu/cikk/2016_03_osz_tel/10_frekvenciaosztogatas>.

[55] For interviews and case studies on these issues see Dorottya Sallai (Egerszegi) and Gerhard Schnyder, 'The Transformation of Post-Socialist Capitalism—from Developmental State to Clan State?' (12 January 2018) <www.papers.ssrn.com/sol3/papers.cfm?abstract_id=3100775>.

[56] József Péter Martin, Gabriella Nagy, and Miklós Ligeti, *Fekete Könyv. Korrupció Magyarországon 2010–2018* (Civitas and Transparency International Magyarország 2018) 96, 121–22.

[57] Pablo Gorondi, 'Huge Pro-government Media Conglomerate Formed in Hungary' (28 November 2018) *AP News* <https://apnews.com/article/budapest-hungary-viktor-orban-newspapers-europe-39028d9c44b64e08a6609b60a8bf7a13>.

nothing new about this, the degree and the conspicuousness of the disparities nowadays go way beyond what was experienced earlier.

(g) Finally, a rather recent trend has been the particularly extensive use of emergency decree powers in reaction to the COVID-19 pandemic[58] and to the war in Ukraine. Furthermore, there are negative impacts on the quality of legislation in general, making frequent amendments necessary, which has a particularly adverse effect on legal certainty.[59]

These examples demonstrate a growing gap between written laws and legal reality: the normativity of formal legal norms is slowly deteriorating in Hungary. This holds true especially in politically sensitive legal areas.[60] Informal extra-legal practices in turn become stronger and stronger, often also contrary to existing laws. Specifically in the field of constitutional law, this means that the gap between constitutional law and constitutional reality is constantly growing: the normativity of Hungarian constitutional law is gradually fading. The forms are still there, but in practice they are slowly being hollowed out: liberal (or at least largely liberal) formal rules mask strongly illiberal everyday practices.[61] Captured institutions (such as the Constitutional Court or the prosecutorial services) are independent on paper, but in fact they act according to the wishes of the leaders of the regime.[62] This behaviour can be manifested not only in formal acts, that is, in their content and in the choice of decision-making form,[63] but also in consciously refusing to

[58] See Csaba Győry and Nyasha Weinberg, 'Emergency Powers in a Hybrid Regime: The Case of Hungary' (2020) 8 The Theory and Practice of Legislation 329, 329 'the Hungarian case stands out', providing further references; see also Tímea Drinóczi and Agnieszka Bień-Kacała, 'COVID-19 in Hungary and Poland: Extraordinary Situation and Illiberal Constitutionalism' (2020) 8 The Theory and Practice of Legislation 171, 171: 'Hungary uses and abuses its Fundamental Law, while Poland is disregarding its binding 1997 Constitution'; cf also Petra Guasti, 'The Impact of the COVID-19 Pandemic in Central and Eastern Europe: The Rise of Autocracy and Democratic Resilience' (2020) Democratic Theory <https://www.berghahnjournals.com/view/journals/democratic-theory/7/2/dt070207.xml?fbclid=IwAR12k7d8prL6Jn2nMqBHGBgxkqPry1Um13b47LGCWKyQseaxP5o_zwzqbSg>, finding that in Hungary and Poland 'the populist leaders instrumentalized the state of emergency to increase executive aggrandizement'.

[59] For the statistics of the modifications of freshly adopted statutes, see Miklós Sebők, Bálint Kubik, and Csaba Molnár, 'A törvények formális minősége—egy empirikus vázlat', in Zsolt Boda and Andrea Szabó (eds), *Trendek a magyar politikában 2. A F idesz és a többiek: pártok, mozgalmak* (MTA TK and Napvilág 2017) 300, 304.

[60] The situation is similar with regard to the Russian Constitutional Court, which is doing decent work in politically irrelevant cases, but in politically important cases it is always a submissive servant of the Putin regime. See Alexei Trochev and Peter H Solomon, 'Authoritarian Constitutionalism in Putin's Russia: A Pragmatic Constitutional Court in a Dual State' (2018) 51 Communist and Post-Communist Studies 201.

[61] András Sajó, *Ruling by Cheating: Governance in Illiberal Democracy* (CUP 2021) 154, 255.

[62] On the steps leading to the currently very strong correlation between the opinion of the government and the opinion of the Constitutional Court, see Szente (n 48) with detailed empirical data.

[63] A central and strong competence of any constitutional court is the annulment statutes. The Hungarian Constitutional Court still has this competence, but in practice its use became very rare.

act.[64] Even in informal acts such as press releases we witness this phenomenon, which can be assumed to have been created specifically on government orders, or at least with prior consultation with the government.[65]

Decision-makers completely lack a sense of responsibility. They are actively dismantling constitutionality (ie the system of legal norms restricting government), while formally upholding constitutional rules, to which they continue to pay lip service.[66]

3. Reasons Explaining the Formation of the Illiberal Regime in Hungary

As with complex political changes in general, the formation of the Hungarian illiberal regime can best be understood as the result of several factors and not just one single cause.[67] The erosion of democracy and the rule of law is a global phenomenon[68] which is multi-causal. Economic, sociological, communicational, and geopolitical factors all play important roles.[69] But why has the Hungarian deterioration been dramatically worse than the 'average' deterioration? We think of several particular reasons.

Instead, the Constitutional Court tends to use softer competences (such as declaring that the legislature omitted to act, and obliging the legislature to act within a deadline).

[64] Regarding various techniques delaying, avoiding, or hollowing out decisions, applied by the Constitutional Court itself, to justify its own failures to act, see Petra Lea Láncos, 'Passivist Strategies Available to the Hungarian Constitutional Court' (2019) 79 Heidelberg Journal of International Law (ZaöRV) 971.

[65] See eg the open letter by the President of the Hungarian Constitutional Court published on 14 December 2021 <https://www.alkotmanybirosag.hu/kozlemeny/az-alkotmanybirosag-elnokenek-allasfoglalasa-a-jogallamisag-vedelmeben>.

[66] On hybrid constitutional regimes (with further references) see eg Roberto N Ortega, 'Conceptualizing Authoritarian Constitutionalism' (2016) 49 World Comparative Law 339; Steven Levitsky and Lucan A Way, *Competitive Authoritarianism: Hybrid Regimes after the Cold War* (CUP 2010); Bozóki and Hegedűs (n 13).

[67] For a literature overview, see Katalin Fábián, 'Why Did Hungarian Politics Become Authoritarian? A Review of Competing and Complementary Responses' (2021) 2 Hungarian Studies Review 216.

[68] See the sobering 2022 World Justice Project Report (on p 8 by Alejandro Ponce): 'The results in this report show that adherence to the rule of law fell in 61% of countries over the past year.'

[69] For further details see András Jakab, 'What Can Constitutional Law Do against the Erosion of Democracy and the Rule of Law? On the Interconnectedness of the Protection of Democracy and the Rule of Law' (2020) 6 Constitutional Studies 5, esp. 8–12 with literature references.

3.1 A Legal-Political Culture with a Weak Immune System

One of the key risk factors for Hungarian constitutionalism has been the legal political culture that failed to stop the erosion. The cultural context in all former socialist countries made the ice thin, which then broke (due to specific political constellations).

The US Constitution, for example, has been a stable and functioning constitution for 230 years now and has withstood severe crises—even a civil war. It was, however, translated into Spanish and became the Argentine Constitution of 1853, under which Argentina was turned very quickly into a dictatorship. Also, the current Austrian Constitution, adopted in 1920, miserably failed after thirteen years. By 1933/4 Austria had already become a fascist state, that is, already before the *Anschluss*. Literally the same constitution was then re-established in 1945, and since then Austrian democracy and the rule of law have been quite strong. This does not mean that rules do not matter. But for a constitutional error (in our case: the combination of the disproportionate electoral system and the easily circumvented constitutional amendment procedure) to be really damaging, you need some unfortunate interplay with other factors.

Empirical surveys point to the fact that the Hungarian population was characterized by an ambivalent (ie partially self-contradictory) attitude towards the law.[70] Citizens do not trust the state and the legal system, but at the same time they still expect the state and the legal system to solve all their problems. On the one hand, they want very detailed and strictly enforced regulations, but if they are specifically about them, they would rather find a smart way to evade the laws and expect privileged treatment. Their attitudes towards the law were embedded in a generally pessimistic, cynical, and anomic social culture. The research also indicates that there might even be a lack of coherence concerning values in a large part of society, even in terms of the most basic principles.

There are characteristics that can be considered a legacy of socialism in Hungarian legal culture. There are also some that perhaps go back even earlier: for example, the fact that the average citizen seems not to dare question official action even in the case of obvious abuse indicates a much older lack of democratic and rule of law traditions. In other words, what we now consider to be the legal culture of the current Hungarian illiberal regime is only partially

[70] See eg György Gajduschek, 'Wild East and Civilised West? Some Indicators of Legal Culture in Hungary, Serbia and the Netherlands: An Empirical Comparative Assessment' (2019) 60 Jahrbuch für Ostrecht 165.

its own; large parts draw on an inherited legal culture from which the current regime feeds as a breeding ground.[71] This cultural problem is of course also true for other former socialist countries, so it is no coincidence that the EU's so-called 'rule of law crisis' broke out in post-socialist EU MSs.

3.2 The Pre-democratic Historical Origins of Hungarian Legal Culture Are Still Present

Some claim that the legal system is more and more reminiscent of that preceding 1945, at least in its rhetoric/narrative. This, however, is not convincing. The most important and genuinely promoted narrative of that time related to the historical (pre-Second World War) Constitution, to which only a few, unsystematic, dishonest, and unfounded references are made today. If this is done, the sole aim is historicizing.[72] Meanwhile, the real—albeit restricted—similarities between current and pre-war actual practices are not sufficient to prove the analogy.

When looking for an archetype that best describes the current legal system, it is more fitting to turn to the socialist era. This is all the more surprising since the allegedly most important reason put forward for adopting the new Fundamental Law was to overcome the previous (1949/1989) socialist (or even 'communist') Constitution.[73] On a political level, the present Hungarian government consistently employs an anti-communist political rhetoric, yet its implied and sometimes also explicit ideas of the law are in fact highly reminiscent of socialist legal doctrine. This is no simple and coincidental similarity, but much rather a clear and identifiable continuity of socialist legal theory, which had in part survived the political change and persisted in Hungarian legal culture.[74] It became visible after 2010, having partly been elevated to the level of official narrative.[75] This continuity is not merely a simple remnant of the past, but the reinforcement of certain characteristics, in part induced by the

[71] Péter Tölgyessy, 'Politika mindenekelőtt: Jog és hatalom Magyarországon' in András Jakab and György Gajduschek (eds), *A magyar jogrendszer állapota* (MTA TK 2016) 32–33.

[72] See eg Hungarian Constitutional Court, Decision 22/2016 (XII.5.). For more details see Tímea Drinóczi, 'Hungarian Constitutional Court: The Limits of EU Law in the Hungarian Legal System' (2017) 11 Vienna Journal on International Constitutional Law 139; Zoltán Szente, 'A historizáló alkotmányozás problémái—a történeti alkotmány és a Szent Korona az új Alaptörvényben' (2011) 4 Közjogi Szemle 1.

[73] See on this 2.2.

[74] For more details, see eg Jakab and Hollán (n 3).

[75] See Tölgyessy (n 71) 17.

similarity of political operation, in particular, statism and voluntarism and in part by the bits and pieces of socialist theory that survived as mental residues.[76]

The official legal doctrine (and in particular constitutional doctrine) at the time of socialism may be briefly summarized in a few simplified assumptions (see below).[77] While we are not claiming that these would form the essence of socialist legal or constitutional theory *in abstracto*, the points listed below seem to be the most relevant for understanding the contemporary legacy of these views in Hungary. The government's approach to the law visibly shuns theoretical underpinnings, and when fragments of it accidentally emerge, it is difficult to piece them together to a consistent, abstract legal doctrine.[78] A number of proponents of the current government from amongst legal scholars actually started their careers as socialist legal theorists and some even continue to work (among others) with such terminology.[79] Meanwhile, different elements of socialist legal theory still tend to resurface, of which we will highlight a few below. Following the description of the different theses we will briefly outline how and to what extent they continue to live on today.[80]

(a) Law is only a technical impediment, and is not a real barrier to politics; it reflects the will of the ruling class—legal instrumentalism, which essentially denies the idea of constitutionalism. Infamous examples are the unbridled use of legislation, including constitution-making for the concrete aims of power politics. The laws on the media, on election procedure, and on political advertising in public spaces are good examples. Also the economic benefit of a restricted interest group like the regulation of gambling, tobacco retail, or different tax laws are illustrative. Legislation bolstering *Kulturkampf* (such as the anti-LGBTQ law, that is Act LXXIX of 2021) mainly seeks to divert public discourse and distract from uncomfortable issues, such as corruption, the state of public health services, and the education system. The instrumentalist concept of the law has only changed in the sense that 'working class' has been replaced

[76] The expression 'mental residues' has been borrowed from Claus Offe, 'Designing Institutions in East European Transitions' in Robert E Goodin (ed), *The Theory of Institutional Design* (CUP 1996) 199, 210.

[77] As regards the use of socialist legal theory in this book, we mean the socialist normativism of Soviet origin. For more detail, see eg John N Hazard, *Communists and Their Law* (CUP 1969); William E Butler, *Soviet Law* (OUP 1988).

[78] As to the 'illiberal state', see below.

[79] For a particular Marxist legal theory, see eg Csaba Varga, 'A joguralom és színeváltozásai idealizáció és ideokratikus nyomásgyakorlás között' (2016) Pázmány Law Working Papers No. 12 <www.plwp.eu/evfolyamok/2016/170-2016-12>, who was one of the best-known Marxist legal theorists before 1990; Béla Pokol, *Globális uralmi rend* (Kairosz 2008), for instance, works with the neo-Marxist theses of Michael Hardt and Antonio Negri.

[80] On the continuing influence of the socialist legacy, with further references, see Jakab and Hollán (n 3).

by 'nation', whose interest may even legitimize formal violations of the law, and in whose interest legislation must be passed in contravention of the principles of Western constitutionalism.

(b) From among the methods of interpretation textual approaches are given preference, since more creative solutions, such as referring to the general aims of the legal text, would provide judges with too much leeway, amounting to antidemocratic methods, in breach of legal certainty. In reality, this is a further symptom that the normative force of legal norms is getting weaker: if you take the task of governing society via law seriously, then judges sometimes need to have a degree of discretion when applying the law. By denying this option, you imply either extremely fast law-making (in order to adjust to new constellations, social facts, or challenges) or, even more often, you will find a non-legal, informal solution (without the need for a proper legal, eg purposive, reasoning). Actually, the original text of the Fundamental Law would have signalled a step forward by encouraging purposive interpretation, which is customary in Western legal cultures and even in Hungary before the Second World War.[81] However, the Fourth and the Seventh amendments of the Fundamental Law were largely aimed at curbing judicial (both the Constitutional Court's and the ordinary courts') power by rewriting the formal rules.[82]

(c) Rejecting the idea of the separation of powers, in preference for the unity of power, or 'democratic centralism'. Officially and somewhat pharisaically, the principle of the separation of powers has been spelled out in the Fundamental Law's text and thus is formally part of the Constitution. On the level of actual practices, however, we are witnessing a clear erosion of the separation of powers. This is hard to pin down with traditional legal methods focusing on formal legal rules, often happening through staffing and informal pressures. In socialist times, constitutional courts were described as elitist and antidemocratic institutions with no original legitimacy. Therefore they should not interfere with political processes, while judges were considered to be mere bureaucrats. Similar views had also been present in Hungarian public discourse and legal thought after the end of socialism, but the openly hostile stance and the tone in which this was voiced on the highest political levels was unprecedented.[83]

[81] András Jakab, 'A bírói jogértelmezés az Alaptörvény tükrében' (2011) 2 Jogesetek Magyarázata 86.

[82] On the fading, but still persisting post-socialist traditions of judicial formalism, see Marcin Matzak, Máryás Bencze, and Zdenek Kühn, 'EU Law and Central European Judges: Administrative Judiciaries in the Czech Republic, Hungary and Poland Ten Years after Accession' in Michael Bobek (ed), *Central European Judges under European Influence* (Hart 2015) 43.

[83] The changes in the legal rules relating to the Constitutional Court since 2010 can largely be explained by the aim of the constitution-maker to distance the Court from politically relevant law-making.

(d) The force of international law is derived from state sovereignty and is secondary to it. This is also something that we are experiencing on a daily basis, starting with the statements portraying the Venice Commission as being part of an international conspiracy led by George Soros, to the state's poster campaigns inciting hate against migrants, the United Nations, and the EU. The latter is derogatorily only referred to as 'Brussels'. But recent years have also seen a parliamentary resolution that harshly criticized a Strasbourg judgment; even though the imposed fine of the judgment was later actually paid to the claimant.[84] Meanwhile, this stance even appears in certain Constitutional Court decisions, with total disregard for the relevant provisions of the Fundamental Law.[85]

While the similarities are apparent, one or two elements may stem from other sources, for example from authoritarian concepts of the law or simply from old-style legal positivism.[86] However, taken together, their origins may be traced back to socialism. Those who are voicing these thoughts (including the Prime Minister himself) received their legal education before 1990, based on sovereigntist socialist doctrines. While it is not impossible that they also had other inspirations (and, in general, the tendency of non-democratic states is to be less friendly towards international law), in combination with the above views about legal interpretation and democratic centralism, these ideas seem to be a socialist legacy in the Hungarian context.

Resistance towards judicial review of parliamentary acts, for example, is also characteristic of classical British constitutionalism—which no longer exists in its original form since the 1998 Human Rights Act and since a moderate fundamental rights-oriented constitutional jurisprudence was introduced. Paying lip service to the British example for the benefit of the Hungarian audience, however, disregards the fact that, lacking a formal constitution, the British system allows for the adoption of any law with a simple majority; that is, it greatly differs from the Hungarian system. Any effort at transplanting the British concept of 'political constitutionalism' would fail in the context of the different institutional

See Fruzsina Gárdos-Orosz, 'Alkotmánybíróság 2010–2015' in András Jakab and György Gajduschek (eds), *A magyar jogrendszer állapota* (MTA TK 2016) 442.

[84] Parl Dec 58/2012. (VII. 10.) OGY hat.

[85] Article Q of the Fundamental Law contains the obligation of conformity with international law. For attempts to neutralize the provision, see Separate Opinion by Justice Béla Pokol, Hungarian Constitutional Court, Decision 34/2013 (XI.22) [83]–[85]; Separate Opinion by Justice Béla Pokol, Hungarian Constitutional Court, Decision 7/2014 (III.7) [113].

[86] Béla Pokol, 'Separation of Power and Parliamentarism in Hungary' (2003) 37 East European Quarterly 67; Béla Pokol, *The Juristocratic State: Its Victory and the Possibilities of Taming* (Dialóg Campus Kiadó 2017).

environment.[87] Also, rejecting judicial creativity was not only characteristic of socialist legal theory, but also an important branch of American scholarly literature: the originalists, which hold a similar view.[88] However, while originalists are trying to unearth the original meaning of certain specific terms, there is no actual sign of this approach in Hungarian practice.

3.3 A Concrete Error in Constitutional Law

Another reason is a concretely identifiable error in Hungarian constitutional law, which arose from the interplay of two norms. The constitutional order before 2010 included a disproportionate electoral system (for the sake of government stability), which together with the comparatively low (two-thirds) constitution-amending majority, opened the legal door for unilateral amendments to the Constitution. However, the constitutional rules alone never explain the erosion of democracy and the rule of law, because they exert their effect together with sociological-political-cultural factors.

3.4 Political Entrepreneurs Abusing the Weak Immune System

Yet another factor is the specific people who made political decisions that led to the current situation.[89] Certain persons, and due to the centralized nature of the Hungarian illiberal regime, mostly a single person, Viktor Orbán,[90] do

[87] On political constitutionalism see eg Richard Bellamy, *Political Constitutionalism: A Republican Defence of the Constitutionality of Democracy* (CUP 2007). For a critical review of the Hungarian reception of the concept, see Attila Antal, 'Politikai és jogi alkotmányosság Magyarországon' (2013) 22 Politikatudományi Szemle 48, with further references; István Stumpf, *Erős állam—alkotmányos korlátok* (Századvég 2014).

[88] See eg Antonin Scalia and Bryan A Garner, *Reading Law: The Interpretation of Legal Texts* (West Group 2011).

[89] For the role of political entrepreneurs (ie someone who takes advantage of the opportunity offered by the political context) see Marianna Kneuer, 'Unravelling Democratic Erosion: Who Drives the Slow Death of Democracy, and How?' (2021) Democratization 1442. The fact that the deterioration of the rule of law and democracy in Hungary is even more significant compared to other countries in the region resulted from the interplay of specific domestic political actors (especially Viktor Orbán) and strong polarization (which is stronger than in the rest of the region). In addition, unfortunate coincidences also played a role (eg the economic crisis of 2008, global political changes in the 2010s)—or to put it differently: there were many worrying signs, but even compared to them, Hungary just got really unlucky to experience the strong deterioration that we have seen.

[90] The permanent volatility of the Hungarian regime (its instability and gradual deterioration) can largely be explained by the Prime Minister's personality traits. It is disputed in the literature whether by nature all hybrid regimes are necessarily unstable (and represent an unsustainable transitional stage

have enormous influence on specific political decisions. However, they are somehow dependent on the cultural context and the development of the cultural environment. It depends on such a context, for instance, to what degree hierarchy is accepted or even expected, paternalism is tolerated, corruption and nepotism forgiven, etc. This cultural profile characterizes not only the supporters of the Hungarian illiberal regime, but the entire Hungarian society on average (ie to a large extent also opposition voters).

3.5 The Paradox of EU Membership: Unintentional Damages to a Fragile Constitutional Democracy

The EU, or rather Hungary becoming an MS of the EU, was in fact a key factor for the erosion of rule of law and democracy in Hungary. First, the instruments of effective external pressure—often called accession conditionality—disappeared with the accession to the EU.[91] While the accession conditionality supported the liberal democratic constitutional system of 1989, the EU accession itself and the trust which comes with it, treating every EU MS as an equally strong and resilient member of the EU, was too much of a burden for liberal democracy in Hungary. The supporting scaffolding has disappeared, and parts of the building have unfortunately collapsed, due to various inputs.

Second, paradoxically, EU accession was harmful even beyond this failure to render assistance to the state of the Hungarian rule of law and democracy.[92] A significant part of the active Hungarian citizens who are sensitive to the values of constitutionalism migrated to the western part of the EU and thus they are less present in the domestic democratic processes. Due to the free

between dictatorship and democracy). For the discussion, see eg Joakim Ekman, 'Political Participation and Regime Stability: A Framework for Analyzing Hybrid Regimes' (2009) 30 International Political Science Review 7.

[91] Formally, there are (and always have been) legal instruments in the hands of the EU against hybrid(izing) regimes, but these always depend on political discretion at some point in the procedure (eg the Commission has no legal obligation to initiate infringement procedures), and since Hungary is already an EU member, its support was often needed in the internal EU decision-making mechanisms (in completely different matters). In other words, a skilfully manoeuvring MS (eg with veto blackmail, supporting votes in other matters, etc) can avoid the strict enforcement of EU law for a long time. See more on the topic in András Jakab and Dimitry Kochenov (eds), *The Enforcement of EU Law and Values: Ensuring Member States' Compliance* (OUP 2017); András Jakab, 'Three Misconceptions about the EU Rule of Law Crisis' (17 October 2022) *Verfassungsblog* <https://verfassungsblog.de/misconceptions-rol/>. The Hungarian hybrid regime has now run out of options to manoeuvre, mostly thanks to developments in Poland and the Russian aggression against Ukraine.

[92] R Daniel Kelemen, 'Appeasement, ad Infinitum' (2022) 29 Maastricht Journal of European and Comparative Law 177.

movement of goods and economic integration Hungary became an interesting place of production for Western European countries. 'Audicracy' is a nickname which describes the negative impact of this phenomenon.

Third, quite likely the largest damage, however, was done by the uncontrolled financial support of the EU. An open door may even tempt a saint, one could say. The enormous amounts handed over to Hungary with little to no control for their adequate use provided incentives to become corrupt, helped the regime to bolster its position, and essentially increased the public acceptance of the Hungarian illiberal regime. To be blunt, financial support by the EU made corrupt practices more tempting, as much more money was on the table. The uneven distribution of the money in turn helped to concentrate more power at the centre. As a by-product of facilitating corruption and concentrating political power, the rule of law and democracy were dismantled continuously.

All factors (3.1–3.5) listed above can only be meaningfully interpreted in relation to each other or in connection with each other. It was not fate that Hungary ended up in today's situation, but, in medical terms, the 'risk factors' were present.

4. Is Hungary a Unique Accident?

It is interesting to see the Hungarian developments in the context of the former socialist countries which are now MSs of the EU. A comparative outlook on former socialist countries in the EU lays bare a generally low immune system in post-socialist EU MSs. Besides Hungary, another country which took an illiberal turn within the EU is Poland. At the moment of closing this manuscript, Poland seems to be recovering, but we cannot be sure whether this is going to last, and Slovakia is now openly taking the illiberal Hungarian path. Further post-socialist EU MSs are in serious danger of following this trend too. For the purposes of comparison we will use the rule of law sub-index of the BTI (the WJP RLI until recently only contained a few former socialist EU MSs and is therefore less appropriate for our comparing time-series).

Figure 2.3 shows that there has been a generic trend over the last ten years of slow but steady deterioration of the quality of the rule of law in previously socialist countries which are now EU MSs. Notable exceptions are the Baltic countries and Romania, which have remained stable (or in the case of Estonia have even slightly improved). On average, however, the socialist legacy has left its traces and the whole region is in decline. Moreover and paradoxically, as

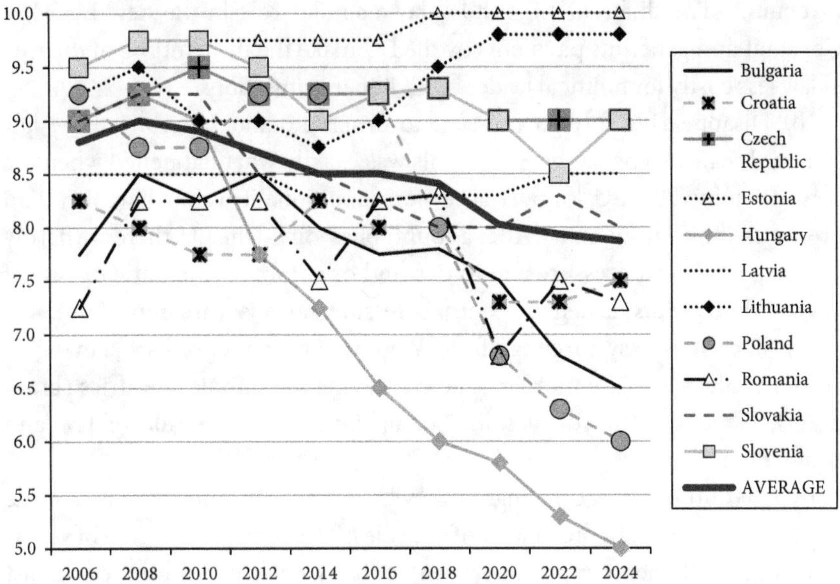

Figure 2.3 The rule of law sub-index of the Bertelsmann Transformation Index (data on previously socialist EU Member States from the period 2006–24)

helpful as the hope of EU membership was, actual EU accession in its concrete form proved to have negative effects on the quality of the rule of law in these countries. Given the time frame of the BTI data presented above, Bulgaria and Croatia are particularly illustrative examples. They joined the EU in 2007 and 2013 respectively. For both countries, the BTI data show a strengthening of the rule of law during the accession period, stagnation after accession, and a fairly steady decline for some time after accession. While it may well be that reasons other than EU membership are important factors in the erosion of the rule of law and democracy, the different timing of the onset of erosion in the post-socialist EU MSs is a strong indicator that EU membership is related to erosion. There are various reasons for such a relation:

(a) An abundance of natural resources, such as oil revenues, contribute to the strengthening of illiberal features: the *ceteris paribus* low economic performance of illiberal regimes (meaning here: countries with lower rule of law values)[93] is masked by oil

[93] The rule of law has a positive effect on economic growth, see Lars P Feld and Stefan Voigt, 'Judicial Independence and Economic Growth: Some Proposals Regarding the Judiciary' in Roger D Congleton and Brigitta Swedenborg (eds), *Democratic Constitutional Design and Public Policy* (MIT Press 2006) 251.

revenues.[94] The different EU funds play a similar role in the new EU MSs. Constant and generous payments by the EU make the dismantling of the rule of law less costly for political leaders with illiberal ambitions.

(b) Disappearing foreign pressure to observe democratic or rule of law standards can also be dangerous.[95] This was exactly what happened when the new MSs joined the EU, for post-accession conditionality is much weaker than pre-accession conditionality. After a country has joined the EU, there are hardly any means to exert pressure and to demand or enforce democratic or rule of law standards. Outside help or external pressure, however, are important.

(c) Since it is easy to emigrate to Western Europe, citizens believing in Western values who are more mobile are leaving their home countries (brain drain), facilitating the dismantling of institutions of the rule of law and democracy.

In light of the above, one might ask: why exactly has Hungary suffered the most severe erosion in the quality of the rule of law in the last couple of years? The cultural elements must have been similarly determined by the socialist past also in other East European EU MSs. The answer is relatively simple: in Hungary a political party and a political leader with illiberal tendencies were able to form a government in 2010 without any formal constraints as they had the constitution-amending two-thirds majority. When similar developments occurred a couple of years later in Poland, many of the measures adopted in Hungary (especially court-packing of the change of personnel in the electoral commission, purging the judiciary with early retirement rules, takeover of the state media and turning it into a propaganda machine, etc) were also adopted in Poland.[96] As a matter of fact, they were not simply similar: they were directly inspired by the Hungarian developments and since the Polish governing party won the 2019 parliamentary elections again, we have witnessed further malicious Hungarian legal transplants, and similar informal measures might follow.[97] The fact that the Polish events provoked a stronger reaction

[94] The question is highly debated in political science, see Michael L Ross, 'Does Oil Hinder Democracy?' (2011) 53 World Politics 325; Thad Dunning, *Crude Democracy: Natural Resource Wealth and Political Regimes* (CUP 2008); Stephen Haber and Victor Menaldo, 'Do Natural Resources Fuel Authoritarianism? A Reappraisal of the Resource Course' (2011) 105 American Political Science Review 1.

[95] Anna Lührmann, Kelly McMann, and Carolien van Ham, 'The Effectiveness of Democracy Aid to Different Regime Types and Democracy Sectors' (2017) 40 V-Dem Institute Working Paper.

[96] For an excellent account of these developments, see Wojciech Sadurski, *Poland's Constitutional Breakdown* (OUP 2019); see also Mirosław Wyrzykowski and Michał Ziółkowski, 'Illiberal Constitutionalism and the Judiciary' in András Sajó, Renáta Uitz, and Stephen Holmes (eds), *Routledge Handbook of Illiberalism* (Routledge 2022) 517 reviewing 'the transformation of the judiciary in illiberal regimes' as well as offering a case study on Poland.

[97] On the concept of malicious legal transplants, see Mathias Siems, 'Malicious Legal Transplants' (2018) 38 Legal Studies 103. For a similar prediction, see Wojciech Sadurski, 'What Happens after the

internationally was to a large extent due to the fact that the Polish governing party failed to achieve the constitution-amending majority in 2015 and some of the measures were therefore clearly (more clearly than in Hungary) a violation of formal rules as enacted by the Constitution.

What we see taking place in Hungary is not an unfortunate and unique accident, but most likely the future for many Eastern European countries. The first casualty was Hungary in 2010, the second was Poland in 2015, and it is not far-fetched to suppose that others like Slovakia due to its change of government in 2023 (and some of the less obvious countries such as Bulgaria, Slovenia, Czechia, or Croatia) could also follow them in the future, unless effective new forms of external pressure (mainly from the EU) can inhibit this.[98]

5. Conclusion

To sum up the main argument of Chapter 2, we wish to highlight two findings. First, historical experience shows that besides honest determination, a radical institutional overhaul of the complete legal system can only be successful in the presence of external pressure. As this pressure was lifted with the accession of Hungary and Poland to the EU, the situation became worse. The illiberal narrative and the worrisome de facto practices in Hungary and other post-socialist EU MSs contributed further to the erosion of the rule of law and democracy in

Polish Elections?' (18 August 2019) *Verfassungsblog* <https://verfassungsblog.de/what-happens-after-the-polish-elections/>; see also John Shattuck, 'The New Global Landscape: Illiberal Regimes and Movements' (2018) 71 Journal of International Affairs 15, 15: 'The Orban model is now being copied across Europe by illiberal movements in Austria, the Czech Republic, France, Italy, the Netherlands, Poland, Romania, and the United Kingdom.'

[98] Some of the methods are actually already available, but Western European political leaders seem to be missing the political will, see Maximilian Steinbeis, 'A Bad Workman Blames His Tools' (9 June 2019) *Verfassungsblog* <https://verfassungsblog.de/a-bad-workman-blames-his-tools/>. New measures can include both formal (like a new EU regulation about cutting funds for violating rule of law standards) and informal ones (like suspension and monitoring of rogue parties by their respective European party families). For critical appraisals of both the currently available options and the solutions to be established in the future, see eg Laurent Pech and Dimitry Kochenov, 'Strengthening the Rule of Law within the European Union: Diagnoses, Recommendations, and What to Avoid' (2019) Reconnect Policy Brief; Dimitry Kochenov and Petra Bárd, 'Rule of Law Crisis in the New Member States of the EU' (2018) 1 Reconnect Working PaperFrom the three negative effects of EU membership mentioned in the main text which are detrimental to the rule of law, only the migration of Eastern European workers into Western Europe has not received much attention so far. Future policies by the EU which would encourage their return into Eastern European EU MSs would definitely help in these countries. Part of the Romanian (relative) success story is the return of workers who have worked and have socialized in Western Europe: they formed a large part of the anti-corruption demonstrators between 2017 and 2019, see 'Romanian Expats Return Home for Major Anti-government Protest, Clash with Police' (10 August 2018) Deutsche Welle <https://www.dw.com/en/romanian-expats-return-home-for-major-anti-government-protest-clash-with-police/a-45034900>.

Hungary. In other words, institution-building should go hand-in-hand with effective EU law obligations undertaken in more sober political moments, in order to guarantee that the political community does not enter into a self-destructive mode at a later point in time. An important step, which has been taken only recently, is to elevate the pressure once again. Withholding considerable financial support from EU MSs which do not guarantee the rule of law and democracy is important in two ways. First, it dries out corruption, which has been an important element of the decline. Second, it reintroduces external pressure. While both are important at the moment, they are not enough to get post-socialist EU MSs back on track. It is essential to contribute to a positive narrative and the readjustment of de facto practices with formal rules which must be in line with EU law. This will take a considerable amount of time.

Second, we should take elements beyond mere rules more consciously into account in post-socialist EU MSs. Since this is not in the interest of incumbent decision-makers, for the time being, overcoming the impasse seems, sadly, unlikely—unless the EU hardens its stance and exercises more efficient forms of external pressure on its MSs where the rule of law has been declining in the last couple of years. External pressure is thus especially needed in post-socialist EU MSs in order to ensure that the three components of formal rules, de facto practices, and narratives work together rather than against each other.

Elevating external pressure from the perspective of the EU necessitates structural changes at EU level. However, in the following chapter we will show why the EU is unlikely to provide the necessary force to improve the situation. A major reason for inaction is that the EU itself suffers from serious rule of law and democracy deficits.[99]

[99] See Chapter 3.

3

Deficits and Erosion of Democracy and the Rule of Law in EU Institutions

1. Introduction

European integration is one of the major success stories of the twentieth century. It is the construct which has helped a continent, prone to war, to live the longest peaceful episode of its modern history.[1] Major parts of this success story were the values of liberal constitutionalism as a uniting force of the divided continent in a common market.[2] The history of the EU began with France, Germany, Italy, and the Benelux countries ratifying the Treaty of Paris, establishing the European Coal and Steel Community led by its own executive branch, the High Authority, in 1951.[3] This development continued when in 1957 the foundation of the European Economic Community (EEC) was—besides the Euratom Treaty—laid out by the so-called Treaty of Rome. Both treaties founded organizations which enjoyed autonomous powers and featured important and innovative legal elements like the doctrine of direct effect, distinguishing these supranational communities from other international organizations. The continuous process of EU enlargement led at its peak to a Union of twenty-eight MSs, of around 514 million people, being then the second largest economy on earth.

For some fifteen years, however, the EU had to face 'its worst economic, financial and social crisis since World War II', leading then EC president Jean-Claude Juncker in 2016 to speak of a 'polycrisis'.[4] Rightly he stated that '[o]ur

[1] John Merriman, *A History of Modern Europe: From the Renaissance to the Present* (3rd edn, WW Norton & Company 2010) 1238–9, 'the most important success of the European Union has been to make war between member states unlikely'.

[2] On the economic dimension, see eg Alan S Milward, *Politics and Economics in the History of the European Union* (Routledge 2005); on the political dimension, see eg Simon Blumer and others, *Politics in the European Union* (5th edn, OUP 2020); on values, see eg Giuliano Amato and others (eds), *The History of the European Union: Constructing Europe* (Hart 2019).

[3] See eg Robert Schütze, *European Constitutional Law* (2nd edn, CUP 2015) 12 ff.

[4] Jean-Claude Juncker, 'Speech by President Jean-Claude Juncker at the Annual General Meeting of the Hellenic Federation of Enterprises (SEV)' (21 June 2016) *Athens* <http://europa.eu/rapid/press-release_SPEECH-16-2293_en.htm> accessed 24 October 2024.

Saving the European Union from Its Illiberal Member States. András Jakab and Lando Kirchmair, Oxford University Press. © András Jakab and Lando Kirchmair 2025.
DOI: 10.1093/oso/9780198954606.003.0004

various challenges—from the security threats in our neighborhood and at home, to the refugee crisis, and to the UK referendum—have not only arrived at the same time. They also feed each other, creating a sense of doubt and uncertainty in the minds of our people.'[5] In the aftermath of this diagnosis the pandemic and the Russian war of aggression against Ukraine came on top of the previous challenges. Not explicitly addressed, but nevertheless strongly interconnected, is what we call the EU's illiberal regime challenge. As has been outlined in Chapter 2, the transformation success story, turning former socialist states into rule of law respecting democracies as EU MSs, has turned out to be another major difficulty for the EU. In view of the other challenges, the huge erosion of the rule of law and democracy in post-socialist EU MSs has long been underestimated. It has been disregarded and treated as a crisis only in the MSs affected. Now that the erosion of democracy and the rule of law in Hungary and Poland is one of the largest worldwide, and it appears that 'ideologically agnostic' politicians seem to endanger also unitary actions in addressing other crises, it has been understood that the EU ought to do something. In her candidate speech to be re-elected as Commission President at the EP, Ursula von der Leyen explicitly included 'the rule of law and the fight against corruption'. She said that these values 'will be at the heart of our work'.[6] This stands in stark contrast to the actions taken by the EU to stop or rather reverse the erosion of democracy and the rule of law in its illiberal MSs. So far, these actions have been too little too late.[7] We contend in this chapter that this passivity cannot be adequately explained by saying 'the EU does not have the necessary legal tools'. Rather, we will aim to show that it is deficits and even erosion phenomena at EU institutions which are the reasons as to why the EU was not able to confront the illiberal regimes among its MSs. We do so by briefly recounting the history of the constitutional dimension of EU law, which arguably unfolded and continues to unfold in two intertwined stories: development of the rule of law and democratization. The ECJ was and continues to be an essential part of these stories, which are not isolated and did not happen in a strict chronological order, but have important overlaps and mutually influence each other in their respective storylines. While in part these are success

[5] Juncker (n 4).

[6] Ursula von der Leyen, Statement at the European Parliament Plenary by President Ursula von der Leyen, candidate for a second mandate 2024–2029, 18 July 2024, European Parliament, available at <https://multimedia.europarl.europa.eu/de/video/statement-by-ursula-von-der-leyen-president-of-the-european-commission-candidate-for-a-second-mandate-2024-2029-atmosphere-in-the-chamber_I259737> accessed 24 October 2024.

[7] Sonja Priebus and Lisa H Anders, 'Fundamental Change beneath the Surface: The Supranationalisation of Rule of Law Protection in the European Union' (2024) 62 Journal of Common Market Studies (early view) 224, 238.

stories, we cannot but point to deficits which are still present and even erosion phenomena which bother the EU too.

After we have spelled out these important strands of development, it becomes questionable as to whether the challenge of a stable rule of law and democracy only concerns the MSs or rather also the EU itself. Discussions of the democratic deficit of the EU were on high tide in the 1980s and 1990s. Even though the Treaty of Lisbon secured important rights for the EP, weaknesses are still present. Among other things, the so-called polycrisis of the EU—namely the economic and financial crisis, the refugee situation, the health and social crisis, and now the largest security and humanitarian crisis since the Second World War—has left its traces on the functioning of the EU too. To some extent, there has even been an erosion of the rule of law and democracy at EU level. It is not only that illiberal regimes are poisoning other MSs (by investing in various foreign media assets or by ruining judicial cooperation through fake judges) and the EU (by electing MEPs in unfair elections or by delegating Trojan horse officials in EU institutions). The illiberal regime crisis is actually a *symptom* of the EU's own constitutional malaise.

2. The Rule of Law: Revisiting a Central Pillar of European Integration

2.1 The Construction of the Rule of Law

The rule of law includes not just questions of the formal rule of law such as judicial independence, enforceability, clarity of legal norms, stability and foreseeability, and certain procedural requirements. In our understanding the rule of law in a wide (thick or substantive) sense comprises also the protection of human rights.[8] By the rule of law, we thus mean a list of requirements aimed at inhibiting the arbitrary use of public authority. In this sense, the rule of law is an important pillar of the constitutional dimension of the EU. Furthermore, the constitutional dimension of the EU rule of law is not merely that at the (horizontal) level of the EU the separation of powers is given, but that also on a vertical level the EU MSs need to justify to the EU that their rule of law remains intact. Precisely this element is an essentially and still heavily contested element of the constitutional dimension of the EU. Before, however, looking

[8] See also our discussion in Chapter 6.

for reasons as to why the EU response to its illiberal MSs is rather weak, we will briefly revisit the establishment of the rule of law within the EU legal order.

The chief architect of the rule of law in the EU is the ECJ, which is responsible for the evolution of the doctrines of direct applicability and primacy. In 1963 the ECJ postulated the autonomy of the Community legal order which was accompanied by the direct effect of EU law on the national laws of the MSs,[9] just like the primary application of EU law.[10] This arguably was the foundation on which the subsequent development of the EU could be successfully based, establishing a strong and effective autonomous legal system.[11] The landmark judgment in this regard was *Van Gend & Loos*, in which the ECJ famously declared as early as 1963 that the 'Community constitutes a new legal order of international law for the benefit of which the states have limited their sovereign rights, albeit within limited fields, and the subjects of which comprise not only the MSs but also their nationals'.[12] In this case, the ECJ stipulated that EU law enjoys direct effect and thus creates individual rights which MSs and their courts must respect.[13] Only a year later, the ECJ added something important to this finding. In *Costa v. E.N.E.L.* the Court stated that the law of the European Community is itself a legal order by postulating the 'autonomy of the Community legal order' when holding that '[b]y contrast with ordinary international treaties, the EEC Treaty has created its own legal system which, on the entry into force of the Treaty, became an integral part of the legal systems of the MSs and which their courts are bound to apply'.[14] The autonomous EU legal order thus was born and important constitutional elements were

[9] See Case 26/62 *NV Algemene Transport- en Expeditie Onderneming van Gend & Loos v Netherlands Inland Revenue Administration* [1963] EU:C:1963:1.

[10] Case 6/64 *Flaminio Costa v E.N.E.L.* [1964] EU:C:1964:66; and Case 11/70 *Internationale Handelsgesellschaft mbH v Einfuhr- und Vorratsstelle für Getreide und Futtermittel* [1970] EU:C:1970:114, paras 3–4; Case 106/77 *Amministrazione delle Finanze dello Stato v Simmenthal SpA* [1978] EU:C:1978:49.

[11] See Eric Stein, 'Lawyers, Judges, and the Making of a Transnational Constitution' (1981) 75 American Journal of International Law 1; and Joseph HH Weiler, 'The Transformation of Europe' (1991) 100 Yale Law Journal 2403.

[12] Case 26/62 *NV Algemene Transport- en Expeditie Onderneming van Gend & Loos v Netherlands Inland Revenue Administration* [1963] EU:C:1963:1, p 12.

[13] *NV Algemene Transport* (n 12), pp 13, 16.

[14] Case 6/64 *Flaminio Costa v E.N.E.L.* [1964] EU:C:1964:66, p 593; the German version states '*Rechtsordnung*'; the French version uses '*ordre juridique*'; cf Opinion 1/91 *Opinion delivered pursuant to the second subparagraph of Article 228 (1) of the Treaty—Draft agreement between the Community, on the one hand, and the countries of the European Free Trade Association, on the other, relating to the creation of the European Economic Area* [1991] EU:C:1991:490, para 2 postulated the 'autonomy of the Community legal order'; compare the German version '*Autonomie des Rechtssystems der Gemeinschaft*'; see furthermore on this Werner Schroeder, *Das Gemeinschaftsrechtssystem: Eine Untersuchung zu den rechtsdogmatischen, rechtstheoretischen und verfassungsrechtlichen Grundlagen des Systemdenkens im Europäischen Gemeinschaftsrecht* (Mohr Siebeck 2002) 104–5 (with further references in nn 6 and 7). Recently see Case C-284/16 *Slowakische Republik v Achmea BV* [2018] EU:C:2018:158, para 33.

already present.[15] Moreover, the ECJ continued by saying that '[t]he integration into the laws of each MS of provisions which derive from the Community, and more generally the terms and the spirit of the Treaty, make it impossible for the States, as a corollary, to accord precedence to a unilateral and subsequent measure over a legal system accepted by them on a basis of reciprocity'.[16] Thereby, the primacy of EU law over MS law was established.

In the *Stauder* case in 1969 the ECJ acknowledged for the first time in EU history that fundamental rights formed part of unwritten general principles of EU law.[17] This important case later climaxed in the establishment of the CFR in the rank of EU primary law, the origins of which can be traced back to this important judgment of the ECJ.

One year later, in 1970, in *Internationale Handelsgesellschaft* the Court explicitly claimed the primacy of EU law even over the constitutional law of its MSs, no matter whether fundamental rights or structural principles are concerned:

> [T]he law stemming from the Treaty, an independent source of law, cannot because of its very nature be overridden by rules of national law, however framed, without being deprived of its character as Community law and without the legal basis of the Community itself being called in question. Therefore the validity of a Community measure or its effect within a Member State cannot be affected by allegations that it runs counter to either fundamental rights as formulated by the constitution of that State or the principles of a national constitutional structure.[18]

In 1978 in *Simmenthal II*, this primacy of EU law over conflicting MS law was finally explicitly spelled out in positive terms. The Court stated that beyond rendering conflicting MS law automatically inapplicable, the adoption of new national legislation which conflicts with EU law is also precluded.[19]

And in 1986, the ECJ referred to the EEC Treaty as 'the basic constitutional charter' of the Community.[20] This was confirmed in 1991: '[T]he [EU] Treaty,

[15] See András Jakab, *European Constitutional Language* (CUP 2016) ch 3.

[16] Case 6/64 *Flaminio Costa v E.N.E.L.* [1964] EU:C:1964:66, pp 593–94.

[17] Case 29/69 *Erich Stauder v City of Ulm—Sozialamt* [1969] EU:C:1969:57.

[18] Case 11/70 *Internationale Handelsgesellschaft mbH v Einfuhr- und Vorratsstelle für Getreide und Futtermittel* [1970] EU:C:1970:114, para 3; see in this regard also Case C-409/06 *Winner Wetten GmbH v Bürgermeisterin der Stadt Bergheim* [2010] EU:C:2010:503, para 61: 'Rules of national law, even of a constitutional order, cannot be allowed to undermine the unity and effectiveness of Union law.' See also Case C-399/11 *Stefano Melloni v Ministerio Fiscal* [2013] EU:C:2013:107, para 59.

[19] Case 106/77 *Amministrazione delle Finanze dello Stato v Simmenthal SpA* [1978] EU:C:1978:49, para 17.

[20] Case 294/83, *Parti écologiste 'Les Verts' v European Parliament* [1986] EU:C:1986:166, p 1365.

albeit concluded in the form of an international agreement, none the less constitutes the constitutional charter of a [Union] based on the rule of law.'[21] In 2008 and 2013 respectively the ECJ firmly established the constitutional dimension of the EU also with regard to international law when deciding that EU regulations freezing the assets of certain terror suspects as instructed by UN Security Council Resolutions violate EU fundamental rights and therefore violate the constitutional character of the EU.[22]

In 1998, in the judgment *IN.CO.GE.'90 ao*, the ECJ finally clarified the legal consequences of a conflict between EU law and MS law. According to the ECJ, EU law enjoys primacy ('*Anwendungsvorrang*') but does not invalidate conflicting MS law ('*Geltungsvorrang*').[23] In the recent *Rimšēvičs* case handed down in 2019 the ECJ potentially took another major step in the process of European integration. For the first time in the history of the EU, the ECJ declared void an act of an MS, namely the decision of the Republic of Latvia to relieve the Governor of the Latvian Central Bank, Mr Ilmārs Rimšēvičs, of office.[24] Commentators have already described this judgment as a 'constitutional moment'[25] which 'should send shockwaves through the circles participating in the discourse on European constitutional law'.[26] For this 'Mephistophelian power of a court to nullify an act of public authority has always been regarded as the ultimate expression of its superior position'.[27] This is certainly true in symbolic terms. However, considering the primacy of EU law and the so-called *Rechtsbereinigungspflicht* of MSs, this is not that different from the ECJ simply declaring the MS had not acted in conformity with EU law. It was already settled case law that national legislators must not enact new national law

[21] Opinion 1/91 *Opinion delivered pursuant to the second subparagraph of Article 228 (1) of the Treaty—Draft agreement between the Community, on the one hand, and the countries of the European Free Trade Association, on the other, relating to the creation of the European Economic Area* [1991] EU:C:1991:490, para 21.

[22] Joined Cases C-402/05 P and C-415/05 P *Yassin Abdullah Kadi and Al Barakaat International Foundation v Council of the European Union and Commission of the European Communities* [2008] EU:C:2008:461, para 285; Case C-584 P, C-593 P, and C-595/10 P *European Commission and Others v Yassin Abdullah Kadi* [2013] EU:C:2013:518.

[23] Case C-10/97 *Ministero delle Finanze v IN.CO.GE.'90 Srl, Idelgard Srl, Iris'90 Srl, Camed Srl, Pomezia Progetti Appalti Srl (PPA), Edilcam Srl, A. Cecchini & C. Srl, EMO Srl, Emoda Srl, Sappesi Srl, Ing. Luigi Martini Srl, Giacomo Srl and Mafar Srl* [1998] EU:C:1998:498, para 21.

[24] Joined Cases C-202/18 and C-238/18 *Ilmārs Rimšēvičs and European Central Bank v Republic of Latvia* [2019] EU:C:2019:139, para 66.

[25] Daniel Sarmiento, 'Crossing the Baltic Rubicon' (4 March 2019) *Verfassungsblog* https://verfassungsblog.de/crossing-the-baltic-rubicon/> accessed 24 October 2024.

[26] Jürgen Bast, 'Autonomy in Decline? A Commentary on Rimšēvičs and ECB v Latvia' (13 May 2019) *Verfassungsblog* https://verfassungsblog.de/autonomy-in-decline-a-commentary-on-rimsevics-and-ecb-v-latvia/> accessed 24 October 2024.

[27] Bast (n 26). Cf On the specificities of this which provide context for this decision, Josef Weinzierl, 'Der EuGH erklärt erstmalig nationales Recht für ungültig—Anmerkung zum Urteil des EuGH v. 26.2.2019, Rs. C-202/18 (Rimšēvičs)' (2019) 54 Europarecht 434.

conflicting with EU law, which includes the duty to adjust national law to EU law.[28] Yet, it is an important showcase for the development of the constitutional dimension of the EU.

The development of the rule of law in the ECJ case law, together with the evolution of the European treaties, for instance in 1986 through the Single European Act, the first major revision of the Treaty of Rome, and the Treaty of Lisbon in 2009, besides many other minor but nevertheless important developments which must be left out here,[29] constitutes an important pillar of the constitutional dimension of the EU.[30] Primacy in its typical form as developed by the ECJ is by now settled case law.[31] However, 'for all its uniqueness and despite the fact that most legal actors have accepted it to a large extent, primacy remains sensitive and contested. This is witnessed by the fact that the attempt to codify it in the Constitutional Treaty failed.'[32] Only Declaration No 17 concerning primacy annexed to the Treaty of Lisbon provides an anchor for this concept in EU primary law.[33]

2.2 Challenges and Erosion of the Rule of Law at EU Level

Another driving force behind the success of European integration is the preliminary reference procedure which rests on the acceptance of important players in MS legal orders applying EU law. MS courts are essential in giving EU law its designed effect within MS legal orders.[34] Hence, the strong position of the ECJ claiming the unconditional primacy of EU law over MS (constitutional) law

[28] See eg Case C-290/94 *Commission of the European Communities v Hellenic Republic* [1996] EU:C:1996:265, para 2; Case 104/86 *Commission of the European Communities v Italian Republic* [1988] EU:C:1988:171, para 12.

[29] As eg the phenomenon of agencification, as described by Paul Weismann, *European Agencies and Risk Governance in EU Financial Market Law* (Routledge 2016).

[30] Cf Koen Lenaerts, 'Constitutionalism and the Many Faces of Federalism' (1990) 38 American Journal of Comparative Law 205; Frederico Mancini, 'The Making of a Constitution for Europe' (1989) 26 Common Market Law Review 595. For the argument that 'by the early 1970's all major constitutional doctrines were already in place', see Weiler (n 11) 2413, n 22.

[31] See eg Case C-409/06 *Winner Wetten GmbH v Bürgermeisterin der Stadt Bergheim* [2010] EU:C:2010:503, para 55 with further reference.

[32] Monica Claes, 'The Primacy of EU Law in European and National Law' in Damian Chalmers and Anthony Arnull (eds), *The Oxford Handbook of European Union Law* (OUP 2015) 178, 178.

[33] This declaration unambiguously states: 'The Conference recalls that, in accordance with well settled case law of the Court of Justice of the European Union, the Treaties and the law adopted by the Union on the basis of the Treaties have primacy over the law of Member States, under the conditions laid down by the said case law.'

[34] See in this regard Morten Rasmussen, 'Revolutionizing European Law: A History of the *Van Gend en Loos* Judgment' (2014) 12 International Journal of Constitutional Law 136. For instance, the Austrian Constitutional Court is quite active in this regard and sent its first preliminary reference request already four years after Austria's accession to the EU, VfSlg 15.450/1999.

depends in a way on organs applying national law.[35] Especially with regard to self-confident national constitutional courts, this adds another perspective.[36]

More than fifty years after *Van Gend & Loos* and *Costa E.N.E.L.* the history of enforcement and supremacy conflicts between the ECJ and the MSs has been fuelled again in light of the recent rule of law and democracy crisis. Forerunners were judicial concepts such as the 'constitutional identity' of MSs[37], '*ultra vires*' and the '*solange* fundamental rights protection', all developed by the German Federal Constitutional Court.[38] An analogous concept is the doctrine of 'controlimiti'[39] developed by the Italian Constitutional Court. Despite these concepts the relationship between the ECJ and the German Federal Constitutional Court could be described—despite all the vicissitudes and small ruptures—as a 'fruitful dialogue'.[40]

This harmonious relationship was shaken to the core on 5 May 2020 by the judgment of the German Federal Constitutional Court on the Public Sector Purchase Programme (PSPP) of the European Central Bank (ECB).[41] For the first time in the history of the EU, the German Federal Constitutional Court declared a judgment of the ECJ *ultra vires*, stating that the ECJ had acted 'objectively arbitrarily' when 'interpreting the treaties in a way which was no longer comprehensible'.[42] Despite the lengthy judgment and this qualification, it is, however, more than questionable whether the PSPP judgment of the ECJ must actually be mandatorily qualified as *ultra vires* in terms of structurally expanding the competences of the EU.[43] On this point the critique of the

[35] While basically MSs accept the primacy of EU law concerning non-constitutional MS law, a lack of knowledge of EU law and more trivial reasons might actually undermine the basic acceptance of the primacy of EU law at least to some extent. See, in this regard Claes (n 32) 187–93 with examples and further references.

[36] See eg Bruno de Witte, 'Direct Effect, Primacy and the Nature of the Legal Order' in Grainne de Búrca and Paul Craig (eds), *The Evolution of EU Law* (OUP 2011) 323, 352–56, pointing towards the rulings of various national Constitutional Courts to establish 'counterlimits' of EU primacy indicating a 'two-dimensional reality' (356).

[37] See on the concept and its origin in German law Monika Polzin, *Verfassungsidentität* (Mohr Siebeck 2018); cf Christian Calliess and Gerhard Van der Schyff (eds), *Constitutional Identity in a Europe of Multilevel Constitutionalism* (CUP 2019).

[38] For a good overview, see Mattias Wendel, *Permeabilität im europäischen Verfassungsrecht: Verfassungsrechtliche Integrationsnormen auf Staats- und Unionsebene im Vergleich* (Mohr Siebeck 2011).

[39] For an analysis of the 'Taricco saga', see eg Giovanni Piccirilli, 'The "Taricco Saga": The Italian Constitutional Court Continues Its European Journey' (2018) 14 European Constitutional Law Review 814.

[40] In this vein, Andreas Paulus, 'Horizontale und vertikale Aufgabenteilung beim Grundrechtsschutz in Europa' in Thomas Groh and others (eds), *Verfassungsrecht, Völkerrecht, Menschenrechte—Vom Recht im Zentrum der Internationalen Beziehungen. Festschrift für Ulrich Fastenrath* (CF Müller 2019) 79, 86.

[41] BVerfGE 154, 17 (*PSPP*).

[42] BVerfGE 154, 17 (*PSPP*) para 112, 116.

[43] Case C-493/17 *Proceedings brought by Heinrich Weiss and Others* [2018] EU:C:2018:1000.

PSPP judgment of the German Federal Constitutional Court is largely justified.[44] It seems that, by declaring the ECJ judgment *ultra vires*, the German Federal Constitutional Court has finally proven that the *ultra vires* control by MSs should not be in the hands of quite a small number of judges speaking in the name of democracy, but rather in the sphere of politics. Hence, when an MS holds that an EU act is *ultra vires*, this should rather be expressed by a democratic decision of the MS because the ECJ has, judicially speaking, the last word on matters of EU competence.[45]

The PSPP decision ignored the fact that the rule of law has been declining in many countries of the world,[46] including several MSs of the EU.[47] The fear that more stable democracies could take such a turn is pervasive in public debate and scholarly discourse.[48] Almost imperceptibly and largely unnoticed, the EC has been showing more and more reluctance to initiate infringement procedures (despite severe violations of EU law), the number of which has declined significantly over the years.[49] Furthermore, the unprecedented removal of Advocate General (AG) Sharpston in 2020 was rightly criticized as being against the law.[50] While Brexit-related solutions for the composition of the ECJ

[44] See the post by Franz C Mayer, 'Auf dem Weg zum Richterfaustrecht? Zum PSPP-Urteil des BVerfG' (7 May 2020) *Verfassungsblog* <https://verfassungsblog.de/auf-dem-weg-zum-richterfaustrecht/> accessed 24 October 2024, asking whether we are on the way to the 'law of the jungle of judges'; or András Jakab and Pál Sonnevend, 'The Bundesbank is under a Legal Obligation to Ignore the PSPP Judgment of the Bundesverfassungsgericht' (25 May 2020) *Verfassungsblog* <https://verfassungsblog.de/the-bundesbank-is-under-a-legal-obligation-to-ignore-the-pspp-judgment-of-the-bundesverfassungsgericht/> accessed 24 October 2024, concluding that it is 'more than likely that this new sort of judicial politics [introduced by the PSPP judgment when 'flagrantly giving up on a paradigm that ensured peace between two of the most important courts in Europe. The paradigm that maintaining one's theoretical position can be combined with a practical way of living together. The paradigm that the rule of law is diminished if state agencies are exposed to contradicting legal obligations both seeking to be supreme over the competing one, and the agencies are forced to make a choice that will inevitably be illegal, one way or another'] will equally hurt European integration and the rule of law'. See furthermore the critical analysis offered in the special issue 'The German Federal Constitutional Court's PSPP Judgment' (2020) 21 German Law Journal.

[45] See on this also Lando Kirchmair, *Rethinking the Relationship between International, EU and National Law: Consent-Based Monism* (CUP 2024) 216.

[46] Mark A Graber, Sanford Levinson, and Mark Tushnet (eds), *Constitutional Democracy in Crisis?* (OUP 2018).

[47] András Jakab and Dimitry Kochenov (eds), *The Enforcement of EU Law and Values: Ensuring Member States' Compliance* (OUP 2017); Armin von Bogdandy and Pál Sonnevend (eds), *Constitutional Crisis in the European Constitutional Area* (CH Beck, Hart and Nomos 2015); Martin Brusis, *Illiberale Drift und Proliferation: BTI-Regionalbericht Ostmittel- und Südosteuropa* (Bertelsmann 2018).

[48] See only Edward Luce, *The Retreat of Western Liberalism* (Atlantic Monthly Press 2017).

[49] See R Daniel Kelemen and Tommaso Pavone, 'Where Have the Guardians Gone? Law Enforcement and the Politics of Supranational Forbearance in the European Union' (2023) 75 World Politics 779; cf Sivaram Cheruvu, 'When does the European Commission Pursue Noncompliance?' (2022) 23 European Union Politics 375, arguing that the Commission strategically delays advancing infringement proceedings when it thinks compliance success might be higher in the future.

[50] See eg Dimitry Kochenov and Graham Butler, 'Independence of the Court of Justice of the European Union: Unchecked Member States Power after the Sharpston Affair' (2021) 27 European Law Journal 262.

had to be found, the way AG Sharpston was removed—initiated by a declaration of MSs[51]—interfered with the independence of the institution in general and, given the nature of the specific situation, also with the mandate of AG Sharpston in particular.[52] Neither the treaties nor the Statute of the Court provide for the distinct possibility of MSs to meddle with the composition of AGs at the Court during their terms of office. They are appointed for a fixed period of six years in accordance with Article 19 (2) TEU and Article 253 Treaty on the Functioning of the EU (TFEU) and their mandate may only be terminated for limited reasons which were not applicable in this case.[53]

3. Democratic Legitimacy in the Wake of European Integration

3.1 Democracy and the EU

The development of the EU legal order in general and the many facets of the rule of law in particular made the need for democratic legitimacy with every step stronger. This development is key to understanding how the relationship between the institutions of the EU and the legislation procedures changed over the decades.

By democratization we mean the establishment and the process of enhancing the effectivity of political accountability of political decision-makers both in the executive (EC) and the legislative (EP and Council). The debates on the lacking democratic legitimacy of the EU led to the creation of the first direct elections to the EP in 1979. In contrast to the rule of law, the most significant improvements of the democratic legitimacy of the EU actually came with modifications by European treaties. Also in terms of democratization the Single European Act in 1986, and even more so the Maastricht Treaty in 1992 as well as in particular the Treaty of Lisbon in 2009, improved the status and

[51] Council of the European Union on 29 January 2020, Declaration by the Conference of the Representatives of the Governments of the Member States on the consequences of the withdrawal of the United Kingdom from the European Union for the Advocates-General of the Court of Justice of the European Union (XT 21018/20).

[52] See for an open letter in support of AG Sharpston (which was authored by one of us) Sandra Hummelbrunner and others, 'In Support of the EU Rule of Law and Advocate General Eleanor Sharpston—An Open Letter' (18 March 2020) *European Law Blog*.

[53] See Hummelbrunner and others (n 52).

the powers of the EP.[54] The political accountability of the Commission, however, is, despite some legal control by the EP, still an open question.

A usual topic in the debate on EU democracy is whether there is a European demos which could be the bearer of EU popular sovereignty.[55] The argument often concerns the factual homogeneity of the EU, simply stating that the EU cannot be a democratic society as it is not homogeneous. There are numerous counter-arguments against *homogeneity*.

(a) According to a well-known classic argument, it is not homogeneity, but rather the opposite *heterogeneity* that is necessary for democracy. In Madison's faction theory (Federalist Paper No 10) different social factions are the guarantee that none of them will have full power and none of them will be oppressed.

(b) Another argument goes along the lines that heterogeneity itself might not be the problem, but only if the heterogeneous groups are fixed (eg along ethnic or religious lines).[56] In this case elections are not elections, but only population censuses. But so far European elections seem not to have moved towards this dead end, so a fear of it would be premature.

(c) A third counter-argument emphasizes the point that even European nation states are no longer as homogeneous as some would like to see them. We are currently living in multicultural societies (not only in the USA or in Switzerland, but in most EU MSs).[57] The requirement of homogeneity (if it goes further than the requirement to accept the rule of law and democracy) would bring up the danger of assimilation and exclusion, or even a friend-enemy distinction within society.[58]

(d) A fourth argument is based on history, stating that most of today's nation states were not formed along ethnic lines: it was rather the other way around. First there was the political unit, and it formed the population into one cultural and linguistic unit.[59] At the time of the French Revolution (1789) half

[54] See Berthold Rittberger, *Building Europe's Parliament: Democratic Representation beyond the Nation State* (OUP 2005); Adrienne Héritier and others, *European Parliament Ascendant: Parliamentary Strategies of Self-Empowerment in the EU* (Palgrave Macmillan 2019).

[55] Answering in the positive: Amaryllis Verhoeven, *The European Union in Search of a Democratic and Constitutional Theory* (Kluwer Law International 2002) 159–89. Opposing the idea of a European demos: Joseph HH Weiler, 'European Democracy and Its Critics: Polity and System' in Joseph HH Weiler, *The Constitution of Europe* (CUP 1999) 264, 265.

[56] Christoph Gusy, 'Demokratiedefizite postnationaler Gemeinschaften unter Berücksichtigung der EU' (1998) 45 Zeitschrift für Politik 267, 279; Anne Peters, *Elemente einer Theorie der Verfassung Europas* (Duncker & Humblot 2001) 712.

[57] Verhoeven (n 55) xi.

[58] Peters (n 56) 704.

[59] The traditional opposing idea originates eg from Johann Gottfried Herder, Friedrich Carl von Savigny, and Friedrich Meinecke based on the rather peculiar German case, where actually common identity came first and then came political unity. See Peters (n 56) 653. In public law scholarship for an early formulation of the necessity of a pre-legal cultural unit of people for state-forming, see Georg

of the population of France did not speak French (instead they spoke Italian, German, Breton, English, Occitan, Catalan, Basque, Dutch), and only 12–13 per cent spoke it correctly. At the time of Italian unification (1861) only 2.5 per cent (!) of the population spoke the Italian that we know today.[60]

(e) A fifth argument concentrates on the logic of democracy: it is based on *individuals* (and not on collectivist units) and the popular unity will be formed first by the democratic procedure itself.[61] So *ethnos* and *demos* are analytically different.[62]

In the light of the above arguments it is very difficult to say that it is conceptually impossible to have a democracy on the EU level because of cultural differences.[63] Hence, what remains is a generally expressed scepticism, which, however, is unfounded conceptually. The main reason for the claim that democracy at the EU level practically would not work is mostly a somewhat dubious claim that the European peoples just would not want it, because they simply would not have the feeling of togetherness with other European peoples. The question mark behind a European demos in this sense concerns the feeling of togetherness (national identity) of European citizens.[64] The critics of the idea of a European demos as formed by procedures can easily point out that separatist Catalan or Scottish nationalists were not impressed by the Spanish or British procedures either, and national identity in general does not necessarily flow from procedures. So the problem is not factual similarity or dissimilarity, but rather identity.[65] And identity still primarily belongs to the nation states.[66]

(a) One possible counter-argument is that national identity is fading in general in the world,[67] so in time the feeling of togetherness will lose its relevance.

Jellinek, *Die Lehre von den Staatenverbindungen* (Hoelder 1882) 263. For a contemporary formulation in the context of the EU see Ernst-Wolfgang Böckenförde, *Welchen Weg geht Europa?* (Carl-Friedrich-von-Siemens-Stiftung 1997) 40–1.

[60] Eric J Hobsbawm, *Nations and Nationalism Since 1780: Programme, Myth, Reality* (CUP 1990) 60–1. For more details see Jakab (n 15) 224–41.

[61] Peters (n 56) 649, n 86, 704, 707. A classic form of this idea is to be found in Emmanuel J Sieyès, *Qu'est-ce que le Tiers État? (1789)* (in English: *Political Writings* (Hackett 2003)) and remained strong in the French republican tradition.

[62] Emerich K Francis, *Ethnos und Demos* (Duncker & Humblot 1965) 77.

[63] We can reason though that a simple Westminster style majoritarian parliamentarism would not be the right choice for the pluralist EU, but a consensual coalition style parliamentarism is better. On the difference between majoritarian and consensus government see Arend Lijphart, *Democracies* (Yale University Press 1984), especially 1–36.

[64] Both arguments have a soft ('not yet') and a radical ('there will never be a European demos') version. Cf Carlos Closa, 'Some Foundations for the Normative Discussion on Supranational Citizenship and Democracy' in Ulrich K Preuß and Ferran Requejo (eds), *European Citizenship, Multiculturalism and the State* (Nomos 1998) 109, 113.

[65] Dieter Grimm, 'Does Europe Need a Constitution?' (1995) 1 European Law Journal 282, 297.

[66] For an empirical survey proving this see Mathieu Deflem and Fred C Pampel, 'The Myth of Postnational Identity: Popular Support for European Unification' (1996) 75 Social Forces 119.

[67] Michael Sandel, *Democracy's Discontent* (Belknap Press of Harvard University Press 1996) 344.

This would, however, be a weak counter-argument. We do not have exact and convincing empirical data about fading national identities, and examples of the opposite can also be presented—especially in light of the pandemic.[68] But even if we had data for it, it would be very difficult to project a certain level of fading to the future as a continuous development.

(b) A more convincing argument says that even in the USA, when the famous words 'We the people' were put on paper, it was nothing more than wishful thinking, or rather political manipulation. So we could similarly attempt it in the EU.[69] We can also point out that nations are imagined or even mythical communities, so it is not a fixed fact, it can even change in time (as happens when an ethnic minority assimilates into the majority).[70] Peaceful methods of identity-building are possible (like having EU sports teams competing against the Americans or the Chinese, winning most of the medals if we counted the EU already as a nation), which could be used in the future. The development of the EU-Citizenship is very important in this regard and might become even more important.[71] We have some doubts whether it could work in the foreseeable future. But it is less relevant here, as our actual point would be that national identity in this strong substantive sense is not absolutely necessary.

(c) What we need is loyalty to or belief in the system, the procedures of democracy (such loyalty is possible only, of course, if the procedures work).[72] It helps the effectiveness of law (so the rule of law), and with adherence to these basic constitutional values (and the connecting emotional identification) it can survive crisis situations too.

[68] For an empirical study on national in-group satisfaction vs collective narcissism during the COVID-19 pandemic, see eg Christopher M Federico, Agnieszka Golec de Zavala, and Tomasz Baran, 'Collective Narcissism, In-Group Satisfaction, and Solidarity in the Face of COVID-19' (2020) 12 Social Psychological and Personality Science 1.

[69] Manfred Zuleeg, 'What Holds a Nation Together? Cohesion and Democracy in the United States of America and in the European Union' (1997) 46 American Journal of Comparative Law 505, 526.

[70] Shown on the example of France by Eugen Weber, *From Peasants into Frenchmen: The Modernization of Rural France, 1880–1914* (Stanford University Press 1976).

[71] See eg Elspeth Guild, *The Legal Elements of European Identity: EU Citizenship and Migration Law* (Kluwer 2004). For the argument of EU citizenship without duties, see Dimitry Kochenov, 'EU Citizenship without Duties' (2014) 20 European Law Journal 482; cf Chris Rumford, 'European Civil Society or Transnational Social Space? Conceptions of Society in Discourses of EU Citizenship, Governance and the Democratic Deficit: An Emerging Agenda' (2003) 6 European Journal of Social Theory 25.

[72] To name national identity as a precondition for democracy is methodologically biased, as it reconstructs the concept of democracy along the concrete sociological features of some democracies. See Jürgen Habermas, 'Remarks on Dieter Grimm's "Does Europe Need a Constitution?"' (1995) 1 European Law Journal 303.

Therefore, the existence of a unified and dominant European political identity is not necessary in order to have a functioning European democracy. There is no doubt that it is useful, but it is not necessary.[73]

3.2 Democratic Deficit and Erosion of Democracy at EU Level

The EU's democratic shortcomings were a major point of discussion in the 1980s and 1990s.[74] Nevertheless, the EP managed to steadily expand its powers.[75] The Treaty of Lisbon especially secured some important improvements, by strengthening the role of the national parliaments and the EP, for instance. An important passage introduced by the Lisbon Treaty to this end holds that the candidate for the President of the Commission has to be *proposed* by the European Council and *elected* by a majority of the EP, taking into account the elections to the EP and after having held the appropriate consultations (Article 17 (7) TEU). Thereby the way has been prepared to state that legally the crucial organ in appointing the Commission President is the EP and not the European Council.[76]

Despite this improvement there is still a 'missing correlation between election and responsibility'.[77] In other words, there are elections, and also a new government (Commission) is set up, but the direct link between the two acts is still missing. There seem to be only two institutional solutions to ensure the virtues of democracy (both loyalty and self-correction): one possibility would be to transform the EU into a presidential system (similar to the USA), the other would be to parliamentarize it.[78] The latter seems to be a more viable option, as the current system is much nearer to the parliamentary system,

[73] On further preconditions of democratization of the EU, such as democratic mentality and interested public opinion (media coverage) see Jakab (n 15) 192–94.

[74] See eg David Marquand, *Parliament for Europe* (Jonathan Cape 1979) 64 ff; Kevin Featherstone, 'Jean Monnet and the "Democratic Deficit" in the European Union' (1994) 32 Journal of Common Market Studies 149.

[75] See eg Rittberger (n 54); Héritier and others (n 54).

[76] See in this vein András Jakab, 'Full Parliamentarisation of the EU without Changing the Treaties: Why We Should Aim for It and How Easily It Can Be Achieved' (2012) 3 Jean Monnet Working Paper 1, 30. Cf the Declaration 11 attached to the Treaty of Lisbon states that 'the European Parliament and the European Council are jointly responsible for the smooth running of the process leading to the election of the President of the European Commission. Prior to the decision of the European Council, representatives of the European Parliament and of the European Council will thus conduct the necessary consultations in the framework deemed the most appropriate.'

[77] Peters (n 56) 627.

[78] Different institutional sub- and in-between types are considered with their advantages by Walter van Gerven, *The European Union: A Polity of States and Peoples* (Hart 2005) 318.

and so only minor institutional changes would be necessary to achieve it.[79] An important step towards solving the problem would thus be to make only the EP responsible for the election of the Commission, whereas the European Council could have a ceremonial role similar to monarchs or presidents in parliamentary systems.[80] The point is not that the *Spitzenkandidaten*-system—a rather specific way of designing political accountability—is the miracle solution to all the problems of democracy in Europe. However, the profound lack of directly attributable democratic political accountability for a key European institution—the EC—is an important problem which became worse with the 2019 elections to the EP.[81]

In addition, and as a consequence of addressing various crises of the EU (the financial crisis, humanitarian challenges of helping refugees, Brexit, the pandemic, the Russian war of aggression against Ukraine, etc), power shifted to the Council, which by its institutional setting is more difficult to hold accountable as a whole.

Last but not least, the EP itself, a self-declared bastion of political morality in Europe, had its own corruption scandal, the extent of which is not yet fully known.[82]

4. Conclusion

We recounted the constitutional dimension of the history of the EU as two intertwined stories, which are, however, not without ruptures. Democratization as well as the development of a vertical rule of law are stories involving many struggles and even (minor) setbacks. The development from a confederal (international) organization into a state-like, centralized (federal) organization particularly concerns the development of the relationship between EU law and MS law. This has been constructed especially by the ECJ in the process of European integration particularly when installing the doctrines of direct applicability and primacy of EU law. In this vein, the ECJ proved to be an essential institutional driving force of European constitutionalism—despite some

[79] See van Gerven (n 78) 344–45.

[80] For more details, see Chapter 7.

[81] While it is true that the EP can exercise a limited degree of political control (see Article 14 (1) TEU), for the most effective method of political control, the vote of no confidence (motion of censure according to Article 17 (8) TEU), a two-thirds majority is necessary. This high threshold has never been achieved in the history of the EU.

[82] For an overview, see eg Suzanne Lynch, 'Anatomy of a Scandal: How "Qatargate" Crisis Shook EU to its Core' (17 December 2022) *Politico* <https://www.politico.eu/article/scandal-qatargate-crisis-european-union-corruption-crisis/> accessed 24 October 2024.

setbacks displayed through a history of enforcement and primacy conflicts with constitutional courts of MSs.

This development of the rule of law has increased the need for democratic legitimacy with each step, that is, it actually led to democratization. And it is key to understanding how the relationship between the institutions of the EU and the legislation procedures changed over the decades. Democratization concerns the establishment and the process of enhancing the effectivity of political accountability of political decision-makers both in the executive (EC) and the legislative (EP and Council) and some form of political identity. This dimension of the EU has also seen considerable improvement over the process of European integration. Important treaty revisions strengthening the EP and developments in parameterization of the EU are considerable developments. Yet, this story is still not over. Important developments such as the decision about the President of the Commission by the EP (instead of the Council) are still in the midst of evolution. Illiberal EU MSs are a particular challenge, as undemocratic EU MSs might compromise also the elections of the EP (as EU MSs which do not meet democratic standards organize these elections).[83]

The evolution of the constitutional dimension of the EU was (and will be) highly dependent on the ECJ, which contributed to the EU constitution in a step-by-step manner. Thus, neither Maastricht nor other important instances of constitutional codifications during the process of European integration seem to be 'constitutional moments' in the sense of turning points in EU constitutional history. Instead, continuous development and adaptation of the judicial component is decisive for constitutional developments (given the existence of a large number of veto players in treaty modification procedures). Treaty modifications (or a respective silence by new treaties with regards to formerly proactive case law) were often just a codification (or a tacit consent) of former judicial case law (or secondary law).

The shortcomings of the rule of law and democracy highlighted in this chapter indicate that due to certain deficits and due to the erosion of some important pillars of the rule of law and democracy at the EU level, the EU cannot actually face illiberal practices in some of its MSs. Some may argue that the peculiar nature of the EU legal order provides some explanation for the EU's failure to function in a fully comparable way to democratic constitutional states (rather than being a clear violation of the rule of law). It may be the case

[83] For a proposal on how to tackle this problem, see András Jakab, 'How to Defend the Integrity of the EP Elections against Authoritarian Member States' (31 March 2019) *Verfassungsblog* <https://verfassungsblog.de/how-to-defend-the-integrity-of-the-ep-elections-against-authoritarian-member-states/> accessed 24 October 2024.

that, depending on the example, some rule of law and democracy deficits in the EU have been built into the system since the beginning of EU integration, to a greater or lesser extent. However, even taking into account the special nature of the EU, we are convinced that we are witnessing an erosion of the rule of law and democracy at the EU level as well. Simply put, whether the EU is conceived of as a federal constitutional state or a supranational organization, it has enormous powers and it must ensure the rule of law and democracy for itself. Only then will it be powerful enough to restore them in all its MSs. In the next chapter we will look at the interdependence of the rule of law and democracy as well as the mutual dependence of both in EU MSs and the EU itself.

4

On the Mutual Dependence of the Rule of Law and Democracy at Both EU and Member State Levels

1. Introduction

In this chapter we argue that the rule of law—in our understanding including also the protection of fundamental rights—and democracy are mutually dependent. Therefore they can only be protected together. Second, safeguarding them at EU level and MS level is inseparably linked. Hence, any severe crisis at one level is most likely to spill over sooner or later to the other level. Third, and this draws on Chapters 2 and 3, slow deterioration (ie erosion) of the rule of law and democracy, not only at MS level but also at EU level, has already happened to a certain extent. Negative trends at MS level and EU level have a mutually reinforcing effect. We call this 'mutual poisoning'. Fourth, and this will prepare for what follows in Chapters 5, 6, and 7, EU constitutionalism ought to develop answers, in our words 'antidotes', to address the challenge of this two-level erosion. For this purpose, we offer an overview of the current state of EU law to withstand erosion and future guidelines for institution-building in the contemporary context of illiberal EU MSs.

2. Two Interrelated Interdependencies: The Danger of Mutual Poisoning

We have contended that it is far too simplistic to talk about the EU's 'rule of law crisis' as we are convinced that it is more fitting to call it an 'illiberal regime crisis'. What has been happening is more of a twin crisis, namely, a slow erosion of *both* democracy *and* the rule of law at both levels, some MSs and the EU too, at least to a certain extent. By focusing exclusively on the rule of law, the debate

Saving the European Union from Its Illiberal Member States. András Jakab and Lando Kirchmair, Oxford University Press.
DOI: 10.1093/oso/9780198954606.003.0005

is missing the point of how democracy and the rule of law mutually support each other.

2.1 Mutual Dependence of the Rule of Law and Democracy

It has been commonly known for some time that the rule of law, and especially certain political fundamental rights, are preconditions for a democratic process.[1] However, one should not forget the reverse causality either: namely, that the rule of law is itself a product of democratic rotation; if governing parties have no fear of being outvoted and finding themselves in opposition, they will inevitably be less and less inclined to respect the separation of powers, particularly judicial independence, and fundamental rights.[2] Moreover, if we understand the rule of law as the negation of unlimited government power, then democratic accountability contributes to it, itself being a limitation on government power.

For the purpose of this book, and as a brief reminder of our definition in Chapter 1, democracy is understood as the concurrent presence of the following qualities of any regime: (a) periodically organized fair and free elections, (b) general and equal suffrage, (c) an actual and legally realistic chance of voting the incumbent government out of office, and (d) voters having a real opportunity and the legal means to inform themselves about the performance of the government. Hence, the upshot is that voters have an actual and legally realistic chance of voting the incumbent government out of office. By rule of law we refer to its formal elements—in particular, predictability, effectiveness, and clarity—as well as substantive elements such as separation of powers and the protection of fundamental rights both formally and in reality. It is evident from these definitions that the two notions include factual and legal elements.[3]

A central proposition of this chapter (and of the entire book) is that these notions are not merely supportive of each other through certain common elements (eg the protection of political rights); rather, they are inseparably linked to the effect that there can be no protection of democracy without protection

[1] For a classic account see John Hart Ely, *Democracy and Distrust: A Theory of Judicial Review* (Harvard University Press 1980). On the indivisible 'Holy Trinity: Democracy, human rights, and the rule of law', see Joseph HH Weiler, 'The European Circumstance and the Politics of Meaning: Not on Bread Alone Doth Man Liveth (Deut. 8:3; Mat 4:4)' (2020) 21 German Law Journal 96.

[2] András Jakab, 'What Can Constitutional Law Do against the Erosion of Democracy and the Rule of Law? On the Interconnectedness of the Protection of Democracy and the Rule of Law' (2020) 6 Constitutional Studies 5; Tom Ginsburg and Aziz Z Huq, *How to Save a Constitutional Democracy* (University of Chicago Press 2018) 14.

[3] See n 11 in Chapter 1 (and the associated main text).

of the rule of law (and vice versa). Thus, the effects of the mechanisms to protect democracy and the rule of law are strongly intertwined.[4] The relationship between democracy and the rule of law is like a (good) marriage: although some structural conflicts exist, one cannot really manage without the other. As a pair, they flourish; and if they fail, they do so together. Potential examples to show the opposite, where the rule of law operates without democracy (eg Singapore), are unconvincing: a closer look reveals that their system fails to meet important substantive rule of law standards.[5]

Hence, the rule of law *by itself* is unable to protect democracy, but well-designed constitutional provisions may be helpful in preventing the erosion in combination with social and political factors such as political culture, strength of civil society, structure of party landscape, etc. Ultimately, what every political community needs is a democratic, rule of law-oriented political morality[6]—one to be defended in the political process, and one that is on the side of both the population and the politicians (and where this is missing, effective external pressure will be necessary). Despite all these issues it boils down to the fact that 'the only way to defend liberal democracy is to fight in elections against those who seek to erode it'.[7]

2.2 Mutual Dependence of the EU and Its MSs

In the context of the EU, the interdependence of the rule of law and democracy is embedded in the process of European integration, which further complicates the situation. It is a commonplace in EU law scholarship to highlight how the EU depends on the MSs, for instance concerning the implementation of EU law on the ground. On the other hand, Brexit showcased how dependent MSs are on being a member of the EU. Decades of legal, economic, and political integration have tied the MSs to the EU and the other MSs, and a divorce is immensely complex and expensive. This has also a bearing on the rule of law and democracy. In this vein, it is important to note that it is mistaken to

[4] On causal effects between democracy and the rule of law see Roberto Rigobon and Dani Rodrik, 'Rule of Law, Democracy, Openness, and Income: Estimating Interrelationships' (2005) 13 Economics of Transition and Institutional Change 533.

[5] See eg Mark Tushnet, 'Authoritarian Constitutionalism' (2015) 100 Cornell Law Review 391.

[6] A democratic, rule of law-oriented political morality means internalized support for democracy and the rule of law.

[7] Similarly, Udo Di Fabio, *Die Weimarer Verfassung: Aufbruch und Scheitern* (CH Beck 2018) 7 asserts: 'even the smartest Constitution is unable to protect from the failure, from the self-destruction of democracy' (translation by the authors).

conceive of what is going wrong in specific EU MSs like Hungary and Poland 'purely as a crisis of the MSs affected'.

The necessity to find compromises on many important issues is another element of this dependence. Compliance with EU law becomes less important in the frame of the 'negotiations' on releasing huge amounts of money, either from the COVID Recovery and Resilience Facility (RRF entitled 'NextGenerationEU') or the usual budget, if other political issues seem more important. This is related to securing a uniform foreign and security policy in the current war of aggression of Russia against Ukraine, for instance. In comparison to politicians of liberal democracies, politicians of illiberal regimes are much more likely to obstruct EU decision-making processes. Examples are the difficulties in consenting on sanctions against Russia, establishing a global minimum tax rate for large multinational groups, the struggle about the precise functioning, scope, as well as coherent application of financial conditionality, or adopting a new multi-annual budget.[8]

3. Mutual Poisoning of the EU and Its Illiberal MSs

The EU constitutional order has been challenged on two levels. There has been an erosion of the rule of law *and* democracy in certain EU MSs,[9] but at the same time we can also witness—often overlooked—deficits and erosion phenomena at EU level.[10]

Almost imperceptibly and largely unnoticed, the EU has become poisoned by the rule of law and democracy crisis of some of its MSs. While sometimes minor setbacks of the rule of law and in other times seemingly unimportant aspects of democracy have deteriorated, this erosion--in combination with the already known deficits of the EU--is the most important reason why the EU was not able to effectively prevent and reduce illiberalism in some of its MSs. We showcased this erosion focusing on democracy and on the rule of law in the previous chapter. Here we wish to highlight that this erosion is inextricably linked to the illiberalism present in some EU MSs.

[8] For an interesting argument, holding that war and existential security threats offer new possibilities for political development, suggesting at the same time to look at the EU from a state-building perspective, R Daniel Kelemen and Kathleen R McNamara, 'State-Building and the European Union: Markets, War, and Europe's Uneven Political Development' (2022) 55 Comparative Political Studies 963; Kathleen R McNamara and R Daniel Kelemen, 'Seeing Europe like a State' (2022) 29 Journal of European Public Policy 1916.

[9] See Chapter 2.

[10] See Chapter 3.

For example, the erosion of democratic accountability in the form of ignoring the EP-*Spitzenkandidat* in 2019 shows how the EU's illiberal MSs have been poisoning the rule of law and democracy at EU level. A decisive reason for the appointment of von der Leyen was the lack of support of Orbán's Fidesz party for the original *Spitzenkandidat*, Manfred Weber.[11] The re-election of the *Spitzenkandidat* Ursula von der Leyen as Commission President in 2024 was made possible by the votes of mainstream parties which are supporting Article 2 TEU values and have required more decisive actions during recent years against illiberal MSs.

Yet another worrisome aspect is the election of Members of the EP through procedures which are not up to democratic standards.[12] If European elections in certain MSs are not fair, this infects EU democracy (in the EP through EP elections, as well as in the EC through both national elections and EP elections).[13] Moreover, the poisoning by infected EU MSs could also constitute a problem for the rule of law on the European level as illiberal MSs too are allowed to participate in the appointment of personnel in EU organs. For instance, the poisoning by infected EU MSs could also constitute a problem for the rule of law as Article 253 TFEU states that Judges and Advocates General are 'appointed by common accord of the governments of the Member States'. Illiberal MSs too are allowed to participate in the appointment of judges to

[11] Andrew Gray, Jacopo Barigazzi, and Maia de la Baume, 'Who Killed the Spitzenkandidat?' (5 July 2019) *Politico* <https://www.politico.eu/article/who-killed-the-spitzenkandidat-european-parliament-election-2019-transition/> accessed 24 October 2024, stating that 'neither Hungary alone nor the four-strong Visegrad Group of central and eastern European governments was big enough to kill the Spitzenkandidat alone'; cf Ben Crum, 'Why the European Parliament Lost the *Spitzenkandidaten*-Process' (2023) 30 Journal of European Public Policy 193, 204 offering the narrative that the European Council reclaimed 'its autonomy in 2019'; see also Pieter de Wilde, 'The Fall of the Spitzenkandidaten: Political Parties and Conflict in the 2019 European Elections' in Sylvia Kritzinger and others (eds), *Assessing the 2019 European Parliament Elections* (Routledge 2020) 37. See furthermore Yvonne Nasshoven, '"To be or not to be?" Das Spitzenkandidatenprinzip in der Europawahl 2019 und zukünftige Szenarien' (2019) 42 Integration 280, 286 providing an overview how diversely the members of the European Council were spread over the European party families in 2019 and identifying two reasons: 'First, the EPP's vote against transnational lists in February 2018 meant both the Liberals and the Social Democrats felt less compelled to support the EPP Spitzenkandidat. Second, Weber's tacit support for Victor Órban and the democratic backsliding in Hungary he orchestrated made him a toxic candidate for other mainstream party groups.'

[12] András Jakab, 'How to Defend the Integrity of the EP Elections against Authoritarian Member States' (31 March 2019) *Verfassungsblog* <https://verfassungsblog.de/how-to-defend-the-integrity-of-the-ep-elections-against-authoritarian-member-states/> accessed 24 October 2024.

[13] Here lies at the same time potential for improvement by not validating mandates of MEPs who have been elected through national procedures which are not up to democratic standards. Cf also John Cotter, 'To Everything There Is a Season: Instrumentalising Article 10 TEU to Exclude Undemocratic Member State Representatives from the European Council and the Council' (2022) 47 European Law Review 69.

the ECJ and usually MS governments do not interfere with the decision of other MSs.[14]

The EU rule of law suffers too particularly from the erosion of the rule of law in EU MSs. The conflict over compliance with the rule of law in some EU MSs has reached a new level of escalation with the decision of the Polish Constitutional Court on 7 October 2021. The Polish Constitutional Court has clearly stated in this decision that Union law does not take precedence over (Polish) national constitutional law. On the contrary, the attempt of the ECJ to 'interfere' in the Polish judiciary would violate (according to the Polish Constitutional Court) the rule of supremacy of the Polish Constitution (in relation to Union law) and the rule that sovereignty must be preserved in the process of European integration.[15] This judgment has been much more explicit than the PSPP decision by the German Federal Constitutional Court referred to in Chapter 3. While the German decision has already been perceived as a judicial earthquake of unprecedented degree, the constitutional courts of the EU's illiberal MSs have somehow used, and some would say misused, this earthquake in order to attempt to reshape the judicial landscape in Europe. Less noticed, however, not less problematic, the Hungarian Constitutional Court has reasoned that the Hungarian government is constitutionally empowered to disapply EU law if it considers that EU law would violate Hungarian constitutional identity.[16] Due to these events and the preceding developments, commentators concluded that 'the functioning of the EU legal order itself is in jeopardy'.[17]

[14] Such common accords are 'acts adopted by Representatives of the Member States, acting not in their capacity as members of the Council of the European Union or of the European Council but as representatives of their governments, and thus collectively exercising the powers of the Member States'. For this reason, the Vice-President of the ECJ concluded in an order that these acts 'are not subject to judicial review by the courts of the Union': Case C-423/20 P(R) *Council of the European Union v Eleanor Sharpston* [2020] EU:C:2020:700, para 26. Therefore, the ECJ could be compromised by Trojan horse judge nominations. The Treaty of Lisbon (Article 255), however, established an advisory panel on judicial appointments. This panel allows for resilience against potential threats to the independence of the ECJ as this hurdle is more than a mere formality. Indeed, some nominated candidates by MSs have been declined. See R Daniel Kelemen, 'Selection, Appointment and Legitimacy: A Political Perspective' in Michal Bobek (ed), *Selecting Europe's Judges* (OUP 2015) 244, 256 explaining changes in the appointment procedure for ECJ judges and pointing to an expert committee composed of a majority of national judges influencing the process.

[15] Polish Constitutional Court, Judgment of 7 October 2021, K 3/21. For an impressive rebuke by twenty-seven retired judges of the Polish Constitutional Court, cf 'Statement of Retired Judges of the Polish Constitutional Tribunal' (10 October 2021) *Verfassungsblog* <https://verfassungsblog.de/statement-of-retired-judges-of-the-polish-constitutional-tribunal/> accessed 24 October 2024.

[16] Hungarian Constitutional Court, Decision 32/2021 (XII.20.). Cf for an analysis, Attila Vincze, 'Unsere Gedanken sind Sprengstoff—Zum Vorrang des Europarechts in der Rechtsprechung des ungarischen Verfassungsgerichts' (2022) 49 Europäische Grundrechte-Zeitschrift 13.

[17] Editorial Comments, 'Clear and Present Danger: Poland, the Rule of Law & Primacy' (2021) 58 Common Market Law Review 1635, 1648.

In order to safeguard the rule of law in certain MSs, or rather in order to face decisions like those referred to in the previous paragraph, the ECJ, quite paradoxically, has had to put the rule of law at the EU level at risk, as it had to stretch its own mandate quite considerably, to say the least, so that it could protect the judicial independence of its individual members.[18] While the consequences of these decisions are, in some ways, to be welcomed—let us just imagine for a second what the situation would look like if the Court had not protected judicial independence at all—it still endangers the rule of law at the EU level. And with every progressive step taken by the ECJ,[19] patience is, unfortunately, wearing thin in other EU MSs, which now have to accept a stronger ECJ position, even if they are 'well behaved'.

The reluctance of the EC to initiate infringement procedures is also much more problematic in the face of illiberal MSs. If severe violations of EU law are not confronted with adequate legal procedures, this invites illiberal practices to unfold unhindered. In addition, the Commission has failed to take adequate steps to safeguard the rule of law in the MSs on countless occasions in recent years.[20] For example, the EC applied the rule of law conditionality mechanism to Hungary only after a long delay and a shaky agreement in the European Council, and released large sums under the CPR, presumably not because the Hungarian rule of law situation had improved, but because of a political bargain.[21] As far as Poland is concerned, the EC was first reluctant to do so and later released the money without any meaningful changes in the relevant statutes. While it is understandable that the Commission wanted to support the pro-EU stance of Donald Tusk, who won the parliamentary elections in 2023, it was somewhat surprising to see large sums being released just because a new

[18] Lando Kirchmair, 'The EU and Its Hybrid Regimes Are Poisoning Each Other' (23 August 2022) *Politico* <https://www.politico.eu/article/eu-hybrid-regime-poison-each-other-democracy-spitzenkandidaten/> accessed 24 October 2024.

[19] For an overview on the case law regarding Article 2 TEU, see eg Luke Dimitrios Spieker, *EU Values Before the Court of Justice: Foundations, Potential, Risks* (OUP 2023) 11 ff.

[20] For the suggestion that the EU should become a 'militant democracy' in face of the long-term failure of EU institutions to defend European values enshrined in Article 2 TEU, see Kim Lane Scheppele, Dimitry Vladimirovich Kochenov, and Barbara Grabowska-Moroz, 'EU Values Are Law, After All: Enforcing EU Values through Systemic Infringement Actions by the European Commission and the Member States of the European Union' (2020) 39 Yearbook of European Law 3.

[21] Regulation (EU, Euratom) 2020/2092 of the European Parliament and of the Council of 16 December 2020 on a general regime of conditionality for the protection of the Union budget [2020] OJ L 433I. For an analysis, see Antonia Baraggia and Matteo Bonelli, 'Linking Money to Values: The New Rule of Law Conditionality Regulation and Its Constitutional Challenges' (2022) 23 German Law Journal 131; Isabel Staudinger, 'The Rise and Fall of Rule of Law Conditionality' (2022) 7 European Papers 721; László Detre, András Jakab, and Tamás Lukácsi, 'Comparing Three Financial Conditionality Regimes and Their Application to Hungary: The Conditionality Regulation, the Recovery and Resilience Facility Regulation, and the Common Provisions Regulation' (2023) 23 Max Planck Institute for Comparative Public Law & International Law (MPIL) Research Paper No 2023-23.

government seems more trustworthy than the old one ('trustworthiness' was neither a supermilestone under the RRF nor a fulfilment of the enabling conditions under the Common Provisions Regulation (CPR)). Not adequately dealing with a bad state of affairs gradually contributes to erosion of the rule of law in MSs, but importantly also undermines credibility and gnaws away at the roots of the rule of law at EU level.

Illiberal MSs are poisoning other MSs, for example by investing into their media assets or by ruining judicial cooperation through fake judges. In addition, illiberal regimes within the EU also poison the EU itself. Thereby they are spreading the poison even more quickly to yet other MSs. The upshot of this mutual poisoning is that the illiberal regime crisis is actually only a symptom for deficits of the EU.[22] These deficits of the rule of law and/or democracy in an MS has negative effects on the rule of law and democracy in other EU MSs, the EU, and vice versa. The EU must ensure the rule of law and democracy for itself. Only then will it be powerful enough to restore them in all its MSs.

Table 4.1 gives an overview of various instances constituting erosion of the rule of law and democracy both at EU level and at MS level.[23]

4. Current State of EU Law to Withstand Erosion

EU law in its current shape leaves room for improvement. Just to provide a few examples: first, in the Article 7 TEU procedure the Council (General Affairs) and the European Council decide at key points of the procedure.[24] Second, the application of various conditionality mechanisms (Conditionality Regulation (CR), Recovery and Resilience Facility Regulation (RRFR), and CPR) raises doubts whether the Commission and the Council are using their decision-making powers for the legally prescribed purposes of these mechanisms in an efficient way.[25] Third, also in the case of infringement procedures, the Commission has political discretion whether to launch them or not—and what we have seen in the last two decades is a stark decline in the number of

[22] See Chapters 3 and 4.

[23] Most of the instances listed in Table 4.1 are not restricted solely to either the rule of law or to democracy, but the two aspects cannot strictly be separated from each other.

[24] See Carlos Closa, 'Institutional Logics and the EU's Limited Sanctioning Capacity under Article 7 TEU' (2020) 42 International Political Science Review 501, 502 arguing that '[b]oth the EP and the Commission can initiate the procedure but in both cases, internal logics (partisanship on the one hand, and calculus about obtaining compliance on the other) condition their performance. The lack of an assertive line from either cannot counterbalance the Member State governments' tendency to inhibit action within the Council.'

[25] Detre, Jakab, and Lukácsi (n 21).

Table 4.1 Erosion phenomena at EU level and MS level

Erosion	Rule of Law	Democracy
EU	• declining number of infringement procedures (enforcement of EU law by the Commission is getting softer) • Commission applying inconsistently the rule of law (budget) conditionality mechanism (application only after a long delay concerning Hungary and releasing money for political reasons unrelated to the rule of law; and against Poland refusing to apply it, even though the Commission was under a legal obligation to do so) • open defiance against the ECJ: the inability of enforcing ECJ judgments in illiberal MSs (despite daily fines) • inadvertently debilitating judicial cooperation and extraditions between MSs via illegally appointed (fake) judges	• the EP is becoming infected with MEPs who have been elected in undemocratic national processes[a] • repeated vetoes and continuous veto threats of EU decisions by illiberal MSs (more and more obstruction of EU democratic processes) • weakening the democratic accountability of the Commission by disregarding the *Spitzenkandidaten*-principle • growing weight of the Council (which is as a whole more difficult to hold politically accountable for its decisions) in decision-making procedures in various crisis situations
MSs (especially, but not only in Poland and Hungary)	• centralizing and politicizing the executive (the civil service is usually conservative, working incrementally and cautiously, providing neutral information and following regulated predetermined, work processes—these are features that authoritarian politicians are inclined to dismantle) • weakening independent institutions (esp ordinary and constitutional courts) through formal legal changes and/or through installing party loyalists • growing corruption • growing anti-rule of law rhetoric (depicting judges as enemies of the people etc) which aims at intimidating defenders of the rule of law informally even without formal legal changes	• eroding the public discourse space (transforming the state media into a propaganda machinery and restructuring the commercial media landscape via takeovers by friendly oligarchs) • attacking non-governmental organizations (NGOs) as agents of international globalized conspiracies (sometimes with the help of new laws) • eliminating or suppressing an effective political competition (gerrymandering, abusing rules on militant democracy or party finance control to disproportionately disadvantage opposition parties as well as excluding or selectively prosecuting the opposition politicians) • restricting academic freedom and the autonomy of universities (as independent fact-finding instances which might be uncomfortable for the government)

[a] This is a prime example as to how interdependent the EU and the MSs level of the rule of law and democracy are, because the EP electoral procedure is governed by national law (see Article 8 of the Electoral Act; as well as Joined Cases C-393/07 and C-9/08 *Italian Republic (C-393/07) and Beniamino Donnici (C-9/08) v European Parliament* [2009] EU:C:2009:275, para 75).

new infringement procedures. MSs have not become more law-abiding, but the willingness of the Commission to launch infringement procedures has declined. The situation increasingly resembles horse trading: if an MS breaches EU law in several matters, then the Commission often looks the other way in half of them, if at least the remaining half will be solved quickly. Political expediency rules over law enforcement.[26]

The ability of the EU constitutional order to withstand erosion can be improved significantly on both levels (EU and MS level). There are well-known legal techniques to improve the constitutional system such as term limits, proportional electoral systems, network of organizationally and financially independent institutions, rules on internal party democracy, reliance on international human rights instruments, anti-corruption rules, multi-layered constitutions, etc.[27] The good news is that it is completely wrong to say that the 'EU does not have the necessary enforcement tools' to fix all this. In fact, it does. It always has. The problem has been that the application of these enforcement mechanisms has, at one point or another, been subject to political discretion.[28]

5. Guidelines for Future Institution-Building in the Contemporary Hungarian Context and Setting the Stage for a Forceful European Response

The greatest difficulty for institution-building lies in the fact that informal elements are not directly accessible, that is, there is no applicable amendment procedure; furthermore they may even sabotage the effects of formal amendments. Some of the challenges of institution-building in Hungary originate from the socialist legacy, while others are determined by cultural traits that even pre-date the socialist era.[29]

[26] Cf R Daniel Kelemen, 'The European Union's Authoritarian Equilibrium' (2020) 27 Journal of European Public Policy 481, 481 stating that '[t]he EU has become trapped in an "authoritarian equilibrium" underpinned by three factors. First, the EU's half-baked system of party politics and its ingrained reluctance to interfere in the domestic politics of its member states help shield national autocrats from EU intervention. Second, funding and investment from the EU helps sustain these regimes. Third, the free movement of persons in the EU facilitates the exit of dissatisfied citizens, which depletes the opposition and generates remittances, thereby helping these regimes endure.'

[27] For an overview, see András Jakab, 'Constitutional Resilience' (October 2022) *Max Planck Encyclopedia of Comparative Constitutional Law* <https://oxcon.ouplaw.com/display/10.1093/law-mpeccol/law-mpeccol-e845> accessed 24 October 2024.

[28] See R Daniel Kelemen, 'Appeasement, ad Infinitum' (2022) 29 Maastricht Journal of European and Comparative Law 177.

[29] On the authoritarian traditions of Hungarian constitutional law before the Second World War, see László Péter, *Hungary's Long Nineteenth Century: Constitutional and Democratic Traditions in a European Perspective* (Brill 2012).

While informal elements may be changed with the help of institutions—a strategy highly reminiscent of the notorious attempt of Baron von Munchhausen[30]—the success of institution-building actually hinges on proper practices and narratives, which in turn rely on the right institutions.[31] The solution lies in the combination of a will to recover and the acceptance of external help. It is crucial for Hungary to abandon the mirage of sovereignty and adapt to Western civilization by undertaking commitments which are concluded in the more sober moments of a nation's history, thereby providing a guarantee that even in less sober times its political elite will not deviate from this course and will not give free reign to its pagan instincts. Unfortunately, such a scenario where political elites come to a compromise is rarely successful and usually follows grave upheavals. Indeed, this also bears the risk of putting the country on the wrong course instead of sobering up elites: an example would be the Trianon Peace Treaty for Hungary (in which Hungary lost two-thirds of its territory after the First World War, and after which liberalism was blamed for the misery of the nation), or the centuries-old struggles and even decline of several Latin American states (where crises only resulted in new crises instead of sobering up).[32]

(a) Unfortunately, there is no magic recipe for institution-building; nevertheless, we may formulate several conclusions that are worth considering. When it comes to *formal rules*, we should learn from the lessons of the recent past and amend constitutional or legislative rules governing the most important constitutional institutions.[33] Instead of comprehensive recodification, the course to take would be a series of small steps.[34] Grand recodifications may have unforeseeable consequences, precisely because institutions are not the sum of their rules, and at the same time, such recodifications exacerbate

[30] For similar considerations, with a somewhat more optimistic terminology, see Alberto Alesina and Paola Giuliano, 'Culture and Institutions' (2015) 53 Journal of Economic Literature 898, 928 and 938, on two-way effects, interdependence, and mutual feedback effects.

[31] 'Thus good citizens make good institutions, and good institutions are "good" to the extent that they generate and cultivate good citizens or the "better selves" of citizens ...'; Claus Offe, 'Designing Institutions in East European Transitions' in Robert E Goodin (ed), *The Theory of Institutional Design* (CUP 1996) 199, 200.

[32] The consensus of the elite can develop in an evolutive manner (eg in Italian and in Belgian politics in the decades after the Second World War) or through explicit symbolic agreements (eg the English Bill of Rights of 1689 or the Spanish Moncloa Pact of 1978). For a number of examples see John Higley and Michael Burton, *Elite Foundations of Liberal Democracy* (Rowman & Littlefield 2006) 55–106 and 139–80.

[33] For many examples and suggestions in this sense, see András Jakab and György Gajduschek (eds), *A magyar jogrendszer állapota* (MTA TK 2016).

[34] For similar conclusions, see András Sajó, 'Az állam működési zavarainak társadalmi újratermelése' (2008) 55 Közgazdasági Szemle 690, 710.

uncertainty, decreasing trust in these institutions.[35] Hence, the success of institutional reforms depends much more on the trust and the actual practices of those concerned than on the quality of individual (otherwise important) detailed rules.[36]

We cannot go into the details of these small steps here, but we will highlight some of the main abstract elements that require legislative or, better yet, constitutional underpinnings: institutional autonomies, transparency, rule-based governance, stability, meritocracy, predictability, slowing down legislation, more stringent rules for preparing legislative bills, constitutional financing guarantees and funds for universities and other educational institutions (with a prohibition on individual aid), constitutional guarantees of internal party democracy, and making the financing of churches and foundations/civil society organizations independent of government decisions. Among others, the reinforcement of these areas through the adoption of formal rules may break down current practices. Opportunities offered by means of closer European integration may play a key role in building formal guarantees, such as integration into the most stringent system of the European Public Prosecutor's Office.

We must also acknowledge that transplanting formal Western regulatory solutions to other countries in an identical form may turn out to be a spectacular failure.[37] This is not to say, 'Hungary is not cut out for the rule of law.' Exactly the opposite is true: the cultural elements presupposed by Western states based on the rule of law must be consciously built step by step, if necessary, through the adoption of formal rules that may or may not exist in Western model states. In other words, where the necessary cultural components are missing, formal rules may have to deviate from those we would otherwise adopt to support

[35] On the dangers of 'designer activism', see David Stark, 'Path Dependence and Privatization Strategies in East Central Europe' (1992) 6 East European Politics and Societies 17.

[36] Offe (n 31) 215.

[37] Stephen Holmes, 'Can Foreign Aid Promote the Rule of Law?' (1999) 8 East European Constitutional Review 68. On the concept of legal transplants see Alan Watson, *Legal Transplants: An Approach to Comparative Law* (University of Georgia Press 1971); Michele Graziadei, 'Comparative Law as the Study of Transplants and Receptions' in Mathias Reimann and Reinhard Zimmermann (eds), *The Oxford Handbook of Comparative Law* (OUP 2007) 441. Michele Graziadei, 'Legal Transplants and the Frontiers of Legal Knowledge' (2009) 10 Theoretical Inquiries in Law 723. For similar conclusions concerning the difficulty of transplanting formal legal rules into a different context of informal institutional elements, see eg Mark van Hoecke, 'Family Law Transfers from Europe to Africa: Lessons for the Methodology of Comparative Legal Research' in John Gillespie and Pip Nicholson (eds), *Law and Development and the Global Discourses of Legal Transfers* (CUP 2012) 273 on how European family law legal transplants failed in Africa because of cultural differences; Pierre Legrand, 'The Impossibility of "Legal Transplants"' (1997) 4 Maastricht Journal of European and Comparative Law 111 (more general), on how the transplant cannot survive the change of context and on how its original meaning will inevitably be lost.

an optimal cultural component,[38] and we may have to opt for the *second best* rule. This holds true for the entire population where dependency on political powers and, in particular, the state must be significantly decreased: for instance, in hospitals', schools', universities', and other cultural and social establishments' independence from party politics, enshrining concrete personal and financial guarantees in different constitutional rules. But it also applies to the elite, where attitudes towards fostering compromise should be strengthened: for instance, with an election system which allows particularly controversial politicians to be voted out by the negative vote of citizens who are otherwise voting for other parties.[39]

(b) On the level of *actual practices*, the imperative of restaffing key constitutional organs such as the Court of Auditors, Constitutional Court, leaders of the prosecuting services, etc—through transparent procedures—is often mentioned. Getting rid of obvious party loyalists of the current illiberal regime (who also in practice have been behaving like party loyalists) would most certainly increase the credibility of the legal order; however, by itself, it will not solve existing problems. In fact, it may even exacerbate them by deepening the sharp division between 'us' and 'them'. What is more important is strict compliance with and enforcement of formal rules.[40] Or to put it differently, we need to re-confirm the normativity of formal legal rules. Even the best formal guarantees will fail where officials are seeking to circumvent them or do nothing in the face of their breach. Stability of formal rules (except for the moment of regime change) is also important—in fact, in some cases even more important than the content of rules.[41]

(c) Finally, perhaps the most important prerequisite is to find an honest and credible *narrative* for the legal system which is acceptable to the entire society. The way the Hungarian society perceives and speaks of the legal system

[38] For similar considerations about formal and informal elements of a constitution, see Adrian Vermeule, 'System Effects and the Constitution' (2009) 123 Harvard Law Review 4.

[39] On the advantageous effect of negative votes (and plural votes) in electoral systems, in an easily comprehensible form, see D21 <http://www.d21.me> accessed 24 October 2024, or in a more academic style with detail, see Dodge Cahan and Arkadii Slinko, 'Electoral Competition under Best-Worst Voting Rules' (2018) 51 Social Choice and Welfare 259; Martin Gregor, 'The Optimal Ballot Structure for Double-Member Districts' (25 September 2013) CERGE-EI Working Paper Series 493 <www.ssrn.com/abstract=2347118> accessed 24 October 2024.

[40] Gretchen Helmke and Steven Levitsky, 'Introduction' in Gretchen Helmke and Steven Levitsky (eds), *Informal Institutions and Democracy: Lessons from Latin America* (Johns Hopkins University Press 2006) 1, 23.

[41] Foreign direct investment in Central Eastern Europe correlates more with the stability of tax rules than with their actual content, see Kelly Edmiston, Shannon Mudd, and Neven Valev, 'Tax Structures and FDI: The Deterrent Effects of Complexity and Uncertainty' (2003) 24 Fiscal Studies 341.

is highly contradictory and this is not just a product of the past few years. In György Gajduschek's words:

> While citizens do not trust the state or the law, they nevertheless rely on these to solve all their problems. They demand extremely detailed regulation and the severe sanctioning of any deviation from the law, however, when it comes to their person, they will gladly circumvent the rules and expect equitable treatment. All this is coupled with a social culture of exceptional pessimism, cynicism and anomie. What we are missing is a consistent value system that is shared by the majority of citizens—even when it comes to the most basic elements of the law (role of fundamental rights and duties, the presumption of innocence). In fact, individuals will often profess values that stand in stark contrast with each other. Members of society agree that society is unfair, yet they are not ready to do anything to change this. Almost every individual is of the view that s/he is better, more moral and law abiding than everyone else.[42]

The fabric of society is glued together with values and prohibitions that may not be directly questioned, but will be cautiously reinterpreted: from an anthropological perspective, these are taboos. In medieval times, Christianity played this role and heretics paid a heavy price. In Western Europe since the end of the Second World War, and following the fall of socialism, on the entire continent, this framework of integration has been made up of the secular taboos of constitutionalism. The twentieth century may be read as the history of experimenting and failing with different secular taboo systems, such as nationalism or socialism. Today, democracy and the protection of fundamental rights (the very reason the Council of Europe was established in 1949) seem to be the only rational narrative for organizing society. No sustainable alternative has emerged, notwithstanding the fact that this narrative has clearly been shaken and has experienced crises, yet these have only served to pinpoint the existence of extremely diverse sources of discontent and frustration. In recent times, the government has invoked sovereignty as an argument to justify corruption cases and to reject without further scrutiny all foreign (including EU and international) criticism regarding the violation of fundamental rights. These references to the people and/or sovereignty are a mere rhetorical tool in the hands of the government to justify their own corruption and violations of

[42] György Gajduschek, 'Jogtudat és értékvilág—mint a magyar jogrendszer környezete' in András Jakab and György Gajduschek (eds), *A magyar jogrendszer állapota* (2016) 95 (translation AJ).

the law. Hence, the notion of sovereignty should be redefined by a new narrative, or, alternatively, references to it should possibly be avoided.[43]

The Hungarian experiment of the illiberal state will only be sustainable in the long run in the event that the grand narrative of the European integration project itself breaks down—either formally or on the level of actual practices. Fortunately, despite all challenges, this does not seem to be a realistic scenario; but whether or not the rebuilding of the Hungarian legal system is successful depends largely on whether Hungary is capable of carrying out the necessary tasks of institution-building. This implies not only elevating the narrative of democracy and the rule of law (including the protection of fundamental rights) to the level of taboo,[44] but also securing the moral foundations of the legal order. Citizens cannot be expected to consider secular constitutional values to be credible and profess them to be their own, if earlier violations and betrayals are left unnamed and unsanctioned.[45] The crucial problem of institution-building in the 1989/90 constitutional system (besides corrupt practices) was that issues of justice, of dealing with the past (ie the narrative), were swept under the carpet following a peculiar interpretation of the formal rules.[46]

[43] András Jakab, 'Neutralising the Sovereignty Question: Compromise Strategies in Constitutional Argumentations about the Concept of Sovereignty before European Integration and Since' (2006) 2 European Constitutional Law Review 375.

[44] For denouncing liberal values, especially the protection of fundamental rights, see eg Viktor Orbán, 'Speech at the 25th Bálványos Summer Free and Student Camp' (30 July 2014) <www.kormany.hu/en/the-prime-minister/the-prime-minister-s-speeches/prime-minister-viktor-orban-s-speech-at-the-25th-balvanyos-summer-free-university-and-student-camp> accessed 24 October 2024; Viktor Orbán, 'Speech at the 14th Kötcse Civil Picnic' (17 September 2015) <www.kormany.hu/en/the-prime-minister/the-prime-minister-s-speeches/viktor-orban-s-speech-at-the-14th-kotcse-civil-picnic> accessed 24 October 2024.

[45] According to empirical studies, the payment of taxes is more likely in a morally acceptable regime, see Lars Feld and Bruno Frey, 'Tax Compliance as a Result of a Psychological Tax Contract: The Role of Incentives and Responsive Regulation' (2007) 29 Law & Policy 102; Valerie Braithwaite, *Defiance in Taxation and Governance: Resisting and Dismissing Authority in a Democracy* (Edward Elgar 2009). On the issue that at the end of communism the economic elite was able to acquire major wealth in ways which were considered by the vast majority of the population to be immoral (for which, however, there was no legal punishment), resulting in a loss of trust in the rule of law, see György Gajduschek, *Rendnek lenni kellene: Tények és elemzések a közigazgatás ellenőrzési és bírságolási tevékenységéről* (KSZK-MKI 2008) 220 and György Gajduschek, 'A közigazgatási bírságolás eredménytelenségéről' (2009) 1 Jogtudományi Közlöny 9. See also György Gajduschek, 'Measuring Cross-Sectorial Law Enforcement Capacity of Regulatory Agencies in Hungary' (2015) 11 Transylvanian Review of Administrative Sciences 108, 122: 'In the end, those following rules may be considered as "losers", and breaking norms may become a norm itself.'

[46] According to Gábor Halmai, 'Rise and Fall of Constitutionalism in Hungary' in Paul Blokker (ed), *Constitutional Acceleration within the European Union and Beyond* (Routledge 2017) 215, 220–23 the main reasons for the failure of liberal democracy in Hungary are the following: lack of human rights culture and liberal democratic traditions, victim culture in the national narrative, lack of economic success, loss of civic or participatory constitutionalism (and too much emphasis on judicial solutions), and a disproportionate electoral system.

Where legal and moral expectations clearly collide—as in the times of socialism, but to a certain degree also during the transition from socialism to the rule of law in 1989/90, and often even after that—both legal and moral norms will be weakened, leading to some degree of anomie.[47] To put it more provocatively and comprehensibly: Hungarian society is in a moral crisis.[48] Therefore, it seems particularly pertinent that the files of the secret services from the time of socialism are dealt with,[49] and that corrupt officials are held accountable, so that public trust can be rebuilt in the constitutional institutions underlying the legal order.[50] We must consciously express moral expectations both towards members of the society and public figures in public discourse,[51] thereby going against some know-all political commentators often appearing in the Hungarian media who interpret violations of various norms by public figures as successfully following the 'logic of politics'. Not only are these *destructive to institutions*, but they also reflect a lack of scholarly understanding of how institutions work.

For this to be successful, it is important to provide new generations of lawyers with the necessary theoretical toolbox.[52] Law is not just a sum of rules to be learned by heart. Currently, law students passing their final exams have a precise knowledge of administrative procedure. However, if you ask them why a state based on the rule of law is superior or what the point of democracy is, they will rattle off a brief truism (perhaps formulated in legalese), but most will

[47] Hungarian society is not only characterized by a low level of trust, but it is also anomic: even if normative expectations are clear, in case of own interests, people easily defy these expectations (more than usual in an international comparison). See István G Tóth, 'A társadalmi kohézió elemei: bizalom, normakövetés, igazságosság és felelősségérzet—lennének …' in Tamás Kolosi and István G Tóth (eds), *Társadalmi riport 2010* (Tárki 2010); Tamás Keller, 'A gazdasági erkölcsösséget szabályozó társadalmi normákról—normakövetés és normaszegés' in István G Tóth (ed), *Európai Társadalmi Jelentés 2. Gazdasági attitűdök* (2009).

[48] With a sociologically more precise expression: 'amoral', see Edward C Banfield, *The Moral Basis of a Backward Society* (Free Press 1958), the classic description of the Southern Italian situation ('amoral familism'). In Banfield's work this means the inability of collective action in the public interest, the irrelevance of any goal beyond the immediate material advantages of the nuclear family, the lack of social trust, nepotism, envy, and suspicion. See also the general attitude in Hungarian society towards corruption that is more lenient than not only the average European, but also the average of Hungary's neighbouring countries. Special Eurobarometer 470. Corruption (2017).

[49] On the unresolved nature of this issue, see eg László Varga, *Világ besúgói, egyesüljetek!* (Polgart 2006); Krisztián Ungváry, *A szembenézés hiánya* (Jaffa 2017).

[50] On this possibility see Tamás Hoffmann, 'Az állami közreműködéssel szerzett tulajdon elvonásának lehetősége a nemzetközi és európai emberi jogi sztenderdek fényében' (2017) MTA Law Working Papers No 17 <www.jog.tk.mta.hu/uploads/files/2017_17_Hoffmann.pdf> accessed 24 October 2024.

[51] See Samuel Bowles and Herbert Gintis, *A Cooperative Species: Human Reciprocity and Its Evolution* (Princeton University Press 2011) on a game theoretical analysis that shows that a low level of altruism and a lack of institutions enforcing altruism lead to weaker communities in conflict situations.

[52] Timothy Snyder, *On Tyranny: Twenty Lessons from the Twentieth Century* (Penguin 2017) 27: 'eternal vigilance is the price of liberty'.

not be able to make a solid case for it.[53] If these are the people who will operate the legal system in the future, they will not be able to lead the way or prevent the erosion of institutions. This is because they do not understand what it is that must be protected and supported beyond the realm of formal rules.[54] Yet institutions must be continuously cared for and nurtured every day, otherwise they will gradually fall into a demise.[55] Lawyers must constantly be aware of this and must not be satisfied by the thought that 'we are only interested in the legal rules as that is our job'.[56]

The bad news is that from among the three main components of institutions it is the system of formal rules that is the easiest to change; this, however, necessitates political action, that is, legislation. Unfortunately, as evidenced by the mechanisms described in the longer quote from Acemoglu at the beginning of Chapter 1, we can hardly expect such action from a political elite that benefits from this situation, where the interplay of weak institutions, circumvention of rules, and distrust are mutually disruptive.[57]

6. Conclusion

The erosion of the rule of law and democracy in certain EU MSs and at the EU level too are mutually reinforcing. It is not only that illiberal regimes are poisoning other MSs, but also that illiberal regimes within the EU are poisoning the EU itself. The reason as to why the EU and its various organs had such a hard time confronting illiberal politicians in some EU MSs is that the EU too has deficits when it comes to the rule of law and democracy and, less noticed, there has also been an erosion of both at the EU level.

If the EU does not want to lose its credibility it has a duty to defend its values (cf Article 2 TEU) to the greatest possible extent.[58] This tension between the

[53] Zoltán Fleck, *Technika vagy érték a jogállam? A jogállami értékek átadása és az előítéletek csökkentése a jogászok és a rendőrtisztek képzésében* (L'Harmattan 2012).

[54] On the negative picture of lawyers as command followers and enforcers see Snyder (n 52) 41.

[55] Vivien Lowndes and Mark Roberts, *Why Institutions Matter: The New Institutionalism in Political Science* (Palgrave Macmillan 2013) 171.

[56] Strangely, in written rules on legal education, we already have this requirement, see Ministerial reg 18/2016. (VIII. 5.) EMMI, pt 7.1.1.c. In reality, however, it is hardly happening. Thus again, making the formal rule is insufficient, but the lawmaker (out of comfortable blindness) considered the job to be done. The rule about overcoming rule-fixation became a victim of rule-fixation itself.

[57] On the relationship between social trust and institutions, see eg Bo Rothstein and Eric M Uslaner, 'All for All: Equality, Corruption, and Social Trust' (2005) 58 World Politics 41.

[58] See Case C-156/21 *Hungary v European Parliament and Council of the European Union* [2022] EU:C:2022:97, para 127: 'The values contained in Article 2 TEU have been identified and are shared by the Member States. They define the very identity of the EU as a common legal order. Thus, the EU

lack of enforcement of the EU on the one hand, and the moral and (implied) legal duty to enhance the rule of law and democracy within its territory on the other, lies at the heart of the debate about EU law to withstand the erosion of the rule of law and democracy. While we should not close our eyes to this, let us not be defeatist. There is room for improvement at EU and at the MS level.

In light of the above, we think of selected tools at EU level which already exist, and which would only have to be adapted to resolve the illiberal regime challenge. We suggest three antidotes to tackle this issue which are currently underrated, but highly promising. Thereby, we do not want to claim that these three antidotes are the only tools which might prove effective. In the complex situation of the multilevel illiberal regime crisis very likely several different aspects are necessary in order to improve the situation. There might be yet other tools which could be of help. For instance, withholding large sums of financial subsidies can be effective incentives to correct certain illiberal measures. However, the three antidotes which we present below are less discussed and do provide for important structural improvements which can have long-lasting effects.

First, we need to better evaluate the situation without whitewashing it. We need an epistemological tool to this end. Fortunately, we can *adapt* the existing EU Justice Scoreboard (Chapter 5). Second, we need to strengthen the protection of fundamental rights in all MSs. A solid guarantee of fundamental rights is important to uphold or restore the rule of law, which in turn also positively influences a democratic culture. We therefore make the case for *completing* the European Fundamental Rights Union by reinterpreting Article 51 (1) of the EU CFR (Chapter 6). Third, the *Spitzenkandidaten*-system should be *stabilized*—not only to ensure the democratic accountability of the Commission, but also because this could approximate the currently undecided and hesitant stance of the Commission to the clearly anti-illiberal-regime stance of the EP. If the winner of the next EP elections were to subsequently be the candidate for election as President of the Commission, an effective institutional incentive for the coherent application of the already existing enforcement tools by the Commission against the EU's illiberal regimes would be created (Chapter 7). We go into more detail on each aspect respectively in Chapters 5, 6, and 7.

must be able to defend those values, within the limits of its powers as laid down by the Treaties.' And para 232: 'Article 2 TEU is not merely a statement of policy guidelines or intentions, but contains values ... which are given concrete expression in principles containing legally binding obligations for the Member States.'

5

Adjusting an Existing Epistemological Tool

How to Transform the EU Justice Scoreboard into an Actual Rule of Law Index

1. Introduction

In the past few years, the rule of law and democracy have been declining in many countries of the world.[1] As we have seen in Chapters 2 and 3 this includes several MSs of the EU as well as the EU itself. The fear that more stable democracies could take such a turn is pervasive in public debate and scholarly discourse.[2] From the analysis in Chapter 1, taking legal institutionalism as a framework, we learned that the study of legal rules yields only partial insight into the state of the rule of law. In particular, in cases of erosion of the rule of law and democracy, the main problem is the slow demise of the normativity of constitutional law, that is, the growing chasm between the constitution and constitutional reality.[3] Amendments to formal legal acts say little about what and how things will change. If we do not want to remain blind to erosion, besides considering the formal rules, we need appropriate epistemological tools which enable us to examine the de facto conduct of addressees of these rules and the narrative accompanying it. The latter includes the social mentality or the political rhetoric regarding constitutional institutions.[4] Fine-tuned constitutional law doctrine is always capable of identifying a de facto breach of the general requirements of the rule of law by the addressees of constitutional rules. However, the question regarding the gravity of such breaches cannot be

[1] Mark A Graber, Sanford Levinson, and Mark Tushnet (eds), *Constitutional Democracy in Crisis?* (OUP 2018).

[2] See Chapter 2, esp n 5.

[3] Cf Chapter 2.

[4] For such an analysis see András Jakab, 'What Is Wrong with the Hungarian Legal System and How to Fix It' (13 July 2018) MPIL Research Paper No 2018-13 <https://ssrn.com/abstract=3213378> accessed 24 October 2024. Cf Strømmen Lile, 'Lost in Operationalisation: Developing Legally Relevant Indicators, Questions and Benchmarks' (2017) 21 The International Journal of Human Rights 1378 quoting Martin Luther King who wrote in 1967 that '[t]he ubiquitous discrimination in his daily life tells him that laws on paper, no matter how imposing their terms, will not guarantee that he will live in "the masterpiece of civilization"'.

Saving the European Union from Its Illiberal Member States. András Jakab and Lando Kirchmair, Oxford University Press.
DOI: 10.1093/oso/9780198954606.003.0006

captured with the standard tools of legal doctrine alone. In order to fully grasp reality, one should also resort to rule of law indices.[5] Unfortunately, the existing rule of law indices, as we will see later in this chapter, are not particularly helpful for the EU's current needs, for different reasons.

While we are not in a position to offer a miraculous solution to the EU illiberal regime crisis in this book, we wish to point to an important and so far largely overlooked element to diagnose rule of law defects. We argue that rule of law indices, if well designed,[6] can be a powerful tool to detect ills in the rule of law of MSs. The introduction of the EU Justice Scoreboard (EUJS) in 2013 has already been an important step in laying the ground for an EU-wide analysis. It was primarily designed to address 'the negative growth spiral' after the 2008 economic and financial crisis.[7] For this reason, the EUJS is currently too concerned with the financial guarantees and the infrastructure of the judicial system, instead of a holistic analysis of the rule of law. Since 2020, however, the EUJS also informs the Annual Rule of Law Report to be presented by the EC.[8]

In this chapter, we suggest how the EUJS should be further developed into a proper rule of law index because this would make the EUJS a considerably more useful tool in the current crisis. Not only could the EUJS play an important role in providing reliable data for political debates, but it could also inform the 'Regulation on a general regime of conditionality for the protection of the Union budget'—which links the protection of the budget of the Union to the generalized deficiencies of the rule of law in the MSs—adopted on 16 December 2020,[9] as well as the 'Regulation establishing the Recovery and Resilience Facility'—providing loans and financial support in order to assist EU MSs to better overcome the coronavirus pandemic—adopted on 12 February 2021[10]. In addition, a sophisticated EUJS which provides a clear and

[5] For a showcase of combining empirical research based on indices with doctrinal rule of law questions, see Tim Ginsburg and Mila Versteeg, 'Constitutional Correlates of the Rule of Law' in Maurice Adams, Anne Meuwese, and Ernst Hirsch Ballin (eds), *Constitutionalism and the Rule of Law: Bridging Idealism and Realism* (CUP 2017) 506.

[6] Cf Kim Lane Scheppele, 'The Rule of Law and the Frankenstate: Why Governance Checklists Do Not Work' (2013) 26 Governance 559 arguing that separate indicators that do not consider the interaction effects amongst them might fail to portray the true monster Frankenstate. For a similar argument, criticizing the 'fallacy of decomposition' see Mark Tushnet, 'Authoritarian Constitutionalism' (2015) 100 Cornell Law Review 391, 409–10.

[7] See Communication from the Commission, The EU Justice Scoreboard. A tool to promote effective justice and growth, COM(2013) 160 final.

[8] See Communication from the Commission, 2020 Rule of Law Report. The rule of law situation in the European Union, COM(2020) 580 final.

[9] See Regulation (EU, Euratom) 2020/2092 of the European Parliament and of the Council of 16 December 2020 on a general regime of conditionality for the protection of the Union budget [2020] OJ L 433I.

[10] See Regulation (EU) 2021/241 of the European Parliament and of the Council of 12 February 2021 establishing the Recovery and Resilience Facility [2021] OJ L 57.

honest picture of the state of the art of the rule of law in EU MSs would make inaction by EU organs, which has been a key problem in the illiberal regime crisis, politically more costly.

Beyond these improvements of the EUJS we argue that the EUJS should also include the EU itself in its analysis. As we have learned from Chapter 3, the EU itself has never been a model student in terms of democracy and the rule of law. There are even erosion phenomena pertaining to the EU itself. Despite these developments we do not have an adequate methodology to observe the functioning of the rule of law and democracy with rather objective tools at EU level. This should be changed by simply including the EU in the analysis of the improved EUJS. A positive side-effect of this move would be an increase in legitimacy by saying that every institution, be it all MSs or the EU itself, is under scrutiny.

2. Why Measure Legal Systems? The Use of Rule of Law Indices

There are a large number of indices that all measure legal systems.[11] This can be explained by four factors. First, one single number can easily sum up complicated questions,[12] so that non-professionals and the press can also use it.[13] We should not underestimate this explanatory character, because this simplification can also contribute to democratic accountability. Second, indices are often also considered as external measures in debates about evaluating reforms or the performance of the government.[14] Because of this, international organizations and NGOs use indices in order to foster and propagate best practices by comparing numbers of different countries. Exemplary countries usually score at the top of the scale set up by these organizations.[15] A side-effect of this

[11] Observing the increasing number of indicators and indices, in other words, the composite indicators, some authors speak about 'indicator fatigue'. See generally Linn Hammergren, 'Indices, Indicators and Statistics: A View from the Project Side as to Their Utility and Pitfalls' (2015) 3 Hague Journal on the Rule of Law 305, 311.

[12] Michaela Saisana and Andrea Saltelli, 'Rankings and Ratings: Instructions for Use' (2011) 3 Hague Journal on the Rule of Law 247.

[13] This is also dangerous because the measured value can also affect reality, for example, news about high levels of corruption can actually boost the acceptability of corruption itself, which can consequently also increase real corruption. See Tom Ginsburg, 'Pitfalls of Measuring the Rule of Law' (2011) 3 Hague Journal on the Rule of Law 269: 'Perceptions can produce their own reality' (270); '[A] bad image can become a self-fulfilling prophecy' (279).

[14] Juan Carlos Botero, Robert L Nelson, and Christine Pratt, 'Indices and Indicators of Justice, Governance, and the Rule of Law: An Overview' (2011) 3 Hague Journal on the Rule of Law 153, 159–60.

[15] For more about this problem in practice, and concerning the question of legitimacy, see Kevin E Davis, Benedict Kingsbury, and Engle Merry, 'Indicators as a Technology of Global Governance'

approach can be seen, for example, when a government solely changes a policy in order to change its score on a scale, without treating the real problem.[16] Third, as already noted in section 1 of this chapter, rule of law indices can show the de facto situation—that is, law in action rather than law in books. They can also show the extent of improvements and deteriorations; and very importantly, these results cannot be discredited as 'simply one opinion'. Rule of law indices aggregate a large number of data, including many expert opinions—if done well—in a transparent and controllable way.[17] Fourth and finally, economists need quantitative data in order to test political-economical correlations, for example between the rule of law and economic performance; therefore, the characteristics of legal systems need to be quantified.[18]

The challenge is that in all these cases we want to measure a phenomenon that is not directly observable, like the rule of law.[19] Fortunately, statistics has several methods to handle this, and over the coming pages we will present this approach, without delving too deeply into the mathematical details. We focus

(2012) 46 Law & Society Review 71; Armin von Bogdandy and Matthias Goldmann, 'The Exercise of International Public Authority through National Policy Assessment: The OECD's PISA Policy as a Paradigm for a New International Standard Instrument' (2008) 5 International Organisations Law Review 241; Tor Krever, 'Quantifying Law: Legal Indicator Projects and the Reproduction of Neoliberal Common Sense' (2013) 34 Third World Quarterly 131; AnnJanette Rosga and Margaret Satterthwaite, 'The Trust in Indicators: Measuring Human Rights' (2009) 27 Berkeley Journal of International Law 253.

[16] Botero, Nelson, and Pratt (n 14) 159. In general, see Andrea Saltelli, 'Composite Indicators between Analysis and Advocacy' (2006) 81 Social Indicators Research 65, 65.

[17] See eg Sakiko Fukuda-Parr, Terra Lawson-Remer, and Susan Randolph, *Fulfilling Social and Economic Rights* (OUP 2015) 17 providing a measurement approach of social and economic rights; they 'find some surprising and counterintuitive relationships between rights fulfillment, on the one hand, and democratic governance, civil and political rights, social spending, economic growth, gender equality, and legal commitments, on the other'. On guidance of how to construct quantitative analysis in the field of human rights law, cf Lile (n 4); Christopher J Fariss and Geoff Dancy, 'Measuring the Impact of Human Rights: Conceptual and Methodological Debates' (2017) 13 Annual Review of Law and Social Science 273 synthesizing theoretical approaches on human rights with theories of measurement, and differentiating a factualist, constructivist, and a constitutive approach. For a major database on all human rights recommendations that are outstanding against EU MSs, see also EU Fundamental Rights Information System, EU FRA (29 July 2024) <https://fra.europa.eu/en/databases/efris/> accessed 24 October 2024. Cf CIRI Human Rights Data Project (29 July 2024) <http://www.humanrightsdata.com/p/data-documentation.html> accessed 24 October 2024; Dimitry Kochenov and Justin Lindeboom (eds), *Kälin and Kochenov's Quality of Nationality Index: An Objective Ranking of the Nationalities of the World* (Hart Publishing 2020).

[18] Tero Erkkilä, B Guy Peters, and Ossi Piironen, 'Politics of Comparative Quantification: The Case of Governance Metrics' (2016) 18 Journal of Comparative Policy Analysis: Research and Practice 319.

[19] Daniel Kaufmann, Aart Kraay, and Massimo Mastruzzi, 'The Worldwide Governance Indicators: Methodology and Analytical Issues' (2011) 3 Hague Journal on the Rule of Law 220: 'inherently unobservable nature'.

on the measurement of the rule of law, but the fundamental methodological problems are similar in the case of other indices measuring legal systems too.[20]

Quantification is not part of the traditional toolbox of a lawyer,[21] and the attitude of lawyers towards statistical methods is also ambiguous, to say the least.[22] On occasions they underestimate the indices because of the extent of simplification—or even discredit them, based on some unlikely outcomes—but at the same time they also admire the unintelligible mathematical models. In the present chapter, we would like to find the golden mean between these two extreme approaches, by using the indices as important tools and as additional information for the better understanding of the overall view, while also treating them with caution and critique.

A remark on terminology: by indicator we refer to a single number or feature, and by index we refer to composite indicators.

3. Methodological Steps

In this part we present the methodological questions based on the legal literature and on the OECD Handbook on Constructing Composite Indicators (2008).[23] The main rule is that the design of the index must be transparent and the methodological choices must be grounded, otherwise the indices are likely to serve pre-established policies.[24]

[20] Eg Jos Blank and others, *Bench Marking in an International Perspective: An International Comparison of the Mechanisms and Performance of the Judiciary System* (2004) <http://siteresources.worldbank.org/INTLAWJUSTINST/Resources/Benchmarking.pdf> accessed 24 October 2024.

[21] Indices can be useful in the field of comparative law too, see Ralf Michaels, 'Comparative Law by Numbers? Legal Origins Thesis, Doing Business Reports, and the Silence of Traditional Comparative Law' (2009) 57 American Journal of Comparative Law 765. But lawyers are usually cautious towards this approach. Other legal academics, linked to an underscoring system, used to emphasize the methodological shortcomings of the indices, eg Bénédicte Fauvarque-Cosson and Anne-Julie Kerhuel, 'Is Law an Economic Contest? French Reactions to the Doing Business World Bank Reports and Economic Analysis of the Law' (2009) 57 American Journal of Comparative Law 811.

[22] See only the example given by Lile (n 4) 1379 referring, for example, to research by Hans Otto Sano and Halta Thelle, 'The Need for Evidence-Based Human Rights Research' in Foons Coomans, Fred Grünfeld, and Menno T Kamminga (eds), *Methods of Human Rights Research* (Intersentia 2009) 96 pointing out that the papers published in the *Human Rights Quarterly* and the *Netherlands Quarterly of Human Rights* (between 2005 and 2007) do not use statistical analyses at all.

[23] OECD Handbook on Constructing Indicators (2008) 20–21 <http://www.oecd.org/std/42495745.pdf> accessed 24 October 2024.

[24] OECD Handbook on Constructing Indicators (n 23). See also René Urueña, 'Indicators and the Law: A Case Study of the Rule of Law Index' in Sally Engle Merry, Kevin E Davis, and Benedict Kingsbury (eds), *The Quiet Power of Indicators: Measuring Governance, Corruption, and the Rule of Law* (CUP 2015) 75, 96–97 holding that 'indicators, though, need to be generally perceived as nonpolitical by most of those who are being measured. Otherwise, they would lose most of their appeal.' Yet Urueña also states that 'it would be silly to attempt to' prevent the numbers produced by indices 'from being used politically'. To the contrary, 'influence of an indicator derives from the fact that it is used by policymakers: otherwise, indicators would remain as a footnote in scholarly journals, with no influence

First, we must note that some steps of index-building presuppose a thorough knowledge of legal doctrine, for example conceptualization, and other steps require expertise in working with quantitative data, for example handling and aggregating data. As there are very few experts who excel at both fields, index-building is usually carried out via team-based work, based on the cooperation of legal experts and data experts, even if they sometimes speak entirely different languages.

3.1 Conceptualization

Before starting the construction of the index, we should clarify what we want to measure.[25] Babbie, quoting Kaplan, places measurable things into three categories: (a) direct observables like the number of seats in a parliament; (b) indirect observables, like the minutes of corporate board meetings which only convey indirect information on what actually happened; and (c) constructs or theoretical creations, such as IQ or government performance.[26] Lawyers have a special expertise in the latter field: one of the main parts of a lawyer's work relates to conceptual analysis.[27] If we want to measure the rule of law, we have to define it.

The exact meaning of the rule of law as a term is, however, contested.[28] It is mostly defined as a list of requirements or legal techniques that aim at inhibiting the arbitrary use of state power.[29] Most characteristically, authors differentiate between formal-procedural (or thin) and material-substantive (or thick) requirements.[30] Somewhat simplistically, the formal-procedural side includes

in real life'. However, while he suggests that indices 'may be transformed into sites of contestation of the definition of what it means to adhere to the rule of law', we rather suggest that due to their political implications it is of utmost importance to use transparent and rigorous methodology.

[25] For our topic, see eg Jørgen Møller and Svend-Erik Skaaning, *The Rule of Law: Definitions, Measures, Patterns and Causes* (Springer 2014) 13–27.

[26] Earl R Babbie, *The Practice of Social Research* (13th edn, Wadsworth 2013) 168–69; Abraham Kaplan, *The Conduct of Inquiry: Methodology for Behavioral Science* (Routledge 2017) 54–56.

[27] András Jakab, 'What Makes a Good Lawyer?' (2007) 62 Zeitschrift für öffentliches Recht 275.

[28] For the difficulty of clearly delineating the values enshrined in Article 2 TEU, see eg Lando Kirchmair, 'Demokratische Legitimität, die EU-Rechtsstaatlichkeitskrise und Vorüberlegungen zu einer transnationalen Gewaltengliederung' (2019) 6 Zeitschrift für praktische Philosophie 171.

[29] For such an understanding, see eg the rule of law report of the Commission COM (2020) 580 final (n 8) 1.

[30] Cf eg Christopher May and Adam Winchester (eds), *Handbook on the Rule of Law* (Edward Elgar 2018) ch 1; Gianluigi Palombella, 'The Rule of Law as an Institutional Ideal' in Leonardo Morlino and Gianluigi Palombella (eds), *Rule of Law and Democracy: Inquiries into Internal and External Issues* (Brill 2010) 4; Randall Peerenboom, 'Human Rights and Rule of Law: What's the Relationship?' (2005) 36 Georgia Journal of International Law 809; Daniel B Rodriguez, Matthew McCubbins, and Barry Weingast, 'The Rule of Law Unplugged' (2009) 59 Emory Law Journal 1455; Brian Z Tamanaha, *On the*

such aspects as the stability of legal rules, compliance, and fair enforcement, whereas the material-substantive side includes foremost fundamental rights, as well as checks and balances. It is not possible and not necessary to enter into debates over the meaning of the rule of law here.[31] Instead, taking into account the goal of our chapter, we need to be aware of the structure of the concept as a list of requirements, and its anti-arbitrariness as a defining goal.

The various concrete definitions that are used by the various rule of law indices are usually based on legal-doctrinal opinions. If the majority of this legal-doctrinal professional community (eg constitutional lawyers of the relevant discourse) find the definition acceptable, for example because it is based on authoritative legal documents, the definition seems to be appropriate.[32] We can, of course, encounter numerous terminological debates[33] about the concept of the rule of law, and because of the contested nature of values we cannot expect a full consensus on this matter.[34] The general advice, however, is that we should use a mainstream definition—when possible—with a small grain of caution. Because of the contested nature of the concept of the rule of law, the difficult task of finding a 'common' opinion among experts can be shortcut by reference to official documents, for example by the EU, the UN, the Council of Europe (CoE), or the EC.

Consequently, some indices diverge concerning the exact definition used, a problem that we will discuss later. Legal indices usually measure the de facto characteristics of a system, so a well-crafted and substantively appealing law with a corrupt, oppressive, or ineffective implementation will underscore on these scales.[35]

Rule of Law: History, Politics, Theory (CUP 2004); Augusto Zimmermann, 'The Rule of Law as a Culture of Legality: Legal and Extra-Legal Elements for the Realization of the Rule of Law in Society' (2007) 14 European Law Journal 10. For a good overview, see Alexandra Timmer, 'Concepts of Human Rights, Democracy, and the Rule of Law: A Literature Review' (28 November 2013) *European Commission* <http://www.fp7-frame.eu/frame-reps-3-1/2013> accessed 24 October 2024.

[31] On these conceptual debates, see eg András Jakab, *European Constitutional Language* (CUP 2016); Jørgen Møller and Svend-Erik Skaaning, *Requisites of Democracy: Conceptualization, Measurement, and Explanation* (Routledge 2011). For various causal relationships, see Roberto Rigobon and Dani Rodrik, 'Rule of Law, Democracy, Openness, and Income: Estimating Interrelationships' (2005) 13 Economics of Transition and Institutional Change 533.

[32] Saisana and Saltelli (n 12) 249.

[33] On this phenomenon in general, there is a lack of consensus and problems of definition in the case of composite indicators, see eg Lovell Cherchye, Wim Moesen, and Tom Van Puyenbroeck, 'One Market, One Number? A Composite Indicator Assessment of EU Internal Market Dynamics' (2007) 51 European Economic Review 749.

[34] Botero, Nelson, and Pratt (n 14) 166 quoting Saisana and Saltelli (n 12) 248: 'composite indicators are value laden constructs'. On the necessary political content of indices, see also Urueña (n 24) 543–84.

[35] As a bad example, we can mention the RTI Rating, 'Global Right to Information Rating' (29 July 2024) <http://www.rti-rating.org> accessed 24 October 2024, in which two NGOs analysed the situation relating to the right to information, but with rather surprising results: Moldova outscored the United Kingdom and Russia performed better than the United States. Despite any disclaimer—such as

3.2 Selecting Data

Once it is clear what will be measured, the data for this measurement has to be found. The quality of a given legal system cannot be measured directly. Therefore, proxies (approximate data) have to be used: the opinion of experts or that of the public—*soft data*—or approximate facts—*hard data*—for example the number of registered crimes, the budget of the courts, frequency of the modification of laws, frequency of the condemnation of a state by an international court of human rights.[36]

The main concern about expert opinions is the choice of experts and the subjectivity of their opinions. This is an especially sensitive problem in politically polarized countries.[37] As a partial remedy a transparent selection method is preferable. For instance, in a country with inter-ethnic tensions, the proportion of the experts should reflect the overall ethnic distribution. Alternatively, the use of as many experts as possible, by random sampling or with the participation of every available expert, is an appropriate way to address the challenge of selecting experts known as selection bias.[38] A further problem is that in case of general questions, which is often characteristic of legal indices, it is not easy to find an expert who is up to date in every field. For example, criminal procedure, which is an important constituent of the rule of law, is usually not well known by constitutional lawyers.[39] In several countries, participation brings risks for the expert too, if for example he or she criticizes the current regime, even if anonymity is granted, obtaining unbiased reports will be more complicated.[40] However, an obvious advantage of acquiring an expert opinion is that wide opinion polls are expensive, hard data are not always available from every single country, and some questions can only be answered by experts.

An important advantage of using opinion polls in the general population is that they also take into consideration the situation of vulnerable groups. Even

that the implementation might differ from the written rule—it is a clear example of how unelaborated goal-setting and conceptualization can make indices completely useless.

[36] Jim Parsons, 'Developing Clusters of Indicators: An Alternative Approach to Measuring the Provision of Justice' (2011) 3 Hague Journal on the Rule of Law 170, 175–6.

[37] Office of the High Commissioner for Human Rights (OHCHR), *The UN Rule of Law Indicators: Implementation Guide and Project Tools* (UN publication 2011) 1 <https://peacekeeping.un.org/sites/default/files/un_rule_of_law_indicators.pdf> accessed 24 October 2024. In politically polarized countries, the results of the polls may vary: a popular government can increase trust in independent institutions, like the courts, and vice versa.

[38] György Gajduschek, 'Miben áll, és mérhető-e a kormányzati teljesítmény?' (2014) 3 Politikatudományi Szemle 97, 110.

[39] On this problem, see OHCHR (n 37) 24.

[40] OHCHR (n 37) 28.

though opinion polls can also be biased, if they are professionally taken then the situation of these groups can be better represented than in expert opinions and in hard data. A further advantage of survey data is that it can also enlighten the differences between hard data and reality.[41] Unfortunately, however, opinion surveys are expensive and the questions are limited—as the general population cannot answer very specific questions. Sampling and measurement in no-go zones (in European countries it is less of a problem) and among vulnerable groups is also complicated. Public opinion is also very fluid, especially if it is influenced by the news.[42] A further critique is the limited possibility of cross-country comparison, due to divergent historical mentalities.[43]

Although the use of hard data is objective, the scope of measurement is very limited. A large proportion of our questions cannot be measured even by using proxy hard data. It can also occur that while something is measurable by hard data, there is no data from a given country. We must also be cautious when using available data for four reasons. (a) Sometimes they are corrupted by the authorities, for example the police sometimes discourage the victims of small crimes where there is a limited probability of success, in order to ameliorate statistics. (b) Sometimes, the measured value has an impact on the question only in extreme cases, for example the budget of courts on the rule of law. (c) Sometimes, it is not at all obvious whether a boost of an objective value has a positive or a negative effect on the phenomenon—the high efficacy of public prosecutors can be indicative of an authoritarian judiciary tradition, while low efficacy can be indicative of incompetent prosecutors. (d) Finally, the partial nature of the data: in other words, objective data is only available on certain special questions, not on all questions, which can lead to arbitrary selection.

Some indices combine the different sources, making the results more robust (see eg the WJP-Index below), and the data sources are also cross-checked, via a method known as triangulation.

3.3 Statistical Analysis

There are different types of data: yes or no (binary data: 1 or 0), points on a given scale[44] (ordinal data, eg the experts of the Freedom House evaluate the

[41] Parsons (n 36) 177.
[42] Parsons (n 36) 178.
[43] Parsons (n 36) 179.
[44] See Babbie (n 26) 155–58, 180–84 setting levels of measurement in itself can be problematic: do we use nominal, ordinal, interval, or ratio measure?

questions on a scale ranging from 1 to 7), percentages (metric data, eg trust in institutions in the Eurobarometer), etc. In order to put all the data in one final index, we have to normalize (homogenize) them.[45] For cross-country comparison, we have to adjust the data according to the size of the given country.[46]

There are several statistical methods for dealing with missing data. We can simply delete the whole row of data; for instance if an expert only answers twenty-four out of twenty-five questions, we can delete all of his or her answers, or we can just leave out the unanswered question. The problems are that: (a) the missing data are usually non-random, for example some experts are afraid of answering several questions—in this case, simply disregarding the missing answer can bias the result; (b) deleting data can also decrease the reliability of the result—that is, an increasing standard error.[47] Therefore, if the quantity of missing data is more than 5 per cent, we can use imputation.[48] If, for example, an expert answered only twenty-four out of twenty-five questions, we can deduce her or his twenty-fifth answer by imputing this answer based on the other answers given by the expert. Or we can use the mean of the answers of the other experts, eventually belonging to the same cluster, based on the similar answers. We can also use a variety of other, more complicated statistical methods, and while each of these methods has a different advantage and inconvenience, we can reduce the bias of the outcomes based on these methods.

We must separately examine the non-arbitrary selection of the indicators, on which the indices are based.[49] Indices based on many but bad indicators—meaning indicators which are actually irrelevant for the concept to be measured—are called 'indicator rich but information poor'.[50] We can test this issue by using multivariate analysis. We examine the relation between the indicators, and the effect of them on the final outcome, in other words on the value of the rule of law index. Besides, we always have to test the influence of

[45] For example, transforming a 0-1 scale into 0-100 means that 1 will be 100, a 0-4 scale into 0-100 means that the value of 1 will be 25, 2 is equal to 50, 3 is 75, and 4 is 100. Another possible method is the standardization that is the rescaling of variables in order to obtain a zero mean and a standard deviation of one.

[46] Saisana and Saltelli (n 12) 251.

[47] Saisana and Saltelli (n 12) 252.

[48] See Roderick JA Little and Donald B Rubin, *Statistical Analysis with Missing Data* (2nd edn, Wiley 2002) on filling in for missing values.

[49] For a detailed look into democracy-indices, see Thomas Müller and Susanne Pickel, 'Wie lässt sich Demokratie am besten messen? Zur Konzeptqualität von Demokratie-Indizes' (2007) 48 Politische Vierteljahresschrift 511. For an overview of various strategies on how to measure democracy, see Jaso Seawright and David Collier, 'Rival Strategies of Validation: Tools for Evaluating Measures of Democracy' (2013) 47 Comparative Political Studies 111. On governance indexes see Rachel M Gisselquist, 'Developing and Evaluating Governance Indexes: 10 Questions' (2014) 35 Policy Studies 513.

[50] OECD Handbook on Constructing Indicators (2008) 25.

the individual variables on the final outcome, in other words, examine the robustness.[51]

We must also deal with outliers, meaning the observations distant from other observations. In many cases, these result from measurement errors. Here too, we can use several statistical methods to handle the problem: we can simply delete the values, use imputation techniques, or introduce a natural logarithm, for example to increase the goodness of fit. Of course, there are some real outliers too. We have to take them into consideration.

Weighting is an important question too. On the one hand, we can sum up the data with the same weight, but some characteristics are more important than others; for instance, concerning the rule of law, that the police cannot shoot innocent civilians arbitrarily is more important than the duration of a legal procedure.[52] On the other hand, it is not easy to find an objective method for weighting—due to a lack of knowledge, and consequently, due to a lack of consensus between experts.[53] When testing indices without weight, using multivariate analysis, we are only able to change them by adding or deleting indicators. In the case of weighted indicators, we can change the weight too, without deleting the indicator. The underlying method of weighting must be clear and explicit too.[54] In several cases, weighting can be implicit too: if for instance, we build strongly correlated indicators into the index, this also results in the weighting of the given question.

In order to lower the influence of extreme values on the final index (considering the example above: in order to avoid overscoring legal systems where the police can kill innocent people, but where other institutions are working well), we can use a geometric mean instead of an arithmetic mean. This allows for greater comparability; that is, the state with the arbitrary police but with a good performance on other scales will not perform better than a similar (slightly underperforming) state without such an extreme value.[55] Instead of

[51] The multivariate analysis mentioned earlier shows the inner correlation structure of the indicators. Analysing robustness on the contrary shows the influence of the indicators and methodological choices—normalization, weighting—on the index.

[52] As an example of a weighted index of the rule of law, see eg Benny YT Tai, 'Developing an Index of the Rule of Law: Sharing the Experience of Hong Kong' (2007) 2 Asian Journal of Comparative Law 1.

[53] Saisana and Saltelli (n 12) 254 writing on the subjective character of weighting. For another source sceptical towards weighting, see OHCHR (n 37) 5. For the methods of weighting, see the OECD Handbook on Constructing Indicators (2008) 31–3; Andrew Sharpe and Brendon Andrews, 'An Assessment of Weighting Methodologies for Composite Indicators: The Case of the Index of Economic Well-Being' (December 2012) CSLS Res Rep, No 2012-10. An example of an index without weights is the Islamic Constitutions Index, see Dawood I Ahmed and Moamen Gouda, 'Measuring Constitutional Islamization: The Islamic Constitutions Index' (2015) 38 Hastings International & Comparative Law Review 1.

[54] Saisana and Saltelli (n 12) 255.

[55] Saisana and Saltelli (n 12) 256. Instead of taking the sum of the values and dividing it by the number of numbers (arithmetic average), we take the *n*th root of the product of *n* numbers (geometric average).

using means, we can also use factor analysis, but the description of this method is beyond the framework of the present study.[56]

We can also build sub-indices from indicators. This is useful because (a) it can diminish misunderstandings and biases, occurring in the case of using isolated indicators, and (b) we can measure the complex and multifaceted characteristic of the institutional functions.[57] We can even build dimensions from sub-indices. These are on a higher level of abstraction than the indicators, but on a lower level compared to the final index—for example, in the case of the rule of law, the efficiency of the justice system, or that of the police. We also can statistically test the relation between the dimensions,[58] also in order to measure the effect on the final index. Here we can use factor analysis, principal component analysis, or Cronbach's alpha test.[59] Thereafter, we can correct the list of indicators, or the weights and the classifications into sub-indices, so that they measure similar but not identical things, with an existent but not full correlation. While building up the final index, we have to allow for the possibility of decomposition too, so that we can deduce from it the basic data and indicators.[60]

3.4 Presenting, Interpreting, and Comparing Results

The results are better represented in charts, but textual information is also needed for their interpretation. We have to keep in mind that the numbers in themselves can only represent the correlation.[61] In order to establish a causal relation on the basis of this, the content needs to be considered further.

Visualization of the results with graphs, for example, can be instructive too, as they can influence (or manipulate) the interpretation and understanding.[62] The results of an analysis extended to multiple countries can be represented on

[56] See Howard Rosenthal and Erik Voeten, 'Measuring Legal Systems' (2007) 35 Journal of Comparative Economics 711.

[57] OHCHR (n 37) 3.

[58] Stefan Voigt, 'How to Measure the Rule of Law' (2012) 65 Kyklos 262.

[59] OECD Handbook on Constructing Indicators (2008) 25–27, 63–82.

[60] OECD Handbook on Constructing Indicators (2008) 16.

[61] A well-known example on the difference between strong correlation and causality: according to superstition, the presence of storks can boost fertility. This belief seems to be confirmed by the data: childbirth is correlated with the number of storks in a given region. In fact, in urbanized regions, the hunting-ground of storks is very limited. Parallel to this, in urban, industrialized regions, the birth rate used to be lower than in rural regions. So there is no causality between the number of storks and number of newborn babies. Babbie (n 26) 94, 442–49, and 483–84.

[62] See eg Alexandru C Telea, *Data Visualization: Principles and Practice* (2nd edn, Routledge 2015); Steffen-Peter Ballstaedt, *Visualisieren: Bilder in wissenschaftlichen Texten* (utb 2012).

a map, or the countries can be classified into clusters. If there are other indices on the same question, we should compare them with our index, and we should also explain the differences.

4. International Indices on the Rule of Law

Here, we present four internationally recognized indices on legal systems.[63] These are the indices of the Freedom House ('Freedom in the World', FIW), the BTI, the World Bank ('Worldwide Governance Indicators', WGI), and the WJP RLI.[64] We have chosen these four indices because they are internationally the best-known ones, and their critical analysis is also helpful for improving the EUJS. In order to give a clear-cut picture, we represent the similarities and differences in Table 5.1[65] In the four indices, we also present the measurement of the rule of law, in order to point out the differences in conceptualization.

The Freedom House index—although it deserves praise for pioneering work, having been established already in 1972, and its almost universal coverage—is methodologically a dinosaur (unclear conceptualization, questions are partly overlapping, partly lack coverage; even the simple awareness of methodological problems seems to be missing). It also fundamentally lacks transparency, as, for instance, it is unclear who the experts are and how they are chosen.

The BTI, in contrast, features a sophisticated methodology. The transparent and global index also elaborates on democracy with a part focusing on the rule

[63] For a historically informed extensive overview, see Peter F Nardulli, Buddy Peyton, and Joseph Bajjalieh, 'Conceptualizing and Measuring Rule of Law Constructs 1850–2010' (2013) 1 Journal of Law & Courts 139.

[64] For the former three, a good overview is given by Peter Thiery, Jenniver Shering, and Wolfgang Muno, 'Wie misst man Recht? Möglichkeiten und Grenzen der Messung von Rechtsstaatlichkeit, Kongressbeiträge' in Josef Estermann (ed), *Interdisziplinäre Rechtsforschung: Kongressbeiträge Wie Wirkt Recht* (Orlux 2009) 141. Concerning Freedom House, for an overview on the historical conditions of the FIW indicator, see Christopher Bradley, 'International Organizations and the Production of Indicators: The Case of Freedom House' in Sally Engle Merry, Kevin E Davis, and Benedict Kingsbury (eds), *The Quiet Power of Indicators: Measuring Governance, Corruption, and the Rule of Law* (CUP 2015) 27 concluding that 'Freedom House's production of its indicator has been motivated primarily by the benefits to reputation and institutional identity that have accrued to the organization as a result of its indicator's prominence and credibility.'

[65] The chart is based on the following literature. For the first three indices: Svend-Erik Skaaning, 'Measuring the Rule of Law' (2010) 63 Political Research Quarterly 449; Thiery, Shering, and Muno (n 64); Kaufmann, Kraay, and Mastruzzi (n 19); and the websites of the indices. For WJP RLI: Jim Parsons and others, 'Developing Indicators to Measure the Rule of Law: A Global Approach. A Report for the World Justice Project' (2008) Vera Institute of Justice; Juan Carlos Botero and Alejandro Ponce, *Measuring the Rule of Law* (2011); EU Justice Scoreboard (29 July 2024) *EC* <http://ec.europa.eu/justice/effective-justice/scoreboard/index_en.htm> accessed 24 October 2024.

Table 5.1 Overview on four internationally recognized indices on legal systems (FIW; BTI; WGI; WJP RLI)

	FIW	BTI	WGI	WJP RLI
Goals (Measured values?).[a]	Global comparative evaluation of *political rights and civil liberties.*	Evaluates and measures the steps of developing countries and countries which are steering social change toward democracy and a market economy.	Aggregate and individual governance indicators.	Measurement of the de facto rule of law, based on the people's experience, not on the legal rules.
For how long, how frequently, and in how many countries?	Yearly since 1972, 195 countries today (+15 disputed or special territories).	Since 2006 two-yearly (a pilot study in 2003), today 137 developing countries and countries in transition (ie every non-member country of the OECD in 1989, provided that the population is over 2 million)	Since 1996, and yearly since 2002, over 200 countries at the present time.	Yearly since 2011 (in 2012/13, a unified biannual report), in 140 countries.
Conceptualization	Political rights: (1) Electoral process, (2) Political pluralism and participation, (3) Functioning of Government. Civil Liberties: (1) Freedom of Expression and Belief, (2) Associational and Organizational Rights, (3) ***Rule of law:*** in common sense with somehow arbitrary elements, (4) Personal Autonomy and Individual Rights.	The final index (Status Index) is composed of a democracy (Political Transformation Index) and market economy (Economic Transformation Index) part. The Political Transformation Index is based on an explicit and philosophically elaborate democracy-concept: (1) Stateness, (2) Political participation, (3) ***Rule of law,*** (4) Stability of democratic institutions, (5) Political and Social Integration.	For the six dimensions of governance: (1) Voice and Accountability, (2) Political Stability and Absence of Violence, (3) Government Effectiveness, (4) Regulatory Quality, (5) ***Rule of law,*** (6) Control of Corruption.	Based mainly on UN-documents, the definition of the rule of law is a system relying on the following four principles: '(1) The government and its officials and agents as well as individuals and private entities are accountable under the law. (2) The laws are clear, publicized, stable, and just; are applied evenly; and protect fundamental rights, including the security of persons and property and certain core human rights. (3) The process by which the laws are enacted, administered, and enforced is accessible, fair, and efficient.

(*continued*)

Table 5.1 Continued

	FIW	BTI	WGI	WJP RLI
	There are four questions on the rule of law: (1) Is there an independent judiciary? (2) Does the rule of law prevail in civil and criminal matters? Are police under direct civilian control? (3) Is there protection from political terror, unjustified imprisonment, exile, or torture, whether by groups that support or oppose the system? Is there freedom from war and insurgencies? (4) Do laws, policies, and practices guarantee equal treatment of various segments of the population?	The four constituents of the rule of law are partially overlapping, according to the traditional legal doctrine: (1) Separation of powers, (2) Independent judiciary, (3) Prosecution of office abuse, (4) Civil rights.	'Rule of law captures perceptions of the extent to which agents have confidence in and abide by the rules of society, and in particular the quality of contract enforcement, property rights, the police, and the courts, as well as the likelihood of crime and violence.'[b] Conceptualization is questionable,[c] it is based rather on formal than substantive criteria. Measuring rule of law on the basis of 23 sources (including the partial indices—and not the main indices—of BTI, FIW, and WJP). Using 86 data units (44 of them are representative, 42 are not). 'Representative indicators are indicators that cover a set of countries in which the distribution of governance is likely to be similar to that in the world as a whole.... In contrast non-representative indicators cover either specific regions (for example the BEEPS survey of transition economies or the LatinoBarometer survey of Latin American countries), or particular income levels (for example the World Bank CPIA ratings that cover only developing countries).'[d]	(4) Justice is delivered timely by competent, ethical, and independent representatives and neutrals who are of sufficient number, have adequate resources, and reflect the makeup of the communities they serve.[e] According to the principles above, they measure 9 factors and 47 sub-factors: (1) Constraints on Government Powers, (2) Absence of Corruption, (3) Open Government, (4) Fundamental Rights, (5) Order and Security, (6) Regulatory Enforcement, (7) Civil Justice, (8) Criminal Justice, (9) Informal Justice (ie traditional, tribal, and religious courts).[f]

	FIW	BTI	WGI	WJP RLI
Selecting data	Expert opinions evaluated with points ranging from 1 to 7, a general *codebook* with the definition of the grades only, not that of the individual questions. The list of experts is not public, the selection is not transparent. Measures 27 questions in 8 groups.	Mainly based on expert opinions, with a standardized codebook. Points ranging from 1 to 10 (with separate instructions for every single question). Not only numbers but a descriptive text (two reports on a country: a foreign and a domestic report, the latter of which also comments on the former); the list of experts is public, but non-transparent. Hard data too, on inflation and education. 17 criteria with 49 questions.	Based on several hundred indicators from 32 different sources.	So-called General Population Polls: 1,000 respondents from the three largest cities of the country, selected by probability sampling. + Qualified Respondents' Questionnaires: on average, 25 legal professionals from each country. The scores from the two types of Questionnaire—when available—were weighted 50%-50%. Selecting experts: two methods: (1) Random sampling from a list of experts like law professors, attorneys, NGO professionals etc., (2) WJP network of practitioners and academics.
Methods of aggregation	Arithmetic mean.	Arithmetic mean.	Aggregation in three steps: (1) Each question is assigned to one of the six indicators, (2) Responses are rescaled between 0 and 1, 1 meaning the best outcome, (3) Constructing a weighted average using an Unobserved Components Model.	Aggregation in five steps: (1) Translating the questionnaire into numbers, (2) Raw country scores aggregated from the individuals (experts or general public), (3) Normalizing the raw data, (4) Aggregating normalized data into factors and sub-factors using simple average, (5) Final ranking of the countries.
Degree of transparency	Low but progressing (not every datum is available on the website, the sub-indices of the rule of law are also inaccessible).	High (all data used is available on the website, with the related part of the country-report).	Very elaborate calculations, but inherits the non-transparency of the sources.	High (data used is available on the website).
Strengths	(1) Data available since 1972, (2) Well-known trademark.	(1) Transparency, (2) The controlling function of the second report, (3) Better conceptualization compared to the FIW, (4) As the last step, an expert committee corrects the data regionally and globally to enable better international comparison.	(1) Elaborated mathematical model, (2) Robust as the change of a single indicator does not severely affect the whole index.	Also focuses on the perception of the rule of law in vulnerable groups, such as in low-income groups. The selection of experts is transparent.

(*continued*)

Table 5.1 Continued

	FIW	BTI	WGI	WJP RLI
Shortcomings and critiques	(1) Geometric mean would be better here than the arithmetic mean. (2) Lack of transparency as the coding below the sub-categories remains non-transparent. (3) The differences between the grades of 1-7 are unclear. (4) Lack of consistency in time: changing questions. (5) The borders between the dimensions are unclear. (6) Selection of experts is not transparent.	(1) Geometric mean would be better here than the arithmetic mean. (2) Not transparent selection criteria of the experts. (3) The Status Index implies that political and economic development are strongly correlated, which is not necessarily true—see China.	(1) Inherits the shortcomings of the original sources. (2) Favours market-economies, because of the numerous market-indicators. (3) Comparison is difficult in time and between countries as the sources are constantly changing. (4) Weak conceptualization. (5) No text, only numbers.	(1) No text, only numbers—except one paragraph interpreting the results in the last version. (2) The Constraints of the Government Powers' sub-index are centred on the presidential systems.
General evaluation of the index	*Old methodology and lack of transparency.*	*Developed methodology, transparent and global index with a part focusing on the rule of law.*	*The method minimizes the subjective elements, except for the selection of indicators; the main focus is not the rule of law.*	*Very elaborate methodology, focusing on the aspects of the rule of law.*

[a] According to Thiery, Shering, and Muno (n 64) 154, the correlation between the FIW and the BTI is very high (0.938), but the WGI correlates with the FIW and the BTI only by 0.664 and 0.663 respectively, which may indicate that the WGI is measuring something different to the other two.

[b] <https://datacatalog.worldbank.org/rule-law-estimate> accessed 24 October 2024.

[c] Especially, critically, Ginsburg (n 13) 271.

[d] Kaufmann, Kraay, and Mastruzzi (n 19) 243.

[e] 'What is the Rule of Law?' (15 July 2021) World Justice Project, <http://worldjusticeproject.org/what-rule-law> accessed 24 October 2024.

[f] They also collect data on the 9th factor (Informal Justice) but they do not take it into consideration in the aggregate index and in the ranking. These systems are especially complicated, and it is not too easy to measure comparably the efficiency and fairness in these cases. Therefore, the aggregate index is made up of 8 factors and 44 sub-factors 'only'.

of law. However, for our purpose, the index is troublesome, as it does not include Western European countries (let alone the EU itself) and thus does not provide for an EU-wide standard, which is an indispensable prerequisite in order to measure the rule of law in all EU MSs with regard to Article 2 TEU. Using the BTI would bear the danger of double standards accusation, and rightly so. Nevertheless, the improvement of the EUJS could profit from the methodology of the BTI.

Similarly, the index of the WJP is also a methodologically sophisticated project. Yet, the WJP index explicitly states that time series cannot be based on it, as the questionnaire of the index is slightly changing year by year. This is a severe limitation. Nevertheless, if an index has the limitation of providing only static information—instead of displaying evolutionary developments—we can still compare the results of the various EU MSs, and we can also compare it to static benchmarks.

A virtue of the WGI of the World Bank is that it minimizes the subjective elements, except for the selection of indicators, some of which, however, are only available for money. Yet, the main focus is not on the rule of law, and the results stem from other indices and indicators; therefore the WGI necessarily inherits the methodological problems of the original indices and indicators that it aggregates. A further problem is that the countries are given a 'percentile rank', which means that a country can easily 'improve' in the ranking if many other countries deteriorate in the actual absolute quality of the rule of law values; or the other way around: it can place lower in the ranking if many other countries actually improve their quality of the rule of law.

5. How to Develop the EUJS into an Index that Can Be Applied by the EU to Deal with Its Illiberal Regimes

5.1 The Unsuitability of Existing Indices for the Illiberal Regimes of the EU

The assessment of the existing indices above has shown that none of them is—albeit for different reasons—suitable for replacing the EUJS as it stands. While the Freedom House Index is outdated, the Bertelsman Index simply does not cover all EU MSs. The WJP's methodology changes over time and, therefore, does not allow an assessment of changes of the rule of law. The WGI are not suitable either, as some MSs' results might look deceptively improving—without an actual improvement—due to the nature of the percentile rank of this index.

Finally, a generic legitimacy problem for the EU with all mentioned indices is that they are done by external bodies. The EU should be able to set its own official standards for itself and its MSs, and not just rely on partly US-based NGOs. This NGO-objection does not apply to WGI. Before we can look into how to improve the EUJS, informed by the presented indices' strengths, we will look at the EUJS's current state of affairs.

5.2 The EUJS as It Stands

The EUJS is an initiative from the EC which was presented for the first time in March 2013.[66] Since 2013, annual reports are published on the independence, quality, and efficiency of justice systems of EU MSs.[67] For the first time, and since 2020, the EUJS also informs 'the Annual Rule of Law Report to be presented by the European Commission'.[68] Continuing this progress it is our proposal to further develop the EUJS into a rule of law index that should actually meet this new strategy[69] with a specific section devoted to judicial independence.

The data for the EUJS largely stems from the European Commission for the Efficiency of Justice (CEPEJ) of the CoE.[70] The CEPEJ was established in 2002

[66] See Conference and Speech by the EU Justice Commissioner Viviane Reding, 'The 2013 EU Justice Scoreboard, Brussels' (27 March 2013) <https://ec.europa.eu/commission/presscorner/detail/fr/SPEECH_13_271> accessed 24 October 2024.

[67] See Communication from the Commission, The EU Justice Scoreboard. A tool to promote effective justice and growth, COM(2013) 160 final. For more information and all the Scoreboards since 2013, see the website of the EC on the 'EU Justice Scoreboard' (29 July 2024) <https://ec.europa.eu/info/policies/justice-and-fundamental-rights/upholding-rule-law/eu-justice-scoreboard_en> accessed 24 October 2024. For an analysis, see Adriani Dori, 'The EU Justice Scoreboard—Judicial Evaluation as a new Governance Tool' MPILux Working Paper 22015 <http://www.mpi.lu/fileadmin/mpi/medien/persons/Dori_Adriani/The_EU_Justice_Scoreboard_-_Judicial_Evaluation_as_a_New_Governance_Tool.pdf> accessed 24 October 2024, speaking about a 'remarkable unexpressed potential' of the EUJS 'as a basis for experimenting with new governance tools in the area of EU Justice'.

[68] '2020 EU Analysis of National Justice Systems' (29 July 2024) EC <https://ec.europa.eu/info/law/better-regulation/have-your-say/initiatives/7566555-2020-EU-Justice-Scoreboard> accessed 24 October 2024.

[69] Communication from the Commission, 2020 EU Justice Scoreboard COM(2020) 306 final, containing, in the foreword, an explicit statement from Didier Reynders, the European Commissioner for Justice, that, '[o]ver the next years of the Commission's mandate, we plan to develop the Score-board further, as well as all the instruments in our rule of law toolbox'.

[70] 'European Judicial Systems, Efficiency and Quality of Justice' (2018) CEPEJ STUDIES No 26 Council of Europe <https://rm.coe.int/rapport-avec-couv-18-09-2018-en/16808def9c> accessed 24 October 2024.

and uses some 170 qualitative and quantitative indicators on the efficiency and quality of justice.[71] It is composed of forty-six experts from all CoE MSs.[72] Further, the data is received from national contact persons and a range of other sources.[73]

This plethora of sources is an issue of concern as various sources increase potential shortcomings, and a homogeneous dataset cannot be guaranteed.[74] In particular the heavy reliance on data from CEPEJ reports, which in turn bases its information on a questionnaire often answered by national correspondents within the ministries of justice, does not provide for objective data.[75] Criticism extends to the informal 'group of contact persons on national justice systems', which is an expert group of the Commission, established in 2013.[76] Also, this group comprises officials of MSs, namely one person from the judiciary and one from the Ministry of Justice. Beyond that, this group must be criticized for a lack of transparency.[77] Furthermore, the data gathered from the European Network of Councils for the Judiciary (ENCJ) depends on the basic functioning of the MSs' rule of law. The substitution of independent judges with party loyalists obviously infiltrates such national sources of data too. Finally, the lack of some data due to the reluctance of some MSs to provide the data is a serious shortcoming of the EUJS,[78] which is a consequence of the design choice to request the data from the MSs—instead of generating the data independently by using experts.

The EUJS originally had a very limited scope and was designed as a general information tool that enhances the effectiveness of MSs' justice systems. It is only since 2020 that the EUJS shall also provide information on the state of the

[71] See Communication from the Commission, The 2019 EU Justice Scoreboard, COM(2019) 198 final, at 2.

[72] Council of Europe European Commission for the Efficiency of Justice (CEPEJ), Council of Europe (29 July 2024) <https://www.coe.int/en/web/cepej/home/> accessed 24 October 2024. The Russian Federation was excluded from the CoE in an extraordinary meeting on 16 March 2022 held by the Committee of Ministers: Resolution CM/Res(2022)2 on the cessation of the membership of the Russian Federation to the Council of Europe.

[73] See The 2019 EU Justice Scoreboard (n 71) 2–3 mentioning 'the group of contact persons on national justice systems, the European Network of Councils for the Judiciary (ENCJ), the Network of the Presidents of the Supreme Judicial Courts of the EU (NPSJC), Association of the Councils of State and Supreme Administrative Jurisdictions of the EU (ACA-Europe), the European Competition Network (ECN), the Communications Committee (COCOM), the European Observatory on infringements of intellectual property rights, the Expert Group on Money Laundering and Terrorist Financing (EGMLTF), Eurostat, the European Judicial Training Network (EJTN), and the World Economic Forum (WEF)' (references omitted).

[74] See also critically Dori (n 67) 24.

[75] Dori (n 67) 25–6.

[76] See Framework for Commission Expert Groups: Horizontal Rules and Public Register, C(2010) 7649 final, SEC (2010) 1360 (10 January 2010).

[77] Dori (n 67) 30.

[78] Dori (n 67) 32.

rule of law in the EU MSs.[79] This becomes crucial as Commission President von der Leyen has also announced a new European rule of law mechanism in 2019 which requires annual reports on the state of the rule of law across the EU.[80] On 30 September 2020 the first Annual Rule of Law Report consisting of country-specific qualitative analyses was published by the EC.[81] Indeed, the aim 'to strengthen common values and the rule of law'[82] also featured very prominently as a top priority of the Finnish presidency.[83] While the EP urged the establishment of an EU mechanism for democracy, the rule of law, and fundamental rights already in June 2015,[84] it now seems that the EC understands the urgency of the situation and has initiated such a European mechanism.[85] While this Rule of Law Report consists of a country-specific qualitative analysis of the major developments in MSs, according to Didier Reynders, then European Commissioner for Justice, it shall 'benefit ... from the quantitative analysis of the Scoreboard where the reader can zoom in on national justice

[79] See in this regard only, Communication from the Commission, Further Strengthening the Rule of Law Within the Union, COM(2019) 163 final, 'The European Semester, complemented by the EU Justice Scoreboard, has proven to be a good framework to develop country-knowledge relating to rule of law and a reflection could take place on whether their potential could be further exploited.' The EP has lauded the Commission for this initiative and called to 'take this exercise forward' already, early on in: Resolution on the EU Justice Scoreboard—Civil and Administrative Justice in the Member States, EP Doc 2013/2117(INI), para 1 (4 February 2014). See also, COM(2020) 580 final (n 8) 3.

[80] See EC <https://commission.europa.eu/document/download/063d44e9-04ed-4033-acf9-639ecb187e87_en?filename=political-guidelines-next-commission_en.pdf> accessed 24 October 2024.

[81] For an overview on the Abstracts, see Rule of Law 2020, Country Reports, EC (29 July 2024) <https://ec.europa.eu/info/sites/default/files/rule_of_law_2020_country_reports_2_web.pdf> accessed 24 October 2024. See also Alexandra Brzozowski, 'Belgium, Germany Make Joint Proposal for EU Rule of Law Monitoring Mechanism' (19 March 2019) *Euractiv* <https://www.euractiv.com/section/justice-home-affairs/news/belgium-germany-make-joint-proposal-for-eu-rule-of-law-monitoring-mechanism/on> accessed 24 October 2024 (Germany and Belgium had put forward a joint proposal for such an annual rule of law peer review in all EU MSs).

[82] See Finland's Presidency of the Council of the European Union <https://valtioneuvosto.fi/documents/11707387/14346258/EU2019FI-EU-puheenjohtajakauden-ohjelma-en.pdf/3556b7f1-16df-148c-6f59-2b2816611b36/EU2019FI-EU-puheenjohtajakauden-ohjelma-en.pdf.pdf> accessed 24 October 2024.

[83] Despite the prominence of the topic, the takeover of the EU Council presidency by Slovenia has demonstrated the difficulty of addressing it. See eg David Herszenhorn and Hans von der Burchard, 'Rule of Law Disputes Cast Shadow over Opening of Slovenia's EU Council Presidency' (1 July 2021) *Politico* <https://www.politico.eu/article/rule-of-law-dispute-shadows-ceremonial-opening-of-slovenias-eu-council-presidency/> accessed 24 October 2024.

[84] As regards the EP, see EP Legislative Observatory, 'Establishment of an EU Mechanism on Democracy, the Rule of Law and Fundamental Rights' *2015/2254(INL)*; Resolution with Recommendations to the Commission on the Establishment of an EU Mechanism on Democracy, the Rule of Law and Fundamental Rights, EP Doc 2015/2254(INL) (25 October 2016); Resolution on the Need for a Comprehensive Democracy, Rule of Law and Fundamental Rights Mechanism, EP Doc 2018/2886(RSP) (14 November 2018).

[85] See Communication from the Commission, Strengthening the Rule of Law Within the Union A blueprint for Action, COM(2019) 343 final. See, however, for a critique of this Communication, Dimitry Kochenov, 'Elephants in the Room: The European Commission's 2019 Communication on the Rule of Law' (2019) 11 Hague Journal on the Rule of Law 423.

systems and information about their independence, quality and efficiency'.[86] In addition to previous editions of the EUJS, and 'in response to the current need for more comparative information for the annual Rule of Law Report and for the monitoring of the National Recovery and Resilience Plans' the Commissioner states that 'this year's [2021] edition goes further. There are new indicators on the digitalisation of justice systems, on the independence of national supreme court judges, on the autonomy of prosecution services and on the independence of lawyers and bars.'[87] Since 2023 the data of the EUJS feeds not only into the annual Rule of Law Report, but additionally to the European Semester and importantly also the Recovery and Resilience Fund.[88] In the foreword of the most recent twelfth edition of the EUJS in 2024 one reads that among the novelties of the current version is 'an overview of authorities involved in the appointment of court presidents and prosecutors, as well as updated information on the composition of national councils for the judiciary and an overview of the powers of national bodies involved in the prevention of corruption, with a specific focus on asset disclosure'.[89]

Despite this rather optimistic trend, there is still a pressing need to methodologically equip the EUJS in order to serve its important purpose. So far, the EUJS still is a rather limited tool focusing on so-called hard data without delving into a deep analysis of the context and background of the rule of law. It focuses on, for example, the 'efficiency of justice systems' by looking at the caseload and estimated length of proceedings, or the assessment of the 'quality of justice systems' by the criteria of accessibility to justice systems and adequate financial and human resources.[90] This is problematic, as thereby the EUJS misses what we described above as an essential element of the rule of law—the informal aspect of 'law in action'. Therefore, while we do not claim that all the criteria in the current EUJS are meaningless, it is nevertheless necessary that the EUJS extends its scope by *actually* measuring judicial independence and further important benchmarks of the rule of law, instead of only highlighting

[86] See Didier Reynders, European Commissioner for Justice, Foreword to The 2021 EU Justice Scoreboard, Communication from the Commission, 2021 EU Justice Scoreboard, COM(2021) 389 final.

[87] The 2021 EU Justice Scoreboard (n 86) 92.

[88] See Communication from the Commission, The 2023 EU Justice Scoreboard, Com (2024) 309, at iii; as well as Communication from the Commission, The 2024 EU Justice Scoreboard, Com (2024) 950, at iii.

[89] The 2024 EU Justice Scoreboard (n 88) iii.

[90] See Communication from the Commission, The 2020 EU Justice Scoreboard, COM (2020) 306 final, at 6 and 21; The 2021 EU Justice Scoreboard (n 86) 7 and 21.

basic features and figures of a justice system or reporting how the general public or companies perceive judicial independence.[91]

The EUJS, as it stands, only measures whether a justice system is generally *capable* of delivering justice. It does not measure, however, whether it is *actually* working as an independent judiciary. Consequently, the outcome of the EUJS for a specific MS might well be a high justice score, as the justice system is well equipped with staff and computers, despite actually not guaranteeing the rule of law due to arbitrary and biased results. Therefore, the EUJS cannot detect whether an MS actually does not want to guarantee an independent rule of law. Or to put it directly, bad justice can be very effective. And while 'the 2020 EU Justice Scoreboard shows updated indicators in relation to legal safeguards on the disciplinary proceedings regarding judges',[92] it is rather misleading to include figures on the 'perceived independence of courts and judges among the general public'[93]—particularly when thinking of biased media—instead of referring to expert opinions.[94] This verdict still holds true despite the improvements made in the EUJS 2021 referred to above by Commissioner Reynders.[95]

In addition, the focus of the EUJS does not meet the broad understanding of the rule of law report published by the Commission. While the latter acknowledges the importance of informal rules for the rule of law, the former relies on formal rules:

> The guarantees of structural independence require rules, particularly as regards the composition of the court and the appointment, length of service and grounds for abstention, rejection and dismissal of its members, in order to dispel any reasonable doubt in the minds of individuals as to the imperviousness of that court to external factors and its neutrality with respect to the interests before it.[96]

Surprisingly, the EUJS openly admits this shortcoming:

[91] Thereby our proposal is more modest than the one by Petra Bárd and others, 'An EU Mechanism on Democracy, the Rule of Law, and Fundamental Rights: Assessing the Need and Possibilities for the Establishment of an EU Scoreboard on Democracy, the Rule of Law and Fundamental Rights', EP Research Paper PE 579328, No 2016-18, which aims at a much broader surveillance tool.

[92] The 2020 EU Justice Scoreboard (n 90) 40.

[93] The 2020 EU Justice Scoreboard (n 90) 41.

[94] This, however, becomes somewhat clearer when comparing these results with the 'perceived independence of courts and judges among companies'. See The 2020 EU Justice Scoreboard (n 90) 42.

[95] The 2021 EU Justice Scoreboard (n 86) 41.

[96] The 2020 EU Justice Scoreboard (n 90) 44. See also The 2021 EU Justice Scoreboard (n 86) 43.

> The figures presented in the Scoreboard do not provide an assessment or present quantitative data on the effectiveness of the safeguards. They are not intended to reflect the complexity and details of the safeguards. Having more safeguards does not, in itself, ensure the effectiveness of a justice system.[97]

Addressing this directly, we disagree with this self-imposed limitation. This actually unnecessarily limits the performance of the EUJS for its newly found purpose of informing the Commission and other EU organs on the actual state of affairs of MSs' justice systems concerning the rule of law. Rightly, the 2020 and the 2021 EUJS state that '[u]ltimately, the effective protection of judicial independence requires a culture of integrity and impartiality, shared by magistrates and respected by the wider society'.[98] This can be depicted in a proper rule of law index. The year 2022 did not change this. Notable innovations are rather new data on the effects of the COVID-19 pandemic on the efficiency of justice systems, as well as data on the accessibility to justice for persons with disabilities. At best, the strengthening of effective justice systems for an investor-friendly business dimension could indirectly contribute to the EUJS living up to the current illiberal regime crisis.[99] How a real rule of law index can be established will be dealt with in the next section.

As the institutional shell of the EUJS already exists, it offers a chance of developing it into something more useful in the current illiberal regime crisis: a rule of law index.[100] In the current shape, the EUJS is, similarly to other actions taken by the EU in the current crisis, more a Sisyphus-like exercise, instead of a serious and reliable tool to measure the rule of law.[101] As another illustration of this rather harsh critique, we would like to point again to the 2019 EUJS

[97] The 2020 EU Justice Scoreboard (n 90) 44. See also The 2021 EU Justice Scoreboard (n 86) 43; as well as Communication from the Commission, The 2022 EU Justice Scoreboard, COM(2022) 234, 43; The 2023 EU Justice Scoreboard (n 88) 45, and The 2024 EU Justice Scoreboard (n 88) 48.

[98] The 2020 EU Justice Scoreboard (n 90) 44; The 2021 EU Justice Scoreboard (n 86) 43.

[99] The 2022 EU Justice Scoreboard (n 97) 1 and 3.

[100] With regards to democracy, the improvement of the EUJS could profit from the sophisticated *V-Dem project*, seen in Varieties of Democracy <https://www.v-dem.net/> accessed 24 October 2024.

[101] For a similar critique, see Israel Butler, 'How to Monitor the Rule of Law, Democracy and Fundamental Rights in the EU' (August 2013) Open Society European Policy Institute 2 <https://www.opensocietyfoundations.org/uploads/aad3f011-e848-4202-8c2b-2103219c31be/how-monitor-rule-law-democracy-and-fundamental-rights-eu.pdf> accessed 24 October 2024. 'These criteria tell us very little about how effectively courts uphold the rule of law in terms of keeping governments' powers in check—a vital function for which the principal criteria would include judicial independence, how easily individuals can access the courts for judicial review, and the scope of the judiciary's authority to review and remedy violations by national authorities.' See also Israel Butler, 'Enforce Respect for the Rule of Law?' (13 December 2012) *Voices*, Open Society Foundation <https://www.opensocietyfoundations.org/voices/justice-scoreboard-effective-mechanism-enforce-respect-rule-law> accessed 24 October 2024, making the critique that 'justice systems as a whole' should be monitored instead of a too narrow focus on civil and commercial courts.

which refers to '[t]he importance for Member States to ensure the independence of national courts, as a matter of EU law'.[102] However, instead of basing a lack of independence on the findings of the EUJS, the report has to refer to 'the recent case law of the Court of Justice of the European Union'.[103] In this vein, the report points for instance to the fact that 'the Court has clarified that the requirement of judicial independence also means that the disciplinary regime governing those who have the task of adjudicating in a dispute must display the necessary guarantees in order to prevent any risk of it being used as a system of political control of the content of judicial decisions'.[104] The 2020 EUJS did not change that. While the 2021 EUJS 'contains new indicators on authorities involved and status of candidates for the appointment of Supreme Court judges',[105] these new figures do not display *actual* independence of judges.[106] The 2022, the 2023, and the 2024 EUJS again introduce new indicators.[107] Despite these adaptations, the EUJS still is not an adequate tool to address the illiberal regime challenge.

5.3 The Steps Necessary to Improve the EUJS

So what should be done? How could we improve the EUJS? The best examples for our purposes are BTI and the WJP. We should therefore approximate the EUJS to those indices.

(a) As we have seen, the main advantage of the rule of law indices is that they can aggregate a list of data into a single number—or a few numbers. So far, the EUJS cannot offer a single numerical value that would inform us about the rule of law in the MSs. Viviane Reding stated that the EUJS 'is not a beauty contest.

[102] The 2019 EU Justice Scoreboard (n 71) 8.

[103] The 2019 EU Justice Scoreboard (n 71) 8.

[104] The 2019 EU Justice Scoreboard (n 71) 8, referring to ECJ, C-216/18 PPU, EU:C:2018:586 (25 July 2018) para 67). Similarly, the ongoing Article 7 TEU procedures and the rule of law framework are only mentioned in passing: The 2019 EU Justice Scoreboard (n 71) 9. See also Alexander Strelkov, 'EU Justice Scoreboard: A New Policy Tool for "Deepening" European Integration?' (2019) 27 Journal of Contemporary European Studies 15, 16 stating that the EUJS is a 'very technical instrument'. But see at 18, 'Being a "soft governance" tool, its added value lies in the provision of a systematic long-term annual overview by collecting information on aspects of national judicial systems, for example, caseload, length of court proceedings, anti-corruption measures and access to justice among disadvantaged groups. At the end, no single ranking is created but rather a comparative overview of how each national judicial system functions.'

[105] The 2021 EU Justice Scoreboard (n 86) 43. Cf similarly The 2022 EU Justice Scoreboard (n 99) 43.

[106] Cf eg The 2021 EU Justice Scoreboard (n 86) 43 and the many references on recent case law of the ECJ.

[107] The 2022 EU Justice Scoreboard (n 99) 43 new indicators concerning the structural independence of judges are '(i) authorities involved and the frequency of potential security checks on judges

It's not about ranking national justice systems.'[108] While it is true that the main purpose is not to make a ranking, without a single number the EUJS remains a half-hearted effort and, thus, merely a pretended action in the illiberal regime crisis. A ranking is just a side-effect of the overarching final numerical values—the index. It is nevertheless an essential tool. If the EUJS does not provide clear-cut figures based on a sophisticated conceptualization, for instance, journalists will do so—without a defendable concept. The 2020 rule of law report from the Commission has been scanned for how often the terms 'concern' and 'serious concerns' appeared in each country's report on a specific MS. This leads to an MS ranking.[109] It is of utmost necessity to clearly highlight if an MS does not fulfil the requirements of the rule of law—and we also need to know by how much it falls short. All MSs have the obligation to guarantee Article 2 TEU values.[110] The equality does not extend to severe shortcomings on which we must turn a blind eye just for the sake of keeping everyone happy. There is no way around this uncomfortable truth.

(b) Independent expert opinions should be the primary data source for the EUJS.[111] The obsession of EUJS with hard data, such as the length of proceedings, is a dead end. Qualities of a legal system cannot be measured based solely on hard data. It is not enough to only include surveys of the general public and companies on the independence of the judiciary—which is albeit not detrimental—in the EUJS either. In addition, especially in countries with rule of law issues, it is also questionable whether the information, hard data, provided by the respective government is reliable. To improve the EUJS significantly, it would be important to include expert opinions, similarly as in the case of all rule of law indices—the WGI is using secondary data, some of which

(Figure 56); (ii) the possibility of higher/Supreme Courts to take decisions on the consistency of case-law on their own initiative (Figure 57); and (iii) the safeguards in place relating to the temporary employment of judges/prosecutors on political posts (Figure 58)'. The 2023 EU Justice Scoreboard (n 88) 44, and The 2024 EU Justice Scoreboard (n 88) 48.

[108] Reding (n 66).

[109] See David M Herszenhorn and Lili Bayer, 'European Commissioner for Justice Didier Reynders Gives a Press Conference on the Annual Rule of Law Report 2020' (30 September 2020) *Politico* <https://www.politico.eu/article/european-commission-report-finds-many-eu-nations-hungary-poland-malta-bulgaria-falling-short-rule-of-law/> accessed 24 October 2024.

[110] This has been clearly pointed out now by the ECJ: Case C-156/21 *Hungary v European Parliament and Council of the European Union* [2022] EU:C:2022:97, para 127. Cf on Article 2 TEU case law Luke Dimitrios Spieker, *EU Values Before the Court of Justice: Foundations, Potential, Risks* (OUP 2023).

[111] But see Mila Versteeg and Tom Ginsburg, 'Measuring the Rule of Law: A Comparison of Indicators' (2016) 42 Law & Social Inquiry 100, for the point that the four rule of law indices they have analysed correlate significantly despite different methodology. While they suggest that expert opinions—and a too-small circle of experts—could be the reason, it might also be the case that several ways lead to Rome.

are based on expert opinions. As for the experts, their selection should focus on credentials that ensure independence: for example scholarly achievements, if there are no doubts about the independence of the judiciary, higher judicial position, or similar.

Many questions that we are interested in cannot be answered based on hard data, for which the EUJS seems to have a very strong preference; maybe because it wants to look 'objective'. Rule of law indices are not 'objective' in the sense that the results would emerge automatically from the data.

(i) First of all, we need to clarify what we want to measure, and to do this, we must make certain conceptual choices. These conceptual choices have to be justified. The WJP and BTI both made sophisticated conceptual choices. They clearly lay out what they mean by the 'rule of law'. This groundwork is missing for the EUJS. You can either borrow the conceptual choices from the two named indices, or you can develop a new, probably very similar, one based on the treaties, especially Article 2 TEU, further EU documents such as the Commission reports on the rule of law, and case law of the ECJ. This is not particularly complicated—as the goal is not to come to terms with the one and only perfect solution, but a working concept. It is also doable in a couple of months with a number of experts and scholars. Even the Venice Commission, or the CEPEJ, can be involved, or their past documents can be used for this purpose.[112]

Therefore, the major shortcoming of the EUJS—in contrast to the most promising methodologically designed BTI—is the following: although the EUJS has been established in the wake of the already ongoing EU illiberal regime crisis, its current objective is not appropriate for providing valid data in order to make conclusions about the true quality of the rule of law in the EU MSs. The EUJS 'focuses on litigious civil and commercial cases as well as administrative cases in order to assist Member States in their efforts to create a more investment, business and citizen-friendly environment'.[113] This does not track what is actually problematic. To put it bluntly, instead of statistically displaying the availability of computers to national courts, it would be important to measure the independence of the judiciary, not in the perception of the general public or companies, but by the assessment of independent experts,[114] or even more the quality of the rule of law writ large.

[112] 'The Rule of Law Checklist' (May 2016) Venice Commission of the Council of Europe <https://www.venice.coe.int/images/SITE%20IMAGES/Publications/Rule_of_Law_Check_List.pdf> accessed 24 October 2024.

[113] The 2019 EU Justice Scoreboard (n 71) 2.

[114] The 2019 EU Justice Scoreboard (n 71) 47 includes for the first time, 'indicators on bodies and authorities involved in disciplinary proceedings regarding judges …, and, as last year [2018], shows an

Consider this example: according to the 2019 EUJS, 'the 2018 European Semester, based on a proposal from the Commission, the Council addressed country-specific recommendations to five Member States relating to their justice system.'[115] These five MSs did not include Hungary or Poland but rather included Croatia, Italy, Cyprus, Portugal, and Slovakia.[116] This is noteworthy as the EUJS itself is meant to inform the European Semester. And indeed, this changed, as in 'the 2020 European Semester, the Council, on Commission's proposal, addressed country-specific recommendations to eight Member States relating to their justice system', namely Croatia, Italy, Cyprus, Hungary, Malta, Poland, Portugal, and Slovakia.[117]

(ii) The method of aggregation should necessarily be based on certain choices, which need to be made on the basis of conceptualization. Sometimes there are several possible ways, but one must be chosen, and reasons must be given for the choice. Again, transparency is key.

(iii) The experts that will deliver the opinions should be numerous, and they should be selected in a transparent way. The selection method of WJP is that experts, who are unpaid, are selected on a random basis from very large lists, including all members of the bar, whereas each selected expert should have the possibility of recommending new ones. The V-Dem project, specialized in measuring democracy, has a country coordinator for every country who selects experts—who are offered a small amount of payment—based on predetermined criteria. There are different ways to make the selection of experts, but in any case, this needs to be done in a transparent way.[118]

indicator on the appointment of judges-members of the Councils for the Judiciary'. Yet, the caveat immediately following this message is again disappointing:

'The figures presented in the Scoreboard do not provide an assessment or present quantitative data on the effectiveness of the safeguards. They are not intended to reflect the complexity and details of the safeguards. Having more safeguards does not, in itself, ensure the effectiveness of a justice system. It should also be noted that implementing policies and practices to promote integrity and prevent corruption within the judiciary is also essential to guarantee judicial independence. Ultimately, the effective protection of judicial independence requires a culture of integrity and impartiality, shared by magistrates and respected by the wider society.' This caveat is repeated—except for a minor grammatical correction. See The 2022 EU Justice Scoreboard (n 99) 43: 'The figures presented in the Scoreboard do not provide an assessment nor present quantitative data on the effectiveness of the safeguards....'

[115] The 2019 EU Justice Scoreboard (n 71) 6.

[116] However, rather ironically, Hungary and Poland are mentioned among those countries which have been financially supported in implementing 'certain justice reforms through the European Structural and Investment Funds (ESI Funds). Since 2007, 16 Member States have used both the European Social Fund (ESF) and the European Regional Development Fund (ERDF) to improve the effectiveness of their justice systems.' The 2019 EU Justice Scoreboard (n 71) 7.

[117] The 2020 EU Justice Scoreboard (n 92) 5, n 18.

[118] We can call such experts the 'Copenhagen Commission', an expression coined by Jan-Werner Müller, 'A Democracy Commission of One's Own, or What it Would Take for the EU to Safeguard Liberal Democracy in its Member States' in András Jakab and Dimitry Kochenov (eds), *The*

(c) Moreover, it is necessary to include the EU itself in the analysis of the EUJS. We have seen in Chapter 3 that it is the erosion of the rule of law and democracy at EU level which hinders the EU in dealing with its illiberal regimes. A very first step towards tackling this problem is to establish a concise method of analysing the problem. This is to include the EU itself in the analysis done by the improved EUJS. This would, first, enable a clear and honest analysis of the situation of the rule of law at EU level. Second, it would enhance the legitimacy of the EU to analyse the actual state of the art of the rule of law in its MSs.

(d) Last but not least, it is not only the rule of law which erodes in EU MSs and to some extent in the EU itself, but also democracy has a hard time. Elections might still be free also in illiberal EU MSs, but they surely are not fair anymore.[119] The EU itself was confronted for a long time with discussion about its alleged democratic deficit. While this is a complex debate, it probably is fair to say that the EU is far from being a democratic model student. There are democracy indices similar to the rule of law indices presented here. Some aspects important for a democracy are even included in some of the analysed indices. However, democracy is too important to be measured as being part of the rule of law only. What would be necessary is to have a sober and as objective as possible index which measures democracy in all EU MSs and the EU itself. The V-Dem project could be an important source of inspiration. However, currently there is no rule of law or democracy index which includes the EU itself as a subject of its analysis.[120] Yet, here again, it would be advisable to construct an index of its own in order to not rely on external data and analysis.

6. Conclusion

It is important to acknowledge that quantifiable findings in themselves cannot provide the basis for automatic action.[121] Instead, the results need to help

Enforcement of EU Law and Values: Ensuring Member States' Compliance (OUP 2017) 234. In Müller's proposal, the Copenhagen Commission, however, would deliver qualitative doctrinal analysis, similar to the Venice Commission.

[119] See Chapter 2.

[120] Even though the V-Dem project enables the illustration of certain trends focusing on the EU, there are no separate surveys for the EU. The values for the EU which are visible in the newest V-Dem database are simply the arithmetic mean of the variable in question of all EU MSs.

[121] As opposed, for example, to constitutional deficit brakes or debt brakes. It is an open question even whether in these areas this automatism is appropriate or not. See András Jakab, 'Sustainability in European Constitutional Law: From Constitutional Challenges and Innovations for Future

prudent doctrinal analysis by providing weights to violations of the rule of law requirements. An improved EUJS could also play a more central role in the political discourse, helping in agenda-setting, and it could pressure recalcitrant MSs and those politicians from other countries who try to defend the indefensible for reasons of party alliances.[122] It could help to determine whether a 'serious and persistent' breach of the rule of law exists according to Article 7 (2) TEU and help courts in finding whether 'general or systemic deficiencies' in the rule of law of an MS are present.[123]

Reliable data can also inform the 'Regulation on a general regime of conditionality for the protection of the Union budget' which was adopted on 16 December 2020.[124] For instance, the principle of a proportionate financial measure enshrined in the new EU rule of law mechanism could be informed by an improved EUJS drawing on rule of law indices. Thereby, the sensitive matter of determining the amount could be supported also by quantitative data. This is important, because the EC will face high political pressure when acting under the new rule of law mechanism. Having the possibility to rely on an improved EUJS, which presents clear data on rule of law breaches in EU MSs based on independent expert opinions, would significantly strengthen the position

Generations' in Marie-Claire Cordonier Segger, Marcel Szabó, and Alexandra R Harrington (eds), *Intergenerational Justice in Sustainable Development Treaty Implementation: Advancing Future Generations Rights through National Institutions* (CUP 2021) 166. In any case, we do not suggest any 'legal automatism'.

122 See precisely for this argument—albeit with reference to a 'democracy scoreboard'—Ulrich Sedelmeier, 'Political Safeguards against Democratic Backsliding in the EU: The Limits of Material Sanctions and the Scope of Social Pressure' (2017) 24 Journal of European Public Policy 337. For proposals to consider already existing indexes for decision-making (but including also a qualitative analysis each time), see Laurent Pech, 'Rule of Law as Guiding Principle of the European Union's External Action' (2012) Centre for Law of EU External Relations Working Paper 2012/3 <http://www.asser.nl/media/1632/cleer2012-3web.pdf> accessed 24 October 2024; Laurent Pech, 'The EU as a Global Rule of Law Promoter' (2016) 14 Asia Europe Journal 7.

123 See Case C-216/18 PPU, *LM* [2018] EU:C:2018:586, para 23, which is also known as *Celmer*, due to the non-anonymized names of the relevant parties in the Irish proceeding *Minister for Justice & Equal v Celmer* [2018] IEHC 119. For a doctrinal analysis of 'systemic deficiency' see the latest Armin von Bogdandy, 'Principles of a Systemic Deficiencies Doctrine: How to Protect Checks and Balances in the Member States' (2020) 57 Common Market Law Review 705, esp 715. For further similar doctrinal suggestions, see, generally, Armin von Bogdandy and Michael Ioannidis, 'Systemic Deficiency in the Rule of Law: What It Is, What Has Been Done, What Can Be Done' (2014) 51 Common Market Law Review 59, and referring to the gravity or the 'systemic' nature of violations, which are, in our view, difficult to establish without quantitative measures, see Armin von Bogdandy and others, 'Reverse Solange—Protecting the Essence of Fundamental Rights against Member States' (2012) 49 Common Market Law Review 489; Iris Canor, 'My Brother's Keeper? Horizontal Solange: "An Ever Closer Distrust among the Peoples of Europe"' (2013) 50 Common Market Law Review 383.

124 See Regulation (EU, Euratom) 2020/2092 of the European Parliament and of the Council of 16 December 2020 on a general regime of conditionality for the protection of the Union budget [2020] OJ L 433I.

of the EC against charges of politically motivated action.[125] That this is important is generally acknowledged by the EUJS. The 2022 EUJS, for instance, explains that the EUJS feeds into the European Semester at least '[w]here the shortcomings identified have macroeconomic significance'.[126] In this realm, according to the 2022 EUJS 'the European Semester analysis may lead to the Commission's proposing to the Council to adopt country-specific recommendations to improve the national justice systems in individual Member States'.[127] Furthermore, the 2022 EUJS hints at the possibility that according to Article 19 (3) (b) and Article 24 (3) and (5) of Regulation (EU) 2021/241, the EUJS might be of relevance for the huge amounts (more than 670 billion Euros in loans and non-repayable financial support) made available through the RRF as an answer to the consequences of the corona pandemic:

> As '[p]ayments to Member States under the performance-based RRF are contingent on the fulfilment of milestones and targets … the Commission therefore has to continuously assess whether the Member States' recovery and resilience plans (RRPs) are implemented satisfactorily in order to contribute to effectively addressing all or a significant number of challenges identified in the relevant country-specific recommendations or challenges identified in other relevant Commission documents adopted in the context of the European Semester.'

Indeed, the data of the 2023 and the 2024 EUJS feed into the RRF. Yet, a significantly improved EUJS would provide considerably better information.

Proper measurement of the rule of law at the EU level is necessary because arguably all current governments of EU MSs will claim that they actually follow the rule of law standards in their respective countries. This, however, is dubious, to say the least. The EU itself too does not face its deficiencies. An EU-wide index can provide for very valuable and largely neutral, or at least

[125] See already András Jakab and Lando Kirchmair, 'How to Quantify a Proportionate Financial Punishment in the New EU Rule of Law Mechanism?' (22 December 2020) *Verfassungsblog* <https://verfassungsblog.de/how-to-quantify-a-proportionate-financial-punishment-in-the-new-eu-rule-of-law-mechanism/> accessed 24 October 2024.

[126] The 2022 EU Justice Scoreboard (n 99) 3.

[127] The 2022 EU Justice Scoreboard (n 99) 3. Cf the reference in footnote 19 stating that 'In the context of the European Semester, the Council, on the basis of the Commission's proposal, addressed country-specific recommendations on their justice systems to seven Member States in 2019 (HR, IT, CY, HU, MT, PT and SK) and eight Member States in 2020 (HR, IT, CY, HU, MT, PL, PT and SK). The Commission also monitors judicial reforms in BG and RO under the Cooperation and Verification Mechanism. There were no country-specific recommendations in 2021 due to the ongoing RRF processes.'

with respect to the EU MSs, comparable data on such claims. Therefore, an improved index would not just be 'useful' or 'helpful' in order to offer additional arguments for triggering certain enforcement tools such as a potential *reverse solange* by the ECJ or the conditionality regulation by the Commission.[128] More importantly, it would make inaction by EU organs, which has been a key problem in the illiberal regime crisis, politically more costly: it would become more difficult for members of the European Council not to act in Article 7 procedures, and it would be politically more embarrassing for the EC not to launch infringement procedures even if formally the move would stay in the Commission's discretion. In order for the EUJS to accomplish such a task, the above-suggested improvements are necessary.

[128] See on this Chapter 6.

6

Completing the European Fundamental Rights Union

Applying the Charter of Fundamental Rights to Purely Domestic Cases

1. Introduction

In this chapter we want to explore whether there is a way to structurally strengthen the rule of law in all MSs. A key aim is to find a way according to which systemic breaches of the rule of law in all MSs, and particularly in illiberal MSs, can be stopped and prevented. So far, as we have seen in Chapter 2, the EU is apparently unable to sufficiently protect the value of the rule of law. A strong protection of the rule of law is, however, necessary in order to stop the mutual poisoning of illiberal and liberal MSs and the EU itself. A solid protection of the rule of law is moreover a question of credibility. The EU simply has the duty to defend the rule of law within the EU—especially the values enshrined in Article 2 TEU.[1] The tension between the EU's lack of enforcement capacity on the one hand, and the (implicit) legal obligation to strengthen the rule of law common to all MSs on the other, will guide this chapter.

The majority of the methods available for the enforcement of the values contained in Article 2 TEU are based on political discretion (exclusion of the political party concerned from its European party family; Article 7 TEU, initiation of infringement proceedings by the Commission; the new rule of law mechanism) and therefore contribute, if at all, only to a limited extent and thus not sufficiently to securing the values mentioned.[2] European politicians,

[1] See Case C-156/21 *Hungary v European Parliament and Council of the European Union* [2022] EU:C:2022:97, para 127; see also Christophe Hillion, 'Overseeing the Rule of Law in the EU: Legal Mandate and Means' in Carlos Closa and Dimitry Kochenov (eds), *Reinforcing Rule of Law Oversight in the European Union* (CUP 2016) 59.

[2] The question as to how to improve democratic accountability at the EU and thus also the political will to contribute significantly to the enforcement of Article 2 TEU values will be the central focus of Chapter 7.

Saving the European Union from Its Illiberal Member States. András Jakab and Lando Kirchmair, Oxford University Press. © András Jakab and Lando Kirchmair 2025.
DOI: 10.1093/oso/9780198954606.003.0007

or rather politicians of EU MSs, find it difficult or are unwilling to intervene decisively. Often opportunistic considerations take hold, and conflicts are ignored or at least played down. Other issues, such as economic ones, seem to be more urgent than the admittedly elusive questions of constitutionalism and its dismantling in one of the MSs. However, we must also expect European politicians to believe in the fundamental values of the EU (Article 2 TEU) and—if necessary—to defend them. 'Fundamental values cannot be compromised.'[3] And yet they are compromised to such an extent that one can seriously question whether these values will be complied with in all MSs without supranational support.[4]

A mechanism that places value enforcement in the hands of politicians is a useful mechanism, but is not sufficient in itself. The potential of legal mechanisms is different from that of political ones. They are not accused of having an ideological agenda—or at least not to the extent that political processes are accused of having one—in spite of the recently inflated rhetoric of Polish politicians who have even (note the irony given the subsequent war of aggression of Russia against Ukraine) fantasized that the Commission would risk Third World War as an accusation against EU institutions engaging in the illiberal regime crisis if it did not greenlight the Polish recovery plan.[5] Judicially guaranteed mechanisms represent the most trustworthy mechanisms for enabling those who are affected to enforce these values. Recently the EC has confronted illiberalism in Hungary by making significant amounts of financial support conditional on improvements in the rule of law. This is an important step in the right direction. Yet, this has been compromised by the release of significant parts of it, largely unrelated to the rule of law concerns at the heart of the conditionality. Even if it had not been the case, this alone would not be sufficient. That the EC seems to be treating Poland differently is already an important indicator that it is not the mistreatment of the rule of law, or at least not primarily the rule of law, which concerns the EC.[6] And even if this were the case it is simply not enough to withhold money and blackmail the compliance

[3] Editorial Comments, 'Clear and Present Danger: Poland, the Rule of Law & Primacy' (2021) 58 Common Market Law Review 1635, 1648.

[4] See Bojan Bugarič, 'Protecting Democracy inside the EU' in Carlos Closa and Dimitry Kochenov (eds), *Reinforcing Rule of Law Oversight in the European Union* (CUP 2016) 82; Christoph Möllers and Linda Schneider, *Demokratiesicherung in der Europäischen Union* (Mohr Siebeck 2018); Lando Kirchmair, 'Demokratische Legitimität, die EU-Rechtsstaatlichkeitskrise und Vorüberlegungen zu einer transnationalen Gewaltengliederung' (2019) 6 Zeitschrift für praktische Philosophie 171.

[5] See Piotr Macej Kaczyński, 'Polish PM Says Commission Risks "World War III"' (26 October 2021) *Euractiv* <https://www.euractiv.com/section/politics/short_news/polish-pm-says-commission-risks-world-war-iii/> accessed 24 October 2024.

[6] Cf the action brought on 29 October 2021 by the EP against the EC. However, this action was discontinued by the EP on 18 May 2022 (C-657/21).

with core elements of the rule of law. As we have learned from Chapter 2, the troublesome ground for many violations of the rule of law is deeply embedded in post-socialist culture and the mere request to install formally adequate laws is not enough. De facto practices and narratives, however, are far more difficult to change than formal laws. Withholding funds is important, and can be very relevant for instance in draining the corruption swamp; however, structural tools to guide the way back to a rule of law culture are desperately needed too. In this chapter we submit that judicial rule of law enforcement mechanisms should be strengthened. This is what completing the Fundamental Rights Union is about. Moreover, we will see that achieving this completion is surprisingly simple.

2. The Illiberal Regime Crisis as a Problem and the Complete Fundamental Rights Union as a Response

The achievements of modern constitutionalism can be seen in several ways. For the purposes of our contribution, we understand them here as answers to societal challenges.[7] Consequently, ideas such as the need to base fundamental rights interventions not only on a legal basis, but also on a proportionality test, can be explained as answers to societal challenges that have developed over the years.[8]

In line with Arnold Toynbee, we regularly see societies facing new challenges for which they try to find the right solutions.[9] By challenge, we refer to a new

[7] See also Paul Kirchhof, 'Der Antwortcharakter der Verfassung' in Michael Anderheiden and others (eds), *Gedächtnisschrift für Winfried Brugger* (Mohr Siebeck 2013) 450. See for a different understanding of the 'answer character of the constitution' in Austrian constitutional law scholarship, András Jakab, 'Verfassungsrechtliche Argumentation' in András Jakab (ed), *Methoden und theoretische Grundfragen des österreichischen Verfassungsrechts* (Verlag Österreich 2021) 214.

[8] Richard A Posner, *The Problematics of Moral and Legal Theory* (The Belknap Press of Harvard University Press 1999) 17 ff. In relation to the given example, Michael Thaler, *Grundlagen und Entwicklung von Verfassungs- und Verwaltungsrecht: Strukturprobleme zum Vergleich Österreich—Frankreich—Großbritannien—USA* (5th edn, Facultas 2020) 45 ff.

[9] Arnold Toynbee, *A Study of History, Vol. 1* (OUP 1934) 271. Although some aspects of Toynbee's work (especially the role of religion, the relationship between civilizations, or certain historical details) have been rightly criticized, his basic model of challenge and response seems to fit the historical facts. For a recent review of Toynbee's work, see Marvin Perry, *Arnold Toynbee and the Western Tradition* (Peter Lang 1996) esp 103–28. A good introduction to his work is provided by CT McIntire and Marvin Perry, 'Toynbee's Achievement' in CT McIntire and Marvin Perry (eds), *Toynbee: Reappraisals* (University of Toronto Press 1989) 3–5. For classic literature and some of his methodological essays, see Ashley Montagu (ed), *Toynbee and History: Critical Essays and Reviews* (Porter Sargent 1956).

circumstance or problem that requires a new method for its resolution.[10] This can take many forms, for example through new inventions or the introduction of new ideas to deal with particular social (order) problems. Seen in this light, the idea of the rule of law could be understood as answering to absolutism.[11] Over time, various definitions of the rule of law have developed.[12] The one key element that has never been questioned is the restriction or combating of the arbitrary use of state power.[13]

In the following, we will argue in favour of a specific judicial enforcement of the rule of law against MSs in which governments have been hijacked by groups working to dismantle the rule of law.[14] We will argue that in order to overcome the crisis of the rule of law, an essential step would be to enable persons in affected MSs to invoke the application of the EU CFR whenever a violation of Article 2 TEU values in MSs provides ground for fundamental rights violations and thus the scope of protection is applicable;[15] in other words, even if the restriction of the scope of protection occurs exclusively through national measures. In this way, individuals could independently counter the erosion of the rule of law. While the traditional interpretation of Article 51 (1) CFR had a balanced division of competence between the EU and its MSs in mind, the disregard of Article 2 TEU values in some MSs provides for the application of the *clausula rebus sic stantibus*: the delicate federal balance of a full fundamental

[10] On such constitutional ideas that previous constitution makers wanted to avoid, see András Sajó, *Limiting Government: An Introduction to Constitutionalism* (Central European University Press 1999) 1 ff.

[11] For more details see András Jakab, 'Breaching Constitutional Law on Moral Grounds in the Fight against Terrorism: Implied Presuppositions and Proposed Solutions in the Discourse on "the Rule of Law vs. Terrorism"' (2011) 9 International Journal of Constitutional Law 58; András Jakab, *European Constitutional Language* (CUP 2016).

[12] Rule of law is often used in an expanded sense, which includes the political ideology of the respective speaker or judge, cf Joseph Raz, 'The Rule of Law and Its Virtue' in Joseph Raz (ed), *The Authority of Law: Essays on Law and Morality* (Clarendon Press 1979) 210.

[13] In the United States, this abuse means abuse of particular interests instead of the aggregated interest of all citizens, see Christoph Möllers, *Die drei Gewalten* (Velbrück Wissenschaft 2008) 29–35. In France the abuse was a danger from the monarchical executive. The US legislature is conceived as representing lobbies or other particular interests, as opposed to France, where the legislature is the people's voice. See Möllers, Die drei Gewalten, 32, 35. For an understanding of the rule of law as the opposite of arbitrariness, see Martin Krygier, 'The Rule of Law: Legality, Teleology, Sociology' in Gianluigi Palombella and Neil Walker (eds), *Relocating the Rule of Law* (Bloomsbury 2009) 45. Brian Z Tamanaha, 'A Concise Guide to the Rule of Law' in Gianluigi Palombella and Neil Walker (eds), *Relocating the Rule of Law* (Bloomsbury 2009) 3, 7–8, understands it as a restriction of government discretion.

[14] For an overview of the possible responses of constitutional law in general and the relationship between democracy and the rule of law in particular, see András Jakab, 'What Can Constitutional Law Do against the Erosion of Democracy and the Rule of Law? On the Interconnectedness of the Protection of Democracy and the Rule of Law' (2020) 6 Constitutional Studies 5.

[15] We do not think that this is the only (magical) way to address this crisis. Hence there are other important steps that would not be rendered meaningless even if the approach advanced here were successful. See eg Chapter 4.

rights protection can only be upheld if both ends stick to the original promise. If this standard is violated in an MS, the EU must close the *lacunae* in order to provide for a sufficient fundamental rights union in Europe.

This is what we mean when we speak of a complete European fundamental rights union. In most cases, the buzzwords 'fundamental rights community' ('*Grundrechtsgemeinschaft*' in German)[16] or 'fundamental rights union' ('*Grundrechtsunion*' in German)[17] express nothing more (but also nothing less) than that the EU is 'more than just a huge economic area'.[18] Common to this understanding is that fundamental rights simultaneously protect individuals from arbitrary exercise of state power and represent 'the expression of a common European conviction of fundamental rights, a European value system'.[19] While the ECJ in its case law initially defined the concepts of legal community ('*Rechtsgemeinschaft*' in German)[20] and now the legal union ('*Rechtsunion*' in German),[21] in this chapter we understand the concept of a

[16] Cf G Hirsch, 'Die Europäische Union als Grundrechtsgemeinschaft' in Rodriguez Iglesias and others (eds), *Mélanges en hommage à Fernand Schockweiler* (Nomos 1999) 177, 187; Christoph Grabenwarter, 'Auf dem Weg in die Grundrechtsgemeinschaft?' (2004) 31 Europäische Grundrechte-Zeitschrift 563, 564, arguing for a favourable position on an understanding of the term 'implementation' in Article II-51 (1) Treaty establishing a Constitution for Europe (TCE), which also affirms the application of Community fundamental rights when acts of the MSs have been adopted in order to restrict a fundamental freedom. Cf for a discussion of this with further references to case law, Dieter Scheuing, 'Zur Grundrechtsbindung der EU-Mitgliedstaaten' (2005) 40 Europarecht 162; cf also for a general use of the term 'fundamental rights community' ('*Grundrechtsgemeinschaft*'), Markus Kotzur, 'Eine Bewährungsprobe für die Europäische Grundrechtsgemeinschaft: Zur Entscheidung des EuG in der Rs. Yusuf u.a. gegen Rat, Europäische Grundrechtezeitschrift 2005, S. 592 ff' (2006) 33 Europäische-Grundrechte Zeitschrift 19, 25; however, see also Markus Kotzur, 'Der Schutz personenbezogener Daten in der europäischen Grundrechtsgemeinschaft: Die korrespondierende Verantwortung von EuGH, EGMR und mitgliedstaatlichen Verfassungsgerichten' (2011) 38 Europäische Grundrechte-Zeitschrift 105, 110, 114, speaking of a constitution of community fundamental rights ('*gemeineuropäischen Grundrechtsverfassung*'), that comprises the fundamental rights of the MSs, the European Convention on Human Rights (ECHR), and the CFR.

[17] Thorsten Kingreen, 'Grundrechtsverbund oder Grundrechtsunion? Zur Entwicklung der subjektiv-öffentlichen Rechte im europäischen Unionsrecht' (2010) 45 Europarecht 338, 354 (discussing the judgments *Mangold* and *Maruko*) understands by the term fundamental rights union that the EU sets its own fundamental rights standards. Cf Stefan Griller, 'Vom Diskriminierungsverbot zur Grundrechtsgemeinschaft? Oder: Von der ungebrochenen Rechtsfortbildungskraft des EuGH' in Metin Akyürek, Dietmar Jahnel, and Gerhard Baumgartner (eds), *Staat und Recht in europäischer Perspektive: Festschrift Heinz Schäffer* (Manz 2006) 203, for an—albeit critical—similar use of the term 'fundamental rights community detention' ('*Grundrechtsgemeinschaft*') as here.

[18] Philipp Terhechte, *Konstitutionalisierung und Normativität der europäischen Grundrechte* (Mohr Siebeck 2011) 1.

[19] Terhechte (n 18) 3, with further reference to Thomas Schmitz, 'Die Charta der Grundrechte der Europäischen Union als Konkretisierung der gemeinsamen europäischen Werte' in Dieter Blumenwitz, Dietrich Murswiek, and Gilbert H Gornig (eds), *Die Europäische Union als Wertegemeinschaft* (Duncker & Humblot 2005) 73; cf Christian Calliess, 'Europa als Wertegemeinschaft—Integration und Identität durch europäisches Verfassungsrecht?' (2004) 59 JuristenZeitung 1033.

[20] Case 294/83, *Parti écologiste 'Les Verts' v European Parliament* [1986] EU:C:1986:166, para 23.

[21] Case C-64/16 *Associação Sindical dos Juízes Portugueses v Tribunal de Contas* [2018] EU:C:2018:117, para 31.

complete fundamental rights union as the realization of unrestricted, so-called 'free fundamental rights', that is, fundamental rights that apply equally to all citizens of the Union also in purely national constellations if this is necessary due to a violation of Article 2 TEU values at the national level.[22]

3. The Scope of Application of the Charter of Fundamental Rights: Article 51 (1) CFR and the Prevailing Doctrine

Article 51 (1) CFR is a central provision—the 'keystone', so to speak—of the CFR.[23] It standardizes its scope of application and restricts it vis-à-vis the MSs. It applies to them, according to the wording of the norm, '*only* when they are implementing Union law'.

Essentially, and quite briefly, three variants of interpretation of Article 51 (1) CFR can be distinguished:

A literal and rather restrictive approach presupposes the actual existence of Union law in the area in question ('implementation') in order to invoke the application of the Charter.[24] Such a restrictive understanding of Article 51 (1) CFR, which would limit the application of the fundamental rights of the Union exclusively to this kind of 'implementation' of Union law, does not only seem to contradict the underlying philosophy of the Charter,[25] but is also more restrictive than the case law of the ECJ on the applicability of fundamental rights (conceived as general principles of law) before the entry into force of the

[22] Kingreen (n 17) 354.

[23] Koen Lenaerts, 'Exploring the Limits of the EU Charter of Fundamental Rights' (2012) 8 European Constitutional Law Review 375, 377. According to Piet Eeckhout, 'The EU Charter of Fundamental Rights and the Federal Question' (2002) 39 Common Market Law Review 945, 954, it is paradoxical to have a general Charter of Fundamental Rights with a limited scope of application.

[24] Steve Peers, 'The Rebirth of the EU's Charter of Fundamental Rights' (2013) 13 Cambridge Yearbook of European Legal Studies 283, 298; Thomas von Danwitz and Katherina Paraschas, 'A Fresh Start for the Charter: Fundamental Questions on the Application of the European Charter of Fundamental Rights' (2017) 35 Fordham International Law Journal 1396, 1409; Peter Huber, 'Unitarisierung durch Gemeinschaftsgrundrechte—Zur Überprüfungsbedürftigkeit der ERT-Rechtsprechung' (2008) 43 Europarecht 190, 196; Martin Borowsky, 'Artikel 51—Anwendungsbereich' in Jürgen Meyer (ed), *Charta der Grundrechte der Europäischen Union* (3rd edn, Nomos 2011) 653–54; Zsófia Varga, 'Az Alapjogi Charta alkalmazási köre I' (2013) Európai Jog 17, 19 with further references. See also Paul Yowell, 'The Justiciability of the Charter of Fundamental Rights in the Domestic Law of Member States' in Peter Huber (ed), *The EU and National Constitutional Law* (Boorberg 2012) 114 ff.

[25] See Ricardo A García, 'The General Provisions of the Charter of Fundamental Rights of the European Union' (2002) Jean Monnet Working Paper 5 <www.jeanmonnetprogram.org/archive/papers/02/020401.pdf> accessed 24 October 2024.

CFR.[26] This scepticism towards this restrictive interpretation is also fuelled by a look at the explanations to the CFR:[27]

> As regards the Member States, it follows unambiguously from the case law of the Court of Justice that the requirement to respect fundamental rights defined in a Union context is only binding on the Member States when they act in the scope of Union law (judgment of 13 July 1989, Case 5/88 Wachauf [1989] ECR 2609; judgment of 18 June 1991, ERT [1991] ECR I-2925); judgment of 18 December 1997 (C-309/96 Annibaldi [1997] ECR I-7493). The Court of Justice confirmed this case law in the following terms: 'In addition, it should be remembered that the requirements flowing from the protection of fundamental rights in the Community legal order are also binding on Member States when they implement Community rules ...' (judgment of 13 April 2000, Case C-292/97, [2000] ECR 2737, paragraph 37 of the grounds). Of course this rule, as enshrined in this Charter, applies to the central authorities as well as to regional or local bodies, and to public organisations, when they are implementing Union law.

This interpretation is therefore not only contrary to the previous case law of the ECJ (as cited above in the explanations), but also contradicts the Charter itself, since Article 53 CFR explicitly states that the Charter may not lead to a lower level of protection of fundamental rights (than that guaranteed in particular by 'Union law', the ECHR, and the constitutions of the MSs).[28] If this

[26] For a detailed comparison with the preceding case law, cf Xavier Groussot, Laurent Pech, and Gunnar Petursson, 'The Scope of Application of Fundamental Rights on Member States' Action: In Search of Certainty in EU Adjudication' (2011) Eric Stein Working Paper <www.era-comm.eu/charter_of_fundamental_rights/kiosk/pdf/EU_Adjudication.pdf> accessed 24 October 2024. On the history of the various drafts of the CFR, see Gráinne de Búrca, 'The Drafting of the European Union Charter of Fundamental Rights' (2001) 7 European Law Review 126.

[27] Explanations relating to the Charter of Fundamental Rights [2007] OJ C 303/17. For a critical assessment of the rather confusing explanations, cf Leonard Besselink, 'The Member States, the National Constitutions and the Scope of the Charter' (2001) 8 Maastricht Journal of European and Comparative Law 68, 76–78. Groussot, Pech, and Petursson (n 26) 19 denounce the explanations on Article 51 CFR as a mixture of different formulas (originally: 'a mixture of various formulas').

[28] Carsten Nowak, 'Grundrechtsberechtigte und Grundrechtsadressaten' in Sebastian Heselhaus and Carsten Nowak (eds), *Handbuch der Europäischen Grundrechte* (Helbing & Lichtenhahn, CH Beck, and LexisNexis 2006) 244–45.

interpretation were to be accepted,[29] it would lead to a reduced level of fundamental rights protection than was the case before the adoption of the Charter.[30]

In *Åkerberg Fransson*[31] the ECJ rebuked voices that advocated for the previously described restrictive interpretation of Article 51 (1) CFR.[32] This judgment clarified the scope of application of the Charter through interpretation and adopted the widely held view in the literature:

> Since the fundamental rights guaranteed by the Charter must therefore be complied with where national legislation falls within the scope of European Union law, situations cannot exist which are covered in that way by European Union law without those fundamental rights being applicable. The applicability of European Union law entails applicability of the fundamental rights guaranteed by the Charter.[33]

A similar, albeit—depending on the interpretation—somewhat more generous view was also previously held by AG Eleanor Sharpston in *Ruiz Zambrano*:

> Transparency and clarity require that one be able to identify with certainty what 'the scope of Union law' means for the purposes of EU fundamental rights protection. It seems to me that, in the long run, the clearest rule would be one that made the availability of EU fundamental rights protection dependent neither on whether a Treaty provision was directly

[29] Eeckhout (n 23) 993; Heidi Kaila, 'The Scope of Application of the Charter of Fundamental Rights of the European Union in the Member States' in Pascal Cardonnel, Allan Rosas, and Nils Wahl (eds), *Constitutionalising the EU Judicial System* (Bloomsbury 2012); Juliane Kokott and Christoph Sobotta, 'The Charter of Fundamental Rights of the European Union after Lisbon' (2010) EUI Working Paper 7.

[30] See for an analysis of the ECJ case law on Article 51 (1) CFR before *Åkerberg Fransson*, which comes to the conclusion that the Court of Justice until then—albeit with brief and sometimes misleading justifications—had essentially already wanted to follow up its case law on the binding force of fundamental Union rights in the form of principles on the MSs, Benedikt Pirker, *Grundrechtsschutz im Unionsrecht zwischen Subsidiarität und Integration* (Nomos 2018) 335 ff, esp 339.

[31] Case C-617/10 *Åklagaren v Hans Åkerberg Fransson* [2013] EU:C:2013:105.

[32] Filippo Fontanelli, '*Hic Sunt Nationes*: The Elusive Limits of the EU Charter and the German Constitutional Watchdog' (2013) 9 European Constitutional Law Review 315; Angela Ward, 'Article 51—Scope' in Steve Peers and others (eds), *The EU Charter of Fundamental Rights: A Commentary* (2nd edn, CH Beck, Hart and Nomos 2021) 1578–81. On the tension between the broad *Åkerberg Fransson* doctrine and the strict approach of the German Federal Constitutional Court, cf Daniel Thym, 'Separation versus Fusion—or: How to Accommodate National Autonomy and the Charter? Diverging Visions of the German Constitutional Court and the European Court of Justice' (2013) 9 European Constitutional Law Review 391.

[33] Case C-617/10 *Åklagaren v Hans Åkerberg Fransson* [2013] EU:C:2013:105, para 21; interestingly, this statement was introduced with a reference to the wording of Article 51 (1) CFR (para 17: 'implementing European Union law') and a confirmation of the previous case law (para 18), which had stated that the CFR would be applicable 'in all situations governed by European Union law' (para 19). For a detailed analysis, see Pirker (n 30) 339 ff.

> applicable nor on whether secondary legislation had been enacted, but rather on *the existence and scope of a material EU competence.* To put the point another way: the rule would be that, provided that the EU had competence (whether exclusive or shared) in a particular area of law, EU fundamental rights should protect the citizen of the EU *even if such competence has not yet been exercised.*[34]

Also in the sense of this interpretation, the prevailing idea is that the application of the Charter was only given when there was a connection to the 'scope of Union law' (*Åkerberg Fransson*) or a 'material Union competence' (AG Sharpston in *Ruiz Zambrano*).[35] This means that the application of the Charter continues to be seen as a safety net and its rights are not seen as 'freestanding rights'.[36] Subsequently, the ECJ—in a slightly weakened form compared to the opinion of AG Sharpston in *Ruiz Zambrano* quoted above—made a further clarification, which means that

> the concept of 'implementing Union law', as referred to in Article 51 of the Charter, presupposes a degree of connection between the measure of EU law and the national measure at issue which goes beyond the matters covered being closely related or one of those matters having an indirect impact on the other.[37]

Thus, there must be a 'a certain degree of connection above and beyond the matters covered' between the MSs' measure and a rule of European law for the Charter to be applicable. In the case law of the ECJ, a certain degree of

[34] Opinion of AG Eleanor Sharpston Case C-34/09 *Gerardo Ruiz Zambrano v Office national de l'emploi (ONEm)* [2010] EU:C:2010:560, para 163. Critical, Michael Dougan, 'Judicial Review of Member State Action under the General Principles and the Charter: Defining the "Scope of Union Law"' (2015) 52 Common Market Law Review 1201, 1226–29.

[35] On the different definitions of the concept of 'scope of application of EU law', cf Sacha Prechal, Sybe de Vries, and Hanneke van Eijken, 'The Principle of Attributed Powers and the "Scope of EU Law"' in Leonard Besselink, Frans Pennings, and Sacha Prechal (eds), *The Eclipse of the Legality Principle in the European Union* (Kluwer 2011) 213; Eeckhout (n 23) 993; Opinion of AG Eleanor Sharpston Case C-34/09 *Gerardo Ruiz Zambrano v Office national de l'emploi (ONEm)* [2010] EU:C:2010:560, para 173.

[36] See Groussot, Pech, and Petursson (n 26) 22 with further references.

[37] Case C-198/13 *Víctor Manuel Julian Hernández and Others v Reino de España (Subdelegación del Gobierno de España en Alicante) and Others* [2014] EU:C:2014:2055, para 34.

connection means more than merely an indirect connection, as just cited.[38] The prevailing opinion in the literature probably also agrees with this.[39]

4. Two Ways of Completing the Fundamental Rights Union

4.1 Pursuing a Treaty Revision

A straightforward way to complete the fundamental rights union would be a treaty revision, which amends Article 51 (1) and discharges Article 51 (2) CFR.[40] The current German government, for instance, seems to be fond

[38] *Åkerberg Fransson* to a certain extent also confirming Case C-206/13 *Cruciano Siragusa v Regione Sicilia—Soprintendenza Beni Culturali e Ambientali di Palermo* [2014] EU:C:2014:126, para 24; see also the concretizing statement in Case C-198/13 *Víctor Manuel Julian Hernández and Others v Reino de España (Subdelegación del Gobierno de España en Alicante) and Others* [2014] EU:C:2014:2055, para 35, 'that fundamental European-Union rights could not be applied in relation to national legislation because the provisions of EU law in the area concerned did not impose any specific obligation on Member States with regard to the situation at issue in the main proceedings'. Cf also the overview of the case law in Claas F Germelmann and Jörg Gundel, 'Die Entwicklung der EuGH-Rechtsprechung zum europäischen Verfassungs- und Verwaltungsrecht im Jahr 2020' (2021) Bayerische Verwaltungsblätter 583, 589, eg with further reference to the order in Case C-32/20 *TJ v Balga Srl* [2020] EU:C:2020:441, para 26. In Case C-66/18 *European Commission v Hungary* [2020] EU:C:2020:792, para 213, the ECJ has also held that MSs also implement Union law when they fulfil obligations under international agreements (in this case the General Agreement on Trade in Services) that are also part of Union law. This also applies to measures taken by MSs that restrict fundamental freedoms (para 214 with further references). To be sure, the case law is complex and diverse. See eg furthermore Joined Cases C-609/17 and C-610/17 *Terveys- ja sosiaalialan neuvottelujärjestö (TSN) ry v Hyvinvointialan liitto ry and Auto- ja Kuljetusalan Työntekijäliitto AKT ry v Satamaoperaattorit ry* [2019] EU:C:2019:981 and the analysis provided by Maxime Tecqmenne, 'Minimum Harmonisation and Fundamental Rights: A Test-Case for the Identification of the Scope of EU Law in Situations Involving National Discretion?' (2020) 16 European Constitutional Law Review 493, 505, summarizing 'that the relationship between the national and EU standards of fundamental rights protection is structured along the lines of the distribution of powers between the EU and its member states in that policy area'. For yet another overview categorizing the case law, see Ward (n 32) 1576 ff.

[39] Hans Jarass, 'Artikel 51' in Hans Jarass (ed), *GRCh: Charta der Grundrechte der Europäischen Union* (4th edn, CH Beck 2021) para 24; cf Martin Borowsky, 'Artikel 51—Anwendungsbereich' in Jürgen Meyer (ed), *Charta der Grundrechte der Europäischen Union* (4th edn, Nomos 2014) 758–60; Emily Hancox, 'The Meaning of "Implementing" EU Law under Article 51(1) of the Charter: *Åkerberg Fransson*' (2013) 50 Common Market Law Review 1411, 1418–27; Filippo Fontanelli, 'National Measures and the Application of the EU Charter of Fundamental Rights—Does curia.eu Know iura.eu?' (2014) 14 Human Rights Law Review 231, 263 ff. For a comprehensive and comparative law analysis, see also Pirker (n 30) 488 ff.

[40] See generally Opinion of AG Eleanor Sharpston Case C-34/09 *Gerardo Ruiz Zambrano v Office national de l'emploi (ONEm)* [2010] EU:C:2010:560, paras 163–73 on the requirement of treaty change for her suggestion presented above. Even though Article 48 TEU speaks only of 'the treaties', this includes any primary EU law, hence also the Charter. See in this vein, Marcus Klamert, 'Article 48 TEU' in Manuel Kellerbauer, Marcus Klamert, and Jonathan Tomkin (eds), *The EU Treaties and Charter of Fundamental Rights: A Commentary* (OUP 2019) para 5; Daniel-Erasmus Khan, 'Artikel 48 EVU'

of such an endeavour when it explicitly states in its coalition contract: 'We want the rights under the EU Charter of Fundamental Rights to be enforceable before the ECJ in future even if a Member State acts within the scope of its national law.'[41] A possible new formulation of Article 51 CFR could be the following: 'The provisions of this Charter are addressed to the institutions, bodies, offices and agencies of the Union with due regard for the principle of subsidiarity and to the MSs as far as necessary for the enforcement of the values enshrined in Article 2 of the Treaty on European Union.' This would clearly express the purpose of the amendment and would also conform to the principle of subsidiarity.

Treaty revisions, however, can be long-winded affairs.[42] Hence, while a reform, to be safe in this case according to an ordinary revision procedure (Article 48 TEU), would bring the benefit of an unquestionable methodological status, it provides no relief in the short or mid-term future. It is also questionable why illiberal MSs would be ready to ratify such an amendment, and for a successful amendment the consent of all MSs is necessary.

We are, however, of the opinion that there is also an alternative way to proceed. As Joseph Weiler convincingly demonstrated some thirty-five years ago when reconstructing the legal history of the European integration: whenever the political channels are under blockade, the ECJ is in the best position to give the necessary push to the process, sometimes with activist moves in its case law.[43] We think that we are exactly in such a situation.

4.2 A Different Take on Interpreting Article 51 (1) CFR

We want therefore to reflect here on whether the interpretation referred to above is set in stone or whether the emergence of a further development of

in Rudolf Geiger and others (eds), *EUV/AEUV: Vertrag über die Europäische Union. Vertrag über die Arbeitsweise der Europäischen Union. Kommentar* (7th edn, CH Beck 2023) para 2.

[41] Koalitionsvertrag zwischen SPD, Bündnis 90/Die Grünen und FDP, 'Mehr Fortschritt wagen. Bündnis für Freiheit, Gerechtigkeit und Nachhaltigkeit', p 132 <https://www.spd.de/fileadmin/Dokumente/Koalitionsvertrag/Koalitionsvertrag_2021-2025.pdf> accessed 24 October 2024 (in German: 'Wir wollen, dass die Rechte aus der EU-Grundrechtecharta vor dem EuGH künftig auch dann eingeklagt werden können, wenn ein Mitgliedstaat im Anwendungsbereich seines nationalen Rechts handelt').

[42] Carlos Closa, *The Politics of Ratification of EU Treaties* (Routledge 2013).

[43] Joseph HH Weiler, 'The Transformation of Europe' (1991) 100 Yale Law Journal 2403.

the interpretation of Article 51 (1) CFR is possible.[44] The further development we have in mind aims to ensure that the 'implementation of Union law' is not understood formalistically, but rather factually. Contrary to initial intuition, there are also possibilities to justify such an interpretation in legal terms. It has already been argued that Union citizenship must include a final guarantee of fundamental rights in cases of *systemic* failure in an MS.[45] This was pointedly depicted in the image of a reversed *solange* jurisprudence. However, it is explicitly outside the scope of Article 51 CFR.[46]

Even though this approach built upon a different doctrinal basis than our suggestion, it is important to address some of the criticism this approach has met insofar as this pertains to the broader picture rather than the doctrinal basis:

(a) It would throw the baby out with the bathwater and stigmatize the 'affected' MSs. Thereby it would also contradict the principle of loyalty according to Article 4 (3) TEU, instead of concentrating on the actual protection of fundamental rights.
(b) A systemic failure of the protection of fundamental rights would in turn require procedures for its protection, the establishment of which necessarily presupposes a decision by a political body. This, however, places the protection of fundamental rights at the mercy of politics.[47]
(c) The use of the *solange* formula, in turn, is seen as a potentially face-saving excuse for inaction.[48] To avoid these objections, we will sketch

[44] See Dougan (n 34) 1210, generally stating in relation to the interpretation of Article 51 (1) CFR that 'the wider the Court's definition (of the scope of Union law), the more compelling we are entitled to expect its justification to be'.

[45] For a first formulation of this idea in the context of the free movement of persons, cf the Opinion of AG Poiares Maduro Case C-380/05 *Centro Europa 7 Srl v Ministero delle Comunicazioni e Autorità per le garanzie nelle comunicazioni und Direzione generale per le concessioni e le autorizzazioni del Ministero delle Comunicazioni* [2007] EU:C:2007:505, paras 20 ff.

[46] Armin von Bogdandy and others, 'Reverse *Solange*—Protecting the Essence of Fundamental Rights against EU Member States' (2012) 49 Common Market Law Review 489. The concept had previously been used in a similar way, albeit with a focus on EU citizenship, by Daniel Halberstam, 'Constitutional Heterarchy: The Centrality of Conflict in the European Union and the United States' in Jeffrey L Dunoff and Joel P Trachtman (eds), *Ruling the World? Constitutionalism, International Law, and Global Governance* (CUP 2009) 326. For an update, see Armin von Bogdandy and Luke Spieker, 'Countering the Judicial Silencing of Critics: Article 2 TEU Values, Reverse Solange, and the Responsibilities of National Judges' (2019) 15 European Constitutional Law Review 391; Armin von Bogdandy and Luke Spieker, 'Protecting Fundamental Rights beyond the Charter: Repositioning the Reverse Solange Doctrine in Light of the CJEU's Article 2 TEU Case Law' in Michal Bobek and Jeremias Adams-Prassl (eds), *The EU Charter of Fundamental Rights in the Member States* (Hart 2020) 525.

[47] For a detailed explanation of the approach and the different procedures, see Armin von Bogdandy and Michael Ioannidis, 'Systemic Deficiency in the Rule of Law: What It Is, What Has Been Done, What Can Be Done' (2014) 51 Common Market Law Review 59.

[48] Dimitry Kochenov, 'On Policing Article 2 TEU Compliance—Reverse Solange and Systemic Infringements Analyzed XXXIII' (2014) Polish Yearbook of International Law 145, 156.

a different approach here:[49] an approach which, through a reinterpretation, would elevate the Charter to a genuine and fully fledged fundamental rights document in the EU if at the national level the fundamental rights protection is hampered due to violations of Article 2 TEU.[50] We make the case for a reinterpretation of Article 51 (1) CFR that ensures the application of the Charter in such cases which thus completes the European fundamental rights union.

5. For a Reinterpretation of Article 51 (1) CFR

If we strive for a fully-fledged community of values from which all citizens would equally benefit, then the Charter should in any case (ie also in purely domestic cases) be fully valid at the domestic level and be applied by national courts—even if there is no systemic failure of fundamental rights protection but 'only' a violation of an Article 2 TEU value. Accordingly, Union fundamental rights protection would still depend on a certain degree of connection between the activity of the MSs and a norm of Union law; however, we understand this connection in such a way that no reduction in fundamental rights protection should occur due to specific competences. In other words, all MSs must always respect the fundamental rights of the CFR and cannot rely on an exclusive competence of an MS to justify a violation of fundamental rights.[51] The certain degree of connection criterion would on the one hand be based on the fact that the EU has ubiquitous influence far beyond its competences. For example, subsidies do not only have an impact in the EU's area of competence. In Poland or Hungary, the dismantling of the rule of law is financed with EU taxpayers' money.[52] It is therefore short-sighted if the certain degree of connection is seen in a formalistic way only 'in all situations governed by EU law but not outside such situations'.[53] With this formalistic understanding of 'implementation', the ECJ 'has no power to examine the compatibility with

[49] This approach is a further development of András Jakab, 'Application of the EU CFR by National Courts in Purely Domestic Cases' in András Jakab and Dimitry Kochenov (eds), *The Enforcement of EU Law and Values: Ensuring Member States' Compliance* (OUP 2017) 252.

[50] It seems that after Opinion 2/13 of the ECJ, the ECHR will not become the 'Bill of Rights' of the EU. Cf Editorial Comments, 'The EU's Accession to the ECHR—a "NO" from the ECJ!' (2015) 52 Common Market Law Review 1.

[51] Jarass (n 39) para 20 refers in this regard to the exclusion of this intended effect in Case C-617/10 *Åklagaren v Hans Åkerberg Fransson* [2013] EU:C:2013:105, para 22, to avoid a circular argument.

[52] See R Daniel Kelemen, 'The European Union's Authoritarian Equilibrium' (2020) 27 Journal of European Public Policy 481.

[53] Case C-390/12 *Robert Pfleger and Others* [2014] EU:C:2014:281, para 33.

the Charter of national legislation lying outside the scope of EU law'.[54] On the other hand, the degree of connection would be established if an MS violates a core value on which the EU is based. By including any violation without the necessity of a systemic deficiency, respect for the principle of equality was ensured. Thereby specific MSs are not stigmatized, but any MS which violates core EU values faces the application of the CFR. Furthermore this would not depend on a political evaluation of the situation, for instance, in the realm of the Article 7 TEU procedure, but would work according to judicial standards.

This means that a comprehensive fundamental rights-based judicial supervisory authority would be introduced throughout Europe. The type of judicial control envisaged would be decentralized in the sense of being exercised by the national courts, which—similar to the case law of the ECtHR—would have a margin of appreciation, whereby compliance with the core of fundamental rights would be monitored by the ECJ. However, their uniform application would be guaranteed by the preliminary ruling procedure.[55] One could therefore also call a protection of fundamental rights understood in this way semi-centralized judicial control.

Such an approach would enable the EU to become a complete fundamental rights union in which no one would be left behind. In this vein, no citizen would be excluded from the community of values due to violations of fundamental rights by an MS in purely national constellations. This would be of no small significance, since fundamental violations of basic rights in Europe are a frightening and at the same time unacceptable denial of the European community of values. The citizens of the MS excluded from the protection of fundamental rights are thus left behind with all the associated consequences, while the rest of Europe saves itself.

Standing up for these citizens is especially important when fundamental rights violations are enshrined in MS constitutions in an almost sacrilegious manner and constitutional courts are staffed with party loyalists who do not care about constitutional arguments and values. Ordinary courts would have the advantage that there are many of them in each country; the personnel is therefore more difficult to replace in terms of party politics and only over a longer period of time. Therefore it would be a great advantage if a single ordinary judge could ask the ECJ for help in the form of a preliminary ruling if

[54] Case C-390/12 *Robert Pfleger and Others* [2014] EU:C:2014:281, para 33.

[55] Thus, even in the case of hijacked MS supreme courts, lower courts would be allowed to submit preliminary references; and supreme courts would have to submit preliminary references in terms of the Cilfit doctrine (Case 283/81 *Srl CILFIT and Lanificio di Gavardo SpA v Ministry of Health* [1982] EU:C:1982:335; cf Case C-561/19 *Consorzio Italian Management and Catania Multiservizi SpA v Rete Ferroviaria Italiana SpA* [2021] EU:C:2021:799).

Union fundamental rights are in some way unjustifiably restricted by national measures.

In the following subsections, we address possible objections, some of which concern efficiency (including alternative ways to better protect fundamental rights) and some of which concern (doctrinal) reasoning.

5.1 Articles 2 and 7 TEU (and to Some Extent also Union Citizenship or the Right to an Effective Remedy) Would Support a Generous Understanding of the 'Certain Degree of Connection' Formula Understood as an Unrestricted Application of Article 51 (1) CFR

The interpretation put forward here contradicts the literal meaning of Article 51 (1) CFR, its current interpretation by the ECJ, and the majority of the literature.[56] Consequently, it is necessary to present some solid arguments in support of it. There seem to be three parallel ways to justify such a broad interpretation of the scope of the Charter: (a) the use of the concept of citizenship of the Union; (b) taking Article 47 CFR seriously; and (c) the use of Articles 2 and 7 TEU as connecting factors. Although these justifications are not mutually exclusive, we believe that the final option has most potential.

Union citizenship is generally seen as a set of rights[57] and, as an 'autonomous' legal status, also seems to replace the requirement of cross-border reference,[58] as the application of EU law is also affirmed in cases without a cross-border element and has evolved to protect citizens from their own MSs.[59] A further step in the same direction would be to state that Union

[56] Cf eg Angelika Schwerdtfeger, 'Art. 51 GRCh' in Jürgen Meyer and Sven Hölscheidt (eds), *Charta der Grundrechte der Europäischen Union* (5th edn, Nomos 2019) para 36; Groussot, Pech, and Petursson (n 26) 23: 'it is simply wrong to affirm that natural and legal persons, following the entry into force of the Lisbon Treaty, have gained the right to institute judicial proceedings on the basis of any provision of the Charter, in any situation, against any national (or EU) public authorities'.

[57] Gianluigi Palombella, 'Whose Europe? After the Constitution: A Goal-Based Citizenship' (2005) 3 International Journal of Constitutional Law 357, 377–82.

[58] Peter van Elsuwege, 'Shifting the Boundaries? European Union Citizenship and the Scope of Application of EU Law' (2011) Legal Issues of Economic Integration 263, analysing Case C-34/09 *Gerardo Ruiz Zambrano v Office national de l'emploi (ONEm)* [2011] EU:C:2011:124. See also the Opinion of advocate general Poiares Maduro Case C-135/08 *Janko Rottman v Freistaat Bayern* [2009] EU:C:2009:588, para 23.

[59] Dimitry Kochenov, 'The Essence of EU Citizenship Emerging from the Last Ten Years of Academic Debate: Beyond the Cherry Blossoms and the Moon?' (2013) 62 International & Comparative Law Quarterly 37, 135.

citizenship triggers the application of the Charter.[60] This approach, however, differs greatly from the traditional approach, which considers the scope of the Charter as a delimited *ratione materiae*.[61]

The right to an effective remedy enshrined in Article 47 CFR has a long tradition in EU law and is accepted as general principle of EU law 'which underlies the constitutional traditions common to the Member States'.[62] It pre-dates the CFR and has an accessory nature. Enforcing compliance with fundamental rights necessitates an effective remedy.[63] This logic might lead to a reinterpretation of the limits of competence, allowing those limits to expand as part of an 'inherent' fundamental rights logic within the Charter. Hence, if a fundamental right of the Charter is violated by an MS, and no effective remedy is provided in that MS, Article 47 CFR could be interpreted to trump a traditional reading of Article 51 (1) CFR—at least in cases of blatant fundamental rights violations. The reason against such a self-standing application of Article 47 CFR is similar to the reason mentioned before in relation to the first approach. Article 47 CFR in conjunction with, for instance, Article 19 (1) TEU as applied by the ECJ, might, however, be a much stronger approach.[64]

Another way to justify the broad application while maintaining the *ratione materiae* requirement would be to invoke Article 7 TEU.[65] Article 7 TEU provides that a special procedure may be initiated in the event of a 'serious and persistent breach' of the fundamental values set out in Article 2 TEU, which also includes respect for human rights. The early warning procedure of

[60] Sara Iglesias Sánchez, 'Fundamental Rights and Citizenship of the Union at a Crossroads: A Promising Alliance or a Dangerous Liaison?' (2014) 20 European Law Journal 464, arguing for an extension of the scope of the Charter to address the problem of reverse discrimination. But see Felix Schulyok, 'The Scope of Application of EU Citizenship and EU Fundamental Rights in Wholly Internal Situations' (2012) Europarättslig Tijdskrift 448. Cf also Stefan Griller, 'Unionsbürgerschaft als grundlegender Status' in Werner Schroeder and Walter Obwexer (eds), *20 Jahre Unionsbürgerscahft: Konzept, Inhalt und Weiterentwicklung des grundlegenden Status der Unionsbürger* (EuR-Beiheft 1/2015) 8, esp 25, calling this a small step for the ECJ but a big one for the Union.

[61] Marek Safjan, 'Areas of Application of the Charter of Fundamental Rights of the European Union: Fields of Conflict?' (2012) EUI Working Papers—Law, 2 <http://cadmus.eui.eu/bitstream/handle/1814/23294/LAW-2012-22.pdf> accessed 24 October 2024. On the dilemma, see Filippo Fontanelli, 'The European Union's Charter of Fundamental Rights Two Years Later' (2011) Perspectives on Federalism 22, 40 ff.

[62] See *Marguerite Johnston v Chief Constable of the Royal Ulster Constabulary*, 222/84, EU:C:1986:206, para 18, in relation to measures of MSs. Cf Tobias Lock and Denis Martin, 'Article 47' in Manuel Kellerbauer, Marcus Klamert, and Jonathan Tomkin (eds), *The EU Treaties and Charter of Fundamental Rights: A Commentary* (OUP 2019) para 2.

[63] Case 222/84 *Marguerite Johnston v Chief Constable of the Royal Ulster Constabulary* [1986] EU:C:1986:206, para 14.

[64] See for further details text at n 89 below.

[65] For a convincing argument in favour of this variant, see Armin von Bogdandy, 'Grundrechtsgemeinschaft als Integrationsziel?' (2002) 56 JuristenZeitung 157, 158.

Article 7 TEU regarding the determination of a 'clear risk of a serious breach' of Article 2 TEU values has so far been applied against both Poland (2017)[66] and Hungary (2018)[67] but without any bite. However, if we take the formula developed in *Åkerberg Fransson* and subsequent case law,[68] then—with reference to Article 2 in conjunction with Article 7 TEU—the application of Article 51 (1) CFR would basically be triggered in the case of any violation of fundamental rights.[69]

5.2 A Reinterpretation of Article 51 (1) CFR Is Inefficient

The solution described above could be objected to in terms of its efficiency from two opposing directions. The first objection would concern the fear that if the protection of fundamental rights were to be placed in the hands of the courts of the MSs, this may not be an effective way to protect fundamental rights, as local courts may not be sufficiently trained or may simply be corrupt.[70] While this is a legitimate concern, it applies to the whole essence of the preliminary reference mechanism, which is considered one of the key mechanisms for the success of the ECJ and EU law in general.[71] While the gatekeeping role of national courts could make the reinterpretation less than perfect, we nevertheless think that through this *additional* means many individuals would

[66] The European Commission has for the first time identified a 'clear risk of a serious breach of the rule of law' due to the 'judicial reform' in Poland and therefore made a proposal to initiate proceedings on 20 December 2017 (COM (2017) 0835 final—2017/0360).

[67] European Parliament resolution of 12 September 2018 on a proposal calling on the Council to determine, pursuant to Article 7(1) of the Treaty on European Union, the existence of a clear risk of a serious breach by Hungary of the values on which the Union is founded (2017/2131(INL)) [2019] OJ C 433, p 66—by 448 votes in favour, 197 against, and 48 abstentions—to declare that there is a risk of a violation of Article 2 TEU values in Hungary. On the legality of not taking into account abstentions for the purpose of achieving the two-thirds majority pursuant to Article 354 TFEU, see Case C-650/18 *Hungary v European Parliament* [2021] EU:C:2021:426.

[68] Case C-198/13 *Víctor Manuel Julian Hernández and Others v Reino de España (Subdelegación del Gobierno de España en Alicante) and Others* [2014] EU:C:2014:2055. On the fact that *Åkerberg Fransson* represents the end of the possibility of being able to refer only to national points of view with fundamental rights, cf Daniel Sarmiento, 'Who's Afraid of the Charter? The Court of Justice, National Courts and the New Framework of Fundamental Rights Protection in Europe' (2013) 50 Common Market Law Review 1267, 1303.

[69] See Allan Rosas, 'When Is the EU Charter of Fundamental Rights Applicable at National Level?' (2012) 19 Jurisprudencija: Mokslo darbu žurnalas 1269, 1282. The author rejected this for practical reasons (high workload) (at 1285).

[70] Carlos Closa, Dimitry Kochenov, and Joseph HH Weiler, 'Reinforcing Rule of Law Oversight in the European Union' (2014) EUI Working Papers RSCAS 17, 21 <http://cadmus.eui.eu/bitstream/handle/1814/30117/RSCAS_2014_25_FINAL.pdf?sequence=3> accessed 24 October 2024.

[71] For a classic position, see Karen Alter, 'The European Court's Political Power' (1996) 19 West European Politics 458.

be empowered, and at least some courts and some judges would actually make use of this possibility. As long as there are at least some independent judges (which is typically the situation in illiberal regimes), this additional option would be helpful.

The second objection relates to concerns that the ECJ would not be able to cope with an increased workload, which would probably occur if an unrestricted application of Article 51 (1) CFR were to be accepted.[72] This is also a justified concern, not only in the context of the topic under discussion. Nevertheless, it would be wrong to reject fundamental rights cases because the ECJ is overloaded with (other) cases. This is simply not a legal argument and should be of little weight, especially when Article 2 TEU values are at risk. Furthermore, just as in all cases when EU law is applied, the bulk of the work would be done by national judges and not by the ECJ.

In addition, even in those MSs in which we have witnessed a violation of Article 2 TEU values, not all fundamental rights are violated constantly. We suggest the application of only those CFR fundamental rights that in the concrete situations are necessary for the protection of Article 2 TEU values—that is, solely as a subsidiary solution.

5.3 MS Conflicts against the Background of the CFR

When the EU takes action, it is often seen as an indicator that there are multiple conflicts between the interests and values of the EU and those of the MSs. However, an application of the CFR as proposed here would be different from most proposals to address fundamental rights problems in MSs.[73] In the context of what is being presented here, the conflict would arise between a government of an MS and a court of an MS. The ECJ would only intervene indirectly through the preliminary reference procedure. It is therefore unlikely (though not impossible) that such situations would be defamed as a fight against the Brussels bureaucracy.[74]

[72] Rosas (n 69) 1285; Eike M Frenzel, 'Die Charta der Grundrechte als Maßstab für Mitgliedstaatliches Handeln zwischen Effektivierung und Hyperintegration' (2014) 53 Der Staat 1, 26.

[73] See eg the proposal for a Copenhagen Commission: Jan-Werner Müller, 'Safeguarding Democracy Inside the EU—Brussels and the Future of Liberal Order, 2012–2013' (2013) Transatlantic Academy Paper Series <www.transatlanticacademy.org/sites/default/files/publications/Muller_Safeguarding Democracy_Feb13_web.pdf> accessed 24 October 2024.

[74] For a formal sanction mechanism (systemic infringement procedures), see Kim Lane Scheppele, 'Enforcing the Basic Principles of EU Law through Systemic Infringement Actions' in Carlos Closa and Dimitry Kochenov (eds), *Reinforcing Rule of Law Oversight in the European Union* (CUP 2016) 105.

5.4 Creeping Assumption of Competence

Critical voices could argue that the suggested interpretation is not covered by the typical methods of legal interpretation as it contradicts the explicit wording of Article 51 (2) CFR stating that '[t]he Charter does not extend the field of application of Union law beyond the powers of the Union'.[75] Some hold, in addition, that the rationale of Article 51 (1) CFR is that all instances when MSs act as 'agents' of Union law shall be comprised by EU fundamental rights.[76] However, instead of a fixation on a grammatical interpretation of what is covered by the word 'implementation', a teleological reading along the lines of the *effet utile* principle must take into account not only the historical intention of the drafters of this provision, but also the changed circumstances since then. Similarly, like the *clausula rebus sic stantibus*, the blatant disregard for fundamental values of EU law enshrined in Article 2 TEU, including fundamental rights violations in EU MSs these days, destabilizes the entire Union legal order. For instance, a purely national violation of the fundamental rights of free media and free elections impacts the autonomy of the EU legal order as national politicians become also European politicians and actors that undermine the liberal values of Article 2 TEU. Hence, a teleological reading of the term 'implementation' in Article 51 (1) TEU ensures the unrestricted application of European fundamental rights in order to safeguard the unhampered implementation of EU law.[77]

Another obvious objection is that, according to Article 6 TEU and Article 51 (1) CFR, the Charter should not be used to extend the competences of the EU.[78] However, if both Article 6 TEU and Article 51 (2) CFR are interpreted in the light of Article 2 TEU, this limitation cannot affect the judicial enforcement of the Charter. Furthermore, the principle of subsidiarity (also mentioned in

[75] For an overview of critical voices of the ECJ's dynamic approach to legal interpretation generally, see Thomas Horsley, 'Reflections on the Role of the Court of Justice as the "Motor" of European Integration: Legal Limits to Judicial Lawmaking' (2013) 50 Common Market Law Review 931, 937 ff. For the clear qualification that '[t]he Charter does not apply to MS activities expressly excluded from the scope of EU law', see Tobias Lock, 'Article 51' in Manuel Kellerbauer, Marcus Klamert, and Jonathan Tomkin (eds), *The EU Treaties and Charter of Fundamental Rights: A Commentary* (OUP 2019) para 8.

[76] See Filippo Fontanelli, 'Implementation of EU Law through Domestic Measures after *Fransson*: The Court of Justice Buys Time and "Non-preclusion" Troubles Loom Large' (2014) 39 European Law Review 682, 684.

[77] While being sceptical about an ideologically driven harmonization of EU fundamental rights, Eleanor Spaventa, 'Should We "Harmonize" Fundamental Rights in the EU? Some Reflections about Minimum Standards and Fundamental Rights Protection in the EU Composite Constitutional System' (2018) 55 Common Market Law Review 997, 1022, also understands them as a 'safety net'.

[78] On this phenomenon in general and with regard to the Charter in particular, see Sacha Prechal, 'Competence Creep and General Principles of Law' (2010) 3 REALaw 5, 16–20.

Article 51 CFR) is only applicable with regard to legislative competence and therefore has no impact on judicial authorities.[79] Thus we would be a further step in the direction of federalization.[80] However, this would not be the actual justification, but rather a side-effect (or a price we should be prepared to pay) of the reinterpretation of Article 51 (1) CFR outlined here.

It must be admitted, however, that the new interpretation of Article 51 (1) CFR would probably fail due to the Polish 'opt-out' in Protocol No 30 concerning Poland. Article 1 of this protocol reads as follows:

> 1. The Charter does not extend the ability of the Court of Justice of the European Union, or any court or tribunal of Poland or of the United Kingdom, to find that the laws, regulations or administrative provisions, practices or action of Poland or of the United Kingdom are inconsistent with the fundamental rights, freedoms and principles that it reaffirms.
>
> 2. In particular, and for the avoidance of doubt, nothing in Title IV of the Charter creates justiciable rights applicable to Poland or the United Kingdom except in so far as Poland or the United Kingdom has provided for such rights in its national law.

While interpretations of the meaning of this Protocol vary, and some have argued that this Protocol would be purely declaratory in nature and would have no legal added value with regard to the regulatory content of Article 51 CFR, these voices would probably not agree to an extension of our interpretation of Article 51 (1) CFR to the Protocol as well. Even if one were to follow our argumentation on the reinterpretation of Article 51 (1) CFR, the explicitly expressed idea with regard to Poland is clear: the CFR should have no effect for purely domestic Polish cases. Conversely, the fact of this opt-out shows that the potential for interpretation that we are arguing here has also been seen in Article 51 (1) CFR before. What remains, in any case, is a clear discrepancy

[79] Groussot, Pech, and Petursson (n 27) 23.

[80] See Aida Torres Pérez, 'The Federalizing Force of the EU Charter of Fundamental Rights' (2017) 15 International Journal of Constitutional Law 1080, 1087, stating that 'marking the boundaries of the Charter is at the core of constitutional bargaining over EU federalism'. For concerns based on US experience, see Allard Knook, 'The Court, the Charter, and the Vertical Division of Powers in the European Union' (2005) 42 Common Market Law Review 367, 374–79. For a comparative perspective, see Mauro Cappelletti, *The Judicial Process in Comparative Perspective* (Clarendon Press 1989) 395: 'There is hardly anything that has greater potential to foster integration than a common bill of rights, as the constitutional history of the United States has proved.' See also, for the centrifugal force of whatever Bill of Rights, Luis María Díez-Picazo, 'Notes sur la nouvelle Charte des Droits fondamentaux de l'Union européenne' (2001) Rivista italiana di diritto pubblico comunitario 665, 674.

with the values in Article 2 TEU, which Poland agreed to uphold by ratifying the Treaties. The recorded Polish opt-out is thus virtually a historical argument for the legal possibility of our reinterpretation (for other MSs than Poland).

6. What the ECJ Has Already Done

The history of the ECJ is marked by activism, in which decisions were taken that—to say the least—were not directly apparent from the text of the Treaty.[81] How did the Court get away with it? What common features can be derived from these progressive decisions?

(a) The arguments used in these cases were mostly teleological in nature, based either on the main purpose of European integration or on the purpose of specific regulations/institutions. The same would apply to the interpretation of Article 51 (1) CFR sketched here: the protection of fundamental rights is intended as a value under Article 2 TEU.

(b) Institutionally, it was usually the EC that initially adopted a certain position, which was then followed by the ECJ.[82] In our case, this would be the Commission's explicitly stated aim to abolish the limits of Article 51 (1) CFR. This has already actually happened: Viviane Reding, then Commissioner for Justice, Fundamental Rights and Citizenship, explicitly proposed this in her speech in Tallinn.[83]

(c) The third factor that makes dynamic decisions more likely is a malfunctioning legislative body.[84] This is also an obvious tick in the box: we see only the pretext of real action, for example in the form of the so-called rule of law framework[85] or the Annual Rule of Law Report[86]—the necessary majority of MSs is still missing.

(d) A common method of developing jurisdiction is to establish it but not claim it, or to use it in a way that does not conflict with a government.

[81] See eg Karen Alter, *Establishing the Supremacy of European Law: The Making of an International Rule of Law in Europe* (OUP 2001).

[82] Eric Stein, 'Lawyers, Judges, and the Making of a Transnational Constitution' (1981) 75 American Journal of International Law 1.

[83] Viviane Reding, 'Observations on the EU Charter of Fundamental Rights and the Future of the European Union' (31 May 2012) Speech/12/403 FIDE Congress in Tallin <http://europa.eu/rapid/press-release_SPEECH-12-403_en.pdf> accessed 24 October 2024, although she wanted to achieve this goal by formally amending the contract.

[84] Weiler (n 43).

[85] See Communication from the Commission, A new EU framework to strengthen the rule of law, COM(2014) 158 final/2.

[86] For the first version, see Communication from the Commission, 2020 Rule of Law Report: The rule of law situation in the European Union, COM(2020) 580 final.

This famously happened in *Marbury v Madison*, but also in *Costa v E.N.E.L.*, where 'the ECJ declared the supremacy of EC law' but 'found that the Italian law … did not violate EC law'.[87] The first step here could probably also be a decision in the format of *Costa v E.N.E.L.*, in which the full applicability of the Charter would be established without proving an actual violation.

We have already seen a similar step—albeit limited in consequence to judicial independence—taken by the ECJ in the case of *Associação Sindical dos Juízes Portugueses v Tribunal de Contas*, where the ECJ held that the material scope of Article 19 (1) second subparagraph TEU applies in '"the fields covered by Union law", irrespective of whether the Member States are implementing Union law, within the meaning of Article 51 (1) of the Charter'.[88] Albeit Poland was not a party in this case, the ECJ clearly had the Polish situation in mind when emphasizing the importance of the principle of effective judicial protection enshrined in Article 19 (1) TEU in conjunction with Article 47 CFR.[89]

(e) In a second step—after establishing jurisdiction in a case without a finding of a violation—a violation would have to be established. The more obvious a violation of fundamental rights is and the more isolated the 'convicted' MS is, the more likely the judgment establishing the violation will be accepted by the MSs.[90] We do not have to be pessimistic to predict that such cases could easily reach the ECJ in the near future.

The ECJ then also applied the principle laid down in the *Associação* case just mentioned 'against Poland'. While it is for the MSs, under the second subparagraph of Article 19 (1) TEU, to 'establish a system of legal remedies and

[87] Karen Alter, 'Who Are the "Masters of the Treaties"? European Governments and the European Court of Justice' (1998) 52 International Organisations 121, 131.

[88] Case C-64/16 *Associação Sindical dos Juízes Portugueses v Tribunal de Contas* [2018] EU:C:2018:117, paras 29, 190. For an overview on the rule of law case law of the ECJ, see Koen Lenaerts, 'The Rule of Law and the Constitutional Identity of the European Union' (speech of 5 March 2023) <https://evropeiskipravenpregled.eu/the-rule-of-law-and-the-constitutional-identity-of-the-european-union/> accessed 24 October 2024. Cf the infringement action brought on 19 December 2022 by the Commission against Hungary (C-769/22).

[89] Case C-64/16 *Associação Sindical dos Juízes Portugueses v Tribunal de Contas* [2018] EU:C:2018:117, para 35.

[90] Groussot, Pech, and Petursson (n 26) 104: 'It must be remembered that the US Supreme Court's "legal coup" took place in rather unique historical circumstances—the persistent segregationist practices in Southern States—which required, in turn, a revolutionary expansion of the scope of the US Bill of Rights.' See also Marta Cartabia, 'Article 51—Field of Application' in William BT Mock and Gianmario Demuro (eds), *Human Rights in Europe* (Carolina Academic Press 2010) 318–19, on similarities between some interpretations of Article 51 CFR and the 'doctrine of incorporation' of US constitutional law.

procedures ensuring effective judicial review in the fields covered by EU law',[91] the ECJ went on to say that:

> [t]he principle of the effective judicial protection of individuals' rights under EU law thus referred to in the second subparagraph of Article 19(1) TEU is a general principle of EU law stemming from the constitutional traditions common to the Member States, which has been enshrined in Articles 6 and 13 of the Convention for the Protection of Human Rights and Fundamental Freedoms, ... which is now reaffirmed by Article 47 of the Charter.[92]

With this, the ECJ has taken an important step in the right direction towards protecting the rule of law by standing up for the independence of the judiciary.

The scope of the issues that can be addressed by means of Article 19 (1) TEU in conjunction with Article 47 CFR is, however, limited. While other fundamental provisions of the TEU, such as Article 10 (1) TEU, could be activated to deal with further problem areas, we aim at a complete protection of fundamental rights, which would also have a spill-over effect on potential future violations, such as those of freedom of the press and media. The step taken by the ECJ in the *Repubblika* ruling is noteworthy.[93] In *Repubblika v Il-Prim Ministru*, the ECJ linked a preliminary ruling by a Maltese court on judicial independence to the promise made at the time of accession to the EU under Article 49 TEU that the Union would be founded on the Article 2 TEU values and thus the obligation of MSs (they 'are thus required to ensure') to avoid any violation of these values.[94] With this, the ECJ has made Article 2 TEU justiciable to a certain extent.[95]

In yet another case the ECJ stated that the Article 2 values 'define the very identity of the EU as a common legal order'.[96] Precisely this is the reason why 'the European Union must be able to defend those values, within the limits of its powers as laid down by the Treaties'[97] and without requiring the MSs 'to

[91] Case C-619/18 *European Commission v Republic of Poland* [2019] EU:C:2019:531, paras 48–50; cf Case C-791/19 *European Commission v Republic of Poland* [2021] EU:C:2021:596, paras 52–53.

[92] Case C-619/18 *European Commission v Republic of Poland* [2019] EU:C:2019:531, para 52.

[93] Case C-896/19 *Repubblika v Il-Prim Ministru* [2021] EU:C:2021:311, paras 60 ff.

[94] Case C-896/19 *Repubblika v Il-Prim Ministru* [2021] EU:C:2021:311, para 64.

[95] For an analysis, see Mathieu Leloup, Dimitry Kochenov, and Aleksejs Dimitrovs, 'Non-Regression: Opening the Door to Solving the "Copenhagen Dilemma"? All the Eyes on Case C-896/19 *Repubblika v Il-Prim Ministru*' (June 2021) Reconnect Working Paper No 15.

[96] See Case C-156/21 *Hungary v European Parliament and Council of the European Union* [2022] EU:C:2022:97, para 127. See also Case C-157/21 *Poland v European Parliament and Council of the European Union* [2022] EU:C:2022:98, para 145.

[97] Case C-156/21 *Hungary v European Parliament and Council of the European Union* [2022] EU:C:2022:97, para 127.

adopt a particular constitutional model governing the relationship and interaction between the various branches of the State'.[98] Instead of rather being 'merely a statement of policy guidelines or intentions', these values 'are given concrete expression in principles containing legally binding obligations for the Member States'.[99] Article 2 TEU becomes more and more a concrete touchstone on the basis of which the ECJ faces illiberal practices in EU MSs.[100]

(f) In parallel to (d) and (e), the ECJ could also develop a discretionary doctrine similar to that of the ECtHR.[101] This would lead to the ECJ only having to intervene in cases where the common minimum level of fundamental rights protection would be violated. Such a doctrine would be similar to the concept of 'systemic deficiency',[102] since both provide a margin of manoeuvre, so to speak. The important difference, however, is that the decision on the limits of the margin of manoeuvre would remain with the judiciary and not with a political body, according to what has been argued here.

In summary, once again the ECJ is called upon to safeguard the rule of law in Europe.[103] In all likelihood, the European institutions will not want to stop such a move by the ECJ. Rather, they appear paralysed and would probably be happy if someone other than themselves were to pull the coals out of the fire. The MSs, after all, have no possibility of doing so. Coalitions of MSs against ECJ rulings and threats of a judicial Armageddon are highly unrealistic. As Marcus Höreth put it:

> non-compliance by Member States was not perceived as a threat by the European Justices but rather a welcome opportunity to develop their judicial regime even further. Member State non-compliance generates legal actions,

[98] Case C-357/19, C-379/19, C-547/19, C-811/19, and C-840/19, *Euro Box Promotion and Others* [2021] EU:C:2021:1034, para 229, and C-430/21, *RS (Effect of the decisions of a constitutional court)* [2022] EU:C:2022:99, para 43.

[99] See Case C-156/21 *Hungary v European Parliament and Council of the European Union* [2022] EU:C:2022:97, para 232; Case C-157/21 *Poland v European Parliament and Council of the European Union* [2022] EU:C:2022:98, para 264.

[100] Cf on Article 2 TEU case law Spieker (n 1); see also Hillion (n 1).

[101] On the exercise of discretion as a special case of the 'deference doctrine', see Andrew Legg, *The Margin of Appreciation in International Human Rights Law* (OUP 2012) 17 ff.

[102] See Armin von Bogdandy, Carlino Antpöhler, and Michael Ioannidis, 'Protecting EU Values' in András Jakab and Dimitry Kochenov (eds), *The Enforcement of EU Law and Values: Ensuring Member States' Compliance* (OUP 2017) 218.

[103] Marcus Höreth, 'Warum der EuGH nicht gestoppt werden sollte—und auch kaum gestoppt werden kann' in Ulrich Haltern and Andreas Bergmann (eds), *Der EuGH in der Kritik* (Mohr Siebeck 2012) 73. On the quasi-impeachability of the ECJ's judgments, see Marcus Höreth , 'The Least Dangerous Branch?' in Mark Dawson, Bruno De Witte, and Elise Muir (eds), *Judicial Activism at the European Court of Justice* (Edward Elgar 2013) 32, 39–40.

> followed by new rulings; non-compliance with important new rulings again generates new litigation and new findings of non-compliance, and so on.[104]

If the European integration process fails, it will not be because of stronger fundamental rights protection. It will fail either for purely economic reasons or because of anti-constitutional and illiberal attempts in some MSs.

With judicial statesmanship, patience for the right cases, and a deliberate strategy, decisive steps towards a complete fundamental rights union could be achieved in the near future. To this end, the ECJ would have to continue to live up to its responsibility both in promoting European integration and the values of the EU.[105]

7. Conclusion

Every society is held together by certain values that are, at least rhetorically, indisputable. Since the end of the Second World War in Western Europe and since the end of communism throughout Europe, the secular values of constitutionalism have had an integrative function. The twentieth century in Europe can also be seen as a time of experimentation and failure with the then new secular taboo systems such as nationalism or socialism. Democracy and the protection of fundamental rights seem to be the only credible options for shaping society in Europe today. Of course, there are endless debates about what these concepts actually mean.[106] But the difficulty of defining the values mentioned in Article 2 TEU should not lead to a situation where these values are simply ignored. There have been and will continue to be attempts to question these values as we have seen especially with the 'ideological agnosticism' currently present in the illiberal regime in Hungary.[107] However, if we want to believe that European integration has a chance, we must stop these attempts before it is too late. If it is allowed in one EU MS, it will be allowed in another and in no time at all the European edifice that rests on these values will crumble surprisingly quickly. Inaction contributes to the erosion of the EU's moral and institutional capital. The apparent tension between the EU's enforcement weakness

[104] Höreth, 'The Least Dangerous Branch?' (n 103) 43–44.

[105] See Mauricio Mandujano Manriquez and Tommaso Pavone, 'Follow the Leader: The European Commission, the European Court of Justice, and the EU's Rule of Law Revolution' (2024) Journal of European Public Policy arguing that the ECJ took the lead and not the EC in tackling the 'rule of law crisis'.

[106] WB Gallie, 'Essentially Contested Concepts' (1956) Proceedings of the Aristotelian Society 167.

[107] See Chapter 2.

on the one hand and its (implicit) legal obligation to strengthen the rule of law in Europe on the other hand has serious consequences.

An application of the CFR if Article 2 TEU values are violated by MSs would give the EU the possibility to put a stop to dangerous tendencies. The ECJ could thus enforce the values of European integration and, through the preliminary ruling procedure, turn all courts of the MSs into local actors that profess and enforce these values. An important part of the solution lies (as so often in the history of the Western constitutional state) with the judiciary. The judiciary is the traditional guardian of the rule of law, which should not be understood as blind adherence to the law, but as a powerful institution whose task is, among other things, to put a stop to the arbitrary use of state power. Under the current institutional circumstances, much of the responsibility lies with the ECJ, which could rise to the challenge by taking further steps towards completing the European Fundamental Rights Union, which could ultimately make the Charter applicable in purely domestic cases if necessary.

7

Applying the *Spitzenkandidaten*-System

How to Address the Illiberal Regime Crisis by Improving Democratic Accountability

1. Introduction

As we have set out in the Introduction, it has long been thought that the EU doesn't have the legal tools to deal with its illiberal regimes. This is, so we contend, false. It does and always has. But tools need to be used. With regard to democracy, the most effective way to actually face its illiberal regimes, the EU must improve itself. New tools are not necessary for this improvement. However, only if the EU improves its own democratic accountability will it be able to face democratic shortcomings in its illiberal MSs. The most suitable way to make that happen is to make sure a *Spitzenkandidat* is running the EC. As Ursula von der Leyen made clear in her statement on 18 July 2024 following the EP plenary vote on her re-election as Commission President, a pan-European campaign is essential. While von der Leyen toured 'from Helsinki to Lisbon, from Bucharest to Rome', there is still some way to go before the *Spitzenkandidaten*-system is firmly established. The 2024 EP elections were an important step.

Nevertheless, until now, the EP doesn't have enough power over the EC. This democratic shortcoming is a major reason as to why the illiberal MSs do not face enough opposition from EU institutions. To put it bluntly, the naive picture that a good EC is fighting against bad illiberal MSs is not true, or at least only part of the picture. The persistence of illiberal regimes is not separate from but a symptom of the EU's own deficits of the rule of law and democracy.[1]

[1] Cf Chapters 2 and 3.

Saving the European Union from Its Illiberal Member States. András Jakab and Lando Kirchmair, Oxford University Press.
DOI: 10.1093/oso/9780198954606.003.0008

2. Why Does the EU Need to Improve Its Democratic Accountability in Order to Address Its Illiberal MSs?

The problem has been that the application of any enforcement mechanism depends at one point or another on politics. This is obviously true for the Article 7 TEU procedure. The way the EU currently is withholding large amounts of EU funding as a leverage in the face of the blatant disregard of the rule of law and democracy in Hungary is another case at hand. Less obvious, however still strongly connected to political will, is a rather selective approach in guaranteeing the unionwide application of EU law by launching infringement proceedings. The trend shows that in recent years the number of such proceedings has declined.[2] In the face of the necessary political will needed, we witnessed that the EU Council of Ministers, the European Council, and the EC at key points chose and keep choosing to act half-heartedly, selectively, late, or not at all. If, exceptionally, they nominally act in defence of EU constitutional values, as they did recently against Hungary and to some extent Poland, then other factors, such as Hungary's continuous veto threats in the shadow of the Ukraine war, seem to be more crucial than the disregard of Article 2 TEU values.[3] In some cases, their inaction even borders on illegality, a breach of their own rules.[4] In other cases the EC is behaving legally, strictly speaking, but its inaction leads to long-term damage. It is still a mystery, for instance, how the EC's legal concerns about a Russian-built nuclear plant in Hungary were suddenly resolved in 2016. The point, however, is that also the introduction of the so-called conditionality mechanism,[5] and the recent withholding of 'new' EU

[2] See R Daniel Kelemen and Tommaso Pavone, 'Where Have the Guardians Gone? Law Enforcement and the Politics of Supranational Forbearance in the European Union' (2023) 75 World Politics 779. Cf Sivaram Cheruvu, 'When Does the European Commission Pursue Noncompliance?' (2022) 23 European Union Politics 375, arguing that the Commission strategically delays advancing infringement proceedings when it thinks compliance success might be higher in the future. Cf Chapter 2.

[3] Gisela Hernández and Carlos Closa, 'Turning Assertive? EU Rule of Law Enforcement in the Aftermath of the War in Ukraine' (2023) 47 West European Politics 967. For a somewhat different (even though not actually necessarily contradicting) explanation according to which the EU turned more assertive, because (1) the domestic national political price of inaction became higher and (2) illiberal MSs proved to be unreliable institutional partners in policy questions, see Michael Blauberger and Ulrich Sedelmeier, 'Sanctioning Democratic Backsliding in the European Union: Transnational Salience, Negative Intergovernmental Spillover, and Policy Change' (2024) Journal of European Public Policy 1.

[4] See Chapter 2.

[5] Regulation (EU, Euratom) 2020/2092 of the European Parliament and of the Council of 16 December 2020 on a general regime of conditionality for the protection of the Union budget [2020] OJ L 433I. For a general analysis, see Antonia Baraggia and Matteo Bonelli, 'Linking Money to Values: The New Rule of Law Conditionality Regulation and Its Constitutional Challenges' (2022) 23 German Law Journal 131; Isabel Staudinger, 'The Rise and Fall of Rule of Law Conditionality' (2022) 7 European Papers 721.

funds (in the frame of the CR, the RRFR, as well as based on the CPR) indicate that still political will is needed.[6]

Democratic accountability structures are supposed to provide institutional incentives. If an EC president receives power primarily from the complacent and politically expedient European Council, then the president's behaviour will most likely follow that of the European Council. On the other hand, if the EP—which has been far more assertive in defending the rule of law and democracy—plays the primary role in legitimizing the President of the EC, then we can rather expect that the President will follow the EP—if for no other reason than getting re-elected as EC President for another five years.[7]

That was the original idea behind the so-called *Spitzenkandidaten*-system: the lead candidate (in German '*Spitzenkandidat*') of the largest EP political party grouping becomes President of the EC. This small change, as we are about to argue in this final chapter, means that the President would receive its political legitimacy primarily from the EP. Its protestations notwithstanding, the EC is not an apolitical body. It has a monopoly on initiating new EU-laws; it has a political agenda in its own policy areas. Its members are mostly top politicians. Its character and its powers make it more similar to a government cabinet than to a technocratic regulatory agency. The question is therefore not whether it is political (it is by design), but where it gets its political legitimacy from.[8]

We emphasize one feature of democracy which is of particular relevance to our purpose: democracy's potential for self-correction. If we want the EU to face its illiberal regimes, we need a certain institutional structure which

[6] For an overview, see László Detre, András Jakab, and Tamás Lukácsi, 'Comparing Three Financial Conditionality Regimes and Their Application to Hungary: The Conditionality Regulation, the Recovery and Resilience Facility Regulation, and the Common Provisions Regulation' (2023) 23 Max Planck Institute for Comparative Public Law & International Law (MPIL) Research Paper No 2023-23.

[7] See Nereo Peñalver García and Julian Priestley, *The Making of a European President* (Palgrave Macmillan 2015) ch 3 on the emergence of the idea.

[8] See eg Morten Egeberg, 'The European Commission' in Michelle Cini and Nieves Pérez-Solórzano Borragán (eds), *European Union Politics* (5th edn, OUP 2016) 125 ff; John Peterson, 'Juncker's Political European Commission and an EU in Crisis' (2016) 55 Journal of Common Market Studies 349 especially highlighting the fact that Jean-Claude Juncker was a *Spitzenkandidat* while acknowledging the increasing dependence on 'EU national capitals in a time of acute crisis'; see also García and Priestley (n 7) 34 'It is difficult not to conclude from this that the Commission is an essentially political institution, admittedly with some important regulatory functions, as is often the case with national governments. With the passage of time, its political role has vastly expanded as new areas of responsibility have been assigned to it, by decisions of member states, by treaty changes and in requests from an ever more powerful European Parliament'; cf Laura Cram, 'The European Commission as a Multi-organization: Social Policy and IT Policy in the EU' (2007) 1 Journal of European Public Policy 195; for an overview, see Simon Hix and Andreas Follesdal, 'Why Is There a Democratic Deficit in the EU? A Response to Majone and Moravcsik' (2006) 44 Journal of Common Market Studies 533.

incentivizes action in this regard. This is to establish a parliamentary system at the EU level.

Such a system seems to be an efficient procedural solution to promote the citizens' interests through the possibility of making elected officials responsible if they did not promote these interests—by not re-electing them, that is, by making them compete on the basis of who could promote the citizens' interests best.[9] Governments can be forced by their electorate to change measures harmful to its interests.[10] In the realm of the illiberal regime crisis within the EU this is an important feature. First, it is not in the interest of citizens in so-called 'net contributor' MSs to throw their—taxpayers'—money into the corruption machinery of illiberal EU MSs. Second, it might be the only possibility for citizens of illiberal EU MSs to profit from free and fair elections, the result of which might contribute to the end of the misery of 'cuckoo politicians' in their home countries.[11] Less obvious, however, equally not in the interest of EU citizens is, third, the mutual poisoning of illiberal EU MSs, the EU, and other MSs.[12] From this insight it is understandable that an increase in democratic accountability makes communities economically stronger.[13] Empirical studies indicate that democracy makes economic growth more likely—except for extremely poor countries.[14]

Expressed with the words of a statement by the Christian Democratic group in the EP published on its website on 24 June 2019: 'A basic principle of democracy is for parties to put forward their programs and candidates so voters can

[9] Robert D Cooter, *The Strategic Constitution* (Princeton University Press 2000) 4, 11, 13, 17, 359–60, 373–74. Cf Amartya Sen, *Development as Freedom* (Knopf 1999) 152: 'no substantial famine has ever occurred in any independent country with a democratic form of government and a relatively free press'.

[10] Karl Raimund Popper, *The Open Society and Its Enemies* (Routledge 2006) vol I 163, 167, and vol II, 90, 143, 434; Christoph Möllers, *Demokratie: Zumutungen und Versprechen* (Klaus Wagenbach 2008) 11, 13.

[11] On the deficit of elections in illiberal EU MSs, see Chapter 2. Also, EP elections are not free and fair for EU citizens in illiberal EU MSs, because national laws govern the election process and so far transnational lists have not been established. See also András Jakab, 'How to Defend the Integrity of the EP Elections against Authoritarian Member States' (31 March 2019) *Verfassungsblog* <https://verfassungsblog.de/how-to-defend-the-integrity-of-the-ep-elections-against-authoritarian-member-states/> accessed 24 October 2024. For the notion of 'cuckoo politicians' who do not act in the interest of the people they represent, see Lando Kirchmair, 'Demokratische Legitimität, die EU-Rechtsstaatlichkeitskrise und Vorüberlegungen zu einer transnationalen Gewaltengliederung' (2019) 6 Zeitschrift für praktische Philosophie 171, 191.

[12] See on this especially Chapter 3.

[13] The idea of equal freedom itself has also economic implications, as it helps competition. Non-discrimination means that the most capable should do the job, only his or her individual achievements count. Protection of private property is necessary for capitalist economic growth. Protection of privacy and freedom of thought contribute to a fearless and creative working environment. Political freedoms ensure democracy, so their economic impact is more indirect than any of the latter. For a deep analysis of these questions with further references, see Cooter (n 9) 241–357.

[14] Elias Papaioannou and Gregorios Siourounis, 'Democratization and Growth' (2008) 118 The Economic Journal 1520.

decide which policies and which leaders they want to put in place. This applies to every level: local, regional, national and European.'[15]

Beyond that democracy strengthens the loyalty of their respective political-community members by giving them a voice in what is happening. Or on a more pessimistic note, even if one contends that this were not the case, we could still speak of the potential of democracy to give people the impression that they had a voice.[16] This is something which was especially important during times of crisis or even war.[17]

Today, both in political scientific and legal analysis, the requirement of democratic legitimacy for the EU is absolutely dominant. The EU itself claims democratic legitimacy in the Preamble, in Articles 2 and 10 TEU. Nevertheless, the 'present stage of European integration in democratic terms reflects a predominant legitimacy of member state polities in the governmental system'.[18] So the question is not whether the authority of the EU has to be democratically legitimized, but *how* we achieve it; that is, what kind of conceptual, procedural, and infrastructural solution we need to achieve it. Hence, does the EU have any other choice to provide democratic legitimacy? Could it base itself on another form of legitimacy in order to address its deficit or the erosion of the rule of law and democracy as exemplified.[19] In the light of Article 10 (1) TEU stating 'The functioning of the Union shall be founded on representative democracy',[20] the answer seems to be in the negative, but as in the literature the alternative option of 'output legitimacy' is sometimes mentioned,[21] we will briefly deal with it here too.

[15] Editorial, 'Spitzenkandidaten and the European Union's System of Government' (2019) 15 European Constitutional Law Review 609, 612–13 quoting EPP Press, release, 'Poll: Citizens want the Council to respect the Spitzenkandidat process' (24 June 2019) <www.epp.eu/press-releases/poll-citizens-want-the-council-to-respect-the-spitzenkandidat-process/> accessed 24 October 2024.

[16] Cooter (n 9) 144.

[17] Albert O Hirschman, *Exit, Voice, and Loyalty: Responses to Decline in Firms, Organizations, and States* (Harvard University Press 1970).

[18] Editorial (n 15) 618 with reference and a normative justification of this state of affairs, see eg Richard Bellamy, *A Republican Europe of States: Cosmopolitanism, Intergovernmentalism and Democracy in the EU* (CUP 2019) ch 4.

[19] See Chapter 3.

[20] The principle of democracy (as many other later treaty provisions) came up first in the case law of the ECJ. See Case 138/79 *SA Roquette Frères v Council of the European Communities* [1980] EU:C:1980:249, para 33: 'the fundamental democratic principle that the peoples should take part in the exercise of power through the intermediary of a representative assembly'; similarly in Case 139/79 *Maizena GmbH v Council of the European Communities* [1980] EU:C:1980:250, para 34.

[21] Eg Fritz W Scharpf, *Demokratietheorie zwischen Utopie und Anpassung* (Konstanz University Press 1970) 21–28; Giandomenico Majone, *Regulating Europe* (Routledge 1996); Daniel Wincott, 'Does the European Union Pervert Democracy? Questions of Democracy in New Constitutionalist Thought on the Future of Europe' (1998) 4 European Law Journal 411, 414.

2.1 Is Output Legitimacy an Alternative to Democratic Accountability?

Output legitimacy means that an authority has to be obeyed because its decisions lead to good (ie acceptable) results.[22] So the main issue is not about the source of the authority but about its use and result. To a certain degree, this enlightened technocratic idea served historically as the basis of the EU.[23] This fits the description of the EU as exercising a technical-regulatory expert type of legislation, rather than a political one. If, for instance, the EC were not a political body but a technocratic regulatory agency which only oversees compliance with the law, it would not even need democratic legitimacy.[24] This argument, however, is becoming weaker by every revision of the founding treaties, but even from the beginning there was potential for a democratic institutional system in European integration.[25]

Beyond this general observation, output legitimacy has concrete weaknesses. One particular weakness is that such an approach is unlikely to perform well over a longer period of time. Output legitimacy—without input legitimacy—likely leads to a concentration of too much power in the hands of a few people for too long a time. If, however, important decisions are taken by

[22] Fritz W Scharpf, *Regieren in Europa* (Campus Verlag 1999) 16–28; Marcus Höreth, *Die Europäische Union im Legitimationstrilemma* (Nomos 1999) 82–87.

[23] On Jean Monnet's approach, see Ernst Haas, *The Uniting of Europe* (Stanford University Press 1958) 456; Kevin Featherstone, 'Jean Monnet and the "Democratic Deficit" in the European Union' (1994) 32 Journal of Common Market Studies 149. For further details on neo-functionalist approaches of legitimacy—concentrating on economic, rationality-driven integration instead of political identity—see Amaryllis Verhoeven, *The European Union in Search of a Democratic and Constitutional Theory* (Kluwer Law International 2002) 14, 65.

[24] Hans Peter Ipsen, *Europäisches Gemeinschaftsrecht* (Mohr 1972) 1044; Hans Peter Ipsen, *Fusionsverfassung Europäische Gemeinschaften* (Gehlen 1969) 64–66. Cf Giandomenico Majone, 'Europe's "Democratic Deficit": The Question of Standards' (1998) 4 European Law Journal 5, 8–10; Andrew Moravcsik, 'The Myth of Europe's "Democratic Deficit"' (2008) 43 Intereconomics: Journal of European Economic Policy 331. The danger of legitimacy based on expert knowledge is that it does not possess a well-defined procedural solution of self-correction; see Robert A Dahl, *Democracy and Its Critics* (Yale University Press 1989) 76. On self-interest of experts, on necessary moral implications of expert-decisions, and on disagreement amongst experts, see Dahl, Democracy and its Critics 61–62, 74, 76.

[25] 'Indeed, it made little sense to provide for the future elections of a Common Assembly responsible under the terms of the ECSC Treaty only for debating coal and steel policy, unless such a body were to evolve into something more far reaching.' Richard Corbett, Francis Jacobs, and Michael Shackleton, *The European Parliament* (3rd edn, Catermill 1995) 8. See also García and Priestley (n 7) 34–35, 'Those who hanker after a supposedly halcyon period when the Commission had merely supervisory functions, ensuring the smooth functioning of the market, the operation of competition rules and the regulation of state aids, are deluding themselves. The Commission was always more than this, even at the outset. But, since the rapid development of common policies in the 1970s and 1980s, the creation of an internal market in goods and services, the underpinning of a single currency with economic convergence and budgetary discipline, and the support for infrastructure and growth required to make a success of enlargement, the Commission's role has expanded beyond recognition, with the usually ready acquiescence of member states, or even at their behest.'

one or a few persons, the likelihood of bad results increases considerably. Just think of China's zero COVID policy—despite the initial praise for handling the pandemic more successfully than democracies—or the decision of Putin to invade Ukraine.[26] In addition, if the reason for obeying an authority is that it is successful, then in the absence of success the political community dissolves very quickly. As opposed to the emotional loyalty produced by democratic procedures giving people voice, there is little to no motivation to stand up for a struggling authority based on output legitimacy. Output legitimacy's survival probability is thus lower than that of democratic legitimacy.

Focusing on our topic it is important to see that on the question of how to handle the illiberal regime crisis of the EU, the European Council and the EP diverge—by a lot. The Parliament strategically has tried to enforce the liberal democratic founding values; the European Council has tried to protect MS autonomy even at the price of the EU's founding democratic values. The EC has landed in-between, continually puncturing hopes that it would finally side with the Parliament. It did not—and it most likely will not, if nothing changes. We contend that these diverging approaches cannot be seen without the underlying procedures according to which these institutions function. To put it bluntly, too much power in the hands of the European Council, be it through deciding things by itself or via too strong an unrestricted influence on the EC, does not provide for good decisions in the illiberal regime crisis of the EU. The reason for this poor record has to do with direct democratic accountability.

2.2 How to Ensure Political Freedoms and Access to Information on Government

Democracy without political freedoms is unlikely to sustain itself.[27] The institutional system of even voting procedures, that is, regular elections, might be similar to functioning democracies, but once someone gets into power—either democratically or through violence—they are unlikely to get voted out of it. In other words, self-correction mechanisms cannot work efficiently;[28]

[26] Francis Fukuyama, 'More Proof That This Really Is the End of History' (17 October 2022) *The Atlantic* <https://www.theatlantic.com/ideas/archive/2022/10/francis-fukuyama-still-end-history/671761/> accessed 24 October 2024.

[27] See Chapter 4 on the mutual dependence of the rule of law and democracy.

[28] Oppression and the lack of political freedoms likely lead to the loss of loyalty too. This might be the case generally, but is especially true in those parts of society—like minorities—which suffer from it.

textbook examples of this were formerly the socialist states (democratic centralism); today the problem of lacking political freedoms resurfaces in illiberal EU MSs.[29]

Political freedoms in turn can be used effectively only if it is easily publicly knowable what the government does: that is, if its work is transparent enough. Otherwise it is hardly possible to think about whether politicians deserve to be voted out of power; that is, the self-correction mechanism cannot work either.

Traditionally, the EU itself was criticized on this basis—for good reasons.[30] After the Treaty of Lisbon, the situation is, however, probably no worse than in most European states:[31] both the meetings of the Council and the EP are now open, and a general right to access to EU documents is also enshrined in Article 15 TFEU. A further general clause on the principle of transparency is now contained in Article 11 TEU.

The major problem these days in this regard is the illiberal EU MSs which restrict the freedom of the press and do not take the principle of transparency seriously. We have demonstrated that the process of European integration has led to a mutual interdependence not only between the rule of law and democracy, but also between the EU and its MSs.[32] Hence, illiberal politics in certain EU MSs spill over to other EU MSs and the EU. If it is not for improving the situation of citizens in illiberal EU MSs it is for the EU's own sake to take measures against illiberal practices in its MSs. We have, thus, argued that in order to address these issues, the Fundamental Rights Union should be completed, meaning that the CFR should be applicable in purely domestic cases too.[33] This is related to our argument in this chapter as the rule of law and democracy in general, as well as political freedoms and the freedom of the press and democratic accountability are mutually dependent.

[29] See Chapter 1.

[30] Eg Fiona Hayes-Renshaw and Helen Wallace, 'Executive Power in the European Union: The Functions and Limits of the Council of Ministers' (1995) 2 Journal of European Public Policy 559; Michael Newman, *Democracy, Sovereignty and the European Union* (C Hurst and Co Publishing 1996) 198; Kieran St C Bradley, 'La transparence de l'Union européenne' (1999) 3–4 Cahiers de droit européen 285.

[31] Stephen C Sieberson, 'The Treaty of Lisbon and Its Impact on the European Union's Democratic Deficit' (2007–08) 10 Columbia Journal of European Law 445, 453–54.

[32] See Chapter 4.

[33] See Chapter 6.

3. How to Establish a Direct Link between Election and Responsibility and Why This Will Benefit the EU 'Response' against Its Illiberal MSs

The central problem hampering the EU 'response' against its illiberal MSs and standing in the way of democratic accountability is what Anne Peters calls 'the missing correlation between election and responsibility'.[34] In other words, there are elections, and also a new government (EC) is set up, but the direct link between the two acts is missing.[35] There seem to be only two institutional solutions to ensure the virtues of democracy: one option is to transform the EU into a US-style presidential system;[36] the other way is to parliamentarize it.[37] In the European context, the latter seems to be easier to reach, as the current system is already much nearer to the parliamentary system.[38]

In the 1980s and 1990s, the EU's democratic shortcomings were a major point of debate.[39] Nevertheless, the EP has acquired step by step more and more powers over the years.[40] In particular, the Treaty of Lisbon was a major milestone that established that the candidate for the President of the Commission has to be *proposed* by the European Council and *elected* by a majority of the EP, taking into account the elections to the EP and after having held the appropriate consultations (Article 17 (7) TEU). Thereby the way has been prepared to state that legally the crucial organ in appointing the Commission President is the EP and not the European Council.[41]

[34] Anne Peters, *Elemente einer Theorie der Verfassung Europas* (Duncker & Humblot 2001) 627: 'mangelnde Korrelation zwischen Wahl und Verantwortung'.

[35] Some authors criticize not only the election of the Commission, but also that a complicated regulatory network with independent (ie not accountable) authorities have the power. See András Sajó, 'EU Networks under the New Constitution, Impact on Domestic Constitutional Structures' in Ingolf Pernice and Jiri Zemanek (eds), *A Constitution for Europe: The IGC, the Ratification Process and Beyond* (Nomos 2005) 183; Joseph HH Weiler, 'To Be a European Citizen: Eros and Civilization' in Joseph HH Weiler (ed), *The Constitution of Europe* (CUP 1999) 324, 349. This is a general problem of supranational influence in domestic affairs (OECD, World Trade Organization, World Bank), which we cannot deal with in this chapter.

[36] For such an approach see Franz C Mayer, 'Presidential Power(s)' in Leonard Besselink, Nicola Lupo, and Mattias Wendel (eds), *Research Handbook on EU Constitutional Law* (Edward Elgar forthcoming).

[37] Different institutional sub- and in-between types are considered with their advantages by Werner van Gerven, *The European Union: A Polity of States and Peoples* (Hart 2005) 318.

[38] See van Gerven (n 37) 344–45.

[39] See eg David Marquand, *Parliament for Europe* (Jonathan Cape 1979) 64 ff; Featherstone (n 23).

[40] See eg Berthold Rittberger, *Building Europe's Parliament: Democratic Representation beyond the Nation State* (OUP 2005); Adrienne Héritier and others, *European Parliament Ascendant: Parliamentary Strategies of Self-Empowerment in the EU* (Palgrave Macmillan 2019).

[41] See in this vein András Jakab, 'Full Parliamentarisation of the EU without Changing the Treaties: Why We Should Aim for It and How Easily It Can Be Achieved' (2012) 3 Jean Monnet Working Paper 1, 30. Cf Declaration 11 attached to the Treaty of Lisbon states that 'the European Parliament and the European Council are jointly responsible for the smooth running of the process leading to the election of the President of the European Commission. Prior to the decision of the European Council,

This would be an important step to strengthen democratic accountability by making only the EP responsible for the election of the EC, whereas the European Council could have a ceremonial role similar to monarchs or presidents in parliamentary systems.[42] This is of great importance as according to Article 17 (6) TEU the Commission President has an enormously powerful role. While the European Council has—in agreement with the Commission President-elect—also a role in adopting a list of candidate commissioners, one for each MS, all Commission members have to appear before parliamentary committees and it is the President of the Commission alone who appoints Vice-Presidents of the Commission and since the Treaty of Lisbon has the power to solely request the resignation of Commission members. According to the treaties, reasons must not be provided for such a decision.[43] Hence, the *Spitzenkandidaten*-system would have enormous democratic impact on the President of the Commission and the Commission as a whole.

Indeed, in the EP elections of 2014 the *Spitzenkandidaten*-principle was decisive and the top candidate of the European People's Party, Jean-Claude Juncker, became the President of the EC.[44] This was an important step forward in terms of democratic legitimacy of the EU.[45] Some even stated that 'a new era

representatives of the European Parliament and of the European Council will thus conduct the necessary consultations in the framework deemed the most appropriate.'

[42] For a similar approach see Francesca E Bignami, 'The Democratic Deficit in European Community Rulemaking: A Call for Notice and Comment in Comitology' (1999) 40 Harvard International Law Journal 415, 463; van Gerven (n 37) 350. The idea goes back almost to the beginning of the EEC; see Walter Hallstein, the first president of the Commission on this issue: 'As a parliamentary democracy, the Community is still imperfect ... because the European Parliament has not yet acquired its full role.' Walter Hallstein, *Europe in the Making* (Allen & Unwin 1972) 40–41. Jean Monnet had a different (functionalist) view on the issue, see above n 23.

[43] Case T-562/12 *John Dalli v European Commission* [2015] EU:T:2015:270, para 157: 'In that connection and as regards the termination of a mandate that, as has been stated in paragraph 133 above, is essentially political in nature, the Commission rightly contends that the expression of a firm intention to exercise, if need be, the power to request a Member of the Commission to resign, which is a discretion conferred on the President of the Commission by the EU Treaty, cannot be considered to be illegitimate pressure affecting the validity or the voluntary nature of the resignation of the person concerned.'

[44] For an excellent political analysis, see Klaus Welle, '25 Years of Spitzenkandidaten: What does the Future hold?' (5 March 2019) *Blog of the Wilfried Martens Center* <https://www.martenscentre.eu/blog/25-years-of-spitzenkandidaten-what-does-the-future-hold/> accessed 24 October 2024; for a detailed description of the process, see also García and Priestley (n 7); cf Sara B Hobolt, 'A Vote for the President? The Role of Spitzenkandidaten in the 2014 European Parliament Elections' (2014) 21 Journal of European Public Policy 1528; Desmond Dinan, 'Governance and Institutions: The Year of the *Spitzenkandidaten*' (2015) 53 Journal of Common Market Studies 93; Thomas Christiansen, 'After the *Spitzenkandidaten*: Fundamental Change in the EU's Political System?' (2016) 39 West European Politics 992, 993–98; Ben Crum, 'Why the European Parliament Lost the *Spitzenkandidaten*-process' (2023) 30 Journal of European Public Policy 193.

[45] See eg Héritier and others (n 40) 75; Michael Shackleton, 'Transforming Representative Democracy in the EU? The Role of the European Parliament' (2017) 39 Journal of European Integration 191.

of European Union politics in which leadership changes result from popular choice rather than bargaining behind closed doors.'[46]

Yet, the elections of the Members to the EP in 2019—which were very much presented as though this *Spitzenkandidaten*-principle were to be followed again[47]—and the process by which the President of the EC was finally selected were a major disappointment for democracy at the EU level.[48] The most important political figure in the EU was promoted almost out of the blue. She was crowned by the governments—or rather some of the governments—of the MSs in the European Council (at high cost), and in the end the Parliament did not have much of a say in the process. The profound lack of directly attributable democratic political accountability for a key European institution—the EC—is an important problem which became worse with the elections to the EP in 2019.

Political analyses 'shy away from identifying any generalizable aspect from the 2019 events. Instead, they underline that the *Spitzenkandidaten*-process remains under-institutionalised and that hence it is an open call how things will unfold in 2024.'[49] In these circumstances, the 2024 elections were a positive development. With the re-election of Ursula von der Leyen, who was the EPP's *Spitzenkandidat* in the campaign, the *Spitzenkandidaten*-system seems to be back. The President of the Commission has now a stronger motivation to be responsive to the EP (as she actually promised in her election speech to the EP on 18 July 2024). In the face of this ambiguous situation, we will briefly

[46] Christiansen (n 44) 993.

[47] European Parliament decision of 7 February 2018 on the revision of the Framework Agreement on relations between the European Parliament and the European Commission (2017/2233(ACI)) [2018] OJ C 463, González Pons Resolution of the EP, 'Revision of the Framework Agreement on relations between the European Parliament and the European Commission', P8_TA(2018)0030, A8-0006/2018; cf Laura Tilindyte, 'Election of the President of the European Commission: Understanding the *Spitzenkandidaten* Process' (April 2019) European Parliament Briefing <https://www.europarl.europa.eu/RegData/etudes/BRIE/2018/630264/EPRS_BRI(2018)630264_EN.pdf> accessed 24 October 2024; Editorial (n 15) 612–13 quoting an EPP press release.

[48] For a critique, see Mark Dawson, 'The Lost Spitzenkandidaten and the Future of European Democracy' (2019) 26 Maastricht Journal of European and Comparative Law 731; cf Eva Heidbreder and Daniel Schade, '(Un)settling the Precedent: Contrasting Institutionalisation Dynamics in the Spitzenkandidaten Procedure of 2014 and 2019' (2020) 7 Research & Politics diagnosing a lack of stable institutions and 'case-specific strategic use of resources' in 2014 and 2019 by the EP and the European Council; Kolja Raube, 'From Dawn to Doom: The Institutionalization of the Spitzenkandidaten-Process During European Elections and Its Final Negation' in Sylvia Kritzinger and others (ed), *Assessing the 2019 European Elections* (Routledge 2020) 19 explaining that 'it was not possible for the European Parliament to maintain the Spitzenkandidaten procedure once its collective interests were overtaken by interests of individual MEPs and parties in the aftermath of the European elections'. See generally also Andreas Føllesdal and Simon Hix, 'Why There Is a Democratic Deficit in the EU: A Response to Majone and Moravcsik' (2006) 44 Journal of Common Market Studies 533 arguing that even the 'thinnest' theories of democracy require a contestation for political leadership and over policy which they argued was not given at EU level when writing in 2006.

[49] Crum (n 44) 198.

revisit three possible objections against the *Spitzenkandidaten*-system and offer reasons as to why these objections are not convincing.

4. Critique and Reply

4.1 Objection 1: There Is Neither a Democracy Deficit Nor an Erosion of Democracy at the EU Level

Some might hold that there is neither a democracy deficit nor an erosion of democracy at the EU. According to such a critique of the *Spitzenkandidaten*-system the Commission has a dual democratic legitimacy.[50] This builds on the European Council, which is democratically legitimized on a national level, and the EP, which is legitimized on a European level. Together they were sufficient to legitimize the authority of the EU. This position, however, misses the point.

First, we can trace back in a long chain—or rather on separate chains[51]—the Commission's authority over ordinary citizens. But the nice metaphysical picture about the 'source of power' being the people is simply a metaphor, which cuts short the debate about the reasons for having a democracy. Instead of the metaphor, we should focus on the actual virtues that make a democracy stronger, especially on its self-correction capacity.

Second, especially in the so-called rule of law and democracy crisis of the EU, it becomes blatantly clear that the European Council has too much influence on the EC. Both are not acting adequately to face the illiberal regimes in the EU. This lays bare that the European Council does not (want) to live up to committing itself to a strong European political response. It is too focused on not intervening in 'internal affairs' of MSs and protecting the short-sighted selfish interests of particular MSs. We have to grant that the old conception of

[50] On the idea of dual democratic legitimacy of EU institutions and legislation, see Winfried Kluth, *Die demokratische Legitimation der Europäischen Union* (Duncker & Humblot 1995) 87; Karl-Peter Sommermann, 'Verfassungsperspektiven für die Demokratie in der erweiterten Europäischen Union: Gefahr der Entdemokratisierung oder Fortentwicklung im Rahmen europäischer Supranationalität?' (2003) Die öffentliche Verwaltung 1009. The idea has even been codified in Article 10 (2) TEU. There is a third option (besides dual legitimacy and purely European legitimacy): legitimacy based purely on national parliaments. In an old-fashioned étatist and radical reasoning, in a surprising manner of *Begriffsjurisprudenz*, the German Federal Constitutional Court followed this approach in its Lisbon Decision. BVerfGE 123, 267 (*Lisbon Treaty*). For one of the many convincing criticisms on the judgments, see Christoph Schönberger, 'Lisbon in Karlsruhe: Maastricht's Epigones at Sea' (2009) 10 German Law Journal 1201.

[51] The chain theory is especially vivid in German constitutional doctrine. See Ernst-Wolfgang Böckenförde, 'Demokratie als Verfassungsprinzip' in Ernst-Wolfgang Böckenförde (ed), *Staat, Verfassung, Demokratie* (Suhrkamp 1991) 300; also BVerfGE 83, 60, 72 (*Ausländerwahlrecht II*); BVerfGE 93, 37, 66–67 (*Mitbestimmungsgesetz Schleswig-Holstein*).

dual democratic legitimacy still might do the job. This works only, however, if one considers the trampling on fundamental rights and the prevention of free and fair elections in all MSs as something which does not concern the EU and unaffected MSs, because there was no danger of further spreading. We do not think that this is the case.[52]

What we need especially in the face of illiberal EU MSs, and actually also generally, is to have a system where European citizens can vote out one government and vote in another (the EC).

4.2 Objection 2: All MSs Agreed to the Values in Article 2 TEU, However, the EU Has No Democratic Means to Enforce These Values

Others might say that all MSs agreed to the values in Article 2 TEU. True, however, the EU has no (democratic) means to enforce these values. In this realm, it could be pointed out additionally that the founding treaties and all their modifications were democratically legitimized, as they have been ratified by their respective democratically elected bodies or organs.[53] What is explicitly included in the treaties is thus obligatory, what goes beyond that has no legal basis. Hence, while it might be true that all MSs promised to stick to the values in Article 2 TEU on which the EU is founded, the hurdles for any intervention in the 'sovereign' realm of MSs have been consciously set very high in Article 7 TEU. While this makes an important point, this is no real solution. The actual issue is whether *currently* the EU is functioning democratically and democracy is still common to all MSs. The origin of a system and the point of entry into a system do not say much about its current functioning. As a matter of fact, democracies are typically born

[52] On the danger of further spreading see R Daniel Kelemen, 'Europe's Authoritarian Cancer: Diagnosis, Prognosis, and Treatment' (2022) Progressive Yearbook 73–82.

[53] Peter Badura, 'Bewahrung und Veränderung demokratischer und rechtsstaatlicher Verfassungsstruktur in den internationalen Gemeinschaften' (1966) Veröffentlichungen der Vereinigung der Deutschen Staatsrechtslehrer 34, 72; Pierre Pescatore, 'Les exigences de la démocratie et la legitimité de la Communauté européenne' (1974) Cahiers de droit européen 499, 508–09; Joseph HH Weiler, 'The Transformation of Europe' (1991) 100 Yale Law Journal 2403, 2472; Hans Heinrich Rupp, 'Europäische "Verfassung" und demokratische Legitimation' (1995) 120 Archiv des öffentlichen Rechts 269, 271; Armin von Bogdandy, *Supranationaler Föderalismus als Wirklichkeit und Idee einer neuen Herrschaftsform* (Nomos 1999) 56; Thomas W Pogge, 'How to Create Supra-National Institutions Democratically' in Andreas Føllesdahl and Peter Koslowski (eds), *Democracy and the European Union* (Springer 1998) 160.

non-democratically.[54] We have seen this in Chapter 1 with the example of the German Constitution. So the democratic origin of the EU and its MSs while acceding to the EU cannot satisfy the requirement for their *current* democratic running. The question about the democratic origins is a different and clearly secondary one. The ECJ clearly stated that the EU is not in a position to require from its MSs 'to adopt a particular constitutional model governing the relationship and interaction between the various branches of the State'.[55] However, because the Article 2 values 'define the very identity of the EU as a common legal order',[56] 'the EU must be able to defend those values, within the limits of its powers as laid down by the Treaties'.[57]

4.3 Objection 3: We Should Rather Make National Parliaments Stronger

A usual claim in the face of the democracy deficit at EU level is that the EU can be made more democratic by making national parliaments stronger. Even Article 12 TEU emphasizes the role of national parliaments in the EU. This, however, is not efficient and thus the wrong direction to take. Efficient control by national parliaments is primarily possible, if decisions in the Council are made by unanimity.[58] But this is less and less the case. Democratic control through some national parliaments is not only inefficient,[59] but it also misses the point, which would be to have a clear and efficient procedure whereby voters can vote

[54] Möllers (n 10) 20.

[55] Case C-357/19, C-379/19, C-547/19, C-811/19, and C-840/19, *Euro Box Promotion and Others* [2021] EU:C:2021:1034, para 229, and C-430/21, *RS (Effect of the decisions of a constitutional court)* [2022] EU:C:2022:99, para 43.

[56] See Case C-156/21 *Hungary v European Parliament and Council of the European Union* [2022] EU:C:2022:97, para 127. See also Case C-157/21 *Poland v European Parliament and Council of the European Union* [2022] EU:C:2022:98, para 145.

[57] Case C-156/21 *Hungary v European Parliament and Council of the European Union* [2022] EU:C:2022:97, para 127.

[58] Carlos Closa, 'Some Foundations for the Normative Discussion on Supranational Citizenship and Democracy' in Ulrich K Preuß and Ferrán Requejo (eds), *European Citizenship, Multiculturalism and the State* (Nomos 1998) 105, 109. National parliaments controlling European institutions (ie not their own government) would be either procedurally cumbersome (why not the EP?), or it would invite national veto players to block EU legislation. Cf for (fortunately shy) misplaced attempts in this direction *Protocol on the Role of National Parliaments in the European Union* and *Protocol on the Application of the Principles of Subsidiarity and Proportionality.*

[59] Joseph HH Weiler, 'Does Europe Need a Constitution?' (1995) 1 European Law Journal 219, 232: 'national procedures to ensure democratic control over international treaties of the State are clearly ill-suited and woefully inadequate to address the problems posited by the European Union'. EU negotiations force national governments to act quickly (to accept or to refuse unforeseeable compromises) in the Council, and afterwards their actions will simply be accepted by national parliaments, where they normally have the majority anyway.

out one and vote in another government. This self-correction mechanism can work efficiently *only* if voters receive the direct question whether they want to keep a team of politicians (a Commission) in power or not. But the question cannot be put in this direct way right now, as the EP just does not have the right to choose (on its own) the members of the Commission. Emphasizing the role of national parliaments is simply another rhetorical form of expressing nationalism.[60] It is the strongest argument to counter the claim for a parliamentary system on EU level,[61] or to counter European integration in general.[62]

But the question is no longer whether we would like to have deep European integration, or whether we want to see decisions made in Brussels about policy issues in Europe. It is already there. The question is rather whether we want to use those democratic mechanisms to run it,[63] which made democratic countries so powerful. If we decide that a parliamentary system is not desirable on an EU level, we are still going to deal with the EU's authority, but this authority will be less efficient and useful for us in the long term.[64] If we think, however, that in the light of the above a parliamentary system is desirable (as we argue it is), then we have to answer the practical question of how to introduce it.

If we convey this on the 2019 case of how the *Spitzenkandidaten*-system was neglected, we have to see that national politics trumped EU democracy, even to the extent that someone became President of the EC who was not involved in the EP elections or EU politics in any way—except for acting as the German minister of family affairs and youth, labour and social affairs, as well as defence. Confronting the presumed fact 'that national leaders are unlikely to allow the EP to reclaim the *Spitzenkandidaten*-process'[65] means nothing less than that

[60] Those who stick to the idea of national states normally see the democratic deficit in the weakness of national parliaments; those who support a European federal state see the democratic deficit in the weakness of the EP. Sieberson (n 31).

[61] It makes sense only as long as there is a possibility of veto in the Council. 'So long as each Member Government can veto a Council decision, if it wants to, there is a sense in which each Member Government [can] be held to account for them by its Parliament. If national vetoes disappear this will no longer be true ... The resulting "democratic deficit" would not be acceptable in a Community committed to democratic principles. Yet such a deficit would be inevitable unless the gap were somehow to be filled by the European Parliament.' Marquand (n 39) 65. For a similar argument (the turn to majority voting unleashed legitimacy problems, veto is democratic), see Joseph HH Weiler, 'Problems of Legitimacy in post-1992 Europe' (1991) Außenwirtschaft 411.

[62] Cf the heavily criticized Lisbon decision of the German Federal Constitutional Court: BverfGE 123, 167 (*Lisbon Treaty*). See Schönberger (n 50).

[63] On the dilemma, see Thomas D Zweifel, *Democratic Deficit: Institutions and Regulation in the European Union, Switzerland and the United States* (Lexington 2002) 142.

[64] Intergovernmental package deals tend to favour partial bureaucratic interests in a non-transparent and uncontrollable way; see Stefan Oeter, 'Souveränität und Demokratie in der "Verfassungsentwicklung" der Europäischen Union' (1995) Heidelberg Journal of International Law 659, 699.

[65] Crum (n 44) 209 making the case for a 'demoi-cratic perspective' and claiming that the 'Spitzenkandidaten-process in 2019 forces us to rethink the parliamentarisation-thesis' (at 198), as well as that 'the limits to the expansion of the EP's powers are inherent in the EU's inter-institutional politics'

we have to work hard for establishing an adequate democratic accountability at EU level.

Finally, for the purpose set out in this chapter, making national parliaments stronger would be desirable, but will not be feasible easily in illiberal EU MSs. This problem requires a comprehensive solution for which we need every political will at EU level. The current withholding of substantial amounts of EU funding is important, but will not contribute to structural changes without additional measures. Political will, which is desperately needed, will not come from stronger national parliaments, at least not in the same strength as it currently comes already from the EP. Hence, to address the illiberal regimes within the EU we need a stronger EP which has more grip on the EC, instead of stronger national parliaments which might not want to 'intervene' in the 'sovereign' realm of other MSs.

5. How to Consolidate the (Re-)Establishment of the *Spitzenkandidaten*-System

The claim for introducing a parliamentary system is furthermore countered by saying that MS governments (or at least some of them) would never give up their power to choose the members of the EC.[66] It is definitely the case that someone rarely gives up power easily. Yet, we have already seen that democracies are rarely born democratic and maybe it is also the case that these MS governments will have to learn that democratic accountability at EU level is necessary. And indeed, the 2024 elections have shown (again) that the *Spitzenkandidaten*-system can work. Furthermore, it is not the case that the re-establishment of the *Spitzenkandidaten*-system would break rules. In addition there are three different types of rules which might underpin the *Spitzenkandidaten*-system: (5.1) explicit treaty rules; (5.2) a tricky lawyerly

(at 200). According to Ben Crum, 'It is time to resolve the Spitzenkandidaten conundrum' (17 February 2022) *Reconnect* <https://reconnect-europe.eu/blog/it-is-time-to-resolve-the-spitzenkandidaten-conundrum/> accessed 24 October 2024; the 'critical problem in resolving the situation lies in the difficulty of thinking of a democratic European Union in a way other than a federalized state in which the European Parliament is the main source of democratic legitimacy, and the European Commission operates under its scrutiny'. He argues in favour of a 'Joint Search Committee'. Calling for a 'consolidation of the channels for political action already available at the level of the Member States' rather than the Spitzenkandidaten-system', is Marco Goldoni, 'Politicising EU Lawmaking? The Spitzenkandidaten Experiment as a Cautionary Tale' (2016) 22 European Law Journal 279, 279.

[66] Simon Hix, *The Political System of the European Union* (2nd edn, Palgrave Macmillan 2005) 62; Crum (n 44).

interpretation of some treaty rules which implies an obligation to leave the choice of Commission members to the EP and to have simply a ceremonial role by the European Council; or (5.3) constitutional conventions.

5.1 Treaty Change

If we want to have explicit treaty rules, then we have to modify the TEU. For that purpose we need the ratification by all MSs. While this might not be impossible, it is still quite far away. At this stage, it is unlikely that an explicit treaty change will explicitly establish the *Spitzenkandidaten*-system for the next EP elections in 2028.[67]

5.2 Reinterpretation of Article 17 (7) TEU

We could rely on the argument that the passage introduced by the Lisbon Treaty should be understood to mean that the candidate for the President of the Commission has to be chosen by the EP. The wording 'taking into account the elections to the EP and after having held the appropriate consultations' (Article 17 (7) TEU) after this reading would actually mean—in the light of the general democratic principle underlying the EU—that *legally* the decisive organ in choosing the Commission members *is* the EP.[68] The European Council in contrast would be reduced to a mere ceremonial role. Such an interpretation would contradict the text of the TEU.

5.3 A Constitutional Convention

The solution which might be the most promising is the following: while the regulation in the Lisbon Treaty is not clear, we could still say that in 2014, at least in prelude to the 2019 EP elections and in the 2024 elections the

[67] On this problem, see Julio Baquero Cruz, 'Alternativas a las condiciones de revisión y entrada en vigor' in Iñigo Méndez de Vigo (ed), *¿Qué fue de la Constitución Europea?* (Planeta 2007) 293; Bruno de Witte, 'The Rules of Change in the European Union: The Lost Balance between Rigidity and Flexibility' in Catherine Moury and Luís de Sousa (eds), *Institutional Challenges in Post-Constitutional Europe* (Routledge 2009) 33.

[68] Emphasizing the treaty change coming with the TEU in favour of the *Spitzenkandidaten*-system without, however, claiming that these changes were an automatism, see Thomas Christiansen, 'EU-Spitzenkandidaten—neue Impulse und ihre Folgen für das politische System der EU' (2015) 38 Integration 26, 27, 29–30; Christiansen (n 44) 993–94.

Spitzenkandidaten-system was adopted. While the reform of the EP elections did not take place before the 2024 elections, the EP adopted a resolution in December 2023 which stressed the importance and the necessity of the *Spitzenkandidaten*-system.[69] Arguably, also because of understanding the importance of direct democratic accountability the European Council held back in favour of the EP. Since then the concept of constitutional conventions as used in British constitutional doctrine comes into play.[70] A particularly fitting example of a constitutional convention in the UK is precisely the appointment of the Prime Minister.

Constitutional conventions can be defined as 'understandings and practices that are not legally binding',[71] as rules of 'political morality'[72] or as 'rules of constitutional morality'.[73] They are something like constitutional soft law, but they are not: there was no law-making procedure.[74] It is rather a habit, which is considered to be obligatory but not in a strict legal sense.[75] It is a certain type of self-restriction, but it can also be forced by other actors onto a constitutional organ.[76] Conventions cannot be enforced directly in a court,[77] but they have an indirect legal effect in interpreting legal rules.[78] Conventions may arise through a series of precedents, but they may arise much more quickly than this, without any previous history as usage.[79] 'A single precedent with a good reason may be enough to establish the rule.'[80]

Conventions are obeyed because they are part of a shared system of values[81] and because their breach would result in political consequences such as the political blame of antidemocratic or unconstitutional behaviour. For our

[69] European Parliament resolution of 12 December 2023 on the European Elections 2024 (2023/2016(INI)) P9_TA(2023)0455, especially recital C–E, para 2-10.

[70] See interestingly on the point of a convention of the constitution, Editorial (n 15) 613 holding that '[t]he rule, which builds on the provision in Article 17(7) TEU according to which the European Parliament must consent to the Commission "as a body" before it can be appointed, is a convention of the constitution developed in practice. It is now a well-established cornerstone of the relations between Commission and Parliament at the beginning of a Commissioner's tenure.... it can be argued the requirement of parliamentary approval of individual members is an unwritten constitutional rule, closely related to Articles 17(7), third indent, and 17(8) TEU: action contrary to this rule would be regarded as unconstitutional.' [Footnotes omitted].

[71] John Alder, *Constitutional and Administrative Law* (5th edn, Palgrave Macmillan 2005) 43.

[72] Geoffrey Marshall, *Constitutional Theory* (Clarendon Press 1971) 9.

[73] Frederick William Maitland, *The Constitutional History of England* (CUP 1908) 398.

[74] Geoffrey Marshall, *Constitutional Conventions* (OUP 1984) 216.

[75] Kenneth Wheare, *Modern Constitutions* (OUP 1951) 179. On the legal or non-legal nature of conventions in detail, see Joseph Jaconelli, 'Do Constitutional Conventions Bind?' (2005) 64 Cambridge Law Journal 149.

[76] Colin Turpin, *British Government and the Constitution* (5th edn, Butterworths 2002) 115.

[77] Albert Venn Dicey, *Introduction to the Study of the Law of the Constitution* (Macmillan 1959) 24.

[78] Marshall (n 74) 14.

[79] Wheare (n 75) 180.

[80] Ivor Jennings, *The Law and the Constitution* (5th edn, University of London Press 1959) 136.

[81] Colin R Munro, *Studies in Constitutional Law* (2nd edn, Butterworths 1999) 61.

current topic, the most relevant example is that from a *legal* point of view, the king could choose anyone for the position of Prime Minister, but by *convention* he should choose as Prime Minister the person who can command a majority support in the House of Commons.[82] He does not breach any law by obeying this convention; he just uses his powers in a way which *also* fits the conventions.[83]

This is exactly what we need now. The election of Commission members should depend on which EP political group(s) have the most seats, and who they (in coalition) want to see in the seats of Commission members. But how can the European Council be forced to adopt such a practice? The mere accusations of antidemocratic behaviour can probably not force them, as they would refer to the literal interpretation of TEU, which favours a non-parliamentary solution. So the solution would simply be that the EP, by using its veto possibilities (or to put it more bluntly: blackmailing capacity), only accepts those concretely (and before the relevant meeting of the European Council already) defined persons as candidates by the European Council, whom the majority of the EP supports.[84] All other candidates will be refused.

The logic of such a change is not unknown to the EU institutions: before Mr Barroso became President of the Commission for the first time (2004), the European Council intended to propose a person from the political left, even though the elections to the EP had been won by the political right. The EP vetoed the idea, and the European Council had to choose someone from the political right. It would only be one step in the same direction (an important and big step, though), if the EP announced that they would accept only one particular person for that position. Such a revolt by the EP would be most likely if the political colour of the European Council and of the EP were to differ, as happened in Mr Barroso's case.[85] In 2004, a second event during the formation

[82] As a matter of fact, the office of Prime Minister itself is also based on constitutional convention; see Andrew Le Sueur and Maurice Sunkin, *Public Law* (Longman 1997) 56.

[83] Conventions in this sense exist also in other countries, but they have their most prominent role in British constitutional life due to the rudimentary legal framework of the British Constitution. Cf James G Wilson, 'American Constitutional Conventions' (1992) 40 Buffalo Law Review 645; Andrew Heard, *Canadian Constitutional Conventions: The Marriage of Law and Politics* (OUP1991); Giuseppe Ugo Rescigno, *Le convenzioni costituzionali* (Cedam 1972).

[84] This would *not* transform the EU into a majoritarian system. In Lijphart's terminology on the difference between majoritarian and consensus government, see Arend Lijphart, *Democracies* (Yale University Press 1984) esp 1–36, a majoritarian system would be similar to the UK. In the EU, however, the majority support would still mean a party coalition, and the quasi-constitutional court control of the ECJ (based on the treaties) would strongly limit the Commission. It would become thus a parliamentary system similar to Germany.

[85] The differing political colour is the default position as voters of domestic opposition parties are more likely to vote at EP elections; see Philip Manow and Holger Döring, 'Electoral and Mechanical Causes of Divided Government in the European Union' (2008) 41 Comparative Political Studies 1349.

of the EC also showed that the EP had the strength to influence substantially the composition of the Commission: criticism from the EP on one of the candidates for Commissioner (Rocco Buttiglione) led Barroso to change its membership and to alter the distribution of portfolios. But what we also need is the EU electorate knowing before the EP elections the candidate Commissioners (and their programmes), so they can choose their parties in light of this.[86] Some might even argue that the *Spitzenkandidaten* debate in 2014, and the success of Jean-Claude Juncker, was the Rubicon and that the EU actually already did become a parliamentary system.[87] What is still missing, however, is the same system for all members of the Commission, that is, knowing not only the *Spitzenkandidaten* but all candidate Commissioners (and their programmes) before the elections. Unfortunately, the formation of the Juncker Commission seemed to go along the traditional MS-dominated (and consequently, in the conceptual frame of European constitutionalism, antidemocratic) way.

The drawback in the 2019 EP elections obviously hampered the idea of a constitutional convention.[88] Nevertheless, this does not mean that the *Spitzenkandidaten*-system is dead. Even though we had to learn that the *Spitzenkandidaten*-system depends on many things and political context and various interests must not be neglected, the EP elections in 2024 were a major step towards the *Spitzenkandidaten*-system actually becoming a constitutional convention. With sufficient preparation for the 2028 elections there is a good chance of finally improving democratic accountability in the EU.

5.4 Suggestions for Reform before the Next EP Elections

An important lesson to be learned from the 2019 and 2024 cases was that the approach of the European parties in choosing their candidates is decisive. Some submit that '[i]f we want a credible *Spitzenkandidaten*-system, we need to have primary elections at the level of European political parties'. And that '[t]he American model could inspire a realistic and impactful mechanism'.[89]

[86] Simon Hix and Bjørn Høyland, *The Political System of the European Union* (3rd edn, Palgrave Macmillan 2011) 152.

[87] For the usual arguments in the *Spitzenkandidat* debate, see András Jakab, 'Why the Debate between Kumm and Armstrong Is about the Wrong Question' (20 June 2014) *Verfassungsblog* <http://www.verfassungsblog.de/debate-kumm-armstrong-wrong-question/#.U6RIbfl_uqg> accessed 24 October 2024.

[88] Ylenia M. Citino, 'Unwritten Rules Shaping the EU's "Form of Government": A Study of Conventions and Their Constitutional Implications' (2023) 30 *Maastricht Journal of European and Comparative Law* 107 (esp 125).

[89] Doru Frantescu and Dan Luca, 'Why the Spitzenkandidaten System Will Have Little Impact in 2024' (14 June 2022) *Euractiv* <https://www.euractiv.com/section/future-eu/opinion/why-the-spitze

Yet others suggest to 'convince the Council of the EU to jointly enforce an electoral reform agenda well before the next European elections' with '[t]ransnational electoral lists' as a key element of this reform.[90]

Indeed, in May 2022 a proposal for transnational lists and a leading candidate, in the form of a new European electoral law, was approved by a 'large majority' in the EP. Fittingly, this is instrumental for the cause and has at the same time been the first ever right of initiative exercised by the EP.[91] Although it seemed 'doable' to implement such a reform before the EP elections in 2024, in the end it did not take place.[92] The needed procedure was just too demanding;[93] only the Volt party presented a 'symbolic' transnational list.[94] Moreover, citizens could only vote for candidates in their respective countries.

nkandidaten-system-will-have-little-impact-in-2024/> accessed 24 October 2024, despite being sceptical about the success of the *Spitzenkandidaten*-system in 2024. Being sceptical too: Editorial (n 15) 609: 'In 2019 the procedure misfired. Although that may not necessarily be the end of it, we argue that for the time being the prospects of further parliamentarisation of the Union's system of government do not look favourable, due to the systemic dominance of the European Council.'

[90] Johanna Edthofer and Paul Schmidt, 'The Future of the EU`s Spitzenkandidaten Procedure' (7 April 2021) Policy Briefs Österreichische Gesellschaft für Europapolitik <https://www.oegfe.at/policy-briefs/the-future-of-the-eus-spitzenkandidaten-procedure/?lang=en> accessed 24 October 2024. Similarly, Paul Schmidt, 'Why the EU's Spitzenkandidaten Procedure Should Be Revived before the Next European Parliament Elections' (29 July 2021) *LSE Europeblog* <https://blogs.lse.ac.uk/europpblog/2021/07/29/why-the-eus-spitzenkandidaten-procedure-should-be-revived-before-the-next-european-parliament-elections/> accessed 24 October 2024.

[91] European Parliament legislative resolution of 3 May 2022 on the proposal for a Council Regulation on the election of the members of the European Parliament by direct universal suffrage, repealing Council Decision (76/787/ECSC, EEC, Euratom) and the Act concerning the election of the members of the European Parliament by direct universal suffrage annexed to that Decision (2020/2220(INL)—2022/0902(APP)) [2022] P9_TA(2022)0129. For an analysis, see Monika Polzin, 'Transnational Lists, Diversity and Quota Regulation: The European Parliament's Proposal for a New Electoral Law' (3 December 2022) *Weekend EU Law Live*.

[92] Eleonora Vasques, 'EU Lawmaker: Electoral Reform "Doable" by 2024 Elections' (16 February 2023) *Euractiv* <https://www.euractiv.com/section/elections/video/eu-lawmaker-electoral-reform-doable-by-2024-elections/> accessed 24 October 2024, relying on Domenec Ruiz Devesa, 'a Spanish member of the European Parliament responsible for legislative text dedicated to the reform and transnational lists'.

[93] Article 223 TFEU: '(1) The European Parliament shall draw up a proposal to lay down the provisions necessary for the election of its Members by direct universal suffrage in accordance with a uniform procedure in all Member States or in accordance with principles common to all Member States. The Council, acting unanimously in accordance with a special legislative procedure and after obtaining the consent of the European Parliament, which shall act by a majority of its component Members, shall lay down the necessary provisions. These provisions shall enter into force following their approval by the Member States in accordance with their respective constitutional requirements. (2) The European Parliament, acting by means of regulations on its own initiative in accordance with a special legislative procedure after seeking an opinion from the Commission and with the consent of the Council, shall lay down the regulations and general conditions governing the performance of the duties of its Members. All rules or conditions relating to the taxation of Members or former Members shall require unanimity within the Council.'

[94] Vincenzo Genovese, 'Volt Party Presents "Symbolic" Transnational List in EU Elections' (8 April 2024) <https://www.euronews.com/my-europe/2024/04/08/volt-party-presents-symbolic-transnational-list-in-eu-elections> accessed 24 October 2024.

The reform is still important. According to an MEP three main objectives of the reform are '"[t]o make a real European debate, ... to give visibility to European political parties" and to "make more real" the process of electing directly the "president of the European Commission"'. A key instrument of the reform is the introduction of transnational lists, which enable EU citizens to elect candidates across the Union.[95] By a real European debate the MEP refers to the fact that according to the current situation, there are rather national debates and often EP elections are not taken seriously enough. This will be changed by a 'pan-European campaign'. 'EU citizens would have two votes in European elections, one for their national constituency and another for the Union-wide constituency.'[96] So, like treaty change, this would be an important option. However, it is challenging because of Article 223 TFEU and the necessity of a unanimous decision by the Council in addition to an approval by all MSs.

5.5 (Positive) Consequences of the *Spitzenkandidaten*-System

Once the re-established *Spitzenkandidaten*-system is consolidated several (positive) consequences might surface.

(a) Politicians running for EP elections will need to work out some understandable and concrete policies to campaign for votes.[97] These policies could be checked on at the following elections, and, if unfulfilled, the Commission could be voted out. This holds true despite another—depending on the view—negative side-effect which would be the personalization of elections.[98]

(b) The respective campaign should be much more about EU policies and with the growth of public interest the media would also cover EU affairs more thoroughly.[99] Indeed, in 2019 '[t]he role of the European political parties

[95] Cf Maria Diaz Crego, 'Transnational Electoral Lists: Ways to Europeanise Elections to the European Parliament' (February 2021) *EPRS Study* <https://www.europarl.europa.eu/RegData/etudes/STUD/2021/679084/EPRS_STU(2021)679084_EN.pdf> accessed 24 October 2024. On the combination with *Spitzenkandidaten*-system, see eg Yvonne Nasshoven, '"To be or not to be?" Das Spitzenkandidatenprinzip in der Europawahl 2019 und zukünftige Szenarien' (2019) 42 *Integration* 280.

[96] Maria Diaz Crego, 'Proposing New Rules for European Elections' (May 2022) *EPRS at a Glance* <https://www.europarl.europa.eu/RegData/etudes/ATAG/2022/729384/EPRS_ATA(2022)729384_EN.pdf> accessed 24 October 2024.

[97] The first time it happens, we probably would not call it a convention, but the second or third time it will become a convention. See above n 80 and the relevant main text.

[98] See generally on this issue Katjana Gattermann and Franziska Marquart, 'Do *Spitzenkandidaten* Really Make a Difference? An Experiment on the Effectiveness of Personalized European Parliament Election Campaigns' (2020) 21 European Union Politics 612.

[99] For a mostly similar view see Hix (n 66) 179–80, 203–04.

was strengthened from that of being service providers to being proactive campaigner'.[100]

(c) With such a transparent and direct link between election and responsibility, that is, with an effectiveness of popular will, the turnout at EP elections might rise too.[101]

(d) Subsequently even the popularity of the EU might grow too.[102]

(e) How European parties select their lead candidates would become much more important.[103]

(f) Despite the rather positive side-effects it should not be overlooked that self-interests of actors can be and indeed were instrumental in supporting the *Spitzenkandidaten*-system too.[104]

[100] Stergios Fotopoulos, 'What Sort of Changes Did the Spitzenkandidat Process Bring to the Quality of the EU's Democracy?' (2019) 18 European View 194.

[101] Hermann Schmitt, Sara Hobolt, and Sebastian Adrian Popa, 'Does Personalization Increase Turnout? Spitzenkandidaten in the 2014 European Parliament Elections' (2015) 16 European Union Politics 347: after conducting 'an EU-wide post-election survey' they conclude their 'findings show that the recognition of the candidates increased the propensity to turn out'. Cf Mattias Kumm, 'Why Europeans Will Not Embrace Constitutional Patriotism' (2008) 6 International Journal of Constitutional Law 117, 130: 'The fact that citizens turn out for [European Parliament] elections at all, knowing that their vote is practically not to change anything, has long puzzled public choice theorists.' Dana Spinant, 'How to Make Elections Sexy: Give Voters a Say in Europe's Top Jobs' (11 February 2004) *European Voice* 12. Turnout at elections is primarily *not* influenced by the public esteem of the institutions concerned; see Mark N Franklin, 'How Structural Factors Cause Turnout Variations at European Parliament Elections' (2001) 2 European Union Politics 309. But turnout is influenced by the stakes of the election; that is why domestic turnout is usually higher than the EP turnout, and why in countries where EU subsidies are higher EP turnout is also higher; see Mikko Mattila, 'Why Bother? Determinants of Turnout in the European Elections' (2003) 22 Electoral Studies 449.

[102] Peter Mair, 'Political Opposition and the European Union' (2007) 42 Government and Opposition 1, especially 12: 'because we are denied an appropriate political arena in which to hold European governance accountable, we are almost pushed into organizing opposition to Europe.'

[103] For an empirical analysis as to how and why Europarties selected lead candidates (*Spitzenkandidaten*) for the 2019 EPt elections, concluding 'that mainly intra-party dissent hampered large democratic reforms', see Wouter Wolfs, Gert-Jan Put, and Steven Van Hecke, 'Explaining the Reform of the Europarties' Selection Procedures for Spitzenkandidaten' (2021) 43 Journal of European Integration 891, 891. Cf Gert-Jan Put and others, 'The Choice of Spitzenkandidaten: A Comparative Analysis of the Europarties' Selection Procedures' (2016) 4 Politics and Governance 9, 9 analysing the selection of leading candidates by the political families in 2014 and concluding 'that the procedures are largely copy-paste from the Europarties' internal procedures for selecting a president.' See also Katjana Gattermann, Claes H de Vreese, and Wouter van der Brug, 'Evaluations of the Spitzenkandidaten: The Role of Information and News Exposure in Citizens' Preference Formation' (2016) 4 Politics and Governance 37, 37 showing 'that three factors enable citizens to formulate a preference for the *Spitzenkandidaten*: news exposure, general EU political information, and campaign-specific information about the *Spitzenkandidaten*.'

[104] Lukáš Hamřík and Petr Kaniok, 'Is It All about European Democracy? The Motives behind the Institutionalisation of the Spitzenkandidaten' (2019) 15 Journal of Contemporary European Research 354.

However, once again, for our purpose the most important consequence would be a politically strengthened EC which owes its strength to the EP (elections).[105]

6. Conclusion

The consolidation of the re-established *Spitzenkandidaten*-system would be a significant improvement for democracy within the EU,[106] and in relation to the EU's ability to face its illiberal MSs. Moreover, it is actually quite easily conceivable. There is no need for a treaty change, nor even a new electoral law. The current legal framework already allows it; consequently, it requires 'only' political work. The idea first emerged in the 2014 EP elections, but then MS governments short-sightedly abandoned it in 2019 in a chaotic and untransparent series of events. And the EP let them get away with it. This change was a huge setback for EU democracy and was a phenomenon of erosion itself.[107] Redoing this setback would be helpful both to rescue the EU from its own illiberal regimes and to end its own democratic accountability malaise.

From this perspective it was important that the *Spitzenkandidaten*-system was taken seriously in the 2024 EP elections. The EP is the organ which has shown much more willingness to confront illiberal MSs than the EC or the European Council—it is of the essence that all future MEPs are convinced that the consolidation of the (re-)established *Spitzenkandidaten*-system is a viable way forward. We need strong, willing, and able politicians in the EP who are ambitious enough to contribute to the consolidation of the re-established direct link between election and responsibility. Facing the illiberal EU MSs provides additional incentives to keep the *Spitzenkandidaten*-system for the next elections in 2028 as well.

Moreover, the *Spitzenkandidaten* system could have a positive knock-on effect for European democracy. If people know that their vote has a greater impact on European politics, they are more likely to take an interest in the EP elections. If the elections become more politically significant, the incentive for European politicians to act in favour of the European electorate will increase.

105 See Alberto Alemanno, 'How Much Better Is Better Regulation? Assessing the Impact of the Better Regulation Package on the European Union—A Research Agenda' (2015) 6 European Journal of Risk Regulation 344, 344 on the 'Juncker Commission': 'Emboldened by the Spitzenkandidaten process, the new European Commission emerges as the most political yet.'

106 For a good overview of the arguments and experiences, see Silvia Kotanidis, *Spitzenkandidaten or the Lead Candidate Process* (European Parliament Research Service 2023).

107 See Chapter 3.

The task is not to hope for morally good politicians, but to design the institutional incentives so that politicians are more likely to do the right thing. The establishment and the process of enhancing the effectivity of political accountability of political decision-makers both in the executive (Commission) and the legislative (EP and Council) is thus of great importance.[108] As politicians are mostly not lacking ambition, we are optimistic that sooner or later this will happen, and that this tendency will regain its track. The right moment when the political colour of the EP and that of the Council is different in order to play out this conflict will nevertheless arrive sooner or later and the 2019 setback might well be overcome. In the words of John Markoff: 'One might anticipate a recapitulation of Europe's nineteenth-century struggles over democratization on a larger scale, in which the power of the EP in Strasbourg in relation to the European bureaucracy becomes a central point of contention.'[109] It is happening here and now, and the outcome is likely to be the same as in the nineteenth century. The sooner, the better.

[108] See eg European Parliament legislative resolution of 3 May 2022 on the proposal for a Council Regulation on the election of the members of the European Parliament by direct universal suffrage, repealing Council Decision (76/787/ECSC, EEC, Euratom) and the Act concerning the election of the members of the European Parliament by direct universal suffrage annexed to that Decision (2020/2220(INL)—2022/0902(APP)) [2022] P9_TA(2022)0129. Cf also the German coalition agreement of the current government on a binding *Spitzenkandidaten*-system: Koalitionsvertrag zwischen SPD, Bündnis 90/Die Grünen und FDP, Mehr Fortschritt wagen. Bündnis für Freiheit, Gerechtigkeit und Nachhaltigkeit, p 104 <https://www.spd.de/fileadmin/Dokumente/Koalitionsvertrag/Koalitionsvertrag_2021-2025.pdf> accessed 24 October 2024.

[109] John Markoff, *Waves of Democracy: Social Movements and Political Change* (Pine Forge 1996) 135.

Conclusion

Why is it that the rule of law and democracy have eroded in Hungary and Poland in recent years? We have suggested in this book that it is their common post-socialist past that has played a decisive role in some of the steepest erosions worldwide. More precisely, it is the post-socialist legal culture that must be examined. In Chapter 1, we used the framework of (legal) institutionalism to demonstrate that beyond formal rules, it is especially important to consider the de facto practices of officials and the accompanying narratives. This demonstrates that while formal legal rules might be (mostly) acceptable and comparable to other liberal democratic constitutions, it is the de facto practices and the narratives which expose the illiberal nature of a regime. Liberal laws are applied in an illiberal (abusive, discriminatory, human rights violating, selective, politically biased) manner. Institutionalism helps to disclose the relevance of such practices.

In Chapter 2, we took a closer look at the Hungarian constitution-making process 2010/11. When looking particularly at the narrative which accompanied this process it turned out that this was deeply dishonest. Neither the necessity to get rid of the 'communist Constitution of 1949' nor to end the 'confusion' following the end of socialism in 1989/90 was truly the reason for adopting the Fundamental Law. Rather, behind the façade of the new Constitution, illiberal practices such as court-packing were easier, less obvious, and therefore politically less costly. By introducing a symbolic political rupture, it also became easier to change de facto practices as just referred to above.

Another lesson to be learned from (legal) institutionalism and the Hungarian case is the necessity for some kind of effective external pressure for institution-building. Such effective external pressure ceased to exist after Hungary's accession to the EU. While EU candidate countries had no choice but to comply with the EU's requirements concerning democracy and the rule of law ('Copenhagen criteria'), after accession, the political bargaining power of the very same countries became much stronger. Even though the EU has always had various legal tools, their triggering has depended on the political discretion of EU institutions, and due to the EU's political dynamics these tools

Saving the European Union from Its Illiberal Member States. András Jakab and Lando Kirchmair, Oxford University Press.
DOI: 10.1093/oso/9780198954606.003.0009

have only been used belatedly, half-heartedly, or not at all. Moreover, EU membership paradoxically weakened democracy and the rule of law also within these countries. First, large sums of uncontrolled EU subsidies enhanced local corruption and sometimes they even bought popularity for illiberal incumbents. Second, the free movement of persons resulted in large cohorts leaving for Western Europe, especially those individuals who would have been more receptive of the liberal values of democracy and the rule of law.

So why then, if the EU is partly to blame for the misery, has it not stopped this downward spiral of illiberalism in some of its MSs? Why has the EU been unable to trigger its existing enforcement tools? How can we explain these unfortunate political dynamics? One key reason—as we argued in Chapter 3—is that the EU itself has deficits concerning the rule of law and democracy. Some of these deficits (especially the deficit in democratic accountability) are well known and actually not particularly new. Others stem from policy changes (such as the declining number of infringement procedures, thereby resulting in an erosion of the formal rule of law at EU level), whereas at certain places the illiberal MSs themselves have weakened the functioning of the EU (via veto threats). Thus not only has the EU kept poisoning its illiberal MSs (with uncontrolled money), but these illiberal MSs have also hampered EU policies and infiltrated EU institutions with Trojan horse officials (the best-known example is the Hungarian Commissioner for Neighbourhood and Enlargement).[1] In certain cases, various threads are intertwined, for example: while in the EP elections in 2014 the *Spitzenkandidaten*-principle was applied and, thus, a direct link between EP elections and democratic accountability was established for the first time, this principle was abandoned in 2019 (which meant an erosion when compared to 2014). While the reasons for this unfortunate 2019 development were complex, one of them was staunch opposition by the illiberal Hungarian Prime Minister. The consequences weigh heavily. While the EP has been an EU organ that has shown much more eagerness to confront the illiberal regimes in the EU, it has had a diminished influence on the EC since the 2019 failure of the *Spitzenkandidaten*-system. This means, again, that the EC has been less bothered by the EP's strong stance against illiberalism, and therefore the EC has been less likely to use the tools at its disposal to fight against illiberal MSs as compared to the hypothetical

[1] Alexandra Brzozowski, 'European Parliament Calls for Investigation into Enlargement Commissioner Varhelyi' (19 January 2023) *Euractiv* <https://www.euractiv.com/section/enlargement/news/european-parliament-calls-for-investigation-into-enlargement-commissioner-varhelyi/> accessed 24 October 2024.

scenario of an EC led by a *Spitzenkandidat*. The poisoning of the EU and its illiberal Members States is mutual. The reintroduction and consolidation of the *Spitzenkandidaten*-system for the 2024 elections is therefore an important step in the right direction.

Despite this positive step, negative developments are still present and are particularly disastrous given that, as shown in Chapter 4, the EU and its MSs are mutually dependent on each other after decades of European integration. In addition, the rule of law and democracy are also mutually dependent. Acknowledging this double interdependence shows that the situation is quite complex and changes on one level also likely influence the other level. You cannot protect the rule of law without protecting democracy and vice versa—both at EU level and at MS level. On the basis of this insight, we offer three antidotes against the mutual poisoning. These antidotes concern different areas which are all in need of improvement.

The first antidote would not only help to have an objective and sober understanding of how severe the situation is, but even more importantly it would make inaction politically more costly by showing this severity. In Chapter 5 we present an EU rule of law index that could emerge from the EU Justice Scoreboard. The erosion of the rule of law and democracy is happening slowly and inconspicuously, so the first challenge is to realize that 'we have a situation'. Exactly for this purpose, rule of law and democracy indices can be powerful tools to depict and visualize this process. Well-known rule of law indices are provided by Freedom House (FIW), the Bertelsmann Stiftung (BTI), the World Bank (WGI), and the WJP (RLI), whereas V-Dem is an important democracy index. While the introduction of the EUJS in 2013 has already been an important step in laying the ground for an EU-wide analysis, we suggest that the EUJS should be further developed into a proper rule of law and democracy index by aggregating expert opinions into a single number.[2] This would make the EUJS a significantly more useful tool in the ongoing EU illiberal regime challenge. Creating such an index would not just be 'useful' or 'helpful' in providing additional arguments for triggering certain enforcement tools, but more importantly, it would make the inaction by EU organs, which has been a key problem in the illiberal regime crisis, politically more costly: it would become more difficult for members of the European Council not to act in Article 7 procedures, and it would be politically more embarrassing for the Commission not to launch infringement procedures (even if formally the

[2] See on this Chapter 5.

move would stay under the Commission's discretion) or to release funds that have been made subject to financial conditionality due to rule of law and democracy concerns. Furthermore, the EUJS should not only evaluate EU MSs, but also the EU itself. This addition would make the tool even more legitimate and, as we have seen, would contribute to understanding and tackling important rule of law and democracy issues at EU level too.

The second antidote is to widen the scope of applicability of the European Charter of Fundamental Rights. This pertains specifically to the rule of law and strives to protect it via a comprehensive strengthening of European fundamental rights (Chapter 6). The enforcement of Article 2 TEU values vis-à-vis MSs could benefit from the application of the CFR also in instances where the current interpretation of Article 51 (1) CFR prevents this. This would be the case if the CFR were also applicable to purely domestic cases, for example—but not only—with regard to fundamental rights-relevant violations related to the values enshrined in Article 2 TEU. In this case, the ECJ, which has already partly taken this path recently, could prevent the violation of core EU values. The most important historical challenge to these values in Europe today is the systematic dismantling of the rule of law and democracy in certain MSs. It is the very purpose of fundamental rights to provide answers to such dangers. When one speaks of the rule of law and democracy, one necessarily also means fundamental rights. The EU should, thus, perceive itself as a complete fundamental rights union. While the traditional interpretation of Article 51 (1) CFR had a balanced division of competence between the EU and its MSs in mind, the disregard of Article 2 TEU values triggers a *clausula rebus sic stantibus*: the delicate federal balance can only be upheld if both ends stick to the original promise made. There exist two ways of completing the European Fundamental Rights Union: treaty revision, on the one hand, and a reinterpretation of Article 51 CFR, on the other. Both ways have in common that only a complete fundamental rights union can establish a system of fundamental rights protection that is uniform and thus equality-preserving in cases where national fundamental rights fail to provide sufficient protection.

Finally, the third antidote, the *Spitzenkandidaten*-system, does not only concern the EU's own democratic accountability, but it would also enhance the likelihood of the EC stepping up against illiberal MSs. The EP (as opposed to the European Council) has an institutional set-up that makes it more likely to step up against illiberal MSs, and if the EP's role is stronger in the election of the EC, then the EC's behaviour is also more likely to be tougher on illiberal MSs (Chapter 7). Therefore, the establishment and the process of enhancing the effectivity of political accountability of political decision-makers both in the executive (EC) and the legislative (EP and Council) is of great importance. To improve the situation in illiberal MSs—especially since it is the EP that is showing much greater willingness to confront illiberal MSs as opposed to the Council—it is essential that all future MEPs are convinced that installing the *Spitzenkandidaten*-system is a viable option. Strong, willing, and able politicians are needed in the EP who will have enough ambition to make this change. In addition, the *Spitzenkandidaten*-system could trigger a positive domino effect for European democracy. If people know that their vote has a stronger impact on European politics, they are more likely to show interest in the EP elections. If the elections become politically more prominent, the incentive for European politicians to act in favour of the European electorate increases. The task is not to hope for morally good politicians, but to shape the *institutional incentives* in a way that makes politicians more likely to do the right thing.

All the three antidotes have in common that they are underrated in the current debate on what to do against the rise of illiberalism within the EU. Furthermore, the implementation of the three antidotes does not require difficult obstacles to be overcome. While admittedly treaty changes might be the cleanest solution, we offer ways as to how all three antidotes could be implemented without much difficulty. Although we are convinced that the current withholding of substantial amounts of financial support is an important step towards taking the problem more seriously, this alone will not suffice and there are no institutional guarantees against the softening of the EU's current (admittedly belated and in its scope still limited) stance. Considering the cultural vulnerabilities of former socialist EU MSs, there is a real danger that illiberalism will not stop at the borders of currently illiberal EU MSs. We have argued in this book, that with the help of the mentioned three antidotes, saving the EU from its illiberal MSs would be considerably more likely.

Bibliography

Ablonczy B, 'Ezermilliárdos kínai adósság: a magyar szuverenitást veszélyezteti a Fudan és a Belgrád-vasút' (21 April 2021) <https://www.valaszonline.hu/2021/04/21/fudan-egyetem-kina-magyarorszag-adossag-geopolitika-elemzes/> accessed 24 October 2024.

Acemoglu D, 'Constitutions, Politics and Economics: A Review Essay on Persson and Tabellini's The Economic Effects of Constitutions' (2005) 43 Journal of Economic Literature 1025.

Acemoglu D and Robinson JA, *Why Nations Fail: The Origins of Power, Prosperity and Poverty* (Crown Business 2012).

Ahmed DI and Gouda M, 'Measuring Constitutional Islamization: The Islamic Constitutions Index' (2015) 38 Hastings International & Comparative Law Review 1.

Albrecht K, Kirchmair L, and Schwarzer V, 'Introduction' in K Albrecht, L Kirchmair, and V Schwarzer (eds), *Die Krise des demokratischen Rechtsstaats im 21. Jahrhundert: Oder wie sich die Geschichte gegen ihr Ende wehrt* (Franz Steiner Verlag 2020) 11.

Alder J, *Constitutional and Administrative Law* (5th edn, Palgrave Macmillan 2005).

Alemanno A, 'How Much Better Is Better Regulation? Assessing the Impact of the Better Regulation Package on the European Union—A Research Agenda' (2015) 6 European Journal of Risk Regulation 344.

Alesina A and Giuliano P, 'Culture and Institutions' (2015) 53 Journal of Economic Literature 898.

Alter K, 'The European Court's Political Power' (1996) 19 West European Politics 458.

Alter K, 'Who Are the "Masters of the Treaties"? European Governments and the European Court of Justice' (1998) 52 International Organisations 121.

Alter K, *Establishing the Supremacy of European Law: The Making of an International Rule of Law in Europe* (OUP 2001).

Amato G and others (eds), *The History of the European Union: Constructing Europe* (Hart 2019).

Antal A, 'Politikai és jogi alkotmányosság Magyarországon' (2013) 22 Politikatudományi Szemle 48.

Arato A, 'Democratic Legitimacy and Forms of Constitutional Change' (2017) 24 Constellations 447.

Avbelj M, 'The Sociology of (Slovenian) Constitutional Democracy' (2017) 1 Hague Journal of the Rule of Law 35.

Babbie ER, *The Practice of Social Research* (13th edn, Wadsworth 2013).

Badura P, 'Bewahrung und Veränderung demokratischer und rechtsstaatlicher Verfassungsstruktur in den internationalen Gemeinschaften' (1966) Veröffentlichungen der Vereinigung der Deutschen Staatsrechtslehrer 34.

Ballstaedt S-P, *Visualisieren: Bilder in wissenschaftlichen Texten* (utb 2012).

Banfield EC, *The Moral Basis of a Backward Society* (Free Press 1958).

Bánkúti M, Halmai G, and Scheppele KL, 'Hungary's Illiberal Turn: Disabling the Constitution' (2012) 23 Journal of Democracy 138.

Baquero Cruz J, 'Alternativas a las condiciones de revisión y entrada en vigor' in I Méndez de Vigo (ed), *¿Qué fue de la Constitución Europea?* (Planeta 2007) 293.

Baraggia A and Bonelli M, 'Linking Money to Values: The New Rule of Law Conditionality Regulation and Its Constitutional Challenges' (2022) 23 German Law Journal 131.

Bárd P and others, 'An EU Mechanism on Democracy, the Rule of Law, and Fundamental Rights: Assessing the Need and Possibilities for the Establishment of an EU Scoreboard on Democracy, the Rule of Law and Fundamental Rights' Eur Parl Research Paper PE 579328, No 2016-18.

Bast J, 'Autonomy in Decline? A Commentary on Rimšēvičs and ECB v Latvia' (13 May 2019) *Verfassungsblog* <https://verfassungsblog.de/autonomy-in-decline-a-commentary-on-rimsevics-and-ecb-v-latvia/> accessed 24 October 2024.

Bayer L, 'Hungary to Take Down Controversial Soros Posters' (12 July 2017) *Politico* <https://www.politico.eu/article/hungary-to-take-down-controversial-soros-posters/> accessed 24 October 2024.

Bayer Z, 'A pápa esze' (2 August 2016) *Mandiner* <https://mandiner.hu/velemeny/2016/08/bayer-zsolt-a-papa-esze> accessed 24 October 2024.

Bell J, 'The Importance of Institutions' in M Adams and D Heirbaut (eds), *The Method and Culture of Comparative Law: Essays in Honour of Mark Van Hoecke* (Hart 2015) 207.

Bellamy R, *Political Constitutionalism: A Republican Defence of the Constitutionality of Democracy* (CUP 2007).

Bellamy R, *A Republican Europe of States: Cosmopolitanism, Intergovernmentalism and Democracy in the EU* (CUP 2019).

Bencze M and Badó A, 'A magyar bírósági rendszer hatékonyságát és az ítélkezés színvonalát befolyásoló strukturális és személyi feltételek' in A Jakab and G Gajduschek (eds), *A magyar jogrendszer állapota* (MTA TK 2016) 441.

Besselink L, 'The Member States, the National Constitutions and the Scope of the Charter' (2001) 8 Maastricht Journal of European and Comparative Law 68.

Bignami FE, 'The Democratic Deficit in European Community Rulemaking: A Call for Notice and Comment in Comitology' (1999) 40 Harvard International Law Journal 415.

Blank J and others, *Bench Marking in an International Perspective: An International Comparison of the Mechanisms and Performance of the Judiciary System* (2004) <http://siteresources.worldbank.org/INTLAWJUSTINST/Resources/Benchmarking.pdf> accessed 24 October 2024.

Blauberger M and Sedelmeier U, 'Sanctioning Democratic Backsliding in the European Union: Transnational Salience, Negative Intergovernmental Spillover, and Policy Change' (2024) Journal of European Public Policy 1.

Blumer S and others, *Politics in the European Union* (5th edn, OUP 2020).

Böckenförde E-W, 'Demokratie als Verfassungsprinzip' in E-W Böckenförde (ed), *Staat, Verfassung, Demokratie* (Suhrkamp 1991) 300.

Böckenförde E-W, *Welchen Weg geht Europa?* (Carl-Friedrich-von-Siemens-Stiftung 1997).

Bogaards M, 'De-democratization in Hungary: Diffusely Defective Democracy' (2018) 25 Democratization 1.

Bohle D and Greskovits B, *Capitalist Diversity on Europe's Periphery* (Cornell University Press 2012).

Borowsky M, 'Artikel 51—Anwendungsbereich' in J Meyer (ed), *Charta der Grundrechte der Europäischen Union* (3rd edn, Nomos 2011) 653.

Borowsky M, 'Artikel 51—Anwendungsbereich' in J Meyer (ed), *Charta der Grundrechte der Europäischen Union* (4th edn, Nomos 2014) 758.

Botero JC, Nelson RL, and Pratt C, 'Indices and Indicators of Justice, Governance, and the Rule of Law: An Overview' (2011) 3 Hague Journal on the Rule of Law 153.

Botero JC and Ponce A, *Measuring the Rule of Law* (2011); EU Justice Scoreboard (29 July 2024) EC <http://ec.europa.eu/justice/effective-justice/scoreboard/index_en.htm> accessed 24 October 2024.

Bowles S and Gintis H, *A Cooperative Species: Human Reciprocity and Its Evolution* (Princeton University Press 2011).

Bozóki A and Hegedűs D, 'An Externally Constrained Hybrid Regime: Hungary in the European Union' (2018) 25 Democratization 1173.

Bozzay B, 'Bencsik András: Ferenc pápa keresztényellenes, meg akarta alázni Magyarországot' (8 June 2021) *telex* <https://telex.hu/belfold/2021/06/08/bencsik-andras-ferenc-papa-meg-akarta-alazni-magyarorszagot-es-keresztenyellenesen-viselkedik> accessed 24 October 2024.

Bradley C, 'International Organizations and the Production of Indicators: The Case of Freedom House' in SE Merry, KE Davis, and B Kingsbury (eds), *The Quiet Power of Indicators: Measuring Governance, Corruption, and the Rule of Law* (CUP 2015) 27.

Braithwaite V, *Defiance in Taxation and Governance: Resisting and Dismissing Authority in a Democracy* (Edward Elgar 2009).

Bruner J, 'The Narrative Construction of Reality' (1991) 18 Critical Inquiry 1.

Brusis M, *Illiberale Drift und Proliferation, BTI-Regionalbericht Ostmittel- und Südosteuropa* (Bertelsmann 2018).

Brzozowski A, 'Belgium, Germany Make Joint Proposal for EU Rule of Law Monitoring Mechanism' (19 March 2019) *Euractiv* <https://www.euractiv.com/section/justice-home-affairs/news/belgium-germany-make-joint-proposal-for-eu-rule-of-law-monitoring-mechanism/on> accessed 24 October 2024.

Brzozowski A, 'European Parliament Calls for Investigation into Enlargement Commissioner Varhelyi' (19 January 2023) *Euractiv* <https://www.euractiv.com/section/enlargement/news/european-parliament-calls-for-investigation-into-enlargement-commissioner-varhelyi/> accessed 24 October 2024.

Bugarič B, 'Protecting Democracy inside the EU' in C Closa and D Kochenov (eds), *Reinforcing Rule of Law Oversight in the European Union* (CUP 2016) 82.

Búrca G de, 'Poland and Hungary's EU Membership: On not Confronting Authoritarian Governments' (2022) 20 International Journal of Constitutional Law 13.

Butler I, 'Enforce Respect for the Rule of Law?' (13 December 2012) *Voices*, Open Society Foundation <https://www.opensocietyfoundations.org/voices/justice-scoreboard-effective-mechanism-enforce-respect-rule-law> accessed 24 October 2024.

Butler I, 'How to Monitor the Rule of Law, Democracy and Fundamental Rights in the EU' (August 2013) Open Society European Policy Institute 2 <https://www.opensocietyfoundations.org/uploads/aad3f011-e848-4202-8c2b-2103219c31be/how-monitor-rule-law-democracy-and-fundamental-rights-eu.pdf> accessed 24 October 2024.

Butler WE, *Soviet Law* (OUP 1988).

Cahan D and Slinko A, 'Electoral Competition under Best-Worst Voting Rules' (2018) 51 Social Choice and Welfare 259.

Calliess C, 'Europa als Wertegemeinschaft—Integration und Identität durch europäisches Verfassungsrecht?' (2004) 59 JuristenZeitung 1033.

Calliess C and Van der Schyff G (eds), *Constitutional Identity in a Europe of Multilevel Constitutionalism* (CUP 2019).

Canor I, 'My Brother's Keeper? Horizontal Solange: "An Ever Closer Distrust among the Peoples of Europe"' (2013) 50 Common Market Law Review 383.

Cappelletti M, *The Judicial Process in Comparative Perspective* (Clarendon Press 1989).

Carp R, 'The Struggle for the Rule of Law in Romania as an EU Member State: The Role of the Cooperation and Verification Mechanism' (2014) 10 Utrecht Law Review 1.

Cartabia M, 'Article 51—Field of Application' in WBT Mock and G Demuro (eds), *Human Rights in Europe* (Carolina Academic Press 2010) 318.

Cherchye L, Moesen W, and Van Puyenbroeck T, 'One Market, One Number? A Composite Indicator Assessment of EU Internal Market Dynamics' (2007) 51 European Economic Review 749.

Cherepanov V, Feddersen T, and Sandroni A, 'Rationalization' (2013) 8 Theoretical Economics 775.

Cheruvu S, 'When Does the European Commission Pursue Noncompliance?' (2022) 23 European Union Politics 375.

Christiansen T, 'EU-Spitzenkandidaten—neue Impulse und ihre Folgen für das politische System der EU' (2015) 38 Integration 26.

Christiansen T, 'After the *Spitzenkandidaten*: Fundamental Change in the EU's Political System?' (2016) 39 West European Politics 992.

Chronowski N and Vincze A, 'Full Steam Back: The Hungarian Constitutional Court Avoids Further Conflict with the ECJ' (15 December 2021) *Verfassungsblog* <https://verfassungsblog.de/full-steam-back/> accessed 24 October 2024.

Chronowski N and Vincze A, 'The Hungarian Constitutional Court and the Central European University Case: Justice Delayed is Justice Denied: Decision of the Hungarian Constitutional

Court of 6 July 2021 and the Judgment of the ECJ of 6 October 2020, Case C-66/18' (2021) European Constitutional Law Review 1.

Citino YM, 'Unwritten Rules Shaping the EU's "Form of Government": A Study of Conventions and Their Constitutional Implications' (2023) 30 Maastricht Journal of European and Comparative Law 107.

Claes M, 'The Primacy of EU Law in European and National Law' in D Chalmers and A Arnull (eds), *The Oxford Handbook of European Union Law* (OUP 2015) 178.

Closa C, 'Some Foundations for the Normative Discussion on Supranational Citizenship and Democracy' in UK Preuß and F Requejo (eds), *European Citizenship, Multiculturalism and the State* (Nomos 1998) 105.

Closa C, *The Politics of Ratification of EU Treaties* (Routledge 2013).

Closa C, 'Institutional Logics and the EU's Limited Sanctioning Capacity under Article 7 TEU' (2020) 42 International Political Science Review 501.

Closa C, Kochenov D, and Weiler JHH, 'Reinforcing Rule of Law Oversight in the European Union' (2014) EUI Working Papers RSCAS <http://cadmus.eui.eu/bitstream/handle/1814/30117/RSCAS_2014_25_FINAL.pdf?sequence=3> accessed 24 October 2024.

Cohen A, 'Viktor Orban's Goulash Energy Policy Makes Hungary Putin's Trojan Horse in Europe' (17 May 2022) *Forbes* <https://www.forbes.com/sites/arielcohen/2022/05/17/viktor-orbans-goulash-energy-policy-makes-hungary-putins-trojan-horse-in-europe/> accessed 24 October 2024.

Cooter RD, *The Strategic Constitution* (Princeton University Press 2000).

Corbett R, Jacobs F, and Shackleton M, *The European Parliament* (3rd edn, Catermill 1995).

Cotter J, 'To Everything There Is a Season: Instrumentalising Article 10 TEU to Exclude Undemocratic Member State Representatives from the European Council and the Council' (2022) 47 European Law Review 69.

Cram L, 'The European Commission as a Multi-organization: Social Policy and IT Policy in the EU' (2007) 1 Journal of European Public Policy 195.

Crum B, 'It Is Time to Resolve the Spitzenkandidaten Conundrum' (17 February 2022) *Reconnect* <https://reconnect-europe.eu/blog/it-is-time-to-resolve-the-spitzenkandidaten-conundrum/> accessed 24 October 2024.

Crum B, 'Why the European Parliament Lost the *Spitzenkandidaten*-Process' (2023) 30 Journal of European Public Policy 193.

Csanádi M and others, *Dynamics of an Authoritarian System: Hungary 2010-2021* (CEU Press 2022).

Cushman F, 'Rationalization Is Rational' (2020) 43 Behavioral and Brain Sciences e28.

Dahl RA, *Democracy and Its Critics* (Yale University Press 1989).

Davis KE, Kingsbury B, and MerryE, 'Indicators as a Technology of Global Governance' (2012) 46 Law & Society Review 71.

Dawson J and Hanley S, 'What's Wrong with East-Central Europe? The Fading Mirage of the "Liberal Consensus"' (2016) 27 Journal of Democracy 20.

Dawson M, 'The Lost Spitzenkandidaten and the Future of European Democracy' (2019) 26 Maastricht Journal of European and Comparative Law 731.

Day A, *States of Disorder, Ecosystems of Governance: Complexity Theory Applied to UN Statebuilding in the DRC and South Sudan* (OUP 2022).

de Búrca G, 'The Drafting of the European Union Charter of Fundamental Rights' (2001) 7 European Law Review 126.

Deflem M and Pampel FC, 'The Myth of Postnational Identity: Popular Support for European Unification' (1996) 75 Social Forces 119.

Detre L, Jakab A, and Lukácsi T, 'Comparing Three Financial Conditionality Regimes and Their Application to Hungary: The Conditionality Regulation, the Recovery and Resilience Facility Regulation, and the Common Provisions Regulation' (2023) 23 Max Planck Institute for Comparative Public Law & International Law (MPIL) Research Paper No. 2023-23.

de Wilde P, 'The Fall of the Spitzenkandidaten: Political Parties and Conflict in the 2019 European Elections' in S Kritzinger and others (eds), *Assessing the 2019 European Parliament Elections* (Routledge 2020) 37.

de Witte B, 'The Rules of Change in the European Union: The Lost Balance between Rigidity and Flexibility' in C Moury and L de Sousa (eds), *Institutional Challenges in Post-Constitutional Europe* (Routledge 2009) 33.

de Witte B, 'Direct Effect, Primacy and the Nature of the Legal Order' in G de Búrca and P Craig (eds), *The Evolution of EU Law* (OUP 2011) 323.

Diaz Crego M, 'Transnational Electoral Lists: Ways to Europeanise Elections to the European Parliament' (February 2021) *EPRS Study* <https://www.europarl.europa.eu/RegData/etudes/STUD/2021/679084/EPRS_STU(2021)679084_EN.pdf> accessed 24 October 2024.

Diaz Crego M, 'Proposing New Rules for European Elections' (May 2022) *EPRS at a Glance* <https://www.europarl.europa.eu/RegData/etudes/ATAG/2022/729384/EPRS_ATA(2022)729384_EN.pdf> accessed 24 October 2024.

Dicey AV, *Introduction to the Study of the Law of the Constitution* (Macmillan 1959).

Díez-Picazo LM, 'Notes sur la nouvelle Charte des Droits fondamentaux de l'Union européenne' (2001) Rivista italiana di diritto pubblico comunitario 665.

Di Fabio U, *Die Weimarer Verfassung: Aufbruch und Scheitern* (CH Beck 2018).

Dimitrijevic N, 'Illiberal Regime Types' in A Sajó, R Uitz, and S Holmes (eds), *Routledge Handbook of Illiberalism* (Routledge 2022) 121.

Dimitrios Spieker L, *EU Values Before the Court of Justice Foundations, Potential, Risks* (OUP 2023).

Dinan D, 'Governance and Institutions: The Year of the *Spitzenkandidaten*' (2015) 53 Journal of Common Market Studies 93.

Dori A, 'The EU Justice Scoreboard—Judicial Evaluation as a New Governance Tool' MPILux Working Paper 22015 <http://www.mpi.lu/fileadmin/mpi/medien/persons/Dori_Adriani/The_EU_Justice_Scoreboard_-_Judicial_Evaluation_as_a_New_Governance_Tool.pdf> accessed 24 October 2024.

Dougan M, 'Judicial Review of Member State Action under the General Principles and the Charter: Defining the "Scope of Union Law"' (2015) 52 Common Market Law Review 1201.

Drinóczi T, 'Hungarian Constitutional Court: The Limits of EU Law in the Hungarian Legal System' (2017) 11 Vienna Journal on International Constitutional Law 139.

Drinóczi T and Bień-Kacała A, 'COVID-19 in Hungary and Poland: Extraordinary Situation and Illiberal Constitutionalism' (2020) 8 The Theory and Practice of Legislation 171.

Dunning T, *Crude Democracy: Natural Resource Wealth and Political Regimes* (CUP 2008).

Editorial, 'Spitzenkandidaten and the European Union's System of Government' (2019) 15 European Constitutional Law Review 609.

Editorial Comments, 'Clear and Present Danger: Poland, the Rule of Law & Primacy' (2021) 58 Common Market Law Review 1635.

Editorial Comments, 'The EU's Accession to the ECHR—a "NO" from the ECJ!' (2015) 52 Common Market Law Review 1.

Edmiston S, Mudd K, and Valev N, 'Tax Structures and FDI: The Deterrent Effects of Complexity and Uncertainty' (2003) 24 Fiscal Studies 341.

Edthofer J and Schmidt P, 'The Future of the EU`s Spitzenkandidaten Procedure' (7 April 2021) *Policy Briefs Österreichische Gesellschaft für Europapolitik* <https://www.oegfe.at/policy-briefs/the-future-of-the-eus-spitzenkandidaten-procedure/?lang=en> accessed 24 October 2024.

Eeckhout P, 'The EU Charter of Fundamental Rights and the Federal Question' (2002) 39 Common Market Law Review 945.

Egeberg M, 'The European Commission' in M Cini and NP-S Borragán (eds), *European Union Politics* (5th edn, OUP 2016) 125.

Ekman J, 'Political Participation and Regime Stability: A Framework for Analyzing Hybrid Regimes' (2009) 30 International Political Science Review 7.

Elkins Z, Ginsburg T, and Melton J, *The Endurance of National Constitutions* (CUP 2009).

Erdmann G and Kneuer M (eds), *Regression of Democracy?* (VS 2011).

Erkkilä T, Peters BG, and Piironen O, 'Politics of Comparative Quantification: The Case of Governance Metrics' (2016) 18 Journal of Comparative Policy Analysis: Research and Practice 319.

Eskridge WN Jr and Levinson S (eds), *Constitutional Stupidities, Constitutional Tragedies* (New York University Press 1998).

Fábián K, 'Why Did Hungarian Politics Become Authoritarian? A Review of Competing and Complementary Responses' (2021) 2 Hungarian Studies Review 216.

Fariss CJ and Dancy G, 'Measuring the Impact of Human Rights: Conceptual and Methodological Debates' (2017) 13 Annual Review of Law and Social Science 273.

Fauvarque-Cosson B and Kerhuel A-J, 'Is Law an Economic Contest? French Reactions to the Doing Business World Bank Reports and Economic Analysis of the Law' (2009) 57 American Journal of Comparative Law 811.

Featherstone K, 'Jean Monnet and the "Democratic Deficit" in the European Union' (1994) 32 Journal of Common Market Studies 149.

Federico CM, Golec de Zavala A, and Baran T, 'Collective Narcissism, In-Group Satisfaction, and Solidarity in the Face of COVID-19' (2020) 12 Social Psychological and Personality Science 1.

Feld L and Frey B, 'Tax Compliance as a Result of a Psychological Tax Contract: The Role of Incentives and Responsive Regulation' (2007) 29 Law & Policy 102.

Feld LP and Voigt S, 'Judicial Independence and Economic Growth: Some Proposals Regarding the Judiciary' in RD Congleton and B Swedenborg (eds), *Democratic Constitutional Design and Public Policy* (MIT Press 2006) 251.

Fleck Z, *Technika vagy érték a jogállam? A jogállami értékek átadása és az előítéletek csökkentése a jogászok és a rendőrtisztek képzésében* (L'Harmattan 2012).

Foa RS and Mounk Y, 'The Danger of Deconsolidation: The Democratic Disconnect' (2016) 27 Journal of Democracy 5.

Fodor GG, '"A rendszer igazságait védem"—Interjú G. Fodor Gáborral' <https://magyarnarancs.hu/belpol/a-rendszer-igazsagait-vedem-93802> accessed 24 October 2024.

Føllesdal A and Hix S, 'Why There Is a Democratic Deficit in the EU: A Response to Majone and Moravcsik' (2006) 44 Journal of Common Market Studies 533.

Fontanelli F, 'The European Union's Charter of Fundamental Rights Two Years Later' (2011) Perspectives on Federalism 22.

Fontanelli F, '*Hic Sunt Nationes*: The Elusive Limits of the EU Charter and the German Constitutional Watchdog' (2013) 9 European Constitutional Law Review 315.

Fontanelli F, 'National Measures and the Application of the EU Charter of Fundamental Rights—Does curia.eu Know iura.eu?' (2014) 14 Human Rights Law Review 231.

Fontanelli F, 'Implementation of EU Law through Domestic Measures after *Fransson*: The Court of Justice Buys Time and "Non-preclusion" Troubles Loom Large' (2014) 39 European Law Review 682.

Fotopoulos S, 'What Sort of Changes Did the Spitzenkandidat Process Bring to the Quality of the EU's Democracy?' (2019) 18 European View 194.

Francis EK, *Ethnos und Demos* (Duncker & Humblot 1965).

Franklin MN, 'How Structural Factors Cause Turnout Variations at European Parliament Elections' (2001) 2 European Union Politics 309.

Frantescu D and Luca D, 'Why the Spitzenkandidaten System Will Have Little Impact in 2024' (14 June 2022) *Euractiv* <https://www.euractiv.com/section/future-eu/opinion/why-the-spitzenkandidaten-system-will-have-little-impact-in-2024/> accessed 24 October 2024.

Frantz E and Kendall-Taylor A, 'The Evolution of Autocracy: Why Authoritarianism Is Becoming More Formidable' (2017) 5 Survival 57.

Frenzel EM, 'Die Charta der Grundrechte als Maßstab für Mitgliedstaatliches Handeln zwischen Effektivierung und Hyperintegration' (2014) 53 Der Staat 1.

Friedrich CJ, 'Rebuilding the German Constitution, I' (1949) 43 American Political Science Review 461.

Fukuda-Parr S, Lawson-Remer T, and Randolph S, *Fulfilling Social and Economic Rights* (OUP 2015).

Fukuyama F, 'The End of History?' (1989) 16 The National Interest 3.

Fukuyama F, *The End of History and the Last Man* (Free Press 1992).

Fukuyama F, 'More Proof That This Really Is the End of History' (17 October 2022) *The Atlantic* <https://www.theatlantic.com/ideas/archive/2022/10/francis-fukuyama-still-end-history/671761/> accessed 24 October 2024.

Gajduschek G, *Rendnek lenni kellene: Tények és elemzések a közigazgatás ellenőrzési és bírságolási tevékenységéről* (KSZK-MKI 2008).

Gajduschek G, 'A közigazgatási bírságolás eredménytelenségéről' (2009) 1 Jogtudományi Közlöny 9.

Gajduschek G, 'Miben áll, és mérhető-e a kormányzati teljesítmény?' (2014) 3 Politikatudományi Szemle 97.

Gajduschek G, 'Measuring Cross-Sectorial Law Enforcement Capacity of Regulatory Agencies in Hungary' (2015) 11 Transylvanian Review of Administrative Sciences 108.

Gajduschek G, 'A közpolitikai célok megjelenése a jogban' in A Jakab and G Gajduschek (eds), *A magyar jogrendszer állapota* (MTA TK 2016) 43.

Gajduschek G, 'Jogtudat és értékvilág—mint a magyar jogrendszer környezete' in A Jakab and G Gajduschek (eds), *A magyar jogrendszer állapota* (2016) 95.

Gajduschek G, 'Előkészítetlenség és utólagos hatásvizsgálat hiánya' in A Jakab and G Gajduschek (eds), *A magyar jogrendszer állapota* (MTA TK 2016) 796.

Gajduschek G, 'Wild East and Civilised West? Some Indicators of Legal Culture in Hungary, Serbia and the Netherlands: An Empirical Comparative Assessment' (2019) 60 Jahrbuch für Ostrecht 165.

Gallie WB, 'Essentially Contested Concepts' (1956) Proceedings of the Aristotelian Society 167.

Galligan DJ and Kurkchiyan M (eds), *Law and Informal Practices: The Post-Communist Experience* (OUP 2003).

García RA, 'The General Provisions of the Charter of Fundamental Rights of the European Union' (2002) Jean Monnet Working Paper 5 <www.jeanmonnetprogram.org/archive/papers/02/020401.pdf> accessed 24 October 2024.

García-Holgado B and Pérez-Liñán A, 'The Weaknesses of Illiberal Regimes' in A Sajó, R Uitz, and S Holmes (eds), *Routledge Handbook of Illiberalism* (Routledge 2022) 925.

Gárdos-Orosz F, 'Alkotmánybíróság 2010–2015' in A Jakab and G Gajduschek (eds), *A magyar jogrendszer állapota* (MTA TK 2016) 442.

Gattermann K, de Vreese CH, and van der Brug W, 'Evaluations of the Spitzenkandidaten: The Role of Information and News Exposure in Citizens' Preference Formation' (2016) 4 Politics and Governance 37.

Gattermann K and Marquart F, 'Do *Spitzenkandidaten* Really Make a Difference? An Experiment on the Effectiveness of Personalized European Parliament Election Campaigns' (2020) 21 European Union Politics 612.

Germelmann CF and Gundel J, 'Die Entwicklung der EuGH-Rechtsprechung zum europäischen Verfassungs- und Verwaltungsrecht im Jahr 2020' (2021) Bayerische Verwaltungsblätter 583.

Ginsburg T, 'Pitfalls of Measuring the Rule of Law' (2011) 3 Hague Journal on the Rule of Law 269.

Ginsburg T and Huq AZ, *How to Save a Constitutional Democracy* (University of Chicago Press 2018).

Ginsburg T and Versteeg M, 'Constitutional Correlates of the Rule of Law' in M Adams, A Meuwese, and E Hirsch Ballin (eds), *Constitutionalism and the Rule of Law: Bridging Idealism and Realism* (CUP 2017) 506.

Ginsburg T, Huq AZ, and Versteeg M, 'The Coming Demise of Liberal Constitutionalism' (2018) 85 University of Chicago Law Review 239.

Gisselquist RM, 'Developing and Evaluating Governance Indexes: 10 Questions' (2014) 35 Policy Studies 513.

Goldoni M, 'Politicising EU Lawmaking? The Spitzenkandidaten Experiment as a Cautionary Tale' (2016) 22 European Law Journal 279.

Goodin RE, 'Institutions and Their Design' in RE Goodin (ed), *The Theory of Institutional Design* (CUP 1996) 28.

Gorges MJ, 'New Institutionalist Explanations for Institutional Change: A Note of Caution' (2001) 21 Politics 137.

Gorondi P, 'Huge Pro-government Media Conglomerate Formed in Hungary' (28 November 2018) *AP News* <https://apnews.com/article/budapest-hungary-viktor-orban-newspapers-europe-39028d9c44b64e08a6609b60a8bf7a13> accessed 24 October 2024.

Grabenwarter C, 'Auf dem Weg in die Grundrechtsgemeinschaft?' (2004) 31 Europäische Grundrechte-Zeitschrift 563.

Graber MA, Levinson S, and Tushnet M (eds), *Constitutional Democracy in Crisis?* (OUP 2018).

Gray A, Barigazzi J, and de la Baume M, 'Who Killed the Spitzenkandidat?' (5 July 2019) *Politico* <https://www.politico.eu/article/who-killed-the-spitzenkandidat-european-parliament-election-2019-transition/> accessed 24 October 2024.

Graziadei M, 'Comparative Law as the Study of Transplants and Receptions' in M Reimann and R Zimmermann (eds), *The Oxford Handbook of Comparative Law* (OUP 2007) 441.

Graziadei M, 'Legal Transplants and the Frontiers of Legal Knowledge' (2009) 10 Theoretical Inquiries in Law 723.

Gregor M, 'The Optimal Ballot Structure for Double-Member Districts' (25 September 2013) CERGE-EI Working Paper Series 493 <www.ssrn.com/abstract=2347118> accessed 24 October 2024.

Greif A, *Institutions and the Path to the Modern Economy: Lessons from Medieval Trade* (CUP 2006).

Griller S, 'Vom Diskriminierungsverbot zur Grundrechtsgemeinschaft? Oder: Von der ungebrochenen Rechtsfortbildungskraft des EuGH' in M Akyürek, D Jahnel, and G Baumgartner (eds), *Staat und Recht in europäischer Perspektive: Festschrift Heinz Schäffer* (Manz 2006) 203.

Griller S, 'Unionsbürgerschaft als grundlegender Status' in W Schroeder and W Obwexer (eds), *20 Jahre Unionsbürgerscahft: Konzept, Inhalt und Weiterentwicklung des grundlegenden Status der Unionsbürger* (EuR-Beiheft 1/2015) 8.

Grimm D, 'Does Europe Need a Constitution?' (1995) 1 European Law Journal 282.

Groussot X, Pech L, and Petursson G, 'The Scope of Application of Fundamental Rights on Member States' Action: In Search of Certainty in EU Adjudication' (2011) Eric Stein Working Paper <www.era-comm.eu/charter_of_fundamental_rights/kiosk/pdf/EU_Adjudication.pdf> accessed 24 October 2024.

Guasti P, 'The Impact of the COVID-19 Pandemic in Central and Eastern Europe: The Rise of Autocracy and Democratic Resilience' (2020) Democratic Theory <https://www.berghahnjournals.com/view/journals/democratic-theory/7/2/dt070207.xml?fbclid=IwAR12k7d8prL6Jn2nMqBHGBgxkqPry1Um13b47LGCWKyQseaxP5o_zwzqbSg> accessed 24 October 2024.

Guild E, *The Legal Elements of European Identity: EU Citizenship and Migration Law* (Kluwer 2004).

Gusy C, 'Demokratiedefizite postnationaler Gemeinschaften unter Berücksichtigung der EU' (1998) 45 Zeitschrift für Politik 267.

Győrffy D and Martin JP, 'Legitimacy and Authoritarian Decline: The Internal Dynamics of Hybrid Regimes' (2022) 70 Problems of Post-Communism 593.

Győry C and Weinberg N, 'Emergency Powers in a Hybrid Regime: The Case of Hungary' (2020) 8 The Theory and Practice of Legislation 329.

Haas E, *The Uniting of Europe* (Stanford University Press 1958).

Haber S and Menaldo V, 'Do Natural Resources Fuel Authoritarianism? A Reappraisal of the Resource Course' (2011) 105 American Political Science Review 1.

Habermas J, 'Remarks on Dieter Grimm's "Does Europe need a Constitution?"' (1995) 1 European Law Journal 303.

Halberstam D, 'Constitutional Heterarchy: The Centrality of Conflict in the European Union and the United States' in JL Dunoff and JP Trachtman (eds), *Ruling the World? Constitutionalism, International Law, and Global Governance* (CUP 2009) 326.

Hallstein W, *Europe in the Making* (Allen & Unwin 1972).

Halmai G, 'Rise and Fall of Constitutionalism in Hungary' in P Blokker (ed), *Constitutional Acceleration within the European Union and Beyond* (Routledge 2017) 215.

Halmai G, 'The Hungarian Constitutional Court betrays Academic Freedom and Freedom of Association' (8 June 2018) *Verfassungsblog* <www.verfassungsblog.de/the-hungarian-constitutional-court-betrays-academic-freedom-and-freedom-of-association/> accessed 24 October 2024.

Halmai G, 'Illiberalism in East-Central Europe' in A Sajó, R Uitz, and S Holmes (eds), *Routledge Handbook of Illiberalism* (Routledge 2022) 813.

Hammergren L, 'Indices, Indicators and Statistics: A View from the Project Side as to Their Utility and Pitfalls' (2015) 3 Hague Journal on the Rule of Law 305.

Hamřík L and Kaniok P, 'Is It All about European Democracy? The Motives behind the Institutionalisation of the Spitzenkandidaten' (2019) 15 Journal of Contemporary European Research 354.

Hancox E, 'The Meaning of "Implementing" EU Law under Article 51(1) of the Charter: *Åkerberg Fransson*' (2013) 50 Common Market Law Review 1411.

Hart Ely J, *Democracy and Distrust: A Theory of Judicial Review* (Harvard University Press 1980).

Hayes-Renshaw F and Wallace H, 'Executive Power in the European Union: The Functions and Limits of the Council of Ministers' (1995) 2 Journal of European Public Policy 559.

Hazard JN, *Communists and Their Law* (CUP 1969).

Heard A, *Canadian Constitutional Conventions: The Marriage of Law and Politics* (OUP 1991).

Heidbreder E and Schade D, '(Un)settling the Precedent: Contrasting Institutionalisation Dynamics in the Spitzenkandidaten Procedure of 2014 and 2019' (2020) 7 Research & Politics.

Helmke G and Levitsky S, 'Informal Institutions and Comparative Politics: A Research Agenda' (2004) 2 Perspectives on Politics 725.

Helmke G and Levitsky S (eds), *Informal Institutions and Democracy: Lessons from Latin America* (Johns Hopkins University Press 2006).

Helmke G and Levitsky S, 'Introduction' in G Helmke and S Levitsky (eds), *Informal Institutions and Democracy: Lessons from Latin America* (Johns Hopkins University Press 2006) 1.

Héritier A and others, *European Parliament Ascendant: Parliamentary Strategies of Self-Empowerment in the EU* (Palgrave Macmillan 2019).

Hernández G and Closa C, 'Turning Assertive? EU Rule of Law Enforcement in the Aftermath of the War in Ukraine' (2023) 47 West European Politics 967.

Herszenhorn DM and Bayer L, 'European Commissioner for Justice Didier Reynders Gives a Press Conference on the Annual Rule of Law Report 2020' (30 September 2020) *Politico* <https://www.politico.eu/article/european-commission-report-finds-many-eu-nations-hungary-poland-malta-bulgaria-falling-short-rule-of-law/> accessed 24 October 2024.

Herszenhorn D and von der Burchard H, 'Rule of Law Disputes Cast Shadow over Opening of Slovenia's EU Council Presidency' (1 July 2021) *Politico* <https://www.politico.eu/article/rule-of-law-dispute-shadows-ceremonial-opening-of-slovenias-eu-council-presidency/> accessed 24 October 2024.

Higley J and Burton M, *Elite Foundations of Liberal Democracy* (Rowman & Littlefield 2006).

Hillion C, 'Overseeing the Rule of Law in the EU: Legal Mandate and Means' in C Closa and D Kochenov (eds), *Reinforcing Rule of Law Oversight in the European Union* (CUP 2016) 59.

Hirsch G, 'Die Europäische Union als Grundrechtsgemeinschaft' in G Iglesias and others (eds), *Mélanges en hommage à Fernand Schockweiler* (Nomos 1999) 177.

Hirschman AO, *Exit, Voice, and Loyalty: Responses to Decline in Firms, Organizations, and States* (Harvard University Press 1970).

Hix S, *The Political System of the European Union* (2nd edn, Palgrave Macmillan 2005).

Hix S and Follesdal A, 'Why Is There a Democratic Deficit in the EU? A Response to Majone and Moravcsik' (2006) 44 Journal of Common Market Studies 533.

Hix S and Høyland B, *The Political System of the European Union* (3rd edn, Palgrave Macmillan 2011).

Hobolt SB, 'A Vote for the President? The Role of Spitzenkandidaten in the 2014 European Parliament Elections' (2014) 21 Journal of European Public Policy 1528.
Hobsbawm EJ, *Nations and Nationalism Since 1780: Programme, Myth, Reality* (CUP 1990).
Hoffmann T, 'Az állami közreműködéssel szerzett tulajdon elvonásának lehetősége a nemzetközi és európai emberi jogi sztenderdek fényében' (2017) MTA Law Working Papers No 17 <www.jog.tk.mta.hu/uploads/files/2017_17_Hoffmann.pdf> accessed 24 October 2024.
Holmes S, 'Can Foreign Aid Promote the Rule of Law?' (1999) 8 East European Constitutional Review 68.
Höreth M, *Die Europäische Union im Legitimationstrilemma* (Nomos 1999).
Höreth M, 'Warum der EuGH nicht gestoppt werden sollte—und auch kaum gestoppt werden kann' in U Haltern and A Bergmann (eds), *Der EuGH in der Kritik* (Mohr Siebeck 2012) 73.
Höreth M, 'The Least Dangerous Branch?' in M Dawson, B De Witte, and E Muir (eds), *Judicial Activism at the European Court of Justice* (Edward Elgar 2013) 32.
Horsley T, 'Reflections on the Role of the Court of Justice as the "Motor" of European Integration: Legal Limits to Judicial Lawmaking' (2013) 50 Common Market Law Review 931.
Howe P, 'Eroding Norms and Democratic Deconsolidation' (2017) 28 Journal of Democracy 15.
Huber P, 'Unitarisierung durch Gemeinschaftsgrundrechte—Zur Überprüfungsbedürftigkeit der ERT-Rechtsprechung' (2008) 43 Europarecht 190.
Hummelbrunner S and others, 'In Support of the EU Rule of Law and Advocate General Eleanor Sharpston—An Open Letter' (18 March 2020) *European Law Blog*.
Iglesias Sánchez S, 'Fundamental Rights and Citizenship of the Union at a Crossroads: A Promising Alliance or a Dangerous Liaison?' (2014) 20 European Law Journal 464.
Ipsen HP, *Fusionsverfassung Europäische Gemeinschaften* (Gehlen 1969).
Ipsen HP, *Europäisches Gemeinschaftsrecht* (Mohr 1972).
Iusmen I, 'EU Leverage and Democratic Backsliding in Central and Eastern Europe: The Case of Romania' (2015) 53 Journal of Common Market Studies 593.
Jaconelli J, 'Do Constitutional Conventions Bind?' (2005) 64 Cambridge Law Journal 149.
Jakab A, 'Neutralising the Sovereignty Question: Compromise Strategies in Constitutional Argumentations about the Concept of Sovereignty before European Integration and Since' (2006) 2 European Constitutional Law Review 375.
Jakab A, 'What Makes a Good Lawyer?' (2007) 62 Zeitschrift für öffentliches Recht 275.
Jakab A, 'A magyar jogi oktatás megújításához szükséges lépések: Reformjavaslat összehasonlító áttekintésre alapozva' (2010) 4 Magyar Jog 204.
Jakab A, 'A bírói jogértelmezés az Alaptörvény tükrében' (2011) 2 Jogesetek Magyarázata 86.
Jakab A, 'Breaching Constitutional Law on Moral Grounds in the Fight against Terrorism: Implied Presuppositions and Proposed Solutions in the Discourse on "the Rule of Law vs. Terrorism"' (2011) 9 International Journal of Constitutional Law 58.
Jakab A, 'Full Parliamentarisation of the EU without Changing the Treaties: Why We Should Aim for It and How Easily It Can Be Achieved' (2012) 3 Jean Monnet Working Paper 1.
Jakab A, 'Why the Debate between Kumm and Armstrong Is about the Wrong Question' (20 June 2014) *Verfassungsblog* <http://www.verfassungsblog.de/debate-kumm-armstrong-wrong-question/#.U6RIbfl_uqg> accessed 24 October 2024.
Jakab A, *European Constitutional Language* (CUP 2016).
Jakab A, 'Application of the EU CFR by National Courts in Purely Domestic Cases' in A Jakab and D Kochenov (eds), *The Enforcement of EU Law and Values: Ensuring Member States' Compliance* (OUP 2017) 252.
Jakab A, 'What Is Wrong with the Hungarian Legal System and How to Fix It' (2018) 13 MPIL Research Paper <https://ssrn.com/abstract=3213378> accessed 24 October 2024.
Jakab A, 'How to Defend the Integrity of the EP Elections against Authoritarian Member States' (31 March 2019) *Verfassungsblog* <https://verfassungsblog.de/how-to-defend-the-integrity-of-the-ep-elections-against-authoritarian-member-states/> accessed 24 October 2024.
Jakab A, 'Informal Institutional Elements as Both Preconditions and Consequences of Effective Formal Legal Rules: The Failure of Constitutional Institution-Building in Hungary' (2020) 68 American Journal of Comparative Law 760.

Jakab A, 'What Can Constitutional Law Do against the Erosion of Democracy and the Rule of Law? On the Interconnectedness of the Protection of Democracy and the Rule of Law' (2020) 6 Constitutional Studies 5.

Jakab A, 'Sustainability in European Constitutional Law: From Constitutional Challenges and Innovations for Future Generations' in M-C Cordonier Segger, M Szabó, and AR Harrington (eds), *Intergenerational Justice in Sustainable Development Treaty Implementation: Advancing Future Generations Rights through National Institutions* (CUP 2021) 166.

Jakab A, 'Verfassungsrechtliche Argumentation' in A Jakab (ed), *Methoden und theoretische Grundfragen des österreichischen Verfassungsrechts* (Verlag Österreich 2021) 214.

Jakab A, 'Three Misconceptions about the EU Rule of Law Crisis' (17 October 2022) *Verfassungsblog* <https://verfassungsblog.de/misconceptions-rol/> accessed 24 October 2024.

Jakab A, 'Constitutional Resilience' (October 2022) *Max Planck Encyclopedia of Comparative Constitutional Law* <https://oxcon.ouplaw.com/display/10.1093/law-mpeccol/law-mpeccol-e845> accessed 24 October 2024.

Jakab A and Bodnár E, 'The Rule of Law, Democracy, and Human Rights in Hungary: Tendencies from 1989 until 2019' in T Drinóczi and A Bień-Kacała (eds), *Rule of Law, Common Values, and Illiberal Constitutionalism: Poland and Hungary within the European Union* (Routledge 2020) 105.

Jakab A and Bodnár E, 'Agonie eines jungen Verfassungsstaates: Die ungarische Verfassung 1989 bis 2019' in E Bos and A Lorenz (eds), *Das politische System Ungarns* (Springer 2020) 55.

Jakab A and Hollán M, 'Socialism's Legacy in Contemporary Law and Legal Scholarship: The Case of Hungary' (2004) 11 Journal of East European Law 95.

Jakab A and Gajduschek G (eds), *A magyar jogrendszer állapota* (MTA TK 2016).

Jakab A and Kirchmair L, 'How to Quantify a Proportionate Financial Punishment in the New EU Rule of Law Mechanism?' (22 December 2020) *Verfassungsblog* <https://verfassungsblog.de/how-to-quantify-a-proportionate-financial-punishment-in-the-new-eu-rule-of-law-mechanism/> accessed 24 October 2024.

Jakab A and Kirchmair L, 'How to Develop the EU Justice Scoreboard into a Rule of Law Index: Using an Existing Tool in the EU Rule of Law Crisis in a More Efficient Way' (2021) 22 German Law Journal 936.

Jakab A and Kirchmair L, 'Two Ways of Completing the European Fundamental Rights Union: Amendment to vs. Reinterpretation of Article 51 of the EU Charter of Fundamental Rights' (2022) 24 Cambridge Yearbook of European Legal Studies 239.

Jakab A and Kochenov D (eds), *The Enforcement of EU Law and Values: Ensuring Member States' Compliance* (OUP 2017).

Jakab A and Sonnevend P, 'The Bundesbank Is under a Legal Obligation to Ignore the PSPP Judgment of the Bundesverfassungsgericht' (25 May 2020) *Verfassungsblog* <https://verfassungsblog.de/the-bundesbank-is-under-a-legal-obligation-to-ignore-the-pspp-judgment-of-the-bundesverfassungsgericht/> accessed 24 October 2024.

Jarass H, 'Artikel 51' in H Jarass (ed), *GRCh: Charta der Grundrechte der Europäischen Union* (4th edn, CH Beck 2021).

Jellinek G, *Die Lehre von den Staatenverbindungen* (Hoelder 1882).

Jennings I, *The Law and the Constitution* (5th edn, University of London Press 1959).

Juncker J-C, 'Speech by President Jean-Claude Juncker at the Annual General Meeting of the Hellenic Federation of Enterprises (SEV)' (21 June 2016) *Athens* <http://europa.eu/rapid/press-release_SPEECH-16-2293_en.htm> accessed 24 October 2024.

Juncker J-C and Timmermans F, *Joint Statement on the Fight against Corruption in Romania* (1 Febuary 2017) <www.europa.eu/rapid/press-release_STATEMENT-17-195_en.htm> accessed 24 October 2024.

Kaczyński PM, 'Polish PM Says Commission Risks "World War III"' (26 October 2021) *Euractiv* <https://www.euractiv.com/section/politics/short_news/polish-pm-says-commission-risks-world-war-iii/> accessed 24 October 2024.

Kaila H, 'The Scope of Application of the Charter of Fundamental Rights of the European Union in the Member States' in P Cardonnel, A Rosas, and N Wahl (eds), *Constitutionalising the EU Judicial System* (Bloomsbury 2012).

Kaplan A, *The Conduct of Inquiry: Methodology for Behavioral Science* (Routledge 2017).

Katalin E, 'Elszabotált nyomozások: 20 fontos ügy, ami megakadt az ügyészségen' (16 September 2021) *Atlatszo* <https://atlatszo.hu/kozpenz/2021/09/16/elszabotalt-nyomozasok-20-fontos-ugy-ami-megakadt-az-ugyeszsegen/> accessed 24 October 2024.

Kaufmann D, Kraay A, and Mastruzzi M, 'The Worldwide Governance Indicators: Methodology and Analytical Issues' (2011) 3 Hague Journal on the Rule of Law 220.

Kelemen RD, 'Selection, Appointment and Legitimacy: A Political Perspective' in M Bobek (ed), *Selecting Europe's Judges* (OUP 2015) 244.

Kelemen RD, 'The European Union's Authoritarian Equilibrium' (2020) 27 Journal of European Public Policy 481.

Kelemen RD, 'Appeasement, ad Infinitum' (2022) 29 Maastricht Journal of European and Comparative Law 177.

Kelemen RD, 'Europe's Authoritarian Cancer: Diagnosis, Prognosis, and Treatment' (2022) Progressive Yearbook 73.

Kelemen RD and McNamara KR, 'State-Building and the European Union: Markets, War, and Europe's Uneven Political Development' (2022) 55 Comparative Political Studies 963.

Kelemen RD and Pavone T, 'Where Have the Guardians Gone? Law Enforcement and the Politics of Supranational Forbearance in the European Union' (2023) 75 World Politics 779.

Keller T, 'A gazdasági erkölcsösséget szabályozó társadalmi normákról—normakövetés és normaszegés' in IG Tóth (ed), *Európai Társadalmi Jelentés 2. Gazdasági attitűdök* (2009).

Khan D-E, 'Artikel 48 EVU' in R Geiger and others (eds), *EUV/AEUV: Vertrag über die Europäische Union. Vertrag über die Arbeitsweise der Europäischen Union. Kommentar* (7th edn, CH Beck 2023).

Kingreen T, 'Grundrechtsverbund oder Grundrechtsunion? Zur Entwicklung der subjektiv-öffentlichen Rechte im europäischen Unionsrecht' (2010) 45 Europarecht 338.

Kirchhof P, 'Der Antwortcharakter der Verfassung' in M Anderheiden and others (eds), *Gedächtnisschrift für Winfried Brugger* (Mohr Siebeck 2013) 450.

Kirchmair L, 'Demokratische Legitimität, die EU-Rechtsstaatlichkeitskrise und Vorüberlegungen zu einer transnationalen Gewaltengliederung' (2019) 6 Zeitschrift für praktische Philosophie 171.

Kirchmair L, 'The EU and Its Hybrid Regimes Are Poisoning Each Other' (23 August 2022) *Politico* <https://www.politico.eu/article/eu-hybrid-regime-poison-each-other-democracy-spitzenkandidaten/> accessed 24 October 2024.

Kirchmair L, *Rethinking the Relationship between International, EU and National Law: Consent-Based Monism* (CUP 2024).

Klamert M, 'Article 48 TEU' in M Kellerbauer, M Klamert, and J Tomkin (eds), *The EU Treaties and Charter of Fundamental Rights: A Commentary* (OUP 2019).

Kluth W, *Die demokratische Legitimation der Europäischen Union* (Duncker & Humblot 1995).

Kneuer M, 'Unravelling Democratic Erosion: Who Drives the Slow Death of Democracy, and How?' (2021) Democratization 1442.

Knook A, 'The Court, the Charter, and the Vertical Division of Powers in the European Union' (2005) 42 Common Market Law Review 367.

Kochenov D, 'EU Citizenship without Duties' (2014) 20 European Law Journal 482.

Kochenov D, 'On Policing Article 2 TEU Compliance—Reverse Solange and Systemic Infringements Analyzed XXXIII' (2014) Polish Yearbook of International Law 145.

Kochenov D, 'The Essence of EU Citizenship Emerging from the Last Ten Years of Academic Debate: Beyond the Cherry Blossoms and the Moon?' (2013) 62 International & Comparative Law Quarterly 37.

Kochenov D, 'Elephants in the Room: The European Commission's 2019 Communication on the Rule of Law' (2019) 11 Hague Journal on the Rule of Law 423.

Kochenov D and Bárd P, 'Rule of Law Crisis in the New Member States of the EU' (2018) 1 Reconnect Working Paper.

Kochenov D and Butler G, 'Independence of the Court of Justice of the European Union: Unchecked Member States Power after the Sharpston Affair' (2021) 27 European Law Journal 262.

Kochenov D and Lindeboom J (eds), *Kälin and Kochenov's Quality of Nationality Index: An Objective Ranking of the Nationalities of the World* (Hart Publishing 2020).

Kokott J and Sobotta C, 'The Charter of Fundamental Rights of the European Union after Lisbon' (2010) EUI Working Paper 7.

Kollmorgen R, 'Post-Socialist Transformations in the Twenthieth and Twenty-First Centuries' in W Merkel, R Kollmorgen, and H-J Wagner (eds), *The Handbook of Political, Social, and Economic Transformation* (OUP 2019) 348.

Koob SA, Jørgensen SS, and Sano H-O, *Human Rights and Economic Growth: An Econometric Analysis of the Rights to Education and Health* (Report of the Danish Institute for Human Rights 2017).

Kopits G, 'Saving Hungary's Finances: Budapest's Four Step-Plan for Fiscal Alcoholics' (4 December 2008) *Wall Street Journal Europe* <https://www.wsj.com/articles/SB122833696970376717> accessed 24 October 2024.

Kotanidis S, *Spitzenkandidaten or the Lead Candidate Process* (European Parliament Research Service 2023).

Kotzur M, 'Eine Bewährungsprobe für die Europäische Grundrechtsgemeinschaft: Zur Entscheidung des EuG in der Rs. Yusuf u.a. gegen Rat, Europäische Grundrechtezeitschrift 2005, S. 592 ff' (2006) 33 Europäische Grundrechte-Zeitschrift 1925.

Kotzur M, 'Der Schutz personenbezogener Daten in der europäischen Grundrechtsgemeinschaft: Die korrespondierende Verantwortung von EuGH, EGMR und mitgliedstaatlichen Verfassungsgerichten' (2011) 38 Europäische Grundrechte-Zeitschrift 105.

Kovács IP, 'Modellváltás a magyar önkormányzati rendszerben' in A Jakab and G Gajduschek (eds), *A magyar jogrendszer állapota* (MTA TK 2016) 583.

Krever T, 'Quantifying Law: Legal Indicator Projects and the Reproduction of Neoliberal Common Sense' (2013) 34 Third World Quarterly 131.

Krygier M, 'The Rule of Law: Legality, Teleology, Sociology' in G Palombella and N Walker (eds), *Relocating the Rule of Law* (Bloomsbury 2009) 45.

Krygier M, 'Illiberalism and the Rule of Law' in A Sajó, R Uitz, and S Holmes (eds), *Routledge Handbook of Illiberalism* (Routledge 2022) 533.

Kumm M, 'Why Europeans Will Not Embrace Constitutional Patriotism' (2008) 6 International Journal of Constitutional Law 117.

Lacatus C and Sedelmeier U, 'Does Monitoring without Enforcement Make a Difference? The European Union and Anti-corruption Policies in Bulgaria and Romania after Accession' (2020) 27 Journal of European Public Policy 1236.

Láncos PL, 'Passivist Strategies Available to the Hungarian Constitutional Court' (2019) 79 Heidelberg Journal of International Law (ZaöRV) 971.

Lánczi A, 'A viccpártok színvonalán áll az ellenzék' (21 December 2015) *Magyar Idők* <https://www.magyaridok.hu/belfold/lanczi-andras-viccpartok-szinvonalan-all-az-ellenzek-243952/> accessed 24 October 2024.

Landau D, 'Abusive Constitutionalism' (2013) 47 University of California Davis Law Review 189.

La Torre M, *Law as Institution* (Springer 2010).

Layman GC, Carsey TM, and Horowitz JM, 'Party Polarization in American Politics: Characteristics, Causes, and Consequences' (2006) 9 Annual Review of Political Science 83.

Legg A, *The Margin of Appreciation in International Human Rights Law* (OUP 2012).

Legrand P, 'The Impossibility of "Legal Transplants"' (1997) 4 Maastricht Journal of European and Comparative Law 111.

Leloup M, Kochenov D, and Dimitrovs A, 'Non-Regression: Opening the Door to Solving the "Copenhagen Dilemma"? All the Eyes on Case C-896/19 *Repubblika v Il-Prim Ministru*' (June 2021) Reconnect Working Paper No 15.

Lenaerts K, 'Constitutionalism and the Many Faces of Federalism' (1990) 38 American Journal of Comparative Law 205.

Lenaerts K, 'Exploring the Limits of the EU Charter of Fundamental Rights' (2012) 8 European Constitutional Law Review 375.

Lenaerts K, 'The Rule of Law and the Constitutional Identity of the European Union' (speech of 5 March 2023) <https://evropeiskipravenpregled.eu/the-rule-of-law-and-the-constitutional-identity-of-the-european-union/> accessed 24 October 2024.

Le Sueur A and Sunkin M, *Public Law* (Longman 1997).

Levitsky S and Way LA, *Competitive Authoritarianism: Hybrid Regimes after the Cold War* (CUP 2010).

Levitsky S and Ziblatt D, *How Democracies Die* (Random House 2018).

Ligeti M, 'Korrupció' in A Jakab and G Gajduschek (eds), *A magyar jogrendszer állapota* (MTA TK 2016) 727.

Lijphart A, *Democracies* (Yale University Press 1984).

Lile S, 'Lost in Operationalisation: Developing Legally Relevant Indicators, Questions and Benchmarks' (2017) 21 The International Journal of Human Rights 1378.

Lindner SH, '"Sich eingereiht"? Wolfgang Hefermehl und der Nationalsozialismus (2016) 17 Jahrbuch der Juristischen Zeitgeschichte 326.

Little RJA and Rubin DB, *Statistical Analysis with Missing Data* (2nd edn, Wiley 2002).

Lock T, 'Article 51' in M Kellerbauer, M Klamert, and J Tomkin (eds), *The EU Treaties and Charter of Fundamental Rights: A Commentary* (OUP 2019).

Lock T and Martin D, 'Article 47' in M Kellerbauer, M Klamert, and J Tomkin (eds), *The EU Treaties and Charter of Fundamental Rights: A Commentary* (OUP 2019).

Lowndes V and Roberts M, *Why Institutions Matter: The New Institutionalism in Political Science* (Palgrave Macmillan 2013).

Luce E, *The Retreat of Western Liberalism* (Atlantic Monthly Press 2017).

Lührmann A, McMann K, and van Ham C, 'The Effectiveness of Democracy Aid to Different Regime Types and Democracy Sectors' (2017) 40 V-Dem Institute Working Paper.

Lynch S, 'Anatomy of a Scandal: How "Qatargate" Crisis Shook EU to its Core' (17 December 2022) *Politico* <https://www.politico.eu/article/scandal-qatargate-crisis-european-union-corruption-crisis/> accessed 24 October 2024.

McIntire CT and Perry M, 'Toynbee's Achievement' in CT McIntire and M Perry (eds), *Toynbee: Reappraisals* (University of Toronto Press 1989) 3.

McNamara KR and Kelemen RD, 'Seeing Europe like a State' (2022) 29 Journal of European Public Policy 1916.

Mair P, 'Political Opposition and the European Union' (2007) 42 Government and Opposition 1.

Maitland FW, *The Constitutional History of England* (CUP 1908).

Majone G, *Regulating Europe* (Routledge 1996).

Majone G, 'Europe's "Democratic Deficit": The Question of Standards' (1998) 4 European Law Journal 5.

Mancini F, 'The Making of a Constitution for Europe' (1989) 26 Common Market Law Review 595.

Manow P and Döring H, 'Electoral and Mechanical Causes of Divided Government in the European Union' (2008) 41 Comparative Political Studies 1349.

Manriquez MM and Pavone T, 'Follow the Leader: The European Commission, the European Court of Justice, and the EU's Rule of Law Revolution' (2024) Journal of European Public Policy.

Marauhn T and Elliesie H (eds), *Legal Transformation in Northern Africa and South Sudan* (Eleven 2015).

March JG and Olsen JP, *Rediscovering Institutions: The Organizational Basis of Politics* (Free Press 2010).

Markoff J, *Waves of Democracy: Social Movements and Political Change* (Pine Forge 1996).
Marquand D, *Parliament for Europe* (Jonathan Cape 1979).
Marshall G, *Constitutional Theory* (Clarendon Press 1971).
Marshall G, *Constitutional Conventions* (OUP 1984).
Martin JP, Nagy G, and Ligeti M, *Fekete Könyv. Korrupció Magyarországon 2010–2018* (Civitas and Transparency International Magyarország 2018).
Mattila M, 'Why Bother? Determinants of Turnout in the European Elections' (2003) 22 Electoral Studies 449.
Matzak M, Bencze M, and Kühn Z, 'EU Law and Central European Judges: Administrative Judiciaries in the Czech Republic, Hungary and Poland Ten Years after Accession' in M Bobek (ed), *Central European Judges under European Influence* (Hart 2015) 43.
May C and Winchester A (eds), *Handbook on the Rule of Law* (Edward Elgar 2018).
Mayer FC, 'Auf dem Weg zum Richterfaustrecht? Zum PSPP-Urteil des BVerfG' (7 May 2020) *Verfassungsblog* <https://verfassungsblog.de/auf-dem-weg-zum-richterfaustrecht/> accessed 24 October 2024.
Mayer FC, 'Presidential Power(s)' in L Besselink, N Lupo, and M Wendel (eds), *Research Handbook on EU Constitutional Law* (Edward Elgar forthcoming).
Mendelski M, 'The EU's Rule of Law Promotion in Post-Soviet Europe: What Explains the Divergence Between Baltic States and EaP Countries?' (2016) 7 Eastern Journal of European Studies 111.
Merriman J, *A History of Modern Europe: From the Renaissance to the Present* (3rd edn, WW Norton & Company 2010).
Michaels R, 'Comparative Law by Numbers? Legal Origins Thesis, Doing Business Reports, and the Silence of Traditional Comparative Law' (2009) 57 American Journal of Comparative Law 765.
Milward AS, *Politics and Economics in the History of the European Union* (Routledge 2005).
Møller J and Skaaning S-E, *Requisites of Democracy: Conceptualization, Measurement, and Explanation* (Routledge 2011).
Møller J and Skaaning S-E, *The Rule of Law: Definitions, Measures, Patterns and Causes* (Springer 2014).
Möllers C, *Demokratie: Zumutungen und Versprechen* (Klaus Wagenbach 2008).
Möllers C, *Die drei Gewalten* (Velbrück Wissenschaft 2008).
Möllers C and Schneider L, *Demokratiesicherung in der Europäischen Union* (Mohr Siebeck 2018).
Montagu A (ed), *Toynbee and History: Critical Essays and Reviews* (Porter Sargent 1956).
Moravcsik A, 'The Myth of Europe's "Democratic Deficit"' (2008) 43 Intereconomics: Journal of European Economic Policy 331.
Morlino L, 'Hybrid Regimes' in A Sajó, R Uitz, and S Holmes (eds), *Routledge Handbook of Illiberalism* (Routledge 2022) 142.
Mounk Y, *The People vs Democracy: Why Our Freedom Is in Danger and How to Save It* (Harvard University Press 2018).
Mounk Y and Foa RS, 'The End of the Democratic Century: Autocracy's Global Ascendance' (2018) 97 Foreign Affairs 29.
Müller T and Pickel S, 'Wie lässt sich Demokratie am besten messen? Zur Konzeptqualität von Demokratie-Indizes' (2007) 48 Politische Vierteljahresschrift 511.
Müller J-W, 'A Democracy Commission of One's Own, or What it Would Take for the EU to Safeguard Liberal Democracy in Its Member States' in A Jakab and D Kochenov (eds), *The Enforcement of EU Law and Values: Ensuring Member States' Compliance* (OUP 2017) 234.
Mungiu-Pippidi A, 'Corruption: Diagnosis and Treatment' (2006) 17 Journal of Democracy 86.
Munro CR, *Studies in Constitutional Law* (2nd edn, Butterworths 1999).
Nardulli PF, Peyton B, and Bajjalieh J, 'Conceptualizing and Measuring Rule of Law Constructs 1850–2010' (2013) 1 Journal of Law & Courts 139.
Nasshoven Y, '"To be or not to be?" Das Spitzenkandidatenprinzip in der Europawahl 2019 und zukünftige Szenarien' (2019) 42 Integration 280.

Newman M, *Democracy, Sovereignty and the European Union* (C Hurst and Co Publishing 1996).

North DC, *Institutions, Institutional Change and Economic Performance* (CUP 1990).

Nowak C, 'Grundrechtsberechtigte und Grundrechtsadressaten' in S Heselhaus and C Nowak (eds), *Handbuch der Europäischen Grundrechte* (Helbing & Lichtenhahn, CH Beck and LexisNexis 2006) 244.

OECD Handbook on Constructing Indicators (2008).

Oeter S, 'Souveränität und Demokratie in der "Verfassungsentwicklung" der Europäischen Union' (1995) Heidelberg Journal of International Law 659.

Offe C, 'Designing Institutions in East European Transitions' in RE Goodin (ed), *The Theory of Institutional Design* (CUP 1996) 199.

Orbán V, 'Speech at the 25th Bálványos Summer Free and Student Camp' (30 July 2014) <www.kormany.hu/en/the-prime-minister/the-prime-minister-s-speeches/prime-minister-viktor-orban-s-speech-at-the-25th-balvanyos-summer-free-university-and-student-camp> accessed 24 October 2024.

Orbán V, 'Speech at the 14th Kötcse Civil Picnic' (17 September 2015) <www.kormany.hu/en/the-prime-minister/the-prime-minister-s-speeches/viktor-orban-s-speech-at-the-14th-kotcse-civil-picnic> accessed 24 October 2024.

Ortega RN, 'Conceptualizing Authoritarian Constitutionalism' (2016) 49 World Comparative Law 339.

Ostrom E, 'An Agenda for the Study of Institutions' (1986) 48 Public Choice 3.

Ostrom E, *Understanding Institutional Diversity* (Princeton University Press 2005).

Palombella G, 'Whose Europe? After the Constitution: A Goal-Based Citizenship' (2005) 3 International Journal of Constitutional Law 357.

Palombella G, 'The Rule of Law as an Institutional Ideal' in L Morlino and G Palombella (eds), *Rule of Law and Democracy: Inquiries into Internal and External Issues* (Brill 2010) 4.

Panyi S and Pethő A, 'Hungarian Journalists and Critics of Orbán Were Targeted with Pegasus, a Powerful Israeli Cyberweapon' (19 July 2019) *Direkt 36* <https://www.direkt36.hu/en/leleplezodott-egy-durva-izraeli-kemfegyver-az-orban-kormany-kritikusait-es-magyar-ujsagirokat-is-celba-vettek-vele/> accessed 24 October 2024.

Pap AL, *Democratic Decline in Hungary* (Routledge 2017).

Papaioannou E and Siourounis G, 'Democratization and Growth' (2008) 118 The Economic Journal 1520.

Parsons J, 'Developing Clusters of Indicators: An Alternative Approach to Measuring the Provision of Justice' (2011) 3 Hague Journal on the Rule of Law 170.

Parsons J and others, 'Developing Indicators to Measure the Rule of Law: A Global Approach. A Report for the World Justice Project' (2008) Vera Institute of Justice.

Paulus A, 'Horizontale und vertikale Aufgabenteilung beim Grundrechtsschutz in Europa' in T Groh and others (eds), *Verfassungsrecht, Völkerrecht, Menschenrechte—Vom Recht im Zentrum der Internationalen Beziehungen. Festschrift für Ulrich Fastenrath* (CF Müller 2019) 79.

Pech L, 'Rule of Law as Guiding Principle of the European Union's External Action' (2012) Centre for Law of EU External Relations Working Paper 2012/3 <http://www.asser.nl/media/1632/cleer2012-3web.pdf> accessed 24 October 2024.

Pech L, 'The EU as a Global Rule of Law Promoter' (2016) 14 Asia Europe Journal 7.

Pech L and Kochenov D, 'Strengthening the Rule of Law within the European Union: Diagnoses, Recommendations, and What to Avoid' (2019) Reconnect Policy Brief.

Pech L and Scheppele KL, 'Illiberalism Within: Rule of Law Backsliding in the EU' (2017) 19 Cambridge Yearbook of European Legal Studies 3.

Peerenboom R, 'Human Rights and Rule of Law: What's the Relationship?' (2005) 36 Georgia Journal of International Law 809.

Peers S, 'The Rebirth of the EU's Charter of Fundamental Rights' (2013) 13 Cambridge Yearbook of European Legal Studies 283.

Peñalver García N and Priestley J, *The Making of a European President* (Palgrave Macmillan 2015).

Perry M, *Arnold Toynbee and the Western Tradition* (Peter Lang 1996).

Pescatore P, 'Les exigences de la démocratie et la legitimité de la Communauté européenne' (1974) Cahiers de droit européen 499.

Péter L, *Hungary's Long Nineteenth Century: Constitutional and Democratic Traditions in a European Perspective* (Brill 2012).

Peters A, *Elemente einer Theorie der Verfassung Europas* (Duncker & Humblot 2001).

Peterson J, 'Juncker's Political European Commission and an EU in Crisis' (2016) 55 Journal of Common Market Studies 349.

Piccirilli G, 'The "Taricco Saga": The Italian Constitutional Court Continues Its European Journey' (2018) 14 European Constitutional Law Review 814.

Pirker B, *Grundrechtsschutz im Unionsrecht zwischen Subsidiarität und Integration* (Nomos 2018).

Pogany I, 'The Crisis of Democracy in East Central Europe: The "New Constitutionalism" in Hungary' (2013) 24 European Public Law 341.

Pogge TW, 'How to Create Supra-National Institutions Democratically' in A Føllesdal and P Koslowski (eds), *Democracy and the European Union* (Springer 1998) 160.

Pokol B, 'Separation of Power and Parliamentarism in Hungary' (2003) 37 East European Quarterly 67.

Pokol B, *Globális uralmi rend* (Kairosz 2008).

Pokol B, *The Juristocratic State: Its Victory and the Possibilities of Taming* (Dialóg Campus Kiadó 2017).

Polyák G and Nagy K, 'A médiatörvények kontextusa, rendelkezései és gyakorlata' (2014) 20 Jura 127 <www.mediakutato.hu/cikk/2016_03_osz_tel/10_frekvenciaosztogatas> accessed 24 October 2024.

Polzin M, *Verfassungsidentität* (Mohr Siebeck 2018).

Polzin M, 'Transnational Lists, Diversity and Quota Regulation: The European Parliament's Proposal for a New Electoral Law' (3 December 2022) *Weekend EU Law Live*.

Popper KR, *The Open Society and Its Enemies* (Routledge 2006).

Posner RA, *The Problematics of Moral and Legal Theory* (The Belknap Press of Harvard University Press 1999).

Powell WW and DiMaggio PJ (eds), *The New Institutionalism in Organizational Analysis* (University of Chicago Press 1991).

Prechal S, 'Competence Creep and General Principles of Law' (2010) 3 REALaw 5.

Prechal S, de Vries S, and van Eijken H, 'The Principle of Attributed Powers and the "Scope of EU Law"' in L Besselink, F Pennings, and S Prechal (eds), *The Eclipse of the Legality Principle in the European Union* (Kluwer 2011) 213.

Preussen W, 'Orbán Backs China's Ukraine Peace Plan' (27 February 2023) *Politico* <https://www.politico.eu/article/viktor-orban-hungary-ukraine-china-peace-plan-russia-invasion/> accessed 24 October 2024.

Priebus S and Anders LH, 'Fundamental Change beneath the Surface: The Supranationalisation of Rule of Law Protection in the European Union' (2024) 62 Journal of Common Market Studies 224.

Put G-J and others, 'The Choice of Spitzenkandidaten: A Comparative Analysis of the Europarties' Selection Procedures' (2016) 4 Politics and Governance 9.

Rasmussen M, 'Revolutionizing European Law: A History of the *Van Gend en Loos* Judgment' (2014) 12 International Journal of Constitutional Law 136.

Raube K, 'From Dawn to Doom: The Institutionalization of the Spitzenkandidaten-Process During European Elections and Its Final Negation' in S Kritzinger and others (eds), *Assessing the 2019 European Elections* (Routledge 2020) 19.

Raz J, 'The Rule of Law and Its Virtue' in J Raz (ed), *The Authority of Law: Essays on Law and Morality* (Clarendon Press 1979) 210.

Reding V, 'Observations on the EU Charter of Fundamental Rights and the Future of the European Union' (31 May 2012) Speech/12/403 FIDE Congress in Tallin <http://europa.eu/rapid/press-release_SPEECH-12-403_en.pdf> accessed 24 October 2024.

Reichel P, *Vergangenheitsbewältigung in Deutschland: Die Auseinandersetzung mit der NS-Diktatur in Politik und Justiz* (CH Beck 2001).

Reuters Staff, 'Hungarian ex-Olympic Champion and Mayor Resigns over Sex Tape' (6 November 2019) *Reuters* <https://www.reuters.com/article/us-hungary-fidesz-mayor-idUSKBN1XG1L8> accessed 24 October 2024.

Rigobon R and Rodrik D, 'Rule of Law, Democracy, Openness, and Income: Estimating Interrelationships' (2005) 13 Economics of Transition and Institutional Change 533.

Rittberger B, *Building Europe's Parliament: Democratic Representation beyond the Nation State* (OUP 2005).

Rixer Á (ed), *Állam és közösség: Válogatott közjogi tanulmányok Magyarország Alaptörvénye tiszteletére* (Patrocinium 2012).

Rodriguez DB, McCubbins M, and Weingast B, 'The Rule of Law Unplugged' (2009) 59 Emory Law Journal 1455.

Rosas A, 'When Is the EU Charter of Fundamental Rights Applicable at National Level?' (2012) 19 Jurisprudencija: Mokslo darbu žurnalas 1269.

Rosenthal H and Voeten E, 'Measuring Legal Systems' (2007) 35 Journal of Comparative Economics 711.

Rosga AJ and Satterthwaite M, 'The Trust in Indicators: Measuring Human Rights' (2009) 27 Berkeley Journal of International Law 253.

Ross ML, 'Does Oil Hinder Democracy?' (2011) 53 World Politics 325.

Rothstein B and Uslaner EM, 'All for All: Equality, Corruption, and Social Trust' (2005) 58 World Politics 41.

Rumford C, 'European Civil Society or Transnational Social Space? Conceptions of Society in Discourses of EU Citizenship, Governance and the Democratic Deficit: An Emerging Agenda' (2003) 6 European Journal of Social Theory 25.

Rupp HH, 'Europäische "Verfassung" und demokratische Legitimation' (1995) 120 Archiv des öffentlichen Rechts 269.

Rüthers B, *Institutionelles Rechtsdenken im Wandel der Verfassungsepochen: Ein Beitrag zur politisch-kritischen Funktion der Rechtswissenschaft* (Gehlen 1970).

Sadurski W, 'How Democracy Dies (in Poland): A Case Study of Anti-Constitutional Populist Backsliding' (2018) Sydney Law School Legal Studies Research Paper No 1 <https://papers.ssrn.com/sol3/papers.cfm?abstract_id=3103491> accessed 24 October 2024.

Sadurski W, *Poland's Constitutional Breakdown* (OUP 2019).

Sadurski W, 'What Happens after the Polish Elections?' (18 August 2019) *Verfassungsblog* <https://verfassungsblog.de/what-happens-after-the-polish-elections/> accessed 24 October 2024.

Safjan M, 'Areas of Application of the Charter of Fundamental Rights of the European Union: Fields of Conflict?' (2012) EUI Working Papers—Law, 2 <http://cadmus.eui.eu/bitstream/handle/1814/23294/LAW-2012-22.pdf> accessed 24 October 2024.

St C Bradley K, 'La transparence de l'Union européenne' (1999) 3–4 Cahiers de droit européen 285.

Saisana M and Saltelli A, 'Rankings and Ratings: Instructions for Use' (2011) 3 Hague Journal on the Rule of Law 247.

Sajó A, *Limiting Government: An Introduction to Constitutionalism* (Central European University Press 1999).

Sajó A, 'EU Networks under the New Constitution, Impact on Domestic Constitutional Structures' in I Pernice and J Zemanek (eds), *A Constitution for Europe: The IGC, the Ratification Process and Beyond* (Nomos 2005) 183.

Sajó A, 'Az állam működési zavarainak társadalmi újratermelése' (2008) 55 Közgazdasági Szemle 690.

Sajó A, *Ruling by Cheating: Governance in Illiberal Democracy* (CUP 2021) 154.

Saltelli A, 'Composite Indicators between Analysis and Advocacy' (2006) 81 Social Indicators Research 65.

Sandel M, *Democracy's Discontent* (Belknap Press of Harvard University Press 1996).

Sano HO and Thelle H, 'The Need for Evidence-Based Human Rights Research' in F Coomans, F Grünfeld, and MT Kamminga (eds), *Methods of Human Rights Research* (Intersentia 2009) 96.
Sarmiento D, 'Who's Afraid of the Charter? The Court of Justice, National Courts and the New Framework of Fundamental Rights Protection in Europe' (2013) 50 Common Market Law Review 1267.
Sarmiento D, 'Crossing the Baltic Rubicon' (4 March 2019) *Verfassungsblog* <https://verfassungsblog.de/crossing-the-baltic-rubicon/> accessed 24 October 2024.
Scalia A and Garner BA, *Reading Law: The Interpretation of Legal Texts* (West Group 2011).
Schabert T, *Boston Politics: The Creativity of Power* (Walter de Gruyter 1989).
Scharpf FW, *Demokratietheorie zwischen Utopie und Anpassung* (Konstanz University Press 1970).
Scharpf FW, *Regieren in Europa* (Campus Verlag 1999).
Scheppele KL, 'The Rule of Law and the Frankenstate: Why Governance Checklists Do Not Work' (2013) 26 Governance 559.
Scheppele KL, 'Enforcing the Basic Principles of EU Law through Systemic Infringement Actions' in C Closa and D Kochenov (eds), *Reinforcing Rule of Law Oversight in the European Union* (CUP 2016) 105.
Scheppele KL, 'Autocratic Legalism' (2018) 85 University of Chicago Law Review 545.
Scheppele KL, Kochenov DV, and Grabowska-Moroz B, 'EU Values Are Law, after All: Enforcing EU Values through Systemic Infringement Actions by the European Commission and the Member States of the European Union' (2020) 39 Yearbook of European Law 3.
Scheppele KL and Morijn J, 'Frozen: How the EU is Blocking Funds to Hungary and Poland Using a Multitude of Conditionalities' (4 April 2023) *Verfassungsblog* <https://verfassungsblog.de/frozen/> accessed 24 October 2024.
Scheuing D, 'Zur Grundrechtsbindung der EU-Mitgliedstaaten' (2005) 40 Europarecht 162.
Schmidt P, 'Why the EU's Spitzenkandidaten Procedure Should Be Revived before the Next European Parliament Elections' (29 July 2021) *LSE Europeblog* <https://blogs.lse.ac.uk/europpblog/2021/07/29/why-the-eus-spitzenkandidaten-procedure-should-be-revived-before-the-next-european-parliament-elections/> accessed 24 October 2024.
Schmitt H, Hobolt S, and Popa SA, 'Does Personalization Increase Turnout? Spitzenkandidaten in the 2014 European Parliament Elections' (2015) 16 European Union Politics 347.
Schmitz T, 'Die Charta der Grundrechte der Europäischen Union als Konkretisierung der gemeinsamen europäischen Werte' in D Blumenwitz, D Murswiek, and G Gornig (eds), *Die Europäische Union als Wertegemeinschaft* (Duncker & Humblot 2005) 73.
Schönberger C, 'Lisbon in Karlsruhe: Maastricht's Epigones at Sea' (2009) 10 German Law Journal 1201.
Schroeder W, *Das Gemeinschaftsrechtssystem: Eine Untersuchung zu den rechtsdogmatischen, rechtstheoretischen und verfassungsrechtlichen Grundlagen des Systemdenkens im Europäischen Gemeinschaftsrecht* (Mohr Siebeck 2002).
Schulyok F, 'The Scope of Application of EU Citizenship and EU Fundamental Rights in Wholly Internal Situations' (2012) Europarättslig Tijdskrift 448.
Schütze R, *European Constitutional Law* (2nd edn, CUP 2015).
Schwerdtfeger A, 'Art. 51 GRCh' in J Meyer and S Hölscheidt (eds), *Charta der Grundrechte der Europäischen Union* (5th edn, Nomos 2019).
Seawright J and Collier D, 'Rival Strategies of Validation: Tools for Evaluating Measures of Democracy' (2013) 47 Comparative Political Studies 111.
Sebők M, Kubik B, and Molnár C, 'A törvények formális minősége—egy empirikus vázlat', in Z Boda and A Szabó (eds), *Trendek a magyar politikában 2. A F idesz és a többiek: pártok, mozgalmak* (MTA TK and Napvilág 2017) 300.
Sedelmeier U, 'Anchoring Democracy from Above? The European Union and Democratic Backsliding in Hungary and Romania after Accession' (2014) 52 Journal of Common Market Studies 105.

Sedelmeier U, 'Political Safeguards against Democratic Backsliding in the EU: The Limits of Material Sanctions and the Scope of Social Pressure' (2017) 24 Journal of European Public Policy 337.

Selznick P, 'Institutionalism "Old" and "New"' (1996) 41 Administrative Science Quarterly 270.

Sen A, *Development as Freedom* (Knopf 1999).

Shackleton M, 'Transforming Representative Democracy in the EU? The Role of the European Parliament' (2017) 39 Journal of European Integration 191.

Sharpe A and Andrews B, 'An Assessment of Weighting Methodologies for Composite Indicators: The Case of the Index of Economic Well-Being' (December 2012) CSLS Res Rep, No 2012-10.

Shattuck J, 'The New Global Landscape: Illiberal Regimes and Movements' (2018) 71 Journal of International Affairs 15.

Sieberson SC, 'The Treaty of Lisbon and Its Impact on the European Union's Democratic Deficit' (2007–08) 10 Columbia Journal of European Law 445.

Siems M, 'Malicious Legal Transplants' (2018) 38 Legal Studies 103.

Sieyès EJ, *Qu'est-ce que le Tiers État? (1789)* (in English: *Political Writings* (Hackett 2003)).

Skaaning S-E, 'Measuring the Rule of Law' (2010) 63 Political Research Quarterly 449.

Smuk P, 'Az Országgyűlés' in A Jakab and G Gajduschek (eds), *A magyar jogrendszer állapota* (MTA TK 2016) 617.

Snyder T, *On Tyranny: Twenty Lessons from the Twentieth Century* (Penguin 2017).

Sólyom L, 'Előszó: Az alkotmányos kultúra szerepe' in A Jakab (ed), *Az Alaptörvény keletkezése és gyakorlati következményei* (HVG Orac 2011) 11.

Sólyom L, *Das Gewand des Grundgesetzes: Zwei Verfassungsikonen—Ungarn und Deutschland* (Berliner Wissenschaftsverlag 2017).

Sólyom L, Lévay M, Szente Z, and Jakab A, Amicus Curiae a Lex Ceu ügyében (12 June 2017) Amicus Curiae in the case of Lex CEU <www.public.mkab.hu/dev/dontesek.nsf/0/af27b40ba3b0b821c1258109003f9b19/$FILE/II_1036_5_2017_%C3%A1ll%C3%A1sfoglal%C3%A1s.002.pdf/II_1036_5_2017_%C3%A1ll%C3%A1sfoglal%C3%A1s.pdf> accessed 24 October 2024.

Sommermann K-P, 'Verfassungsperspektiven für die Demokratie in der erweiterten Europäischen Union: Gefahr der Entdemokratisierung oder Fortentwicklung im Rahmen europäischer Supranationalität?' (2003) Die öffentliche Verwaltung 1009.

Sonnevend P, Jakab A, and Csink L, 'The Constitution as an Instrument of Everyday Party Politics: The Basic Law of Hungary' in A von Bogdandy and P Sonnevend (eds), *Constitutional Crisis in the European Constitutional Area* (Springer 2015) 33.

Spaventa E, 'Should We "Harmonize" Fundamental Rights in the EU? Some Reflections about Minimum Standards and Fundamental Rights Protection in the EU Composite Constitutional System' (2018) 55 Common Market Law Review 997.

Spinant D, 'How to Make Elections Sexy: Give Voters a Say in Europe's Top Jobs' (11 February 2004) *European Voice* 12.

Stanley B, 'The Thin Ideology of Populism' (2008) 13 Journal of Political Ideologies 95.

Stark D, 'Path Dependence and Privatization Strategies in East Central Europe' (1992) 6 East European Politics and Societies 17.

Staudinger I, 'The Rise and Fall of Rule of Law Conditionality' (2022) 7 European Papers 721.

Stein E, 'Lawyers, Judges, and the Making of a Transnational Constitution' (1981) 75 American Journal of International Law 1.

Steinbeis M, 'A Bad Workman Blames His Tools' (9 June 2019) *Verfassungsblog* <https://verfassungsblog.de/a-bad-workman-blames-his-tools/> accessed 24 October 2024.

Strelkov A, 'EU Justice Scoreboard: A New Policy Tool for 'Deepening' European Integration?' (2019) 27 Journal of Contemporary European Studies 15.

Stumpf I, *Erős állam—alkotmányos korlátok* (Századvég 2014).

Szente Z, 'A historizáló alkotmányozás problémái—a történeti alkotmány és a Szent Korona az új Alaptörvényben' (2011) 4 Közjogi Szemle 1.

Szente Z, 'The Political Orientation of the Members of the Hungarian Constitutional Court between 2010 and 2014' (2016) 1 Constitutional Studies 123.

Szente Z, 'The Twilight of Parliament—Parliamentary Law and Practice in Hungary in Populist Times' (2021) 1 International Journal of Parliamentary Studies 127.

Tai BYT, 'Developing an Index of the Rule of Law: Sharing the Experience of Hong Kong' (2007) 2 Asian Journal of Comparative Law 1.

Tamanaha BZ, *On the Rule of Law: History, Politics, Theory* (CUP 2004).

Tamanaha BZ, 'A Concise Guide to the Rule of Law' in G Palombella and N Walker (eds), *Relocating the Rule of Law* (Bloomsbury 2009) 3.

Tecqmenne M, 'Minimum Harmonisation and Fundamental Rights: A Test-Case for the Identification of the Scope of EU Law in Situations Involving National Discretion?' (2020) 16 European Constitutional Law Review 493.

Telea AC, *Data Visualization: Principles and Practice* (2nd edn, Routledge 2015).

Terhechte P, *Konstitutionalisierung und Normativität der europäischen Grundrechte* (Mohr Siebeck 2011).

Thaler M, *Grundlagen und Entwicklung von Verfassungs- und Verwaltungsrecht: Strukturprobleme zum Vergleich Österreich—Frankreich—Großbritannien—USA* (5th edn, Facultas 2020).

Thiery P, Shering J, and Muno W, 'Wie misst man Recht? Möglichkeiten und Grenzen der Messung von Rechtsstaatlichkeit, Kongressbeiträge' in J Estermann (ed), *Interdisziplinäre Rechtsforschung: Kongressbeiträge Wie Wirkt Recht* (Orlux 2009) 141.

Thorpe N, 'Jozsef Szajer: Hungary MEP Quits after Allegedly Fleeing Gay Orgy' (1 December 2020) *BBC News* <https://www.bbc.com/news/world-europe-55145989> accessed 24 October 2024.

Thym D, 'Separation versus Fusion—or: How to Accommodate National Autonomy and the Charter? Diverging Visions of the German Constitutional Court and the European Court of Justice' (2013) 9 European Constitutional Law Review 391.

Tilindyte L, 'Election of the President of the European Commission: Understanding the *Spitzenkandidaten* Process' (April 2019) European Parliament Briefing <https://www.europarl.europa.eu/RegData/etudes/BRIE/2018/630264/EPRS_BRI(2018)630264_EN.pdf> accessed 24 October 2024.

Timmer A, 'Concepts of Human Rights, Democracy, and the Rule of Law: A Literature Review' (28 November 2013) European Commission <http://www.fp7-frame.eu/frame-reps-3-1/2013> accessed 24 October 2024.

Tölgyessy P, 'Politika mindenekelőtt: Jog és hatalom Magyarországon' in A Jakab and G Gajduschek (eds), *A magyar jogrendszer állapota* (MTA TK 2016) 17.

Torres Pérez A, 'The Federalizing Force of the EU Charter of Fundamental Rights' (2017) 15 International Journal of Constitutional Law 1080.

Tóth IG, 'A társadalmi kohézió elemei: bizalom, normakövetés, igazságosság és felelősségérzet—lennének…' in T Kolosi and IG Tóth (eds), *Társadalmi riport 2010* (Tárki 2010).

Toynbee A, *A Study of History, Vol. 1* (OUP 1934).

Trochev A and Solomon PH, 'Authoritarian Constitutionalism in Putin's Russia: A Pragmatic Constitutional Court in a Dual State' (2018) 51 Communist and Post-Communist Studies 201.

Turpin C, *British Government and the Constitution* (5th edn, Butterworths 2002).

Tushnet M, 'Authoritarian Constitutionalism' (2015) 100 Cornell Law Review 391.

Ugo Rescigno G, *Le convenzioni costituzionali* (Cedam 1972).

Uhl H, 'Das "erste Opfer": Der österreichische Opfermythos und seine Transformationen in der Zweiten Republik (2001) 30 Austrian Journal of Political Science 19.

Ungváry K, *A szembenézés hiánya* (Jaffa 2017).

Urueña R, 'Indicators and the Law: A Case Study of the Rule of Law Index' in S Engle Merry, KE Davis, and B Kingsbury (eds), *The Quiet Power of Indicators: Measuring Governance, Corruption, and the Rule of* Law (CUP 2015) 75.

van Elsuwege P, 'Shifting the Boundaries? European Union Citizenship and the Scope of Application of EU Law' (2011) Legal Issues of Economic Integration 263.

van Gerven W, *The European Union: A Polity of States and Peoples* (Hart 2005).

van Hoecke M, 'Family Law Transfers from Europe to Africa: Lessons for the Methodology of Comparative Legal Research' in J Gillespie and P Nicholson (eds), *Law and Development and the Global Discourses of Legal Transfers* (CUP 2012) 273.

Varga C, 'A joguralom és színeváltozásai idealizáció és ideokratikus nyomásgyakorlás között' (2016) Pázmány Law Working Papers No 12 <www.plwp.eu/evfolyamok/2016/170-2016-12> accessed 24 October 2024.

Varga L, *Világ besúgói, egyesüljetek!* (Polgart 2006).

Varga Z, 'Az Alapjogi Charta alkalmazási köre I' (2013) Európai Jog 17.

Varga ZA, *Eszményből bálvány? A joguralom dogmatikája* (Századvég 2015).

Varol OO, 'Stealth Authoritarianism' (2015) 100 Iowa Law Review 1673.

Varol OO, 'Stealth Authoritarianism in Turkey' in MA Graber, S Levinson, and M Tushnet (eds), *Constitutional Democracy in Crisis?* (OUP 2018) 339.

Vasques E, 'EU Lawmaker: Electoral Reform "Doable" by 2024 Elections' (16 February 2023) *Euractiv* <https://www.euractiv.com/section/elections/video/eu-lawmaker-electoral-reform-doable-by-2024-elections/> accessed 24 October 2024.

Verhoeven A, *The European Union in Search of a Democratic and Constitutional Theory* (Kluwer Law International 2002).

Vermeule A, 'System Effects and the Constitution' (2009) 123 Harvard Law Review 4.

Versteeg M and Ginsburg T, 'Measuring the Rule of Law: A Comparison of Indicators' (2016) 42 Law & Social Inquiry 100.

Vincze A, 'Unsere Gedanken sind Sprengstoff—Zum Vorrang des Europarechts in der Rechtsprechung des ungarischen Verfassungsgerichts' (2022) 49 Europäische Grundrechte-Zeitschrift 13.

Vincze A and Varju M, 'Hungary: The New Fundamental Law' (2012) 18 European Public Law 437.

Voigt S, 'How to Measure the Rule of Law' (2012) 65 Kyklos 262.

von Bogdandy A, *Supranationaler Föderalismus als Wirklichkeit und Idee einer neuen Herrschaftsform* (Nomos 1999).

von Bogdandy A, 'Grundrechtsgemeinschaft als Integrationsziel?' (2002) 56 JuristenZeitung 157.

von Bogdandy A, 'Principles of a Systemic Deficiencies Doctrine: How to Protect Checks and Balances in the Member States' (2020) 57 Common Market Law Review 705.

von Bogdandy A, Antpöhler C, and Ioannidis M, 'Protecting EU Values' in A Jakab and D Kochenov (eds), *The Enforcement of EU Law and Values: Ensuring Member States' Compliance* (OUP 2017) 218.

von Bogdandy A and Goldmann M, 'The Exercise of International Public Authority through National Policy Assessment: The OECD's PISA Policy as a Paradigm for a New International Standard Instrument' (2008) 5 International Organisations Law Review 241.

von Bogdandy A and Ioannidis M, 'Systemic Deficiency in the Rule of Law: What It Is, What Has Been Done, What Can Be Done' (2014) 51 Common Market Law Review 59.

von Bogdandy A and Sonnevend P (eds), *Constitutional Crisis in the European Constitutional Area* (CH Beck, Hart and Nomos 2015).

von Bogdandy A and Spieker L, 'Countering the Judicial Silencing of Critics: Article 2 TEU Values, Reverse Solange, and the Responsibilities of National Judges' (2019) 15 European Constitutional Law Review 391.

von Bogdandy A and Spieker L, 'Protecting Fundamental Rights beyond the Charter: Repositioning the Reverse Solange Doctrine in Light of the CJEU's Article 2 TEU Case Law' in M Bobek and J Adams-Prassl (eds), *The EU Charter of Fundamental Rights in the Member States* (Hart 2020) 525.

von Bogdandy A and others, 'Reverse Solange—Protecting the Essence of Fundamental Rights against EU Member States' (2012) 49 Common Market Law Review 489.

von Danwitz T and Paraschas K, 'A Fresh Start for the Charter: Fundamental Questions on the Application of the European Charter of Fundamental Rights' (2017) 35 Fordham International Law Journal 1396.

Ward A, 'Article 51—Scope' in S Peers and others (eds), *The EU Charter of Fundamental Rights: A Commentary* (2nd edn, CH Beck, Hart and Nomos 2021) 1578.
Watson A, *Legal Transplants: An Approach to Comparative Law* (University of Georgia Press 1971).
Weber E, *From Peasants into Frenchmen: The Modernization of Rural France, 1880–1914* (Stanford University Press 1976).
Weiler JHH, 'Problems of Legitimacy in post-1992 Europe' (1991) Außenwirtschaft 411.
Weiler JHH, 'The Transformation of Europe' (1991) 100 Yale Law Journal 2403.
Weiler JHH, 'Does Europe Need a Constitution?' (1995) 1 European Law Journal 219.
Weiler JHH, 'European Democracy and Its Critics: Polity and System' in JHH Weiler, *The Constitution of Europe* (CUP 1999) 264.
Weiler JHH, 'To Be a European Citizen: Eros and Civilization' in JHH Weiler (ed), *The Constitution of Europe* (CUP 1999) 324.
Weiler JHH, 'The European Circumstance and the Politics of Meaning: Not on Bread Alone Doth Man Liveth (Deut. 8:3; Mat 4:4)' (2020) 21 German Law Journal 96.
Weinzierl J, 'Der EuGH erklärt erstmalig nationales Recht für ungültig—Anmerkung zum Urteil des EuGH v. 26.2.2019, Rs. C-202/18 (Rimšēvičs)' (2019) 54 Europarecht 434.
Weismann P, *European Agencies and Risk Governance in EU Financial Market Law* (Routledge 2016).
Welle K, '25 Years of Spitzenkandidaten: What Does the Future Hold?' (5 March 2019) *Blog of the Wilfried Martens Center* <https://www.martenscentre.eu/blog/25-years-of-spitzenkandidaten-what-does-the-future-hold/> accessed 24 October 2024.
Wendel M, *Permeabilität im europäischen Verfassungsrecht: Verfassungsrechtliche Integrationsnormen auf Staats- und Unionsebene im Vergleich* (Mohr Siebeck 2011).
Wheare K, *Modern Constitutions* (OUP 1951).
Wincott D, 'Does the European Union Pervert Democracy? Questions of Democracy in New Constitutionalist Thought on the Future of Europe' (1998) 4 European Law Journal 411.
Wilson JG, 'American Constitutional Conventions' (1992) 40 Buffalo Law Review 645.
Wolfs W, Put G-J, and Van Hecke S, 'Explaining the Reform of the Europarties' Selection Procedures for Spitzenkandidaten' (2021) 43 Journal of European Integration 891.
Wuthrich FM and Ingleby M, 'Pushback Against Populism: Running on "Radical Love" in Turkey' (2020) 2 Journal of Democracy 24.
Wyrzykowski M and Ziółkowski M, 'Illiberal Constitutionalism and the Judiciary' in A Sajó, R Uitz, and S Holmes (eds), *Routledge Handbook of Illiberalism* (Routledge 2022) 517.
Yanovskiy M and Ginker T, 'A Proposal for a More Objective Measure of De Facto Constitutional Constraints' (2017) 28 Constitutional Political Economy 311.
Yowell P, 'The Justiciability of the Charter of Fundamental Rights in the Domestic Law of Member States' in P Huber (ed), *The EU and National Constitutional Law* (Boorberg 2012) 114.
Zakaria F, 'The Rise of Illiberal Democracy' (1997) 76 Foreign Affairs 22.
Zimmermann A, 'The Rule of Law as a Culture of Legality: Legal and Extra-Legal Elements for the Realization of the Rule of Law in Society' (2007) 14 European Law Journal 10.
Zsolt B, 'Bizalom, legitimitás és jogkövetés' in A Jakab and G Gajduschek (eds), *A magyar jogrendszer állapota* (MTA TK 2016) 837.
Zuleeg M, 'What Holds a Nation Together? Cohesion and Democracy in the United States of America and in the European Union' (1997) 46 American Journal of Comparative Law 505.
Zweifel TD, *Democratic Deficit: Institutions and Regulation in the European Union, Switzerland and the United States* (Lexington 2002).

Index

For the benefit of digital users, indexed terms that span two pages (e.g., 52–53) may, on occasion, appear on only one of those pages.

The manufacturer's authorised representative in the EU for product safety is Oxford University Press España S.A. of el Parque Empresarial San Fernando de Henares, Avenida de Castilla, 2 – 28830 Madrid (www.oup.es/en or product.safety@oup.com). OUP España S.A. also acts as importer into Spain of products made by the manufacturer.

www.ingramcontent.com/pod-product-compliance
Lightning Source LLC
LaVergne TN
LVHW011819200926
848484LV00005B/1242

* 9 7 8 0 1 9 8 9 5 4 6 0 6 *